THE RULE OF LAW IN AFGHANISTAN

Missing in Inaction

How, despite the enormous investment of blood and treasure, has the West's ten-year intervention left Afghanistan so lawless and insecure? The answer is more insidious than any conspiracy, for it begins with a profound lack of understanding of the rule of law, the very thing that most dramatically separates Western societies from the benighted ones in which they increasingly intervene.

This volume of essays argues that the rule of law is not a set of institutions that can be exported lock, stock and barrel to lawless lands, but a state of affairs under which ordinary people and officials of the state itself feel it makes sense to act within the law. Where such a state of affairs is absent, as in Afghanistan today, brute force, not law, will continue to rule.

WHIT MASON consults internationally on political development and directs the project on justice in peace-building and development in the Centre for Interdisciplinary Studies of Law, University of New South Wales, Sydney. He was a founding member of the UN's justice coordination office in Kandahar and works as an adviser to the United States Institute of Peace's dispute resolution program in Afghanistan.

THE RULE OF LAW IN AFGHANISTAN

Missing in Inaction

Edited by

WHIT MASON

CAMBRIDGE UNIVERSITY PRESS
Cambridge, New York, Melbourne, Madrid, Cape Town,
Singapore, São Paulo, Delhi, Tokyo, Mexico City

Cambridge University Press
The Edinburgh Building, Cambridge CB2 8RU, UK

Published in the United States of America by Cambridge University Press, New York

www.cambridge.org
Information on this title: www.cambridge.org/9781107003194

First published 2011

Printed in the United Kingdom at the University Press, Cambridge

A catalogue record for this publication is available from the British Library

Library of Congress Cataloguing in Publication data
The rule of law in Afghanistan: missing in inaction / edited by Whit Mason.
p.   cm.
Includes bibliographical references and index.
ISBN 978-1-107-00319-4 – ISBN 978-0-521-17668-2 (pbk.)   1. Rule of law – Afghanistan.
2. Justice, Administration of – Afghanistan.   3. Afghan War, 2001–   I. Mason, Whit.
KNF2020.R85   2011
958.104′71 – dc22   2010041670

ISBN 978-1-107-00319-4 Hardback
ISBN 978-0-521-17668-2 Paperback

CONTENTS

CONTRIBUTORS

SHAFIULLAH AFGHAN was formerly the top aide to Kabul's slain chief of police, Akrem Khakrezwal, governance adviser in the Canadian Provincial Reconstruction Team, and program associate in UNAMA's justice office coordination office for southern Afghanistan. He currently heads an independent consulting firm in Kandahar.

COLIN DESCHAMPS is now working on the national solidarity program in the World Bank's Kabul office. At the time of writing, he was the Natural Resource Management Research Officer at AREU.

JOEL HAFVENSTEIN was formerly head of operations for USAID's alternative livelihoods program in Helmand; author of *Opium Season: A Year on the Afghan Frontier* (2009); then director of Tearfund, Afghanistan. He and his wife are now walking the length of Britain.

MICHAEL E. HARTMANN is senior adviser and manager, Criminal Justice Program, UN Office on Drugs and Crime, Afghanistan (2008–10). He was formerly acting chief of UNAMA's rule of law unit (2007–08), US State/INL-JSSP adviser to the Attorney-General of Afghanistan (2005–07), and UNMIK international prosecutor appointed to the Supreme Court of Kosovo (2000–05). He worked on justice reform in Bosnia and Herzegovina for the UN and ABA-CEELI from 1997 to 2000, and was a senior Fulbright Scholar (criminal law) in Lahore, Pakistan (University of Punjab Law College) in 1996. In the US, he served as a San Francisco assistant district attorney from 1983 until he joined the UN in Bosnia. Hartmann was a senior fellow for the US Institute of Peace in 2003, and adjunct faculty at the law schools of the University of California at Berkeley, UC Hastings and USF.

DAVID J. KILCULLEN is an author and a consultant on counter-insurgency and counter-terrorism. A former Australian army officer, he left that army as a lieutenant-colonel in 2005 and is now a principal of the Crumpton Group. During 2007, he served in Iraq as senior counter-insurgency adviser, Multinational Force, Iraq – a civilian position on the personal staff of US Army General David Petraeus responsible for planning and executing the 2007–08 joint campaign plan which drove the Iraq War troop surge of 2007. He has a PhD in political anthropology from the University of New South Wales. He has written extensively about counter-insurgency and complex interventions, including the critically acclaimed *The Accidental Guerrilla: Fighting Small Wars in the Midst of a Big One* (2009).

AGNIESZKA KLONOWIECKA-MILART is on leave as a judge in her native Poland. For twelve years she served with the UN, first as a legal monitor in the UN Mission in Bosnia, then as a judge appointed to the Supreme Court of Kosovo (2000–08.) From 2008 to 2010, she was engaged with UNODC helping the Afghan Ministry of Justice redraft Afghanistan's criminal procedure code. From 2006 to the present, she has served as an international judge on the UNAKART ECCC, the Supreme Court Chamber of the Khmer Rouge tribunal in Cambodia. She is a judge with the EULEX mission in Kosovo.

MARTIN KRYGIER, Gordon Samuels Professor of Law and Social Theory and Co-Director, Centre for Interdisciplinary Studies of Law, is one of the world's leading authorities on the rule of law in countries in transition. In 1997 he delivered the Australian Broadcasting Corporation's Boyer Lectures. His work spans several fields, including legal, political and social philosophy, communist and post-communist studies, and the history of ideas. He is the author, co-author or editor of many books.

WILLIAM MALEY, AM, is professor and, from 1 July 2003, Foundation director of the Asia-Pacific College of Diplomacy, Australian National University. He taught for many years in the School of Politics, University College, University of New South Wales and the Australian Defence Force Academy, and has served as a visiting professor at the Russian Diplomatic Academy, a visiting fellow at the Centre for the Study of Public Policy at the University of Strathclyde, and a visiting research fellow in the Refugee Studies Programme at Oxford University. He is also a barrister of the High Court of Australia, a member of the executive committee of the Refugee

Council of Australia, and a member of the Australian committee of the Council for Security Cooperation in the Asia Pacific (CSCAP). In 2002, he was appointed a Member of the Order of Australia (AM). He is the author of many books on Afghanistan and international relations, and regularly contributes to media around the world.

WHIT MASON has lived and worked outside his native US since 1989. He edited newspapers in Siberia and the Russian Far East, was a staff writer at *Asiaweek* magazine in Hong Kong, and reported for CBS News from Bosnia and South Korea. As a fellow of the Institute of Current World Affairs, Whit lived in Istanbul and wrote about the nexus between religion and politics in Turkey, Iran and the southern Balkans for three years. He worked in Kosovo first for the International Crisis Group and then as a speechwriter and adviser to the head of the UN mission, about which he co-authored a critically acclaimed book, *Peace at Any Price: How the World Failed Kosovo* (2006). He led a large media development project in Azerbaijan, and was communications and outreach director for USAID in Pakistan. In 2008 he opened the UN's justice coordination office for southern Afghanistan. He is a non-resident fellow of the West Asia program of the Lowy Institute for International Policy, Sydney, for which he co-authored Lowy Institute Paper 25, *Zealous Democrats: Islamism and democracy in Egypt, Indonesia and Turkey* (2008). Whit is a founding member of the Centre for Interdisciplinary Studies of Law of the UNSW Faculty of Law. He has spoken on international relations at many prestigious institutions, including NATO, the UN's Division of Peacekeeping Operations, the Folke Bernadotte Academy in Sweden, the Wilson Centre for Scholars, and Harvard University. He is a regular contributor to media in Australia and internationally. Whit is the Research and Lessons Learned Program Manager, Asia Pacific Civil–Military Centre of Excellence, Australia.

SHAHMAHMOOD MIAKHEL was formerly Deputy Minister of the Interior, Government of the Islamic Republic of Afghanistan; a senior governance adviser, UNAMA; and currently Chief of Party, Kabul, US Institute of Peace.

GRETCHEN PETERS is a journalist and author of *Seeds of Terror: How Terror is Bankrolling the Taliban and al Qaeda* (2009).

ALAN ROE is an adjunct research fellow at the School for Environmental Research, Charles Darwin University, Northern Territory, and did his

PhD in geography at Durham University, UK. At the time of writing, he was senior research manager for Natural Resources Management at the Afghanistan Research and Evaluation Unit in Kabul.

SUSANNE SCHMEIDL is a sociologist and Afghanistan specialist. She was formerly project director of the Global Warning and Response Net (Global WARN) at Swisspeace. She worked for nearly four years until the end of 2005 as the country representative for Swisspeace in Afghanistan, working mainly with two Afghan organisations – the Afghan Civil Society Forum and the Tribal Liaison Office – that she helped set up. She also advised and supported other civil society organisations and served on the Board of Rights and Democracy, an organisation funding women's projects in Afghanistan. Previously she worked as senior research analyst for the FAST early warning unit at Swisspeace, where she was responsible for South Asia and special projects such as developing conflict early warning and response mechanisms for the Inter-Governmental Authority on Development in the Horn of Africa. She received her MA and PhD in sociology from Ohio State University (1989 and 1995), and worked at the Centre for Refugee Studies (York University, Canada) as a postdoctoral researcher (1995–96), coordinator of the prevention/early warning unit (1996–97), coordinator of the interim secretariat of the Forum on Early Warning and Early Response (1996–97), and technical consultant for the food and statistics unit of the UN High Commissioner for Refugees (1997). She has published in the areas of Afghanistan, civil society, refugee migration, conflict early warning and peace-building, and human security, including edited volumes with Howard Adelman, *Early Warning and Early Response* (1998), and Cirû Mwaûra, *Early Warning and Conflict Management in the Horn of Africa* (2002).

GRAEME SMITH is the former Kandahar-based correspondent for *The Globe and Mail*, Canada's national newspaper. He was stationed in Afghanistan from 2006 to 2009. Previously he was based in Moscow. His many awards include three National Newspaper Awards, Canada's highest prize for print journalism, and the annual Michener Award for public service given by the Governor-General of Canada. His multimedia series, *Talking to the Taliban*, gave viewers the opportunity to watch forty-two insurgents discuss why they fight, and made public the raw video of each interview along with accompanying articles and short documentaries. The project won several prizes, including an Emmy for new approaches to news and documentary.

BARBARA J. STAPLETON is a political adviser to the Office of the EU Special Representative for Afghanistan. She studied Middle East history and politics at the School of Oriental and African Studies at London University, and completed her LLM in the international law of human rights at the University of Essex in 1991. She spent the 1980s working in Eritrea, Iranian Kurdistan, Pakistan, Burma and the Thai-Cambodian border. From 1992 to 1997 she was a consultant to the BBC series *Human Rights, Human Wrongs*. She moved to Afghanistan in October 2002, joining ACBAR, the main NGO coordination body based in Kabul, as advocacy and policy coordinator. In May 2006, she joined the office of the Special Representative of the EU for Afghanistan in Kabul as a senior political adviser.

ASTRI SUHRKE is a senior researcher, Christian Michelsen Institute, Bergen, Norway. Before moving to the institute in 1992, she was a professor of international relations at the American University in Washington DC, and has been an associate at the Carnegie Endowment for International Peace. She has written widely on peace-building, forced migration and the politics of humanitarian action. She is currently working on a book on international assistance to Afghanistan entitled *The Limits of State-building*. Her most recent publications are *Roads to Reconciliation* (2005) (co-editor with Elin Skaar and Siri Gloppen); *Conflictual Peacebuilding: Afghanistan Two Years After Bonn* (2004) (with Arne Strand and Kristian Berg Harpviken); and *Eroding Local Capacity: International Humanitarian Action in Africa* (2003) (with Monica Kathina Juma).

FRANCESC VENDRELL, CMG, is a Spanish diplomat with vast experience working in societies in conflict, including as Special Representative of the UN Secretary-General from 2000 to 2001 and the EU's Special Representative to Afghanistan from 2002–08. He graduated in law at the University of Barcelona, continued studying at King's College London, and graduated in modern history at the University of Cambridge. He was director of the International Law Academy of The Hague in 1979. In 1968 he joined the diplomatic corps in the UN, and was appointed head of the documentation services of the general secretariat in Europe and America from 1987 to 1992. Among other positions in the upper body, he was the personal representative of the Secretary-General in the peace processes in El Salvador and Nicaragua (1989–91), Guatemala (1990–92) and East Timor (1999). He has participated in diplomatic missions in the Caucasus (1992) and Haiti (1993), and was director of the political affairs division for East Asia and the Pacific (1993–97) and the combined Asia-Pacific division (1998–99). In 1999 he became responsible for the attendance office at the UN Secretary-General for Political Affairs in the Asia-Pacific, Americas and Europe. In 2002 he received the Cross of St George.

PREFACE AND ACKNOWLEDGEMENTS

This book has its origins in a brief conversation in the Kabul headquarters of the United Nations Assistance Mission in Afghanistan (UNAMA) two days before Christmas in 2008. I was rushing to Seattle to see my father, David Mason, who was reaching the end of a 14-month struggle with cancer. Not knowing how long I would be gone, I delayed my departure by a day in order to convey the most important things I had learned in the six months after establishing the UN's justice coordination office in Kandahar. I explained the urgency of devising a recruitment strategy to fill the 90 per cent of posts in the formal justice system that remained empty, of ending arbitrary detention, of engaging with the customary justice system, and several other recommendations widely shared by Afghans in the south. The person then presiding over UNAMA's rule of law department smiled and said: 'Whit, if anything could be done about any of these problems, don't you think that someone would have done it in the past seven years?' Thanks to my erstwhile colleague for providing such unforgettable inspiration.

In fact, many people have recognised profound mistakes as the intervention has stretched out, and many have suggested better ways of proceeding. The Project on Justice in Peace-building and Development in the Centre of Interdisciplinary Studies of Law (CISL), University of New South Wales, brought several of the brightest of these people together for a symposium, 'Catalysing the Rule of Law in Afghanistan: Challenges and Opportunities', on 3 and 4 September 2009 in Sydney. The symposium was co-sponsored by CISL and the Asia-Pacific Civil-Military Centre of Excellence. CISL co-director (and contributor) Martin Krygier deserves special thanks for his support to the symposium, and for proposing some years ago that we co-author a paper on violence and the rule of law, many elements of which have germinated and influenced this book. The symposium, and hence this book, never could have happened without the generous support of the University of New South Wales, its Law

Faculty and the faculty's dean, David Dixon. Mike Smith, executive director of the Asia-Pacific Civil-Military Centre of Excellence, and Christine Brooks, UNSW Law Faculty's very capable events coordinator, also lent indispensable support to the symposium.

The contributors came from Afghanistan, Europe, North America and other parts of Australia, and together produced an event remarkable for its sincerity, candour and passion. After the symposium, all the contributors generously agreed to revise and further develop their papers for a book. To those we have added two that were not originally presented in Sydney. Needless to say, this book would not have been possible without the contributors' thoughtfulness and generosity with their overtaxed energy and time. Nienke van Schaverbeke of Cambridge University Press and the anonymous readers also demonstrated impressive flexibility in embracing a rather unconventional proposal. The book has been improved by helpful comments from Kim Ross and David Brody and from the thoughts and support of my wife, Amanda Wilson.

My biggest thanks go to Jeremy Gilling, proofreader extraordinaire, whose fast, thoughtful and meticulous copy editing and unfailing good humour allowed this book to be published while its subject remained the focus of intense and consequential debate.

It goes without saying that this book is for the people of Afghanistan.

Introduction

WHIT MASON

Inevitably, for an ambitiously interdisciplinary book, this one is bound to be mislabelled. It may be shelved under 'law' or 'international relations' or perhaps, now that the country has become the focus of such voluminous study, under 'Afghanistan'. Its real genre is 'mystery'.

The mystery, involving millions of victims and at least thousands of suspects, is this.

Since the attacks of September 11, 2001, NATO and allied countries, led by the US, have considered it strategically imperative to help create a government in Afghanistan that is supported by the population and committed to not allowing terrorists to use the country as a safe haven. The richest, most powerful countries in the world have duly sacrificed hundreds of their own people's lives and spent billions of dollars[1] to help secure Afghanistan and bring it a modicum of justice. And what, in terms of the human security and justice that is the *sine qua non* of stability, has it all achieved? The government has issued a decree granting immunity to the legions of warlords and gunmen who have tormented their own people for decades. The President's people stuffed ballot boxes to see him re-elected in a thoroughly discredited process. Prisons are full of people who have committed no crime but are too poor to bribe their way out of trouble, while serious criminals can pay enough to avoid ever serving their sentences. Just over half of Afghans fear for their safety in their local area (Asia Foundation 2009), and many feel more secure and are more optimistic about justice prevailing in areas controlled by the Taliban, whose regime they knew and mostly loathed. The countries where the rule of law prevails have done their best to share their blessed political

---

1 According to the Brookings Institution's Afghanistan Index (Livingston, Messera and O'Hanlon 2010), the Western coalition had suffered 1,709 military fatalities by April 2010; the US alone had spent over $51 billion on its intervention.

culture, and the result has been impunity, corruption and violence on a catastrophic scale. Who – or what – dunnit?

To try to unravel this mystery, this book harnesses an unusually broad array of perspectives, experiences and disciplines. The book's sixteen contributors represent nine nationalities from four continents, five women and eleven men. The treatment is profoundly interdisciplinary, not only in that it draws experts and participant-observers from many disciplines and from no academic discipline whatsoever, but also in that the individual contributors themselves each bring more than a single disciplinary or experiential perspective to their respective questions. Kilcullen is an anthropologist and a retired Australian army colonel; Krygier and Maley studied law but bring a philosophical temperament to broad questions about society and the state; Suhrke is a political scientist and a former journalist who was in Kabul when Najibullah was president; Klonowiecka-Milart and Hartmann are experienced legal development specialists and, respectively, judge and prosecutor; Vendrell is a veteran diplomat and a constitutional lawyer; and so on. The chapters by Vendrell, Miakhel, Afghan and Smith are essentially memoirs, which complement the other chapters by relating what their authors have seen and heard themselves during many years in post-Taliban Afghanistan. The diversity of the contributors' backgrounds makes their focus and agreement on several key themes all the more compelling.

A vast conspiracy is not among the explanations any of the contributors to this book put forward for the international community's spectacular underperformance. Individual governments, much less broad international alliances, are not sufficiently coordinated to orchestrate a conspiracy. Despite the diversion of resources to Iraq, the effort made in Afghanistan has been substantial and sincere. The actual reasons for failure are deeper and more insidious than any conspiracy, for they begin in the mind.

Despite good intentions, the West's expenditure of blood and treasure has failed to give the country's people what they crave most – security, which includes protection against the arbitrary assertion of power by the state itself or by rich, well-armed or well-connected individuals or groups. Reasons for this failure overlap with those for other priorities of this and other recent would-be transformational interventions – short political and budgetary cycles, Western polities' dearth of stamina, and so on.

The international intervention has operated as if the Afghan government shared its agenda and merely lacked technical expertise and resources. As a result of this politically driven myopia, the billions the international community has invested in the rule of law have failed to dent criminal impunity, which has been actively sustained by powerful self-interested Afghans.

But even more important than these factors, the failures of the massive investment in Afghanistan to foster security and justice – the inextricability of which has been too little understood – are grounded in the very shallow understanding of the rule of law that has animated them. Only such a misunderstanding can explain, for example, how a unit of the UN Assistance Mission in Afghanistan that has dealt with nothing beyond technocratic interventions in the court system could call itself 'the rule of law unit', or how a foreign government could imagine it was fostering the rule of law by building a new courthouse even while paying protection money to a private militia and backing a warlord as governor.

Early on in interventions in failing states, intervening forces typically realise that their challenge outstrips their governments' political will and begin looking for shortcuts. The 'breathtakingly mechanistic' (Carothers 2006: 21) approach that results appears to be premised on a belief that if they spend enough money on politically uncontroversial, technocratic steps to strengthen the apparatus for administering the system (or systems) of justice, this modest investment will be repaid with most of the virtues we associate with the rule of law in civil, stable societies. Or perhaps policymakers simply have no idea what else to do, and so operate as if they believed what they cannot really. This book aims to disabuse practitioners of belief in political alchemy – or convince them of the folly of operating as if they had this belief – and to develop a more nuanced, sophisticated understanding of the rule of law as a state of affairs in which people feel it makes sense for them to act within the law.

These misunderstandings and self-delusions are common to what Brian Tamanaha (2009: 29) calls 'the rule of law enterprise'. 'UN doctrine [reflecting prevailing practice in IGOs and Western aid agencies] . . . has consistently advanced "institution- and capacity-building" as the primary means by which the rule of law may be established or strengthened in post-conflict situations. This approach is principally one of institutional enforcement, based around state-sanctioned enforcement structures such as arrest, detention and prosecution mechanisms' (Bull 2008: 51).

This approach derives, as Krygier notes, from understanding the rule of law as an appliance rather than a way of interacting. Policymakers find it congenial to imagine the rule of law as a collection of things that can be imported wholesale because that relieves them of the much more daunting challenge of tinkering with the myriad and nebulous arrays of incentives people in the society have for treating one another civilly or otherwise.

Before going further, it may be helpful to clarify what is and is not meant by the 'rule of law' in this book. Some people who know Afghanistan protest that it has had the rule of law because it has, or has had, systems of law that claim to be authoritative. Virtually every society in the world, including the most lawless, has many laws. What is special about those lucky societies where the rule of law prevails is not that they have laws but that the laws, rather than more brutish forms of power, actually rule. As with a game of cards, you can tell if laws rule by looking at the outcomes – and, based on their perceptions of these, of the players' willingness to continue playing; if one player wins every hand, you can assume the rules are being systematically violated, even if you have not yet determined how. Similarly, if in a dispute a weaker person has a reasonable chance of prevailing over a stronger one, and in their daily lives the weaker and stronger conduct themselves accordingly, one can assume that the rule of law is at work without knowing anything about what laws are operating.

International efforts to foster the rule of law in Afghanistan reflect the common stress on 'laws' rather than 'rule'. Most investments in fostering the rule of law in Afghanistan have produced negligible progress because they have all been narrowly directed towards institutional development of the justice sector, even as other elements of the international-Afghan government partnership have acted in ways that undermine the rule of law – specifically, by supporting warlords and creating the conditions in which the narco-economy has flourished.

Another misunderstanding of the nature of justice concerns its interaction with insurgency. Lakhdar Brahimi, who was the UN Secretary-General's Special Representative for Afghanistan during the beginning of the international intervention, expressed the view that one had to choose between peace and justice, and that peace must come first. Referring to atrocities allegedly committed during the US-backed offensive by the Northern Alliance that ended the Taliban regime, 'Brahimi said in some cases accountability must take "second place to peace and stability. You can choose to please yourself and make statements of principle, or you can see . . . in a given moment and place what is possible"' (Constable 2002).[2]

---

2 Nine years after thousands of Taliban were allegedly killed in shipping containers after having surrendered to Rashid Dostum (BBC 2009), a man in Kandahar, at the opposite end of the country, cited the lack of investigation of this act, much less punishment for it, as one of the reasons that he and many other Pashtuns, who make up approximately half the population and the ethnic base of the insurgency, despise the Karzai government.

Many of the essays in this book bear witness to the falseness of the supposed dichotomy between peace and justice and the rule of law on which justice is based. To suggest a trade-off between peace and the rule of law is to misunderstand what people everywhere seem to demand in exchange for the minimal support that a stable political order requires. Pascal famously wrote that 'justice without force is powerless; force without justice is tyranny'. Nine years after the toppling of the Taliban, Afghanistan suffers from both powerless justice and tyrannical force, with virtually no evidence of the virtuous marriage of the two in the form of either enforced justice or justly applied force.

The contest between building a state in Afghanistan that is ruled by law and the forces of lawless entropy remains undecided. Since this story is not over, contributors recommend changes in approach that they believe would improve the chances that the story might yet reach a happier conclusion. While none of the contributors claims that Afghanistan could now be flourishing to the degree we might wish, all agree that the world has not even taken many of what would have been the most obvious steps had policymakers viewed Afghanistan through the eyes of the people who live there.

Overview of papers

Krygier argues that the rule of law in society is a precious value that supports a state of affairs in which interpersonal interaction can be civil, restrained, and conducted without suspicion, hostility or fear. The conventional focus on institutions, training and building is of limited value because the rule of law does not emanate primarily from judicial institutions – though they play vital roles as well – but exists in the practices, structures, perceptions and people who surround the law, and are affected by it (or not) wherever they are. All the chapters that follow will be more richly appreciated in light of this understanding.

Kilcullen argues that the provision of security – understood as safety combined with predictable order – has been the basis of many statebuilding processes through history, and that in conflict environments people tend to support whatever regime demonstrates the greatest capacity to influence their security.

Vendrell argues that the international community made serious mistakes even before the Bonn process (specifically refusing to hold an international conference before the fall of the Taliban), and that these mistakes are integral to the current difficulties. The ability of the Northern Alliance to wrest the lion's share of political positions resulted in the return to power of notorious warlords of the pre-Taliban era. The President was allowed to arrogate excessive power. On the international side, the 'carving up' of the sectors of assistance and delegation to NATO member states undermined unity of purpose in the international effort and defied coherence in planning. Due to a lack of knowledge about Afghanistan, as well as prioritising short-term security over long-term political development, the US and its allies formed inappropriate partnerships with strongmen, and created a distribution of power that was antithetical to their long-term interests and objectives.

Maley notes that the Afghan culture of subservience to power (as opposed to a culture of legality) was not well understood by the international community, and had important consequences for the implementation of the justice programme. Further, there was tension between the rule of law, which was concerned with imposing limits on the exercise of power, and state-building, which was concerned with a concentration of power. Maley argues that the failure to form a clear vision of the kind of state that the international community was trying to help generate in Afghanistan, to contemplate whether such a state was actually viable and, if so, the full range of interventions required, vitiated efforts in particular sectors. The resulting incoherence proved vulnerable to manipulation by a powerful elite in the Afghan government. Issues of justice and rule of law, which are essential to the state's legitimacy, were never made priorities before their neglect had done enormous damage to the evolving counter-insurgency/state-building effort.

Hartmann argues that the problem of corruption and impunity throughout the current government in Afghanistan, including the judiciary, prosecution and police, is both a major symptom of the absence of the rule of law and a serious impediment to establishing it. Hartmann criticises the self-interest and disorganisation of the international community, which resulted in uncoordinated and erratic strategies for reforming and caused more problems than they solved. He also highlights the symbiosis in four areas that worked to prevent establishment of the rule of law, each contributing to and nurturing the others: insecurity, narcotics, corruption, and the failure to end impunity.

Peters describes the political economy of the opium trade as contributing more directly to the security problem in Afghanistan than the international community generally realises. Drug-related corruption is severe among the Afghan national police and reaches the highest levels of officialdom. The UN Office on Drugs and Crime estimated the Taliban earns between 300 and 400 million dollars a year, and that profits from smuggling activities could reach half a billion dollars a year in cash and commodities when the combined revenue – from kidnapping, extortion and gun-running – is included. Peters calls for pursuing the money men at the top of the pyramid, in both Afghanistan and Pakistan.

Hafvenstein argues that efforts to promote the rule of law have been undermined by the misapprehension that the insurgents play a bigger role in the drug trade than Afghan government officials. In fact, Hafvenstein says, the state-trafficker nexus is more important than the insurgent-trafficker nexus. The consequence of this reality is that individuals whom the international community expected to play leading roles in establishing the rule of law instead have compelling incentives to undermine it. Despite some positive results from poppy eradication efforts, he questions current measures of success for progress against the drug trade (poppy-free cover). He argues that eradication policies have divided communities across the southern poppy belt and driven many poor farmers to join the Taliban, and he calls for a focus on interdiction rather than eradication and a reduced emphasis on counter-narcotics operations, which drive up the value of huge stockpiles now controlled by government officials. (This exemplifies the approach based on Afghans' perceptions, which runs throughout this book.)

Schmeidl argues that international forces in Afghanistan have generally pushed a reform agenda that has alienated the rural majority both culturally and politically. Privileging individual over communal rights, according to this view, is an inappropriate model for Afghanistan, where individual rights have always been subordinated to the family and community. A balance needs to be found between individual rights and the communal interests of the Afghan people for any reform programme to be acceptable and sustainable. She identifies the tendency to look for quick fixes and the contradiction between short-term goals and the long-term nature of political-cultural change as important impediments to effective policy.

Schmeidl assesses the effectiveness and fairness of traditional, informal justice mechanisms and the formal, state-administered justice system. The majority of all disputes (especially property disputes in rural areas) are dealt with by the *jirga/shura*, and Schmeidl argues that Afghans broadly regard the system as familiar, consistent, predictable and efficient, which leads to its solutions being respected. Afghans regard the formal system, by contrast, as limited in reach and scope (it can address rights but not reconciliation), costly, inefficient, inconsistent and corrupt. On the other hand, it does offer the potential (rarely realised in practice) for checks and balances against the inherent power imbalances and favouritism of the informal, male-dominated system. The informal system is also unable to reign in strongmen, and prioritises communal rights over those of the individual. Schmeidl recommends a collaborative, hybrid model in which the formal and informal systems complement one another.

Miakhel writes that a lesson from Afghanistan has been that the rule of law is not a luxury and justice not a side issue, and that Afghans lost faith in the peace process when they did not feel safe, whether from combat, crime or state predation. Miakhel argues that the root causes of conflict often stem from social injustice, violations of law and state officials' abuse of power. In the context of Afghanistan, addressing these root causes through establishing and supporting the rule of law and a legitimate and effective justice system is vital, given the long history of failure by its rulers to provide human security and social justice to the population, and a historical cycle of oppression and violence.

Deschamps and Roe present the findings from a multi-year project the overall objective of which was to help reduce land-related insecurity and vulnerability by strengthening the Afghan government's capacity to facilitate the resolution of land conflicts. A typology of land disputes is developed and five representative pilot cases selected for further study. The chapter establishes a framework for understanding land conflict, and investigates a variety of resolution mechanisms.

Suhrke compares state-building as a project to state-building as a historical process. After considering the role of outside pressure in the state-building experiences of Japan and Turkey, she provides clear evidence that state-building as a foreign assistance project suffers from inherent contra-dictions, and that these were intensified by the insurgency in Afghanistan. She identifies the contradictions in the state-building process as control versus ownership; dependency versus sustainability; dependency versus democracy; effectiveness versus legitimacy; and, a final cross-cutting con-tradiction, the building of the Afghan national army (ANA). The dis-proportionate resource allocation to the ANA while civilian institutions remain comparatively weak, its significant and nationally unsustainable size (with even greater numbers being called for to counter the insur-gency), and its extreme reliance on foreign funds (raising questions of whose army it is) are important factors that undermine the international community's objectives to increase the legitimacy, control and effective-ness of the Afghan political apparatus.

Picking up on the theme of legitimacy, Stapleton argues that an effec-tive justice sector and rule of law are integral to the legitimacy of the state, and that elections are used as a secondary source of legitimacy. The blatant manipulation by all sides of the recent election process in Afghanistan had been damaging to ultimate rule of law objectives, and the international community's handling of the election result was considered critical in terms of its ongoing credibility. Stapleton extends the theme with a critique of provincial reconstruction teams (PRTs), which have been heavily promoted as a means of facilitating tangible results in reconstruction and development, extending the authority of the central government and thereby indirectly improving the security situation in Afghanistan. Stapleton argues that the incoherence of the broader international civil-military strategy (going as far back as the Bonn process) manifests in a diverse range of PRT models that reflect individual national priorities rather than a cohesive, mutually reinforcing strategy.

Hartmann and Klonowiecka-Milart explain how, since 2001, Afghan law has been extensively revised and amended, with heavy input from foreign jurists, including whole laws being drafted by foreigners and adopted by Afghanistan. Despite the late establishment of a mechanism for Afghan-international consultation, this process is still not used in the drafting of most laws. These laws fail to take account of Afghanistan's cultural, political and legal traditions and environments. Hartmann and Klonowiecka-Milart, both deeply involved in this process, call for a technical and quasi-political process to build support for the laws and codes being drafted, and to ensure that Afghans will regard them as their own.

The final two chapters, by Graeme Smith and Shafiullah Afghan, offer two finer grained pictures of a single key province, Kandahar. It is hard to overstate the importance of Kandahar in Afghanistan's historical imagination. It is where Ahmed Shah Durrani first conjured an independent Afghanistan in 1747, and where Islamist veterans of the anti-Soviet *jihad* formed the Taliban in the early 1990s (with considerable help from Pakistan's Inter-Services Intelligence or ISI), and where the Taliban leadership continued to hold court even after they had conquered Kabul.

Smith recalls travelling between Kabul and Kandahar in 2005, which would have been unthinkable in late 2009, illustrating the rapid deterioration of the security situation in Afghanistan. He describes personal experience of six kinds of justice at work in Kandahar, highlights linkages and cross-fertilisation between the formal and informal systems, and illustrates the huge challenges facing the credibility and capability of the formal system in particular. Smith writes that the use of torture by officials and the ill-considered use of special forces have heightened rather than ameliorated the sense of lawlessness in the province.

Smith describes opinion polling in Kandahar as 'criminally flawed', and argues that the international community needs to admit its ignorance of what the people of Afghanistan actually want. What could the Taliban offer that might be attractive? Smith believes that ordinary Afghans would say: foreigners out; justice; and not much else. The 'not much else' implies retaining the freedom to pursue illicit activity and reject modern practices.

Afghan recounts his observation that most people who fight alongside the Taliban have been driven into the insurgents' arms by abusive state officials, police and soldiers. The West has once again supported the wrong leaders, and this has seriously undermined its credibility and the stated objectives of the intervention. Tribes that found themselves on the wrong side of government officials often felt they had little option but to join forces with the Taliban for security and protection of their livelihood. He argues that in Afghans' eyes, legitimacy is not based on abstract preconceptions, but on the demonstrated ability to deliver the most basic necessities of social life.

These chapters make a powerful interdisciplinary assault on the status quo, the cumulative impact of which is greater than the sum of its considerable parts. Focusing such a diversity of perspectives on the mystery of why efforts in the rule of law area have yielded such poor results in Afghanistan yields benefits that could not be achieved by legal scholars specialising in rule of law promotion alone.

Two of the field's leading lights, Thomas Carothers and Brian Tamanaha, have argued that rule of law promotion is not, in fact, a field. Tamanaha writes:

> Law and development is a poorly constructed category that lacks internal coherence. Every legal system everywhere undergoes development (and regression), so there is nothing special about this; meanwhile, the multitude of countries that have been targeted for law and development projects differ radically from one another. Hence there is no uniquely unifying basis upon which to construct "a field". Law and development work is better seen, instead, as an agglomeration of projects perpetuated by motivated actors supported by funding.
>
> (Tamanaha 2009: 6)

Carothers agrees. There is a great deal of activity under the rule of law rubric, 'yet it is not a field if one considers a requirement for such a designation to include a well-grounded rationale, a clear understanding of the essential problem, a proven analytic method, and an understanding of results achieved' (Carothers 2006: 28).

The actual practice of rule of law promotion remains gravely under-theorised, despite insightful recent work such as that of Stromseth (2008) and Bull (2008). One of the obstacles to the development of better understandings of practitioners, which is necessary to allow for further refinement by theorists, is that academic writing on rule of law promotion does not start with the same reference points or scope of concerns as practitioners. Practitioners' concerns are both narrower and broader than those of scholars. '"Rule of law" programming has become shorthand for all interventions targeting legal institutions, a synonym for work on "the justice sector". As used in contemporary practice, it is really shorthand for the rule of lawyers rather than the rule of law in the classic sense, though of course the two projects can overlap' (Ginsburg 2010: 1). Unless a project to improve the justice sector does overlap with promoting the rule of law 'in the classic sense', the former misses its own point.

Another set of practitioners, the senior diplomats, military officers and aid officials who set the broad course of an intervention and seek the benefits of the rule of law 'in the classic sense', generally operate as if that central part of their mandate were being well looked after by the legal specialists who are in fact narrowly focused on the justice system. The architects of interventions need to understand that those working on the justice sector alone cannot possibly deliver the benefits they seek, and that creating the conditions for the rule of law to make sense must colour everything they do.

The most sophisticated scholars, for their part, stress the 'extreme interrelatedness of everything with everything else in a society' (Tamanaha 2009: 5). Since even if a legal scholar could know about 'everything', she can hardly be expected also to know about 'everything else'; it can only be useful for insights on nearly everything to be allied within a single volume. But it is to be hoped that amid this diversity, readers will recognise the salience of a small number of principles that differentiate conditions in which acting within the law makes sense from those where spurning or ignoring the law does. Fostering and maintaining the rule of law will always be immensely difficult, but we may find that its essence is simpler than has generally been thought.

References

Asia Foundation (2009). *Survey of the Afghan People*

BBC (2009). 'The Afghan shipping-container "massacre"', 13 July 2009, http://news.bbc.co.uk/2/hi/south_asia/8147977.stm

Bull, Carolyn (2008). *No Entry Without Strategy.* United Nations University Press

Carothers, Thomas 2006. *Promoting the Rule of Law Abroad: In Search of Knowledge.* Carnegie Endowment for Peace

Constable, Pamela (2002). 'Report of mass Afghan graves won't be probed, envoy says. UN official cites danger and weakness of government', *Washington Post Foreign Service,* 28 August 2002

Ginsburg, Tom (2010). 'In defence of imperialism?', draft of presentation at NOMOS conference, New Orleans, 6 January 2010

Livingston, Ian S., Messera, Heather L. and O'Hanlon, Michael (2010). *Brookings Afghanistan Index,* 8 April 2010, www.brookings.edu/~/media/Files/Programs/FP/afghanistan%20index/index.pdf

Stromseth, Jane, Wippman, David and Brooks, Rosa (2008). *Can Might Make Rights? Building the Rule of Law after Military Interventions.* Cambridge University Press

Tamanaha, Brian Z. (2009). 'The primacy of society and the failures of law and development', Legal Studies Research Paper series, Paper 09–0172, December 2009

PART I

The scope and nature of the problem

2

Approaching the rule of law

MARTIN KRYGIER

In a way, rule of law promotion is booming. A lot of people and organisations are contracted to work on it, a lot of money is spent on it, a lot of academics study it. And yet it is hard to boast of much success in actually fostering it, much less conjuring it *ex nihilo* or next to *nihilo*.

That should not be surprising. The rule of law is not a natural fact but a rare achievement, and there are many forces that militate against it. And Afghanistan is not the easiest place to start.

It is not at all clear, however, whether such 'hard facts'[1] are the only source of our problems. Some, at least, derive from limitations we bring to the world. To put it bluntly, and fortunately in the words of another: in the business of rule of law promotion, 'we know how to do a lot of things, but deep down we don't really know what we are doing'.[2]

The authors in this book have a lot to tell us about the quest for the rule of law in Afghanistan; what is going on, what has been attempted, what was wise, what was stupid, what has failed, what has succeeded. They alert us, again and again, to facts that need to be recognised and often have not been, and to specific tactics and strategies, well or ill adapted to those facts.

I am not a specialist on Afghanistan and have not done research on how these significant facts play out on that rocky ground. However, I have thought for some time about the rule of law and attempts to promote it in various, often uncongenial, settings. I have come to believe that, among the many huge difficulties in seeking to catalyse the rule of law where it has not existed or has not been strong, some of the biggest occur in

---

1 On 'hard facts' and our tendency to exaggerate them in relation to 'crafting democracy', see Di Palma 1990.
2 Thomas Carothers (2005: 15) attributes this phrase to 'a colleague who has been closely involved in rule-of-law work in Latin America for many years'.

our heads, rather than in the field; better perhaps, first in our heads and *then* in the field. Though these errors have practical consequences, they are at bottom *conceptual* mistakes. Indeed, they dramatically illustrate the falseness of the dichotomy between conceptual clarity and worldly pragmatism. It turns out that, as was once alleged of love and marriage, you can't have one without the other.

Before considering some of these mistakes, I sketch several ways in which a contemporary polity can lack the rule of law. After all, the rule of law is typically invoked as a contrast term, to be compared with life without it. So it helps to reflect on what it might mean, in contemporary conditions, to lack it. All the more since it is precisely these sorts of conditions that prevail in Afghanistan, as they generally do in the places where the most ambitious attempts to promote the rule of law take place. I will then consider some highly prevalent misconceptions of the rule of law held by, among others, many who seek to bring it to just such places. I follow that by suggesting a different approach. After pouring some lukewarm water on the common tendency to attribute all our problems to 'culture', I conclude by recommending a form of 'contextual universalism' in relation to the rule of law.

Rule without law

One way a society could lack the rule of law is for it to lack law. In such a society, and of course I am exaggerating to clarify the distinction, law would simply be irrelevant to the exercise of power, which is exercised without legal authorisation or excuse. This is the thought that under-lies the old distinction between limited authoritarian government and tyranny. Thus the great eighteenth-century thinker Montesquieu (1989: book 2, chapter 1) distinguished between monarchies, 'in which one alone governs, but by fixed and established laws', and 'despotic government [in which] one alone, without law and without rule, draws everything along by his will and his caprices'. He preferred the former, and so should we all. Even an authoritarian monarch, in Montesquieu's sense, is preferable to a tyrant.

In the late twentieth century, many people argued that the great divide ran not between systems led by a law-bound monarch and those topped by a despot, but between governments chosen by the people through regular elections – democracies – and all the rest. However, there are plenty of societies, especially after the 'third wave' of democratic transformations, with many trappings of democracy, but without the rule of law. And the trappings are not necessarily simply cosmetic. Elections are free, votes are counted, and yet leaders rule according to their own whim and caprice. Such 'illiberal democracies' (Zakaria 1997: 22–43) abound. One might object that they are not 'real' democracies, since true democracy requires a variety of rights and freedoms to enable citizens to form and act upon their own opinions, and only law can make them secure. I believe that case can be made, but the deficiencies of illiberal democracy will not be made good simply by having fairer elections and votes better counted. Something else is needed, and it has to do with law. For that matter, without changes that have to do with law, the elections can't be fairer and the votes won't be better counted.

A third lawless option is found in those countries where neither the people nor a single person or group rules; indeed, where no one rules but many fight. Afghanistan is one such society, but it is by no means alone. 'Failed states' are common and, as thinkers from Thomas Hobbes onwards have warned us, they are terrible places to be. Again, and obviously, the law does not rule in a failed state. Conversely, a state in which the law can plausibly be said to rule is highly unlikely to have failed.

In between all-powerful and powerless states, there are many available pathological permutations where states have power enough to do ill but are too weak to do good. Thus, for example, Timothy Snyder has recently written of Ukraine:

> The fundamental question here . . . is the establishment of the rule of law. Gogol identified the problem in his comic play, *The Government Inspector*: the state is too weak to be predictable, but strong enough to be arbitrary.
>
> (Snyder 2010: 36)

I stress that I am speaking of contemporary polities. There is plenty of evidence that, in the absence of the hot breath of modernity, small or nomadic or what used to be called 'stateless' (Fortes and Evans-Pritchard 1948; see also Krygier 1980: 27–59) pre-modern societies, without our sorts of institutional apparatus – legislatures, executives, judiciaries – nevertheless contrived to protect their members from familiar dangers (unfamiliar dangers, particularly unprecedented and overwhelming ones such as alien invasions, are a different matter), and encouraged certain sorts of necessary cooperation, without a war of all against all. We might not recognise the means by which these ends are accomplished as legal, but that is of little moment compared to their accomplishment and the life this makes possible. It is an empirical question how these ends are achieved, a normative one how well, and an urgent contemporary problem whether and how they can still be achieved in societies disrupted by, among other things, modernity.

For there are ecological limits to doing without states and law, one to do with size, the other with modernity (which also affects size).[3] Beyond a very small size, societies will develop institutionalised apparatuses of rule, or states. This is inevitable, and in modern societies it is also in principle good. We *need* states with adequate powers to do what only they can do.[4] This includes protecting citizens from other citizens, their own states from other states, and other states from temptation. This Hobbesian insight has not yet been washed away by the tides of globalisation or the tremors of September 11. On the contrary.

However, those in control of such states are able to amass great power, which it is difficult to restrain routinely without the institutionalisation of countervailing measures, among them institutions that check and balance, and conventions that embed and support such restraints. Unrestrained, it is reasonable to fear states, as it is to fear any one or thing with unrestrained power.

Moreover, large societies generate coordination problems no longer amenable to purely informal resolution on the basis of common understandings. Common knowledge fades with complexity and distance. Certainly, and this is a major claim of this chapter, rules of law are never self-sufficient, unmoved movers, and they are never sufficient for whatever good we want either; but in large societies, they can contribute to lessening fear and confusion, both of which would be natural and reasonable without them. They don't do this *necessarily*, for rules of certain sorts can do as much harm as rules of other sorts do good, and you need a lot besides rules, but rules are arguably necessary though insufficient planks in the bulwark against social chaos.

Further, modernity militates against the endurance of small societies on the basis of their internal social control mechanisms alone. It destroys many and renders others ineffective. Among other things that wreak such destruction, modern states and law do. There is abundant evidence of that, and such destruction and erosion have occurred in many parts of the world. Australian Aborigines, Native Americans, the whole of Africa, lived, for better or worse, in a different moral, political, social and economic universe before modernity hit them than since.

---

3 This and the next paragraph are drawn from Krygier 2004: 259–60.
4 On this, see especially Holmes 1995b, Sunstein and Holmes 1999, and Weiss and Hobson 1995.

What became of that universe was simply unimaginable before the hit happened.

For though size is an important part of this, it is only a part. Other parts include the thinning of cultural density, competition from other options, freedom of movement, infections and corruptions of every literal and metaphorical sort. So, again for better or worse, there are many places where the impetus to institutionalise ways to protect and facilitate the rule of law has by now become indispensable, if only to restrain the power of the institutions they presuppose.

Rule *by* law

It is pretty obvious that lawlessness in any of the varieties sketched above is antithetical to the rule of law. However, the mere existence of law by itself does not necessarily bring the rule of law. In many states, law has been conceived of, and is wielded, as an instrument for repression or at least top-down direction of subjects, and little more. Indeed, law has often been a very useful vehicle (and at times equally useful camouflage) for the exercise of unrestrained and uncivilised power. Where this is so, law does not rule but is an instrument of rule; in the common distinction, rule is *by* and not *of* law.

Of course, this is always partly so. Modern states are not sporting umpires, simply enforcing the rules of the game. They have their own barrows to push. Much law serves as an instrument of bureaucratic and governmental goals in every modern welfare state. However, differences of degree count for a great deal. Where such a state is constrained by effective and independent legal institutions, professions and traditions, we are a world away from a polity, such as the former Soviet Union, where legal restraint on the power of the Communist Party was for long periods not merely non-existent but unthinkable. Indeed, it was illegal given the 'leading role' constitutionally accorded the party. So though there was plenty of law about, its legal subordination to a supra-legal authority vitiated the role that defines the rule of law and makes it precious.

Under communism, law was often, alas, plentiful and unavoidable. The problem was its character and how it was used. It appears that many despotisms find law very useful precisely to the extent that it renders subjects, but not their rulers, legally accountable. 'Under the rule of [Soviet] strict apparatchiks', as Marina Kurkchiyan (2003: 36) has vividly demonstrated, 'the bureaucratic invention known as "the power of paper" became a highly developed art form'. And the power of paper was power indeed.

The Russian, not merely the Soviet, tradition is particularly striking in its starkly top-down, instrumental view of law, but it is far from unique. More rare, indeed, are regimes where laws, or a substantial proportion of them, *are* available for the protection, guidance and use of citizens, where this is widely assumed to be the case and thought properly to be so. In these regimes, the cluster of values known as the rule of law is strongly institutionalised. That is to say, it is infused in the institutions of law, and to a considerable extent in those of everyday life as well. It is not a figleaf or a luxury option solely for the rich and powerful. It is, rather, a significant part of 'the way we do things here', and there is likely to be resistance – normatively fuelled resistance – to doing otherwise.

Politically pliable, draconian, discriminatory laws; incompetent, venal, weak, suborned administrators of law; rulers who, to adapt Juergen Habermas's distinction (1986: 212), use law solely as a 'steering medium' for the effective exercise of power, leaving no room for it to serve as an 'institution' of the everyday world itself, available to citizens as a resource and protection in their relations with the state and with each other; laws which, against other sources and forms of power, simply do not *count* either as restraints on power or as resources in everyday life – none of these forms or positions of law, and they are hardly rare, is likely either to restrain or to civilise power.

Alternatively, a legal order might embody laws that do restrain some things, or in some spheres, or in relation to some people, yet in doing so contribute to a larger tyranny. One example is what Ernst Fraenkel called a 'dual state'; dual for it includes both a 'normative' and a 'prerogative' component (1941: xiii). In the former, 'an administrative body endowed with elaborate powers for safeguarding the legal order' governs some classes, races or domains. The latter wields 'unlimited violence unchecked by any legal guarantees' over other classes, races, or everyone in other domains (such as politics). In such orders, the 'prerogative state' has the final word, though it might often find it useful to allow the normative state to operate routinely in particular areas of life. Nazi Germany was Fraenkel's example; South Africa under apartheid a more recent one. These are all examples where laws might be hard to avoid, but the rule of law is hard to find.

Wherever the rule of law has been absent for any of these reasons, success in generating it would both face hefty challenges and be a blessing. Those with unrestrained power are reluctant to bow to restraint. Those used to unrestrained power – even as its victims – are often unlikely to believe things can be otherwise, and certainly unaccustomed to behaving in ways that might ensure they could be otherwise. They may not even think it should be otherwise. Those with too much power will not allow law to 'rule'; those with too little can't make law rule. 'Hard facts' of these and other kinds are, alas, easy to find.

Misconceptions

Whoever would seek to generate the rule of law faces daunting tasks, then, even if they knew what they should do. But how often is this the case? Our talents for engineering the rule of law from a standing start, let alone against prodigious handicaps, are inconspicuous. Where have we done it? What should we do to do it? These, notwithstanding the amount of money and effort devoted to it, are not questions to which anyone has obviously successful answers: neither retail, in any particular country, nor wholesale, in benighted 'transitional' countries as a class. I don't either. I am more confident, however, that we approach much closer to answers if first we disabuse ourselves of certain misconceptions about the rule of law that are remarkably common.

There is a deep and widespread misconception about the rule of law that is hard to avoid in what are today optimistically called transitional societies, particularly for promoters of the rule of law, anxious for results and a winning formula that might be franchised. This is not just a theoretical problem, but one with real practical consequences.

The misconception I have in mind is to think of the rule of law as a kind of technology, a product to be installed. And since it is the rule of law we are dealing with, legal technology. The question then becomes: what are the features of this legal gizmo that we want to export and install? Legal philosophers emphasise lists of particular formal characteristics: laws must be clear, prospective, non-contradictory, capable of performance, and so on.[5] Lawyers typically point to particular legal institutions, commonly those that seem to have worked at home.[6] Rule of law promoters develop checklists of aspects of legal institutions to attend to

---

5 See, for example, Fuller 1964 and the huge literature this book has generated. There is much controversy in that literature about whether Fuller has rightly characterised the moral significance of these elements, but very little – too little – about whether they are the most important indicators of the rule of law (see Krygier 2010: 107–34).

6 The classic English source of home-and-institution-based understandings of the rule of law is Dicey 1959.

and spend money on: court reforms, legal education, training of judges and lawyers, design of constitutions and legislation.

Why is it a mistake to start that way? Well, one reason for scepticism is that for the billions of dollars spent on reforms that seek to 'build' (an assumption-rich success word in itself) the rule of law in hard places, we don't have many success stories. Sometimes the product – courts (not to be confused with courthouses) and so on – has turned out to be hard to construct. Sometimes the foundations are a bit wobbly. Other times edifices are erected but no one pays them much attention; they're not where the action is. That could be because the rule of law is hard to build, which it clearly is. It also could be that we're trying to do the wrong thing because we're thinking in the wrong way.

First, if it makes sense to think of the rule of law as technology at all, it has to be understood as a distinctive kind of technology: an *interaction* technology, not a production technology, to borrow a distinction from the American political theorist Stephen Holmes. And interaction technology is harder to transplant, harder to generate, with more and more varied effects than production technology. Perhaps that is why, though Toyotas look much the same all over the world, they behave very differently on different roads and with different drivers. While both production and interaction can go awry, production is much easier to change.

Patterns of interaction and interactional contexts vary dramatically between societies. If you want to affect them, it is now coming to be admitted, you can't assume that institutions that work in one place will work similarly in another. There are many reasons for that. One is that transplanted laws and institutions are typically outgrowths of, and in their day-to-day workings are encrusted with, much in the way of traditions, assumptions, conventions, customs and cultural givens that their routine workings depend upon. Much of this is taken for granted as apparently natural and unregistered, and in any event cannot easily be packaged for shipment with written laws and institutions on their travels. Those laws and institutions then land in territory where much that is already firmly embedded, unbeknown to the exporters, is unwelcoming.

However, catalysing the rule of law depends on things working in the particular place you're in; indeed, in that place that is the only thing that ultimately matters, not their pedigree. As Aesop advises: *hic Rhodus, hic salta* (roughly, if you claim you can perform a certain impressive feat somewhere, go ahead and perform it here). That means they must mesh with a lot else that is going on in there, and that you need to know something about what is going on. Societies where the rule of law does not prevail do not have open posts ready for the rule of law to fill; they have other roles that are already occupied, and which in many cases can continue in their current form only for as long as the rule of law is held at bay. The failure to recognise this means that a lot of 'best practice' models that do the circuit end up as useless junk in places to which they are ill adapted.

The Harvard jurist Lon Fuller (1964) was inclined to think of architecture rather than technology when he thought of law.[7] He spoke of lawyers as social architects, but he might have pressed the metaphor more strongly than he did. Like so many lawyers, he concentrated on the structure of the formal law, though he often showed awareness that there was more to it. After all, like any architect, social ones should know a good deal about the terrain for which they design. The quality of their materials will not always compensate for the swamps or sands on which they must try to build, the barrenness and inhospitable nature of some terrains, the treacherousness of others, the presence of uncongenial structures, among them social structures, that are difficult to remove and yet also difficult to replace. Architects should also know something of the tastes, preferences, understandings and purposes of those for whom, ostensibly, they are building.

In some countries (communist Bulgaria as a matter of fact; but not a huge amount has changed in this regard (Ganev 2009: 263–83)), law is thought of as 'like a door in the middle of an open meadow. Of course, you could go through the door, but why bother?' Such ingrained dismissiveness presents a challenge to an architect who would like his building to be used – even better, useful. A major problem of transitional architecture is to get people to approach the door, let alone go through it. Enticing people who have had either bad experiences with doors or no experience but have heard vaguely menacing rumours about them is harder than most door-loving architects can ever imagine. Some think the door leads nowhere; others that one is bound to get lost, or lose, in there; others fear other dangers there; others still that it is not designed for people like them. If, as in many Soviet republics, 'politics [and equally law] was not something you did; it was something other people did to you' (MacFarlane 2003: 72), the task of making the law inviting is an uphill struggle. And if the law or citizens themselves are surrounded by predatory beasts, that too might affect issues of institutional design and construction. It would

---

7 This paragraph is taken from Krygier 2010: 122. In this section, I have drawn on this article and on Krygier and Mason forthcoming.

be an odd architect who proudly disdained knowledge of where and for whom his buildings are likely to be erected. Yet legal philosophers, lawyers and, until recently, rule of law promoters do it all the time, and not accidentally. Many evidently consider neither the client nor the site to be any of their business.

Moreover, neither technology nor even architecture captures a fundamental truth about what is necessary to catalyse the rule of law: some of its deepest conditions, and even more its most profound consequences, are not found within legal institutions. On conditions, the rule of law grows, needs nurturing, and has to be in sync with local ecologies. It can't just be screwed in, though it can be screwed up, and it depends as much on what's going on around it, on the particular things in that ecological niche, as on its own characteristics. This is a larger point than it seems, and even larger still when one comes to consequences.

After all, whether a refrigerator or indeed a building works can be found by looking inside it. However, whether the rule of law has claim in a society is a matter found in its broader reaches: interactions between citizens and the state, and of equal if not more importance, between citizens themselves. For the law never rules unless it rules in the world around it. If that doesn't occur, no amount of internal elegance of design is worth a bean.

Who would say the rule of law is in good shape in Afghanistan? And does anyone think that much would be different if only it turned out that the criminal code was perfectly drafted?[8] Unlikely, for the rule of law depends on a lot going right outside official practices and institutions, and a lot of what it depends upon is not what we conventionally take to be legal. And that should be no surprise. It is merely an example of Amartya Sen's salutary reminder, in his influential speech to the World Bank, that:

> Even when we consider development in a particular sphere, such as economic development or legal development, the instruments that are needed to enhance development in that circumscribed sphere may not be confined only to institutions and policies in that sphere... If this sounds a little complex, I must point out that the complication relates, ultimately, to the interdependences of the world in which we live. I did not create that world, and any blame for it has to be addressed elsewhere.
>
> (Sen 2000: 10)

8 For reflections on this very experience, see chapter 14 in this volume, 'Lost in translation: legal transplants without consensus-based adaptation' by Michael E Hartmann and Agnieszka Klonowiecka-Milart.

This is not a truth restricted to benighted countries struggling to see glimmers of the rule of law. It is universal. The life of the law, even in the well-appointed homes of its exporters, lies outside official institutions as much as, arguably more than, it does within them.

It is a banal observation, yet still important to acknowledge, that the major effects of central legal institutions, where they *have* major effects (which, as we have seen, is not everywhere), occur outside those institutions. That being the case, it should be just as obvious, but is rarely so to the lawyers charged with promoting the rule of law in inhospitable climes, that those effects are to variable extents and in varying ways dependent on the ways state laws interrelate with, and are refracted, amplified and nullified by, existing non-state structures, norms, networks and attitudes. There is nowhere where everyone is straining to hear just what the legislature and the courts have to say on most actual or potential sources of conflict. Even if people saw a reason to pay special attention to these sources, there are many other generators of noise, some of it often louder and closer at hand than that generated by the law of the state. And states themselves make a lot of noise, much of it outside the law or contrary to the rule of law.

Whenever law stakes a claim to rule, then, there are many sources of potential normative, structural, cultural and institutional collaboration and competition in every society, and they, and their interplay, differ markedly between (and often within) societies. How people will interpret the state's law and respond to it, how highly it will rate for them in comparison with other influences – these things depend only partly on what it says, how it says it, and what the law is intended by its makers to do. In complex and variable ways, people's responses to state law depend on how, in what form and with what salience and force that law is able to penetrate all these intervening media, how attuned to it putative recipients are, and how dense, competitive, resistant or hostile to its messages they might turn out to be.

This is not to say that state law is unimportant. It is often crucially important, but how important, and even if important, in what ways its effects work out in the world, are heavily dependent on the complex social, economic and political contexts into which it intervenes. That is a universal truth. Recognition of it requires from many people a major reconceptualisation of what it might mean for law to rule, where we might find it, what it depends upon, and what we need to know to understand it. Such reconceptualisation has scarcely and somewhat haphazardly begun to filter into the rule of law promotion industry.

Finally, and most important, the problem with *starting* by thinking of the rule of law as institutional technology is that it can obscure or lead one to forget why anyone should want it. Organisational theorists have a name for the phenomenon: 'goal displacement'. It has many incarnations, but its general form goes roughly like this: Once upon a time, people seek to achieve something valuable, then they put rules and institutions in place in order to achieve it. In no time at all, everyone, and particularly those enmeshed in the institutions, thinks only of the rules and institutions, quite ignoring their point. Then people export the rules and institutions because they are old, or good, or well-pedigreed, or come from a presti-gious country, or just because they are there. That's no way to catalyse the rule of law.

Means, ends and states of affairs

I believe the rule of law is better approached by beginning with the complex of values that animate its pursuit, that seem worth pursuing, rather than with some canonical set of features that, in any particular case, may or may not turn out to serve them. We should ask *why* anyone would want something we call the rule of law; in other words, put ends before means rather than the other way around. If, after all, we have no answer to that question, it's hard to see why we should bother, and harder still to convince sceptical societies that they should. Put simply, what is the *point* of the rule of law.

It is not as though no one has asked this. Now that the rule of law is modish, it is recommended for all sorts of purposes: economic develop-ment, human rights, democracy, just to name a few common candidates. It is, however, not always obvious – certainly not uncontested – that the rule of law, even if we were to know how to generate it, does produce these marvels (see for example Davis and Trebilcock 2008: 895–946; Peeren-boom 2005: 809–945). My suggestion is that we start more modestly and closer to home. Whatever *external* ends the rule of law might or not generate, there are goals *immanent* in the concept, part of its mean-ing. If they are hard to enumerate exhaustively, it is not hard to make a start.

The concept of the rule of law, whatever else can be said about it, has to do with the way power is exercised. There are many views of what ways qualify; I will continue to be modest, and aim low. There might be much more to the rule of law than this, but for millennia, and at least since Aristotle, people have noticed one salutary distinction in particular:

that between circumstances in which power can be exercised *arbitrarily* and those where law – not on its own, but together with other social agencies, actors, institutions and norms – plays a real role in channelling the exercise of power, and in particular in constraining the possibility of its arbitrary exercise. We can argue about what else – economic benefits, security, human rights and so on – might flow from this rare achievement; my claim is simply that it is of the essence of the rule of law that it prevents power being used arbitrarily.

Now if constraint on the possibility of arbitrary power is a core rule of law value, what matters is that it happens. If it were to occur naturally or as a gift of God, we could do nothing or we could pray. Since neither seems sufficient, we look to, among other things, institutions; but we do so *not* because there is some sacrosanct set of them to be reproduced, whatever their consequences, and labelled the rule of law, but only to the extent that they lead to lessening the possibilities of power being exercised arbitrarily. Since that is our goal, a particular set of institutions is in principle neither *necessary*, since it is a contingent matter whether or not any particular set will deliver what is valued, nor sufficient, since it is certain that laws and 'parchment institutions' (Carey 2000: 735–61) can deliver little on their own. They need a vast social collaboration to be effective, and in many societies, willing collaborators are hard to find or hard to organise effectively.

In other words, whether and to what extent the rule of law can reasonably be said to exist depends only derivatively and contingently on whether judges are trained in particular ways, or on how legislation is framed. Rather, it turns on the extent to which a particular and salutary *state of affairs* in the world is sustained, one in which (at a minimum, and this could be added to and elaborated) law contributes effectively to constraining and channelling uses of power – political, social and economic – so that the possibilities of its arbitrary exercise and abuse are significantly diminished. It is *this* state of affairs, or something like it, that most matters to so many desperate denizens of zones of conflict and hoped-for transition who value the rule of law, however achieved. I commend this ideal (not especially controversial in the tradition of thought on the rule of law, but open to revision and elaboration) as well nigh universal in application. No one benefits from unrestrained abuse of power, aside (perhaps and not always) from the abuser.

If we can attain some clarity about what we are after when we seek the rule of law, and we believe that institutions can help us attain it, there are then significant questions we can ask about what institutions might need to be able to do to help achieve such ends, what conditions they need to be able to fulfil. I nominate four, but the list is indicative only.

One is *sufficient scope*: who the institutions can reach; who, if anyone, is beyond their grasp. To the extent that wielders of significant power are beyond the scope of the institutions, the rule of law suffers grievously.

Another is *character*: are the laws of such a form that – not alone, of course, but in collaboration with other forces and norms in the society – they are likely to aid self-guidance and coordination among citizens, *and* limit the ways in which power is exercised? Here the philosophers' lists are pertinent: you need to be able to know the law at the time you contemplate action, understand its requirements, conform to them (without breaking some other law), be confident that their terms will frame their application, and so on.

A third has to do with *application*: do officials enforce the rules in ways coherent with their meaning?

And finally, fundamental but not much pursued by lawyers and many promoters of legal institutions, *social salience*: however well or ill crafted, law needs to *count* as a restraint on social power. This is not merely a question of legal enforcement, but of obedience and, more subtle but fundamental, normative significance in the thoughts of masses of citizens as they transact their everyday lives with each other. Whether the law does count or not and in what ways it does and doesn't, as we have seen, cannot be read off from its formal qualities. After all, if, as in many transitional societies, state law has very restricted reach, its formal quality may not count for much. Conversely, if conditions *beyond* the institutions blunt, divert or challenge the sway of the law in people's thoughts and lives, to that extent too, however majestic the institutions, the impact of the law will be diminished, sometimes to vanishing point.

Only in the light of some clarity about these two questions – what do we want, and what do we need from institutions to get it – does it make sense to move to ask a third question: what do we have or can we craft, here and now, to help us do so. This is a particular, socially and politically contingent, matter. The answer will differ from society to society. Indeed, the question cannot be answered without looking beyond legal institutions to the societies in which they function, the ways they function there, and what else happens there that interacts with and affects the sway of law. For the rule of law to exist, still more to flourish and be secure, many things beyond the law matter. And since societies differ in many ways, so will those things.

The practical problem becomes how to design arrangements that serve such ends in particular circumstances. Since societies, histories, practices, traditions and institutions differ, and many such differences have effects, so too will the answers that make sense at one time or another, one place or another. That at least is a lesson that might be gleaned from the manifest challenges in seeking to build the rule of law in 'transitional' societies. Even with clarity about the goal, means vary, and too often we have no idea what they might be. Unfortunately, too much discussion of the rule of law has started and stopped with unwarranted confidence in a particular set of means.

Culture

Theorists and practitioners are gradually acknowledging, if not yet embracing, the importance of contextual particularities (see the fine discussion in Tamanaha 2008). It is no longer news in the literature on rule of law promotion, though it has taken much longer to be reflected in practice, that legal institutions cannot on their own do all the heavy lifting of the rule of law. That recognition is all to the good. However, there is a tendency to move from an exaggerated focus on legal institutions as the solution to the all-purpose catch-all grab-bag of 'culture' as the problem. This exchange of simplistic diagnosis for simplistic cure is not an improvement. Just as legal institutions are only part of the solution, so culture is only part of the problem. In either case, mistaking the part for the whole is unwise.

What blocks and what facilitates – what *has* blocked and what has facilitated – the attainment of such an attractive state of affairs as the rule of law? A common answer, in even the most enlightened treatments of this question, revolves around the nebulous notion of 'culture': lack of 'legal culture', 'civil culture' or just having a culture without the right 'cultural' elements and full of the wrong ones. Thus, we are told that 'the rule of law is not something that exists "beyond culture" and that can be somehow added to an existing culture by the simple expedient of creating formal structures and rewriting constitutions and statutes. In its substantive sense, the rule of law *is* a culture' (Brooks 2004: 2275 and 2285). Similarly, in their excellent book, *Can Might Make Rights?*, Stromseth, Wippman and Brooks (2006: 75) repeatedly and rightly stress that '"promoting the rule of law" is an issue of norm creation and cultural change as much as an issue of creating new institutions and legal codes'. They devote a chapter to 'creating rule of law cultures', in which they emphasise that 'the rule of law is as much a culture as a set of institutions, as much a matter of the habits, commitments and beliefs of ordinary people as of legal codes. Institutions and codes are important, but without the cultural and political commitment to back them up, they are rarely more than window-dressing' (Stromseth, Wippman and Brooks 2006: 311).

This is all true and important, and everything Stromseth, Wippman and Brooks say about how to generate a 'rule of law culture' is illuminating. The rule of law is bound up with all those fundamental aspects of a state and society that determine the extent to which it is rational for a person to behave civilly and within the law. And culture is part of that. The rule of law cannot prevail on the basis of every citizen making a daily calculation of the relative merits of behaving legally and illegally and almost all of them concluding each time that it makes sense to remain within the law. Norms, routine expectations, common understandings and reactions that are 'second nature' are all of crucial importance, and these are commonly encoded in and transmitted by culture. As Philip Selznick (1999: 37) observes, 'the rule of law requires a culture of lawfulness, that is, of routine respect, self-restraint and deference'.

Where institutions and rules of restraint are strong, a large part of that strength typically flows not directly or solely from the institutions and rules themselves, but from the traditions in which they were formed and from the culture that they themselves generated. These traditions and this culture grow around and encrust the rules and institutions, shaping the routine expectations of participants and observers. Moreover, the wider social efficacy of official law requires not merely that elites observe and seek to enforce it, but also that it enter into the normative structures that nourish, guide, inform and coordinate the actions of ordinary people: people who do not merely comply resentfully when they feel they might otherwise be punished, but who comply happily (enough) even when they are confident they will not be.

These understandings, expectations and traditions that make rules and institutions meaningful and effective in turn gain strength from their often invisible pervasiveness. Where thickly institutionalised constraints do exist – indeed, typically where they do their best work – they are often not noticed, for they are internalised, by both the powerful and those with less power, as the normal ways to behave. Limits are not tested because people cannot *imagine* that they should be.

However, it pays not to exaggerate with culture. In a great deal of talk about the rule of law, indeed, in a great deal of use of the concept of culture generally, 'culture' operates as a residual category. It is the bag into which everything apart from rule of law recipes is thrown, and to which cursory and usually ritual deference is given before the important 'hard' stuff is taken up. Alternatively, it is blamed when that hard stuff deflates. This simultaneously diminishes the significance of the specific items in the culture bag while exaggerating their imperviousness to change. It should also be noted that culture can change and be changed by forces and pressures not themselves elements of culture.

Consider first the concept. Much that we call culture in connection with the rule of law – willingness to trust in the law, or its absence; expectations that the law will matter – has other than cultural sources. They are embedded in social structures, networks, institutions, and the ways all of these operate and interconnect and, when they do, change. Certainly, sometimes people fail to rely on the state, or trust political elites, because of deeply embedded cultural distrust of, hostility to and alienation from them. At other times, however, they distrust them because they are untrustworthy, whether because they work in crooked ways or just fail to work. It is actually rational in such circumstances to distrust them, and unless they can be changed, it will remain so, notwithstanding our attempts to enhance benighted local 'culture'. Indeed, too much emphasis on problems of 'culture' might simply blind us to the real problems that remain to be addressed. To categorise all these potential challenges as 'cultural' is to homogenise them misleadingly, and to forget that often a lot more (and a lot else) than culture is involved and needs to be addressed (see Holmes 1995a).

On the other hand, even when culture is the right category to use, we should be careful not to reify it as some vast and insurmountable impediment to change. Often culture is taken to be homogeneous, organic, slow-moving and inescapable, and to say we are confronted with hostile or inhospitable political or legal culture is simply to say the game's up. Were culture as impervious to change as is often imagined, we all may as well hang up our boots and watch events take their preordained course. But cultural sensitivity is not the same thing as cultural determinism. Sensitivity might encourage 'piecemeal social engineering', which would be a salutary alternative to the zealous exporting of institutional models. Determinism is likelier merely to encourage despair.[9]

---

9 See Krygier 1999: 77–105. Amartya Sen (2007: ch 5) is typically wise about these questions.

32 MARTIN KRYGIER

Conclusion

The upshot of these reflections is this: with regard to the rule of law, it pays to be a contextual universalist: universalist about the value of it; deeply contextual about how to get there. What is precious about the rule of law is not this or that bit of legal stuff, but an outcome, a state of affairs, in which the law counts, at least as a reliable restraint on the exercise of power, and arguably as more than that as well. What conspires to generate such a state of affairs is complex and mysterious, and will vary from place to place and time to time. What doesn't vary is that it will depend on many things *outside* what we commonly regard as legal institutions. They will certainly include social forces and institutions, and they may include institutions we wouldn't recognise as legal but which do some of the same work.

In societies where the rule of law has long been secure, the fact that it is misconceived might not matter too much, since to a considerable extent it runs on its own steam. However, in conflictual, post-conflict and transitional societies, where efforts are made to catalyse the rule of law, these problems can be catastrophic. For those most urgently seeking the rule of law are in the end concerned not with a package of legal techniques but with an *outcome*: that salutary state of affairs where law counts in a society as a restraint on power. Afghanistan is a place where such restraint on power is conspicuous by its absence, and sadly will probably be for some considerable time to come.

References

Brooks, Rosa (2004). 'The new imperialism: Violence, norms and the "rule of law"', *Michigan Law Review*, 101

Carey, John (2000). 'Parchment, equilibria and institutions', *Comparative Political Studies*, 33

Carothers, Thomas (2005). 'The problem of knowledge', in Carothers, Thomas (ed.), *Promoting the Rule of Law Abroad. The Problem of Knowledge*. Washington DC: Carnegie Endowment for International Peace

Davis, Kevin E. and Trebilcock, Michael J. (2008). 'The relationship between law and development: Optimists versus skeptics', *American Journal of Comparative Law*, 56

Di Palma, Giuseppe (1990). *To Craft Democracies. An Essay on Democratic Transitions*. Berkeley: University of California Press

Dicey, Alfred (1959). *Introduction to the Study of the Law of the Constitution*, 10th edn (1st edn: 1889). London: Macmillan

Fortes, Meyer and Evans-Pritchard, E.E. (eds.) (1948). *African Political Systems*. Oxford University Press

Fraenkel, Ernst (1941). *The Dual State*. New York: Oxford University Press

Fuller, Lon (1964). *The Morality of Law*. New Haven: Yale University Press

Ganev, Venelin (2009). 'The rule of law as an institutionalised wager: Constitutions, courts and transformative social dynamics in Eastern Europe', *The Hague Journal on the Rule of Law*, 1: 2

Habermas, Juergen (1986). 'Law as medium and law as institution', in Teubner, Gunther (ed.), *Dilemmas of the Welfare State*. Berlin: de Gruyter

Holmes, Stephen (1995a). 'Cultural legacies or state collapse? Probing the post-communist dilemma', Collegium Budapest/Institute for Advanced Study, public lecture no. 13, November 1995

Holmes, Stephen (1995b). *Passions and Constraint*, Chicago: University of Chicago Press

Krygier, Martin (1980). 'Anthropological approaches', in Kamenka, Eugene, and Erh-Soon Tay, Alice (eds.), *Law and Social Control*. London: Edward Arnold

Krygier, Martin (1999). 'Institutional optimism, cultural pessimism and the rule of law', in Krygier, Martin and Czarnota, Adam (eds.), *The Rule of Law after Communism*. Dartmouth: Ashgate

Krygier, Martin (2004). 'False dichotomies, real perplexities, and the rule of law', in Sajó, András (ed.), *Human Rights with Modesty. The Problem of Universalism*. Leiden/Boston: Martinus Nijhoff

Krygier, Martin (2010). 'The Hart-Fuller debate, transitional societies and the rule of law', in Cane, Peter (ed.), *The Hart-Fuller Debate. 50 Years On*. Oxford: Hart Publishers

Krygier, Martin, and Mason, Whit (forthcoming), 'Violence, development and the rule of law', in Mavrotas, George (ed.), *Security and Development*. Cheltenham: Edward Elgar Publishers

Kurkchiyan, Marina (2003). 'The illegitimacy of law', in Galligan, Denis and Kurkchiyan, Marina (eds.), *Law and Informal Practices*. Oxford University Press

MacFarlane, S. Neil (2003). 'Politics and the rule of law in the Commonwealth of Independent States', in Galligan, Denis and Kurkchiyan, Marina (eds.), *Law and Informal Practices*. Oxford University Press

Montesquieu, Baron de (1989). *The Spirit of the Laws*, Cohler, Anne M, Miller, Basia Carolyn and Stone, Harold Samuel (eds. and translators) (1st edn, 1748). Cambridge University Press

Peerenboom, Randall (2005). 'Human rights and rule of law. What's the relationship?', *Georgetown Journal of International Law*, 36

Selznick, Philip (1999). 'Legal cultures and the rule of law', in Krygier, Martin and Czarnota, Adam (eds.), *The Rule of Law After Communism*. Aldershot: Ashgate

Sen, Amartya (2000). 'What is the role of legal and judicial reform in the development process?', Washington DC: World Bank Legal Conference, 5 June 2000

Sen, Amartya (2007). *Identity and Violence. The Illusion of Destiny*. New York: WW Norton & Co

Snyder, Timothy (2010). 'Gogol haunts the new Ukraine', *New York Review of Books*, 25 March 2010

Stromseth, Jane, Wippman, David and Brooks, Rosa (2006). *Can Might Make Rights?* New York: Cambridge University Press

Sunstein, Cass and Holmes, Stephen (1999). *The Cost of Rights*. New York: Norton

Tamanaha, Brian Z (2008). 'The primacy of society and the failures of law and development', keynote address, conference on the rule of law, Nagoya University, Japan, 13 June 2008, forthcoming in *Cornell Journal of International Law*

Weiss, Linda and Hobson, John (1995). *States and Economic Development*. Cambridge: Polity Press

Zakaria, Fareed (1997). 'The rise of illiberal democracy', *Foreign Affairs*, November–December 1997

3

Deiokes and the Taliban*

Local governance, bottom-up state formation and the rule of law in counter-insurgency

DAVID J. KILCULLEN

Herodotus of Halicarnassus, writing in the fifth century BC in Book 1 of his *Histories*, gave an account of Deiokes whom he identified as the first king of the Medes:

> There was a certain Mede named Deiokes, son of Phraortes, a man of much wisdom, who had conceived the desire of obtaining to himself the sovereign power. In furtherance of his ambition, therefore, he formed and carried into execution the following scheme. As the Medes at that time dwelt in scattered villages without any central authority, and lawlessness in consequence prevailed throughout the land, Deiokes, who was already a man of mark in his own village, applied himself with greater zeal and earnestness than ever before to the practice of justice among his fellows. It was his conviction that justice and injustice are engaged in perpetual war with one another. He therefore began his course of conduct, and presently the men of his village, observing his integrity, chose him to be the arbiter of all their disputes. Bent on obtaining the sovereign power, he showed himself an honest and an upright judge, and by these means gained such credit with his fellow citizens as to attract the attention of those who lived in the surrounding villages. They had long been suffering from unjust and oppressive judgments; so that, when they heard of the singular uprightness of Deiokes, and of the equity of his decisions, they joyfully had recourse to him in the various quarrels and suits that arose, until at last they came to put confidence in no one else.
>
> (*Herodotus* 1954: 54ff)

Herodotus is describing a member of a local elite, a 'man of mark in his own village', using the delivery of justice – dispute resolution, mediation, settling of disputes among the community – as a means to acquire local legitimacy and political power. In this traditional society, one where people lived 'in scattered villages without any central authority', he does

---

* Parts of this chapter have been previously published by Oxford University Press in David Kilcullen, *Counterinsurgency* (2010). Reproduced with permission.

this not by developing an elaborate court, but from the bottom up. Herodotus continues:

> The number of complaints brought before him was continually increasing, as people learnt more and more the fairness of his judgments, Deiokes, feeling himself now all important, announced that he did not intend any longer to hear cases . . . Hereupon robbery and lawlessness broke out afresh, and prevailed through the country even more than heretofore; wherefore the Medes assembled from all quarters, and held a consultation on the state of affairs. The speakers, as I think, were chiefly friends of Deiokes. [A snide little aside there from Herodotus.] 'We cannot possibly,' they said, 'go on living in this country if things continue as they now are; let us therefore set a king over us, that so the land may be well governed, and we ourselves may be able to attend to our own affairs, and not be forced to quit our country on account of anarchy.' The assembly was persuaded by these arguments, and resolved to appoint a king.
>
> (*Herodotus* 1954: 54ff)

Here we see Deiokes starting to translate the social good and community service of dispute resolution, mediation and order into popular support on a local level, and thence into the formal authority, rule of law and political structure of a state – in this case, a monarchy founded on law. Herodotus again:

> It followed to determine who should be chosen to the office. When this debate began, the claims of Deiokes and his praises were at once in every mouth; so that presently all agreed that he should be king. Thus Deiokes collected the Medes into a nation, and ruled over them alone.
>
> (*Herodotus* 1954: 54ff)

Herodotus seems to be tapping into a long-standing trend here, one that links the origins of insurgency warfare with the origins of government: local non-state actors gaining influence through the local exercise of law and order, especially dispute resolution and mediation, and then translating that influence into formal political authority through processes of state formation from the bottom up.[1]

Counter-insurgency theory: a detour

One of the seminal theorists of counter-insurgency was Bernard Fall, who fought in the French Resistance in World War II and later in French

---

1 When the Prophet Mohammed originally moved to Medina, where he established the first Islamic community, it was to work as a mediator for the city's Jewish community. The role of mediator has been highly esteemed throughout Islamic history.

Indochina, and was killed in February 1967 while doing research in South Vietnam. Two years earlier, Fall had written: 'When a country is being subverted it is not being outfought; it is being out-administered' (Fall 1965: 36). Or, we might say, when a government is losing to an insurgency, it isn't being outfought; it's being out-governed. This is one of the neater expressions of an insight that is fundamental to counter-insurgency theory, namely that insurgents challenge the state by making it impossible for the government to perform its functions, or by usurping those functions – most commonly, local-level political legitimacy, the rule of law, monopoly on the use of force, taxation, control of movement, and regulating the economy. Robert S. Thompson and David Galula, two leading classical theorists, described counter-insurgency as a competition for government, with both the state and the insurgent trying to mobilise and control the population.

> The communists, or shall we say, any sound revolutionary warfare operator (the French underground, the Norwegian underground, or any other European anti-Nazi underground), most of the time used small-war tactics – not to destroy the German army, of which they were thoroughly incapable, but to establish a competitive system of control over the population.
>
> (Fall 1965: 22)

Fall, Galula and Thompson all shared the insight that counter-insurgency is a competition for governance between a state and an armed non-state challenger. Given this, it becomes very important, in actually running a counter-insurgency campaign, to compare the strength and effectiveness of the insurgents with that of the government they are fighting. The level of benefits the insurgents can deliver, or be perceived to deliver, to the population effectively defines the government's standard of success.

But it is hard to compare the state and an insurgency if one thinks in structural terms. *Structurally*, governments are very different from insurgent movements. Governments have fixed locations, a capital, provincial and district offices, a bureaucracy and public service, armed forces and police, and so on, whereas the insurgents may have only a shifting and shadowy network of cadres, fighters, sympathisers and supporters. They're usually smaller than governments, and it's often difficult to pin down exactly how many fighters they can put in the field at any one time. So all of that makes it extremely hard to compare relative strength and effectiveness.

Joel Migdal (1988) solved this problem for us by taking a *functional* rather than *structural* approach. He identified four functions of government: it has to penetrate society, regulate social relationships, extract resources, and apply those resources to identified group ends. These functions are relevant to any form of governance, including non-state governance systems like tribes or clans, and of course the functions are independent of structure. The beauty of this approach is that these same four functions mirror exactly what insurgents also have to do if they want to establish that competitive system of control that Fall talks about – which makes it much easier to compare the relative strengths of governments and their insurgent competitors.

Just less than twenty years after Migdal, Stathis Kalyvas (2006) examined this same phenomenon from the standpoint of the third actor in the insurgency triad: the local non-combatant population. Using an exhaustive series of fieldwork studies from numerous conflicts, he showed that one of our common assumptions – namely, that insurgent movements are strongest in areas where people support the insurgents' ideology, while governments are strongest in areas where people have a positive view of the state – actually reverses the causality of what really happens. The insurgents are not strongest where people support them: rather, people support them where they are strongest. Likewise, people support the government in areas where government presence is strongest: support *follows* strength, not vice versa.

Obviously, this finding has important implications for traditional 'hearts and minds' and 'battle of ideas' approaches, where combatants try to make people like them in order to gain their support. Kalyvas shows that that's not how it works at all. He focuses on the same concerns Herodotus talks about – the fear of disorder and anarchy – and shows that local populations in an insurgency are in a lethally uncertain environment, buffeted on all sides by armed groups who want their support and will kill or punish them if they don't get it. Community leaders are forced to cooperate with the strongest local group, and to switch sides as needed, as a means to survival.

When I read Kalyvas, it reminds me of conversations I have had with Afghan tribal elders and community leaders over the years. Once, last year, I was with a local leader and eleven of his district elders. This man had fought with the Taliban and had just defected to the government side a couple of weeks before. We were all sitting down talking about the situation, and I asked him what made him decide to leave the Taliban and join the government. He said: 'Oh, you don't get it. I wasn't with the Taliban before, and I'm not with the government now. I was always just trying to protect my people, to look after them. Before, I thought we were better off with the Taliban. Now, we think we're better off with the government – but that could change.' This is a classic 'swing voter' approach. Other people take a 'hedging' approach: in both Pakistan and Afghanistan, I've talked to Pashtun leaders from tribes where most families have one son fighting with the Taliban and one with the government, just to cover both bases.

Kalyvas unpacks the motivation that drives people like this tribal leader to behave in this way, and his work shows that people will do almost anything, and support almost anyone who can reduce that feeling of fear and uncertainty by establishing a permanent presence, through a predictable system of rules and sanctions that allow people to find safety by compliance within a set of guidelines. Even if those guidelines are harsh and oppressive, if people know they can be safe by following a certain set of rules, they will flock to the side that provides the most consistent and predictable set of rules. Obviously, people don't want to be oppressed, and they want to be treated kindly and have a prosperous life. But as Kalyvas shows, these are actually secondary considerations; what people most want is security, through order and predictability, and they will kill to get it.

We could describe what we're talking about here as a theory of normative systems in counter-insurgency – something I'm grateful to my colleague, Professor Erin Simpson, for pointing out to me. Or, following Bernard Fall's usage, we might talk about 'systems of competitive control'. If you add into the mix Migdal's functionalist state-in-society approach and Kalyvas's insight that support follows strength, and throw in for good measure Mao Zedong's observation that 'political power grows out of the barrel of a gun', then we come to a pretty good understanding of what it takes to prevail in an insurgency: what I call 'the theory of competitive control'.

The theory of competitive control

Simply put, the theory of competitive control is this: in irregular conflicts (that is, conflicts in which at least one warring party is a non-state actor), the local armed group that a given population perceives as most able to establish a normative system for resilient, full-spectrum control over violence, economic activity and human security is most likely to prevail within that population's residential area.

In other words, whoever does better at establishing a resilient system of control, which gives people order and a sense of security where they sleep, is likely to gain their support, and ultimately win the competition for government.

Let me explain 'resilient full-spectrum control' with reference to al Qaeda in Iraq (AQI). AQI, just like any other insurgent or terrorist group, tried to gain control by manipulating and controlling Iraq's Sunni population, whom they saw as their power base. And they did that through a system of rules and sanctions based on a particularly severe and de-contextualised form of Shari'a that was alien to the population. It included rules such as: if someone in an area they controlled smoked, they would cut his fingers off; if a woman pushed her headscarf back behind her hairline, AQI would throw acid in her face; if a man failed to give them his daughter in marriage, they would cut his head off; if they suspected someone of being a spy, they would skin him alive in public; if a tribal leader refused to cooperate with them, they would bake his seven-year-old son alive in an oven. All these things actually happened in Iraq in 2006–07, and in fact they did even more heinous things. The point is that AQI had a system of control based almost entirely on intimidation. They terrorised people, and they had tight control in areas where they could maintain that fear over the population, and – as Kalyvas would have predicted – where there was a threat to the Sunni community from Shi'a death squads, people even actively supported AQI out of fear that, horrific though they were, the alternative of being on the wrong side of those with guns by virtue of your creed was worse.

But the control AQI established was in a very narrow band, relying solely on intimidation. Their range of options was a toggle switch: they could either cut your head off or *not* cut your head off. Beyond that, they were basically incapable, and this made their control very brittle. When coalition forces finally succeeded in breaking their reign of terror and lifting the pall of fear off the community, people turned on AQI in a flash and destroyed them.

Contrast this with an organisation like Hezbollah, which has a much more resilient, full-spectrum system of control. They have a terrorist wing, and they *will* kill you if you step out of line. But they also have a community militia that will protect you and keep crime down, they have charities that will help you if you are poor, they can get you a job, teach your children in their schools, treat you in their hospital if you are sick, and represent you in parliament through their political party. And you can watch their television channel, *al-Manar*, listen to their radio station and read their newspaper. Al Qaeda were thugs; Hezbollah – and groups like them, including *Jaysh al-Mahdi*, and Muqtada al-Sadr's Shi'a movement in Iraq – are much, much more than that. In fact, they are acting very much like a government, which is after all another normative system based on wide-spectrum systems of control.

AQI and Hezbollah are at opposite ends of the spectrum, with the Taliban somewhere in between. But the Taliban are far closer to Hezbollah in their approach than to AQI.

The rule of law is clearly the ultimate normative system of control. It lays down rules, associates each rule with a sanction if you break the rule, sets up a system of published laws that aid predictability and consistency, and establishes a judiciary – in democracies, an independent judiciary – and a police force, prisons, lawyers, judges and so on, all in the interests of making people feel safe and secure through a standardised and ordered normative system. This is a huge factor in social stability that ultimately becomes the basis for government. Rule of law in this sense, as Deiokes clearly knew, is literally the foundation of both the state and social order.

Now someone might say that, with this statement, I have admitted that government is just another oppressive protection racket, no better or worse than rebels, insurgents or so-called terrorists. Those who conduct counter-insurgency operations are no better than the enemy, these critics would say, and they are engaged in a fundamentally illiberal and oppressive activity because, like the insurgents, they are trying to establish a system of control. States, with their police and courts and armies and parliaments, according to this view, are just like insurgents, except that they own the means of legitimacy.

Functionally, as Migdal would have it, there is certainly some equivalence. But drawing any moral equivalence between what insurgents do, such as beheading people or baking children alive, and what legitimate responsible governments do, such as enforcing the speed limit or taxation regulations or upholding the laws against homicide and robbery, is gravely misplaced. The rule of law, processes of state formation, and the character of the state, all play essential roles in making these functionally similar structures normatively distinct.

Counter-insurgency mirrors the state

Insurgency, according to current US military doctrine, is 'an organised movement aimed at the overthrow of a constituted government through the use of subversion and armed conflict . . . Stated another way, an insurgency is an organised, protracted politico-military struggle designed to weaken the control and legitimacy of an established government, occupying power or other political authority while increasing insurgent control' (US Army and US Marine Corps 2006: paras 1–2). *Counter-insurgency*, meanwhile, is just an umbrella term that describes the full range of measures that governments take to defeat insurgencies. These can be political, administrative, military, economic, psychological or informational, and are almost always used in combination. There's no standard set of techniques in counter-insurgency. On the contrary, counter-insurgency techniques mirror the character of the state that uses them.

Nazi Germany's approach to irregular warfare illustrates this fact dramatically. In his account of anti-partisan warfare on the Eastern Front, Ben Shepherd (2004) found that many German commanders recognised the need to protect, win over and cooperate with the local population, and treat them with respect and consideration, so as to reduce support for the partisans. A study of operations by the 221st Security Division of Army Group Centre found that 'numerous Eastern Army figures already [in 1941] saw the potential for support in a tentatively pro-German population. They also saw the need for a more sensible, measured prosecution of occupation and security policy in order to exploit it' (Shepherd 2004). This led some units all of the time, and most units some of the time, to engage in population security, hearts and minds, and civic action operations that tried to protect and win over the locals in ways that would be familiar to any modern counter-insurgent. Colonel Reinhard Gehlen wrote in 1941 that 'if the population rejects the partisans and lends its full support to the struggle against them, no partisan problem will exist' (Shepherd 2004).

Yet these commanders' efforts were continuously undermined by the rapacious and genocidal nature of the Nazi state. 'The effectiveness of all these efforts was blunted by the fact that they never posed a fundamental challenge to ruthless economic interests [which led the Germans to despoil the East, leaving the population starving and destroying the economy] or to racist preconceptions of the population [which contributed to mass violence against non-combatants] . . . The ruthless, ideological and exploitative dynamic of Nazi occupation policy in the east, then, proved an implacable obstacle' (Shepherd 2004:118–19) to effective counter-insurgency. As Walter Laqueur said, 'partisan leaders . . . would have found it much more difficult to attract recruits had the Germans treated the population decently, but this would have been quite incompatible . . . with the character of the Nazi leaders, their doctrine and their aims' (quoted in Grenkevich 1994: 111).

Counter-insurgency, then, mirrors the state: any given state's approach to counter-insurgency depends on the nature of that state, and the concept of 'counter-insurgency' can mean entirely different things depending on the character of the government involved. I would submit that this means that while good governments can do counter-insurgency badly, bad governments cannot do it well. Oppressive governments tend to enact brutal measures against rebellions, military dictatorships tend to favour paternalistic or reactionary martial law policies, while liberal-democratic states tend to be quick – perhaps too quick – to hand control to locally elected civilians in a bid to return to 'normalcy'. You only need compare the approach taken by Syrian President Hafez al-Assad in crushing the *ikhwan* at Hama in 1982, or by Saddam Hussein in massacring Kurdish civilians at Halabja in 1989, with British policy in Northern Ireland or our own policies in Iraq and Afghanistan to see this. Counter-insurgency *can* be oppressive and inhumane, but it is not inhumane by definition; whether it is depends on the character of the state or states involved.

Top-down versus bottom-up: Somalia versus Somaliland

Until recently it has been rare for counter-insurgents to compare notes with peace-building specialists, members of the international development community and rule of law experts. This is changing, but one of the side effects of that academic stovepiping has been that, even though Herodotus was writing about these matters more than 2,500 years ago, we currently lack a generally recognised theory of opposed nation-building, or of bottom-up state formation. Because of this, when the international community becomes involved in reconstruction and stabilisation, institutions like the UN, World Bank, IMF and governments tend to focus on top-down, state-centric processes that have a structural focus on putting in place the central, national-level institutions of the state, rather than a functional focus on local-level governance functions.

Recent experience in Iraq, Afghanistan and the Horn of Africa (specifically, the different experiences of Somaliland and Somalia) actually suggests that bottom-up, civil society-based programmes that focus on peace-building, reconciliation and the connection of legitimate local non-state governance structures to wider state institutions may have a greater chance of success in conflict and post-conflict environments than traditional top-down programmes that focus on building the national-level institutions of the central state.

For example, as the anthropologist Ioan Lewis (2008) has shown, in Somalia since 1992, the international community has engaged in a series of failed attempts at top-down nation-building that have been captured and perverted by local elites, many of whom were the same warlords who made the problem in the first place. Meanwhile, just to the north in Somaliland, a series of local clan peace deals in 1992 led to district-level agreements in 1993, regional charters, and the formation of provincial and then 'national' government in 1994. This has resulted in a relatively high degree of peace, order, economic recovery and the rule of law in Somaliland and to some extent in Puntland, despite lack of international recognition and involvement. In fact, Somalia is virtually a laboratory test case, with the south acting as a control group against the experiment in the north. We have the same ethnic groups, in some cases the same clans or even the same people, coming out of the same civil war and the same famine and humanitarian disaster, resulting from the collapse of the same state, and yet we see completely different results arising from a bottom-up peace-building process based on local-level rule of law, versus a top-down approach based on putting in place a 'grand bargain' at the elite level.

Likewise, in Iraq in 2007, the coalition forces during the surge went in with the intent to create security for Iraqis, which would then lead to a national-level peace deal, a 'grand bargain' that would resolve the conflict. Instead, the opposite occurred: a series of local agreements and reconciliation processes that created peace and security at the local level (with our security presence acting as a critical enabler, as Kalyvas predicted) resulted in an improvement in security overall. These enforceable local agreements are just another form of normative system, sanctioned by society and upheld in a very similar manner to the rule of law. Notably, police, courts and a judicial system, along with local representative councils, were some of the first institutions that these communities found it necessary to create.

The Taliban and the rule of law

Finally, we come to Afghanistan, and here we have seen exactly the same dynamics prevail. International assistance efforts focused on building police, courts, ministries and institutions at the level of the central state – and international aid programmes – became bogged down in bureaucracy, duplication and inefficiency. This created a vacuum at the local level, which after 2005 the Taliban increasingly filled. They came in at the grassroots level and took over the functions of security, mediation, dispute resolution and community policing, and they brought the world's most convenient and attractive cash crop – the poppy – to the Afghan farmer. The Taliban thus successfully sidestepped our top-down approach, and were able to outgovern the Karzai government at the local (and functional) level.

To paraphrase Bernard Fall, in Afghanistan the government is losing to the Taliban, and it's losing because it's being outgoverned rather than outfought. Following are some examples.

Across the south of Afghanistan today, about fifteen Taliban Shari'a law courts are operating at the local level. Now when you hear the term 'Shari'a court', you may think of people having their hands cut off for stealing, women being stoned for adultery, beheadings and so on. And that *does* happen. But in fact, the bulk of the work of these courts concerns what in the official system would be commercial or civil cases rather than criminal ones. The Taliban courts issue title deeds and resolve land disputes, settle water and grazing disputes, handle inheritances and family law, and issue identity cards and even passports (in the name of the Islamic Emirate of Afghanistan). They deliver a local dispute resolution and mediation service, with a reputation for harsh but fair and swift justice. In other words, these courts form part of a resilient, full-spectrum system of control. They are in fact doing precisely what Deiokes did and, like him, they are translating local dispute resolution and mediation into local rule of law, and thus into political power.

According to Sarah Chayes (personal communication, Kabul 2009), who was long based in Kandahar, there is a Taliban court just outside the city that formally subpoenas people to testify in court, and people go – even from within the supposedly coalition-controlled urban area of Kandahar City – because they know they'll be punished if they don't by local Taliban enforcement squads who act, and work, a lot like local police. There is in fact a silent campaign of intimidation, coercion and control happening right under the noses of the Afghan government and International Security Assistance Force. So who's in charge in Kandahar? In some places local warlords or drug dealers, in some places the Taliban, but clearly not the government. Even where the government does wield power, officials' power is based more on their personal stature and connections than on their official positions.

In Migdal's terms, the Taliban have penetrated society, and are playing a major role in regulating social relationships. They are also extracting resources and applying these resources to identified group ends. Taliban tax assessors, associated with the local Taliban governors whom the Taliban have appointed for each village and district, go out on a regular basis and assess people's property and crops and then levy taxes – usually around 10 per cent – in a firm but generally equitable manner. At the local level, the Taliban are acting a lot like a government.

How is the actual government doing? Most analysts agree that the Afghan government levies no taxes, relies largely on corruption and shakedowns of the population, has no functioning local court system, doesn't have a presence at the local level in about two-thirds of the country, and when it does have a presence, its local representatives tend to act so corruptly or oppressively that they alienate the population. And that's even leaving aside the significant loss of legitimacy resulting from last year's deeply flawed presidential election. In terms of Migdal's functional approach, the Taliban are the real government of much of Afghanistan. We can beat the Taliban in any military engagement, but we're losing in Afghanistan not because we're being outfought, but because the Afghan government is being outgoverned. Unless we take drastic action to counter corruption, prevent abusive and oppressive practices by local officials (especially the police), reform local-level systems and create legitimate local government structures that can function in the interests of the population, there's little doubt that we are eventually going to lose.

Two other things that the Taliban have done really demonstrate that they understand the government's weakness in this area, and that they see the importance of the competition for local legitimacy. First, again according to Sarah Chayes (personal communication, Washington DC 2009), the Taliban have established an ombudsman system where, if a local Taliban commander behaves abusively, people can complain and can have their complaint heard by an independent authority, the Taliban commander involved will be punished and the injured parties will be compensated. This push for fairness and accountability is a direct challenge to the state. The Taliban are saying, through deeds and words, as part of a sophisticated communications strategy: 'The government will exploit you and abuse you, and their allies, the coalition forces, will bomb you, and there's really nothing you can do about it. We Taliban might be harsh, but we are from here, we are part of your society, we're not going anywhere, and we are fair, predictable and just.'

Second, the Taliban has a code of conduct, the *layeha*, that reads a lot like a military justice code or a set of field service regulations. We first saw this in 2006, and back in May of this year, our forces in Helmand province captured an updated and expanded version of it. This is a set of rules, guidelines for behaviour, admonitions to treat the population fairly, and a set of authorities that lay out how Taliban groups are to operate. This is a normative system that the local people know about, and, combined with the ombudsman system and the Taliban court system, it means that there is a high degree of accountability. This doesn't mean the Taliban are not oppressive and menacing as well. They will put a gun to people's heads and force them to comply. But then, a lot of local-level officials and drug dealers and warlords and other people associated with the government are oppressive and predatory as well. Since this is a *competition* between two sides, to win, one side only has to be better than the other.

Some conclusions

Herodotus's account of Deiokes is something of an archetype – a semi-mythical description of how the rule of law, the delivery of justice and the establishment of a locally legitimate presence are intimately connected with each other, and how they become the foundation not only of a social order, but of the state itself. As Fall, Galula and Thompson have shown, counter-insurgency is a competition for government, and as Migdal and Kalyvas showed, one wins that competition by penetrating society, regulating people's actions through a normative system of rules and sanctions that create predictability and order, and establishing a presence that causes people to feel safe and makes them flock to one's side. As the Nazi experience shows, a regime can get things right at the level of counter-insurgency technique, but if the state is fundamentally oppressive, corrupt or illegitimate, these features will express themselves in the counter-insurgency strategy and fatally undermine it.

As I have said in describing my theory of competitive control, which I first articulated in 2006, the side that best establishes a resilient, full-spectrum system of control that can affect security, rule of law and economic activity at the local level is most likely to prevail. And as our recent experience in Afghanistan, Iraq and Somalia shows, in places where local people have taken a bottom-up peace-building approach based on local, enforceable agreements among local groups and normative systems that protect the community from threats and disorders, the results have been far better than in places where the international community has taken a top-down approach focusing on the institutions of the central state. And yet, that top-down approach nevertheless seems to be the international community's default setting in these types of situations.

These observations yield three implications. First, those working in counter-insurgency and counter-terrorism need to start talking more with the peace-building and development community, and all of these groups need to talk much more with the rule of law community. These academic and policy communities have been stovepiped for far too long, and the more we share insights, the better we'll do in the field. We need to reconsider our theories of top-down state-building, and recognise what empirical evidence from the field is telling us: that bottom-up, community-based, civil society approaches are having much greater success than top-down state-based approaches. This doesn't mean we can do without central government structures, but it does mean we need to put a lot more effort into bottom-up issues, especially those related to the rule of law.

Second, in terms of Afghanistan, all of this suggests that we need to put the top priority on anti-corruption, governance reform, creating a functioning government at the local level, and establishing sufficient presence to make people feel safe. Until now we have had policies that have focused on fighting the main force Taliban and extending the reach of the Afghan government. But as we've seen, it is not the guerrillas' military capacity that poses the biggest challenge, but its capacity – and inclination – to outgovern the Afghan government. If our strategy is to extend the reach of a government that is corrupt, is oppressing its people and is by virtually every measure failing them, then the more successful we are in extending its reach, the worse things are going to get.

Finally, we need to recognise that we're facing a crisis of legitimacy here, founded on a failure to connect at the local level with ordinary Afghans. Our efforts have been captured by an elite – the same warlords that the Taliban overthrew in 1996, along with a new crowd of corrupt and oppressive officials and power brokers – and that elite is doing what elites generally do: exploiting the population rather than maintaining a system that serves common interests, much less acting out of a sense of *noblesse oblige*. The result of the presidential election in August 2009 underscored this fact, and revealed to the international community something that many Afghans have known since the inception of the current regime in 2002.

I don't think the war is lost, and I don't think the situation is hopeless. The additional troops and resources, more civilian specialists, more money and better leadership that the international community is putting into Afghanistan will create a window of opportunity. But I do think we have to urgently seize that opportunity, and use it to focus on fixing what's wrong at the local level of the Afghan government, or that window will close again and it will all be for naught, and the cost to the Afghan people, regional stability and Western credibility will be immense. We can still turn this around, but we have to act now, and we have to focus on governance, rule of law, anti-corruption, and protecting the people at the local level. It's not rocket science, and these are hardly original ideas. But translating them into action is very difficult, and we have no time to lose.

References

Fall, Bernard B. (1965). 'The theory and practice of insurgency and counterinsurgency', *Naval War College Review*, April 1965

Grenkevich, Leonard (1994). *The Soviet Partisan Movement, 1941–44*. London: Frank Cass

Herodotus: The Histories (1954), translated by Aubrey de Selincourt. Harmondsworth: Penguin Books

Kalyvas, Stathis N. (2006). *The Logic of Violence in Civil War*, Cambridge Studies in Comparative Politics. Cambridge University Press

Lewis, Ioan M. (2008). *Understanding Somalia and Somaliland: Culture, History, Society*. New York: Columbia University Press

Migdal, Joel S (1988). *Strong Societies and Weak States: State-Society Relations and State Capabilities in the Third World*. Princeton University Press

Shepherd, Ben (2004). *War in the Wild East: The German Army and Soviet Partisans*. Cambridge, MA: Harvard University Press

US Army and US Marine Corps (2006). *Field Manual FM 3–24/MCWP 3-33.5 Counterinsurgency*, December 2006

PART II

The context

Where we started

4

The international community's failures
in Afghanistan

FRANCESC VENDRELL

It is becoming painfully obvious that the objectives that some of us diplomats and perhaps key member states of the international community
were pursuing in Afghanistan after September 11, 2001, and which most
Afghans were yearning for, will fail to be achieved. This is in spite of
the enormous investment of lives and money since 2001. This disparity
between investment and achievement demands explanation.

In seeking to explain our failures, it has been tempting for some to
claim that what we had set ourselves to achieve was overly ambitious, that
Afghanistan was never going to become 'another Switzerland' (as if that
was what we were aiming at). This line argues that it was a mistake to
attempt to 'impose' a Western style of governance on what had always
been a tribal society devoid of governmental, let alone representative,
institutions.

But this critique, however comforting to us, ignores Afghanistan's history. Between 1919 and the end of the 1970s, Afghanistan had civilian
institutions both at the centre and in the regions, including the period
1963 to 1973 when parliament was elected by universal suffrage with a
government responsible to it. Describing Afghanistan as a hopeless case
further overlooks the fact that Afghanistan is a multi-ethnic society, that
the tribal system only functioned in the areas inhabited by the Pashtun,
and that, in the course of years of conflict, the authority of tribes, elders
and *jirgas* (dispute-resolving bodies made up of all adult men in a group)
has been eroded. Today the tribal system is regarded as an anachronism by
most educated Afghans. Rather than rushing to divest ourselves of responsibility for the current situation and to shift the blame to the Afghans,
then, it might be worthwhile to reflect on how the UN, the US and its
Western allies have contributed to driving Afghanistan toward its current
calamitous state.

The first error occurred before the Bonn conference. Immediately after
the attack on the World Trade Centre, I had urged UN headquarters to

convene without delay a meeting, along the lines of what was later to take place in Bonn,[1] to sketch out a road map for the post-Taliban period. In my mind, this should have included the establishment of an Afghan interim authority (preferably with HM Zahir Shah as titular chair), which would be accorded Afghanistan's seat at the UN and would, inter alia, request the Security Council to dispatch a multinational force to those parts of Afghanistan vacated by the withdrawing Taliban. The urgency of creating a representative body to make such a request lay in the need to prevent the Northern Alliance (NA) from taking over two-thirds of the country, thus presenting us with a fait accompli. Much time was wasted in the mistaken belief that the Taliban would hold on to power for longer than it did, and because it was felt that neither the NA nor the Rome group around the former king was sufficiently representative. In the event, by the time the Bonn conference finally convened with largely the same delegations in late November, all major cities with the exception of Kandahar had fallen to the NA. The NA, which before the US-led intervention had held just 10 per cent of Afghanistan's territory in the far north, was thus able successfully to claim the lion's share of the ministries in the interim administration. This, in turn, meant that many ministries, governorships and key positions in the Afghan national army, the Afghan national police and the local administration were left under or appointed to largely non-Pashtun warlords and commanders, the very people who were despised and dreaded by Afghans for the atrocities and sleaze that had characterised their rule in the mid-1990s. Thus, from the start of the Bonn process, impunity for corruption and abuse became the norm.

A quiet controversy erupted both before and during the conference about the future UN role in the implementation of the Bonn agreement. Some of us forcefully argued for a heavy footprint on the model of Cambodia, East Timor, Bosnia or Kosovo, convinced that, after years of conflict and misrule, the Afghan people were ready for a strong international role that would do away with both warlord and Taliban rule, reconstruct their

---

1 The Bonn conference, formally known as the Agreement on Provisional Arrangements in Afghanistan Pending the Re-establishment of Permanent Government Institutions, brought together the leaders of the Northern Alliance and other prominent Afghans not associated with the Taliban regime to agree on steps for reconstituting a national government, which the country had lacked since 1979. It created a thirty-member Afghan interim authority to rule for six months, after which it would be replaced by a transitional authority for two years. Within eighteen months of the inception of the TA, a *loya jirga* (grand assembly) would decide on a new constitution.

country, and assist in building up rule of law institutions. But we were overruled by those favouring a 'light footprint', in which the Afghans would be 'in the lead', a politically correct slogan that in practice ensured that the process would be led not by genuine representatives of the Afghan people, but by a group of mostly rapacious individuals. Afghans saw the international community's support for transferring power to the worst villains in their country and drew the natural conclusions.

At Bonn, the participants had requested the Security Council to despatch an international force that would be deployed first to Kabul and then to other urban centres vacated by the Taliban. However, when the Security Council met in mid-December to discuss the request, the US insisted that the International Security Assistance Force (ISAF) be limited to Kabul, presumably to ensure that the US-led Enduring Freedom Coalition would have a free hand in the rest of the country. In so doing, the US curtailed the number of allied forces at a time when, with fresh memories of September 11, many Western governments were readier than they would be two years later, with their attention focused on Iraq and elsewhere, to make a larger contribution to the military effort.

One important component of any nation-building exercise must surely be to ensure that the central government enjoys the monopoly of the means of violence. Yet in Afghanistan, the international community never took this task seriously. Instead of creating a special armed unit within ISAF to receive and either keep or destroy surrendered weapons, the disarmament, demobilisation and reintegration process, in the pursuit of the light footprint, was entrusted to the Afghan Ministry of Defence. At the time the ministry was headed by Marshal Fahim, the most powerful of Afghanistan's warlords and today Karzai's first Vice-President. And so the 60,000 dubious NA combatants went through the charade of handing their (inevitably) oldest weapons to their erstwhile commander in his capacity as defence minister! Nor has the successor process, DIAG (disbandment of illegal armed groups), fared any better, with both ISAF and the coalition, whose cooperation would be essential in case of any resulting security problems, showing little or no interest in becoming involved. One suspects that one reason for the US and NATO's indifference has been the continued ties which some of them maintain with warlords and commanders, whose cooperation they regard as useful in providing intelligence and who, in a bizarre reversal of roles, are remunerated for providing security to the very forces whose supposed task is to provide security to the population. It is little wonder, therefore, that on those rare occasions when senior foreign envoys dare ask President Karzai to improve governance and take meaningful steps against corruption, they meet with deaf ears, either because of the President's genuine fear of antagonising strongmen whom he has now learned to cultivate or because he is aware, as in the case of his brother in Kandahar,[2] of the ties that he and others maintain with the CIA or other foreign military or intelligence services.

For those who bemoan our failure to place greater reliance on Afghanistan's tribal system, an opportunity to revive the system and counter Pashtun perceptions that they were the losers in Bonn would have been the return of Zahir Shah as head of state in 2002. The old King, who died in 2007, enjoyed great popularity and respect at the time, his reign between 1933 and 1973 being nostalgically remembered by many Afghans as their country's golden age. Having proved some foreign cynics wrong by returning from exile in the spring of 2002, the king appeared set to be elected head of the Afghan transitional administration by a large majority of the participants at the emergency *loya jirga* (ELJ) when it convened in June of that year. Some senior US and UN diplomats thought otherwise. Citing the opposition of some NA warlords (who, expecting to be deprived of their power, had found themselves lionised instead by the international community and, in violation of the rules of procedure, allowed to dominate the proceedings of the *loya jirga*), the US and UN representatives prevailed on Zahir Shah to declare that he would not accept the position of head of state even if such were offered to him by the ELJ. This deprived Afghanistan of a highly influential voice who might have balanced the influence of the mullahs or breathed new life into the tribal system. It would also have led to the establishment of a prime minister, most likely Hamid Karzai, and a cabinet responsible to parliament. Instead, marginalising Zahir Shah at Bonn was the first step toward the Islamic Republic (with its ingrained Islamic ideology) that would eventually be proclaimed in the 2004 constitution, a document drafted by an unelected body largely beholden to a group of Jihadi strongmen. Alongside this overt Islamist orientation, the establishment of

---

2 Ahmed Wali Karzai (AWK), a younger half-brother of President Karzai, is regarded as the key power-broker in the south. This is less attributable to his holding the position of chairman of Kandahar's Provincial Council (a largely powerless body) than to having used his family ties with the President to further his accumulation of wealth and power through a variety of means widely believed to be illicit, including ties to the opium trade. AWK denies all these allegations.

a highly centralised presidential system concentrated power in the hands of one person, when what was desirable in a multi-ethnic, bilingual society such as Afghanistan was a decentralised parliamentary system that would spread power among the various ethnic groups.

Despite this accretion of self-inflicted political handicaps, Western governments remained determinedly optimistic about Afghanistan. Afghanistan, unlike Iraq, which had absorbed so much of their attention in the meantime, they insisted, was or was soon bound to become a success story. President Musharraf's assurances that Pakistan had reversed its decades-old policy of supporting the Taliban and/or Gulbuddin Hekmatyar, the most violent of the mujaheddin parties, were taken at face value, despite evidence that both had found refuge in Pakistan. Equally, the West seemed oblivious that the close ties being rapidly developed between India and Afghanistan were feeding Pakistan's decades-old paranoia of being sandwiched between two enemies, which had been the main reason for Pakistan's longstanding effort to maintain a docile regime in Kabul.

There were other failures as well. Having decided that in Karzai the West had found some kind of miracle man, we proceeded to rely on him without either giving him the means to stand up to the warlords or building the institutions that could sustain him. Too little attention was paid to the need to rapidly train a professional Afghan police. The reform of the judiciary languished, while attempts to establish an independent civil service have been unsuccessful. Impunity flourished. Justice was regarded as incompatible with, rather than a necessary complement to, stability. A 'transitional justice action plan', strongly supported by the office of the EU Special Representative and some European countries, was never taken seriously by the US – nor therefore by the Karzai government. In the absence of DIAG, it was always going to be difficult to implement, but a vetting system that would exclude from official positions persons broadly regarded as having committed war crimes or crimes against humanity was never seriously put in place. Nor was there any attempt to support those reformist and pluralistic Afghan civil society elements that could become the nucleus of political parties which would serve as a counterweight to the jihadist *Tanzim*, and who would be in place to follow through on our work when we finally left Afghanistan.

Economic reconstruction, in the meantime, failed to focus on either agriculture or job-creating projects, while huge quantities of money were wasted in overheads paid to private firms and corporations through which many donors, the US in particular, channelled their assistance.

The struggle against narcotics was always going to be slow and hard. It was certainly not helped by the US emphasis until recently on eradication, an expensive and corruption-prone procedure, which alienated poor Afghan farmers without seriously hurting the big drug lords, when greater focus on interdiction and subsidies for legal crops would have led to more positive results.

The 2004 presidential elections, held largely under UN auspices, in which some 70 per cent of Afghans cast their vote, were rightly seen as broadly free and fair, and produced the first legitimate government in over thirty years. Pressure from the Bush administration to hold them ahead of the US elections in November so it could parade them as proof of US achievements forced the postponement to the following year of the more complicated parliamentary elections. This resulted in an electoral calendar under which presidential and parliamentary elections cannot be held concurrently, at great logistical and financial cost. When in the autumn of 2005 elections for parliament took place, they were held, at President Karzai's insistence, under a rarely used electoral system called the single non-transferable vote (SNTV),[3] which discourages the development of political parties and led to a fragmented parliament in which majorities have often been built through bribery. A half-hearted effort to vet candidates to exclude those linked to armed groups, which received no support from either ISAF or the US-led coalition, led to the exclusion of a few relatively innocuous candidates, while those who posed a real threat were able to run successfully. This time the elections, in which voter turnout was less than for the presidential, were tainted by intimidation, sloppy electoral administration and a failure to apply basic safeguards in the voter registration, while in some provinces there was clear evidence of ballot-stuffing. As a result, many Afghans expressed doubts that those declared winners had validly received the most votes. Already disappointed at the President's failure to institute major reforms during the year he had run the country unimpeded by a parliament, public cynicism about Western commitment to representative government deepened.

Events beginning in 2006, and particularly since early 2008, have opened the eyes of Western governments to the sad realities in

---

3 Under a single non-transferable vote system, each voter casts one vote for each candidate, but each electoral district includes more than one seat. Candidates with the highest totals win seats. The inevitability of vote-splitting under SNTV makes it difficult for any party to win a majority of seats in a given district.

Afghanistan. And yet, despite the arrival of a new administration in Washington, one wonders at the continued lack of foresight. The growing insurgency in the south and east of Afghanistan was always bound to turn the presidential elections in 2009 and parliamentary elections in 2010 into nightmare scenarios. Some of us had warned that the Independent Electoral Commission (IEC) was anything but independent, its members having all been appointed by the President through a twisted interpretation of the relevant provision in the constitution. We also argued that security conditions would prevent genuine elections in at least half of the country's Pashtun districts, leading either to colossal fraud if they were included or to the disfranchisement of major sections of the largest ethnic group if excluded. With conditions not existing for the holding of credible elections, it seemed desirable to convene in early 2009 a round table composed of key Afghan figures, together with representatives from parliament and of civil society, to decide how to proceed. The fact that Karzai's term of office expired on 22 May 2009 facilitated such an initiative. It was not to happen. The international community ignored all the warning signals, went along with the extension of President Karzai's mandate, did not condition its $300 million support for the electoral process on changes in the composition of the IEC, and appeared to be taken by surprise either at the scale of the fraud or at the coarseness of the methods used for its perpetration. And when, after ten weeks of procrastination, Karzai grudgingly accepted that he had failed to win an absolute majority of the votes, he was hailed as a statesman by those very Western leaders who had been most critical of him, and who used to wring their hands at the prospect of the prolongation of his rule for five more years.

You would think that the West would at least be looking for a formula that would ensure that the parliamentary elections were not as farcical as those in 2009, and would have warned Karzai of the need to involve parliament in a reformed IEC. If that was done at all, it met with a presidential rebuff. Not only has he refused to change the composition of the electoral commission, but he has now arrogated to himself the power to appoint all the members of the Electoral Complaints Commission which, composed of five members, three of them appointed by the Special Representative of the Secretary-General, had been the one body willing to challenge the validity of the presidential vote. The meek response of the international community to the President's challenge leads one to conclude that the next parliamentary elections, again held under SNTV, will end up being paid for by the West, and result in an even lower turnout than the approximately 30 to 35 per cent in the presidential elections, and in a pliable parliament. And, sadly but predictably, there will be those in the West who will raise their hands at the incapacity of the Afghans to develop democratic institutions, while our own publics, faced with our incoherent policy, will increasingly demand our early withdrawal from Afghanistan.

5

The rule of law and the weight of politics

Challenges and trajectories

WILLIAM MALEY

From the time of Aristotle, an enduring theme in political theory has been the desirability of a government of laws, not of men (Aristotle 1976). Taken up by David Hume during the Scottish Enlightenment (Hume 1985), it found its way into the modern concept of constitutionalism, in which the separation of powers and the rule of law stood as bulwarks against the threat to liberty posed by the existence of arbitrary power. But it is not simply in Western circles that such thinking can potentially resonate. A persistent refrain in the post-2001 era in Afghanistan has been disgust at injustice and the abuse of power, and pleas to make faster progress in building a system to constrain such abuse, which we call the rule of law. Yet amid all the challenges that have confronted Afghanistan's transition, this has proved to be perhaps the most troubling. The landscape is replete with actors who engage in hideous abuses with total impunity. This poses the question of how the rule of law can be expected to prevail when the weight of power and politics is so heavy.

My aim in this chapter is to explore some of these complexities in the Afghanistan context. The central point of the chapter is that it is important not to lose sight of the crucial significance of the rule of law as a constraint on the abuse of power. As a political principle, the rule of law goes beyond an affirmation of the desirability of an orderly society, and beyond the desirability of a minimally functioning judiciary. It is concerned with how those concerned with giving effect to law comport themselves, and how this contributes to the character of the polity more generally.

The chapter is divided into six sections. The first offers an overview of broad approaches to conceptualising the rule of law. The second looks briefly at concepts of law, and notes the presence in Afghanistan of a diverse range of norms, principles and rules, grounded in a range of sources that might qualify as 'law' in the eyes of some significant social group. The third looks at some of the broad challenges that establishing the rule of law in Afghanistan might be expected to face, and the fourth looks at how the development of Afghan political life since 2001 has compromised the quest to give effect to the rule of law, with blame resting not only with Afghan political actors, but also with international actors that have proved fitful in their commitments and inconsistent in their signalling. The fifth examines the 2009 Afghan presidential election as a manifestation of these failings. The final section offers some brief conclusions.

Approaches to the rule of law

What the expression 'the rule of law' might mean has long been the subject of robust scholarly debate. The idea of the rule of law has a venerable history in a range of different legal and political environments. In Europe, it echoed through German concepts such as the *Rechtsstaat* and Russian concepts such as the *pravovoe gosudarstvo*.[1] However, the modern idea of the rule of law in English-speaking countries is very much associated with the writings of the Oxford legal scholar A.V. Dicey, who in his 1885 *Introduction to the Study of the Law of the Constitution* not only argued for the importance of what he called 'conventions of the constitution' (see Maley 1985: 121–38), but also developed an account of the rule of law which required that law be ascertainable, prospective, and enforced by a distinct judiciary. In referring to the rule of law, he emphasised 'the absolute supremacy or predominance of regular law as opposed to the influence of arbitrary power', and the 'equal subjection of all classes to the ordinary law of the land' (Dicey 1952: 202). Dicey did not, however, offer much to explain what the doctrine of the rule of law actually was. Was it itself *part of* 'the law', or was it something else? This was a question taken up rigorously by the liberal theorist F.A. Hayek, who argued that the rule of law was a *metalegal* rather than legal principle, a normative political ideal by which real-world systems could be appraised and evaluated (Hayek 1960: 205–7).

This in turn opened the question of whether the rule of law meant the rule of *just* or *good* law, where a failure to meet some standard of justice could lead to the assertion that a particular mooted law was no law at all. The experiences of Nazi Germany (Buchheim 1968: 19) and of the USSR, where laws were promulgated in detail, but purely as instruments

---

1 On the theory of the *Rechtsstaat*, see Hayek 1955. On Russian thought, see Walicki 1987: 364–74.

of state power, ensured that these kind of issues remained a live subject of debate (Ioffe 1985: 202–22; Ioffe's study can be contrasted with the extreme formalism of Butler 1983). More recent writings have sought to distinguish 'thick' from 'thin' accounts of the rule of law. Scholars such as Joseph Raz and Charles Sampford have argued in favour of 'thin' accounts that focus on the way in which law operates, rather than on substantive values that laws might embody (Raz 1979: 210–29; Sampford 2006: 52–5). This approach, which avoids the loss of connotative precision that can flow from 'conceptual stretching' (Sartori 1970: 10, 333–53), prompted Raz to identify eight key components of the rule of law:

- All laws should be prospective, open, and clear.
- Laws should be relatively stable.
- The making of particular laws (particular legal orders) should be guided by open, stable, clear and general rules.
- The independence of the judiciary must be guaranteed.
- The principles of natural justice must be observed.
- The courts should have review powers over the implementation of the other principles.
- The courts should be easily accessible.
- The discretion of the crime-preventing agencies should not be allowed to pervert the law (Raz 1979: 214–18).

In theory, it might be possible to meet these standards even in an autocratic system. In practice, however, it is striking that autocrats have typically seen an independent judiciary seeking to observe the principles of natural justice as a threat. From totalitarian examples such as Hitler's Germany or the USSR under Stalin, to more recent cases such as the intimidation of the judiciary in Malaysia under Dr Mahathir or Zimbabwe under President Mugabe, it is clear that even a 'thin' version of the rule of law makes those with dictatorial aspirations feel distinctly uncomfortable.

Nonetheless, the success of rulers such as these in subordinating nominally 'independent' judiciaries to their will drives home a further crucial point: mere *formal* independence is not enough to give effect to the principle of the rule of law. Of course, in systems such as the Soviet, it is debatable whether there was even much formal independence, given that the Soviet constitutions of 1936 and 1977 enshrined the leading role of the Communist Party of the Soviet Union as a constitutional doctrine (Unger 1981); and a similar point might be made about the role of the *Führerprinzip* in Nazi Germany. But even where judiciaries are formally independent, they will cease to function as such unless they are infused with a culture of legality, and a disposition to exercise the independence that they formally enjoy.

This is not simply a problem for autocracies: it can emerge as a challenge even for democracies in times of national crisis. There, the temptation to argue that extraordinary circumstances require extraordinary measures can pose a profound threat to the rule of law. This was famously captured in a withering dissent by Lord Atkin in the English wartime case of *Liversidge* v. *Anderson*:

> I view with apprehension the attitude of judges who on a mere matter of construction when face to face with claims involving the liberty of the subject show themselves more executive-minded than the executive... It has always been one of the pillars of freedom, one of the principles of liberty for which on recent authority we are now fighting, that the judges are no respecters of persons, and stand between the subject and any attempted encroachments on his liberty by the executive, alert to see that any coercive action is justified in law.
>
> (*Liversidge* v. *Anderson* [1942] AC 206, 244)

It is by now a commonplace observation that the 'war on terror' of the Bush administration inaugurated a period in which attempts by the courts to oversee the exercise of executive power were not welcomed (Goldsmith 2007), and it is notable that in the case of *Rasul* v. *Bush*, a majority of the US Supreme Court felt the need to repeat the ringing words from a generation earlier of Mr Justice Jackson, who had been the chief US prosecutor before the International Military Tribunal at Nuremberg: 'Executive imprisonment has been considered oppressive and lawless since John, at Runnymede, pledged that no free man should be imprisoned, dispossessed, outlawed or exiled save by the judgment of his peers or by the law of the land' (*Rasul* v. *Bush* 542 US 466, 474 (2004)). One can only wonder what impact the need to reiterate this point has had in countries where the US and its allies were nominally committed to re-establishing the rule of law.

The defence of the rule of law need not rest simply on its capacity to apply a brake to autocrats. There is equally a line of argument that defends it on consequentialist grounds, arguing that a society in which the rule of law is honoured will display other desirable attributes as a result. One area where this is particularly notable is that of economic development (Haggard, Macintyre and Tiede 2008: 205–34). This approach links

economic dynamism to the capitalist system of exchangeable private property rights and to markets as devices for the processing of information
and the allocation of resources.[2] While possession may seem to be nine-
tenths of the law, private property rights themselves are creatures of a
legal framework and have the potential to open the door to innovative
forms of economic activity, such as the mortgaging of property to raise
funds that can then be invested entrepreneurially. (This lies at the heart
of the case made by the Peruvian economist Hernando de Soto for the
regularisation of de facto control of property (de Soto 2001), although
de Soto's work has itself been questioned by scholars who emphasise the
complexities involved in such an exercise (Otto 2009: 173–94).) Furthermore, economic progress may contribute significantly to the generation
of *political legitimacy*, conceived as generalised, normative support. It is
simply not the case that in all political systems, it is procedural outcomes
(such as election victories) that endow either the system itself or a government operating in it with legitimacy (see Barfield 2004: 263–93 and
Maley 2009: 111–33). It can be post-election performance that determines
a regime's legitimacy, and to the extent that conformity with the rule of
law produces economic goods that benefit significant population groups,
it can contribute to both legitimacy and stability.

In transition processes in disrupted states, there has been a great deal
of emphasis on the importance of rebuilding the rule of law. In more
recent usage, the term 'building the rule of law' has sometimes been used
simply as a synonym for establishing some sort of justice system and
judiciary. To a degree, this has grown out of dissatisfaction with simplistic
models of 'democratisation' that seemed almost to treat the mere holding
of a free and fair election as sufficient to establish a stable, pluralistic
polity (Maley 2006a: 683–701). But recent experience shows that the rule
of law may also be difficult to export (see for example Bull 2008) – an
unsurprising conclusion given the importance of developing a culture
of legality – and to sustain it may require what one scholar has called a
'self-enforcing equilibrium' (Weingast 1997: 245–63). If no one expects
anyone else to follow the law, there is little likelihood that law will play
much of a role in shaping behaviour. This is especially a problem where
established states have broken down, which brings us directly to the case of
Afghanistan.

2 On information, see Hayek 1948 and Scott 1998. On markets more generally, see Baumol
  2002.

Law in Afghanistan

In many parts of the world, it is broadly clear what makes up the body of a country's law, although questions may arise as to how the law should be interpreted or understood, and issues such as the continued role of established rules in indigenous or minority communities may need to be addressed. A great deal of legal theory has been directed at explaining what is distinctive about law, and what its sources might be. H.L.A. Hart, for example, depicted law as a union of primary and secondary rules grounded 'in an ultimate rule of recognition providing authoritative criteria for the identification of valid rules of the system' (Hart 1961: 245), with the rule of recognition existing 'only as a complex, but normally concordant, practice of the court, officials and private persons in identifying the law by reference to certain criteria' (Hart 1961: 107). Marmor has recently argued that rules of recognition in Hart's sense, varying from jurisdiction to jurisdiction, are 'surface conventions' which instantiate 'deep conventions' of a systemic variety, such as common law or continental law (Marmor 2009: 171–5). This usefully draws attention to the traditional dimension of law, which has been highlighted by scholars such as Martin Krygier (1988a: 179–91 and 1988b: 20–39).

When we come to Afghanistan, however, we confront a decidedly confused situation in which it is far from clear that there is any single rule of recognition on which to rely, and in which arguably there is a long-standing tension, reflecting a multiplicity of *deep* conventions, between different kinds of rules that have carried weight in Afghan society. In May 1997, this writer visited a functioning court in the town of Balkh in northern Afghanistan that captured some of these confusions. On the one hand, the judge (*qadi*) was applying *Hanafi* Sunni jurisprudence to rule on a commercial dispute between two parties. On the other hand, as he openly admitted, his standing to do so arose from his having been appointed to the position by the then local 'strongman' or 'warlord', Abdul Rashid Dostam.[3] He had no connection to any kind of 'state', and historical civil codes did not figure in his legal reasoning. And while Dostam certainly held power locally, it was not on the strength of his 'Islamic' credentials, which were extraordinarily thin, but on the basis of backing from Uzbek co-ethnics. While the parties in the case at hand were seemingly quite happy to accept the *qadi*'s rulings, any attempt to provide a simple account of the sources of his juridical authority could have proved

---

3 On Dostam's administration, see Giustozzi 2009: 103–205.

quite daunting. Historically, law has had a range of different sources in Afghanistan, and the more recent experience of state failure and foreign intervention has only complicated the situation.

The longest-standing source of law in Afghanistan has certainly been Islamic law, or Shari'a, which is subtle and complex, with a venerable history (see Hallaq 2005 and 2009). The predominant school in Afghanistan has been the *Hanafi* school, and it has been applied over a long period of time. Ashraf Ghani, who served as Afghanistan's Finance Minister from 2002 to 2004, has documented the important roles of Shari'a courts in state-building in the late nineteenth century, through a process he described as the 'bureaucratisation of the *qadi*' (see Ghani 1983: 354–6). The strength of Shari'a in an environment such as Afghanistan is its resonance with Islam as a way of life (Barfield 2005: 213–39), but it is not a simple set of rules that can be formulaically applied by amateurs. A high level of sophistication is required for a defensible application of Shari'a, and such sophistication is not readily available in the Afghan context, something demonstrated all too clearly by the crude attempts of the Taliban to enforce Shari'a law. But that said, it would be a mistake to conclude that Shari'a stands or falls as a relevant force merely on the strength of the quality of formalised enforcement mechanisms. On the contrary, one can argue that even in the absence of such mechanisms, Shari'a played an important role in the 1980s in Afghanistan by underpinning the acceptance and the performance of contractual obligations by ordinary citizens in a way that allowed a circular flow of income to take place in a petty market economy.

A second source of law in Afghanistan has historically been the state. As state formation occurred, the temptation for rulers to position themselves as authoritative sources of guidance for the public undoubtedly grew. In the late nineteenth century, Amir Abdul Rahman Khan would issue proclamations embodying his commands on a range of issues, sometimes legitimated by reference to divine inspiration (Edwards 1996: 78–125). With the promulgation of constitutions in 1923, 1931 and 1964, the development of formal institutions for the enactment of laws progressed considerably. These did not wipe out Islam as a force relevant to the identification of the law; indeed, article 64 of the constitution of 1964 provided that no law should be repugnant to the 'basic principles' (*asasat*) of the 'sacred religion of Islam', while article 69 provided that where no statute law existed, the provisions of the '*Hanafi* jurisprudence of the Islamic Shari'a' should be considered as law. They did, however, open the door both to the development of a code of laws identifiable through an official gazette, and for the development of a legal profession trained in the application of laws developed in this way (see Kamali 1985 and Weinbaum 1980: 39–57). It is nonetheless important to appreciate the limits of the practical writ of state legal codes. As one informed observer has put it: 'In theory, state law has always applied to all residents of Afghanistan equally, but, in practice, government institutions were found almost exclusively in urban areas and in provincial centres of administration. The latter's direct control rarely reached beyond the limits of the towns where local officials were stationed' (Barfield 2008: 359). This problem, troubling enough before 1978, became vastly worse after the communist coup of April 1978, and then the Soviet invasion of Afghanistan in December 1979 saw large tracts of the countryside slip out of the control of the Kabul regime.

It was in this context that a third strand of law came into its own, namely customary law within particular communities. The most extensively documented form of customary law in Afghanistan undoubtedly was and is the set of tribal codes (*Pushtunwali*) that prevails with the Pushtun ethnic group, given effect through the institution of the *jirga*, a problem-solving assembly of male tribal members. Such codes reflect the predominance in many parts of Afghanistan of *governance* rather than *government*: 'governance' structures enjoy local legitimacy even without having received the imprimatur of the state. Enforcement, rather than deriving from the state, would be individually grounded, based on norms of revenge and giving rise to the risk of blood feuds;[4] ostracism from the tribe functioned as an ultimate sanction (Barfield 2008: 355). In some cases, of course, there might not be customary rules on hand that were manifestly pertinent to a dispute that had arisen; in such circumstances, it might make more sense to refer to 'alternative dispute resolution procedures' rather than to the application of customary law. It is in this grey area that numerous problems of principle can easily arise, especially if dispute resolution is achieved at the expense of the rights of some vulnerable individual, such as a young woman offered in marriage to resolve a dispute between two clans:[5] here, the means used to resolve the dispute would be at odds with both state law and the *Hanafi* school of Shari'a.

---

4 For a discussion of this phenomenon, see Elster 1990: 862–85. A spectacular example of norms of revenge in Afghanistan has recently been reported from within the family of President Karzai himself (Risen 2009).
5 On exchange marriage, see Tapper 1991: 141–56. On the extreme vulnerability of women in contemporary Afghanistan, see United Nations Assistance Mission in Afghanistan 2009.

An example such as this serves also to remind us of certain legal obligations to which Afghanistan was and is subject. These arise out of international law. Afghanistan has long been a recognised political unit with an international legal personality, capable of assuming international obligations. This it did on numerous occasions through ratifying or acceding to treaties and conventions; and in addition, it would also be subject to the requirements of customary international law, and peremptory norms of international law (*jus cogens*). A whole range of human rights instruments to which Afghanistan is a party could be challenged by actions to resolve disputes through customary institutions (Maley 2008a: 89–107). Here we find a further tension with which those committed to promoting the rule of law in the post-Taliban era have had to struggle.

Challenges in establishing the rule of law

The potential tension between international law and domestic law points to one of the most troubling difficulties in seeking to establish the rule of law in Afghanistan, namely the existence of competing models of legitimacy. A major challenge in the post-2001 era has been to find ways of re-establishing the position of *state-based* legal rules in the face of bodies of law with greater religious or traditional resonance. In this particular area, there is an underlying tension also between different models of legitimacy and legitimation. From the point of view of the international community, the December 2001 Bonn agreement between non-Taliban political groups, an agreement subsequently endorsed by the UN Security Council in Resolution 1383, provided the foundation for the reconstitution of political authority, a process that led to the adoption of the 2004 constitution embodying international human rights standards, and to the holding of presidential and parliamentary elections in 2004 and 2005 (see Maley 2006b: 30–55). However, from the point of view of ordinary Afghans, the institutions and rules generated by this process did not necessarily enjoy any particular legitimacy, especially given that the capacities of the new Afghan state remained limited, and its influence in many parts of Afghanistan was weak when compared with the power of (often unappealing) local power-holders. In such circumstances, the legitimacy of state-based law cannot simply be assumed; it is up to the state to ensure that it is applied in such a way as to satisfy ordinary people's craving for meaningful justice.

This is not, however, merely an abstract issue, for as well as there being different bodies of 'law' in Afghanistan, there are also different systems for its administration. In many parts of the country, as well as the new state-based judicial system put in place after 2001, there are institutions of what one can call the 'informal justice sector', which enjoy no particular formal standing but may be the preferred choice for ordinary people seeking to solve problems. This has created a great quandary. On the one hand, the informal sector has been viewed with considerable unease, if not outright suspicion, on the part of civil society actors who see it as compromising a range of hard-won human rights gains. On the other hand, it tends to enjoy higher levels of confidence from citizens. A 2009 survey conducted for the Asia Foundation showed that 79 per cent of respondents agreed that the local *jirga* or *shura* was accessible to them, while only 68 per cent said this of the state courts; 69 per cent judged the local *jirga* or *shura* effective at delivering justice, while only 51 per cent said this of the state courts; 72 per cent labelled the local *jirga* or *shura* 'fair or trusted', while only 50 per cent said this of the state courts; and 64 per cent stated that the local *jirga* or *shura* resolved cases 'timely and promptly', while only 40 per cent said this of the state courts (see Asia Foundation 2009: 85, 89).

Alongside these survey data sits abundant anecdotal evidence of per-ceived corruption in the state-based system, with attendant frustration on the part of litigants who feel that money can buy positive outcomes, irrespective of the merits of a legal case (see for example Richburg 2010 and Watson 2006). It is for this reason that increasing attention has been applied to whether the informal sector might be harnessed to serve the delivery of justice, albeit with adjustments to protect the rights of groups that might otherwise be highly vulnerable (see United Nations Develop-ment Program 2007 and Wardak 2004: 319–41) – although recourse to the informal sector has been resisted by the Afghan supreme court (see Suhrke and Borchgrevink 2009: 228). However, the case for using the informal sector does not rest purely on the failings of the formal sector. At the level of 'deep convention', one could argue that the adversarial-punitive orien-tation of the state-based sector lacks some of the investigative-restorative features that are sometimes found in the informal sector, which arguably are more appropriate in poor societies, where imprisonment of bread-winners might devastate the lives of many vulnerable people.[6]

A further point, easily overlooked, is that the circumstances of the transition after 2001 created a very substantial *demand* for fair and just

6 For a practical example involving the former Special Representative of the United Nations Secretary-General in Afghanistan, see Suskind 2008: 345–6.

problem-solving mechanisms, which would have stressed even a well-established judicial system. Over a period of more than two decades, Afghanistan had experienced some of the most extensive population displacement of any country in the world, involving not only millions of Afghans as refugees in neighbouring countries, but also substantial internal displacement (Schmeidl and Maley 2008: 131–79). As refugees have returned, all too often they have found other people in possession of land or buildings that they believed to have been theirs. The result has been a complex pattern of disputes that any legal system would find difficult to resolve quickly, if only because of the obscurity or ambiguity of the evidence available to help resolve matters (see Deschamps and Roe 2009 and Wily 2003).

Beyond this, it is important to recognise the complexity involved in attempting to restore a justice system. It is far from sufficient to focus simply on the building of a judiciary. Effective judiciaries are nested in more complex institutional environments, in which it is necessary to bring some degree of coordination to policing, witness protection, adjudication, enforcement of judgments, and penal and corrections policy. Weakness in any of these spheres is likely to compromise prospects for progress in the others. In post-2001 Afghanistan, this coordination was complicated still further by the adoption of a 'lead nation' model of support for reconstruction, in which Italy was given responsibility for judicial system reform while Germany took responsibility for the reform of policing. After years of effort, there was little to show in either sphere, with policing little better than a disaster area (see ICG 2007, ICG 2008, Mani 2003 and Wilder 2007: 108–26).

But this was not the only area in which international actors fell short of adequately assisting the building of the rule of law in Afghanistan. In two other respects, involving both word and deed, what one could loosely call the 'international community' engaged in inconsistent signalling about what was important. The first related to the Afghan constitution of 2004. The language of constitutionality in Western states has often emphasised the fundamental character of a constitution, captured in expressions such as the German *Grundgesetz*. Yet many international actors treated the Afghan constitution as something that should be malleable to suit the convenience of the wider world. This surfaced over the issue of the timing of the 2009 elections. In almost any codified constitution, one is likely to find some provisions that are rather vague, and the 2004 constitution is no exception. But not all provisions are vague, and one of the most explicit, contained in article 61, made it absolutely clear that President Karzai's term in office expired on 22 May 2009.[7] This had in fact been clear since his election in 2004. However, the wider world had not geared up to provide electoral assistance that matched this constitutional timetable, and international actors thus endorsed the postponement of elections until 20 August 2009. This blasé approach to explicit constitutional requirements sent a very poor message to Afghan observers, namely, that even the most fundamental law was able to be twisted. This in turn reinforced their sense of how the world was always destined to work, based on at least thirty years of conflict: that might trumps right.

In another sphere also, international actors sent out dangerous signals: on the issue of impunity. In the absence of a status of forces agreement, international forces in Afghanistan effectively functioned beyond the reach of Afghan law, putting at risk the liberty of ordinary Afghans, something poignantly captured in the 2007 Academy Award-winning documentary *Taxi to the Dark Side*, which told of the death in US custody of an innocent Afghan taxi driver named Dilawar.[8] When foreign militaries are a significant presence in a society, they will inevitably be observed by locals seeking to gain a sense of what it is that the wider world values. It is therefore important that, by word and deed, they signal a commitment to the rule of law. Obfuscation and prevarication in the face of suspected violations of international humanitarian law should never be attempted or accepted. As Telford Taylor observed, the laws of war are not a one-way street (Taylor 1993: 641). This problem was magnified in Afghanistan by the abusive behaviour of various private security companies, which reinforced the impression that those who were well-connected were above the law.[9]

Afghan politics after 2001

In discussions of the practical challenges in re-establishing a judicial system in Afghanistan, the political dimensions of the problem have often been overlooked, or at least downplayed. Yet as Thier has argued: 'In Afghan history, there is neither practical experience with judicial independence in the state system, nor a political ethos to support it' (Thier 2007: 66). When one examines the course of political development since

7 For the text of the constitution in parallel English and Dari versions, see Yassari 2005: 269–329. Article 61 can be found at 290–1.
8 For details on this case, see Golden 2005.
9 See Brooking and Schmeidl 2008: 208–14. For further discussion of the challenges posed by private security companies, see Singer 2003 and Avant 2005.

2001, it becomes clear that little attention has been paid to the need to constrain state power at either central or local levels, and, as a result, abuse of power has become a serious source of angst for ordinary citizens, who find themselves relatively powerless. It is arguably this area of failure in the rebuilding of the rule of law that has done the most to compromise the legitimacy of the transition process. One explanation, of course, is an unduly narrow conception of what building the rule of law involves. It is easy to define building the rule of law in terms of a range of technical tasks and objectives – establishing and running training facilities for judges and lawyers, building and equipping courthouses, and setting up procedures for documentation and information management – which lend themselves readily to benchmarking and assessment against performance indicators (Fukuyama 2010: 42). Progress in these areas is desirable, but falls short of guaranteeing an independent judiciary with a commitment to an ethos of legality.

One specific difficulty is that the central thrust of Afghanistan's constitutional and political development has been towards the consolidation of power and away from the establishment of checks and balances. Central to this has been a presidential politics of personalised networking rather than institution-building. The 2004 constitution established a strong presidential system, albeit in the context of a state whose extractive, regulatory and distributional capacities remained weak. This was vigorously supported by the US, apparently keen to have an obvious partner with whom to deal (Suhrke 2008: 630–48). While a two-chamber national assembly was included in the constitutional framework, its effective powers were limited, and ministers in the government were not 'responsible' to the parliament in the sense of the government depending on a majority in the legislature for its survival. Furthermore, the appointment of officials at provincial levels lay solely within the discretion of the president. This proved highly problematic for a reason not immediately connected to the constitution itself. In early 2002, the US had blocked the expansion beyond Kabul of the 'international security assistance force' for which the Bonn agreement had contained provision. Faced with the threat of spoiler behaviour by petty local power-holders, Karzai had little option but to seek to avert immediate spoiler problems by offering these actors positions within the state. The last thing that they brought with them was any interest in respecting the rule of law or being constrained by it. The most egregious example of such a figure was probably Gul Agha Sherzai in Kandahar (see Chayes 2006 and Maass 2002), but many others fitted the same description. From a military point of view, fidelity to the president seemed to bring more immediate and palpable returns than fidelity to law. The de-legitimating effects of the abuse of power by these plenipotentiaries of the state can hardly be overemphasised.[10] It is they who often personify 'the state' to ordinary Afghans, and most seem to have had no grasp of Robert Layton's fundamental insight that 'trust is a fragile resource' (Layton 2006: 169).

This problem is compounded by the problem of financial corruption, which comes not so much in the form of expropriation of central state resources as in the pervasive form of grand bribery. Petty bribery has a long history in Afghanistan: as one writer has put it, 'not all forms of corruption are equally harmful or equally wrong in the eyes of most Afghans . . . It seems probable the people will tolerate corruption if the state can deliver some tangible benefits to them and their families' (Goodhand 2008: 416). In the justice sector, however, grand bribery is utterly corrosive, for in most matters, one party's gain is another party's loss, and the perception that a case was lost because of illegitimate inducements to the court will inevitably create a burning sense of rage and contempt for the empty rhetoric of justice. Corruption in a legal system is devastating for the system's credibility: it replaces a culture of legality with a culture of graft. Yet in poor countries with rampant inequality, such an outcome is quite likely (Uslaner 2008). In Afghanistan, this problem has been particularly aggravated by the revival of the narco-economy, which has generated vast sums in the hands of drug barons that can then be used to subvert the very system that should exist to bring such criminal actors to account.

President Karzai has proved ineffectual in the face of such problems, not because there is any evidence that he is at all corrupt himself, but rather because his personalistic style of politics meshes so closely with a de-institutionalised system that he is not the person to charge with the task of developing institutions of accountability that limit his own power. His conception of politics owes far more to Plato than to Montesquieu. As a result, he has ridiculed studies of corruption, and painted 'Afghan sovereignty' and 'Afghanisation' as the solutions to pursue. And at one level, his concerns are legitimate. A great deal of corruption in Afghanistan has been fuelled by reckless injections of cash from Western donors with only the weakest of financial controls, often in ways that bypassed the Afghan state. But it is also the case that simplistic solutions based on respect for Afghan sovereignty have little to offer, for sovereignty itself is a far more complex and multidimensional phenomenon than such discourse would suggest. The erosion of state capacities as a result of

10 For an egregious but by no means atypical example, see Lewidge 2009: 81–3.

globalisation has undermined any notion of absolute state dominion except in such odd places as North Korea, and it is questionable whether states have historically enjoyed the sovereign capacities that they often claimed (Krasner 1999). Furthermore, recent sovereignty discourse has arguably been democratic in its thrust, seeking to undermine the more audacious claims of rulers to lie beyond the reach of checks and balances (see Pemberton 2009 for a recent elaboration of this argument). In the Afghanistan case, given the ferocity of the challenges that fragile local institutions confront, there is a strong case for mechanisms of 'shared' sovereignty in which formalised international involvement bolsters the capacity of local bodies to constrain the abuse of power.[11] That shared sovereignty could be both a reinforcement for the rule of law and a threat to arbitrary power was brought out clearly by the experience of the 2009 Afghan presidential election.

The 2009 Afghan election: some implications for the rule of law

All elections in principle are law-governed exercises. Without a framework of rules that gives meaning to the act of marking a ballot paper, the exercise would be little more than one of calligraphy. Even in autocratic systems where elections are forms of political theatre rather than mechanisms for changing rulers peacefully, such rules can be found, and, in consolidated democracies, one looks to a country's constitution for guidance as to what offices might need to be filled, and then to electoral law to learn by whom elections are to be conducted, how eligibility to stand for office or to vote is to be determined, and what procedures are to be followed to count votes, resolve disputes and certify final outcomes. Given that competitive elections create both winners and losers, a credible election depends heavily on the existence of an appropriate legal framework to ensure that outcomes are free and fair, and the independence of electoral authorities is a key requirement of such a framework (see Elklit and Svensson 1997: 35). In Afghanistan, on paper there was much to praise in the post-2001 environment. The 2004 constitution provided in article 156 for an independent election commission (*Komision-e mustaqel-e entakhabat*), and the electoral law (*Qanun-e entakhabat*) that applied in 2009 provided for a separate electoral complaints commission, three of whose five members were international experts nominated by the Special

---

11 For more detailed discussion, see Krasner 2004: 85–120. Shared sovereignty can involve the use by multiple states of a single judicial organ, such as the judicial committee of the Privy Council – see Maley 2008b: 294.

Representative of the UN Secretary-General. In form, therefore, Afghan law provided for checks and balances through a shared sovereignty model. However, transplanting electoral regulation is a difficult task, and so it proved in Afghanistan (Maley 2003: 479–97).

In 2004, when Afghanistan's first presidential election was held, the prevailing framework operated quite effectively, and President Karzai was elected to office with 55.4 per cent of the vote. Virtually everything worked in his favour. Asia Foundation research suggested that 64 per cent of the population felt that the country was heading in the right direction (Asia Foundation 2004: 21), and it would have been astounding if Karzai had not secured a victory. By 2009, the situation was very different. The Asia Foundation's polling suggested that only 42 per cent of respondents felt that the country was heading in the right direction (Asia Foundation 2009: 3). The former foreign minister, Dr Abdullah, had emerged as a serious and articulate challenger to the incumbent president. There was every reason to conclude that the 2009 election would be much more closely fought than the election of 2004, and that the stakes would be very high not just for President Karzai, but for a whole host of presidential associates and appointees who lacked independent power bases and depended on a Karzai victory for their own political survival. Yet it was in this environment that the running of the election, a task that in 2004 had been formally delegated to a joint electoral management body with heavy UN involvement, was assumed by the Independent Election Commission (IEC).

The result was to prove catastrophic. With members appointed by presidential decree, the IEC made only the meekest show of attempted independence, and the chair of the commission, Dr Azizullah Lodin, was a long-term Karzai partisan whose behaviour in the run-up to the election reflected his partisan involvement (see ICG 2009: 9–10 and Kippen 2008: 9). (Indeed, when it seemed likely that a runoff election between Karzai and Abdullah would be required, Lodin openly stated that 'Karzai is going to win' (Filkins 2009a).) Under the commission's gaze, Karzai supporters executed one of the most spectacular exercises of electoral fraud in modern electoral history.[12] Low turnout made plenty of ballot papers available

---

12 The UNDP/ELECT Team, deployed to assist the electoral process, noted the 'low capacity of the IEC, the political bias of the IEC commissioners and senior managers and the blatant political stance taken by Afghan ministries and the security forces', and referred to the IEC as 'an inexperienced and – in the end – deeply flawed – institution whose leadership felt no compunction about changing results, ignoring fraud and perpetrating wrong conduct': see Response of UNDP/ELECT Team to Mid-Term Evaluation (Kabul: UNDP/ELECT, November–December 2009) pp. 1, 16." Maley was a registered election observer, credited to Democracy International.

to the fraudsters, and the main technique used was the age-old one of ballot-box stuffing: 'The operation in Spin Boldak was coordinated by the provincial head of the border police, who had reportedly vowed to deliver the vote in the six border districts under his responsibility. On the night before the elections, a large number of ballot boxes were taken to his compound, where IEC staff members were made to fill them with ballots marked in favour of the incumbent and a number of selected provincial candidates. The full ballot boxes were delivered to the polling stations the next morning. Polling staff were obviously aware that this was against procedures, but felt unable to protest.'[13] The European Union Election Observer Mission stated that its own findings confirmed 'that large-scale ballot stuffing took place at polling station level and that despite the legal provisions on fraud detection and mitigation measures established by the IEC, hundreds of thousands of fraudulent votes were accepted at the tally centre, and were included among the preliminary official results posted on the IEC's website' (European Union Election Observer Mission to Afghanistan 2009). In its initial results tally, the IEC awarded Karzai a victory with 54.1 per cent of the vote.

The Electoral Complaints Commission was confronted with the challenge of addressing this problem, and despite intense pressure on the Afghan members from ministers in the Karzai government, it proceeded to do so. Of the 5.66 million votes that were (allegedly) cast, over 1.3 million were invalidated on the grounds of fraud, with over 75 per cent of these invalidated votes having been cast for Karzai. This reduced Karzai's total to less than 50 per cent, and triggered the requirement for a runoff vote. However, in the face of demands that Lodin be replaced, and that polling places that had witnessed fraud in the first round of voting be closed for the runoff, Karzai proved entirely obdurate (see Boone 2009b; Constable 2009; Starkey 2009), doubtless bolstered by the lamentable performance of a range of international actors who on 20 October publicly praised him as a 'statesman' for agreeing to the runoff, even though this was no more than the constitution required. Dr Abdullah eventually withdrew in a dignified fashion from a process that had become a farce. President Karzai, doubtless realising how close a shave he had had, issued a decree in February 2010 to remove the international element from the Electoral Complaints Commission (for initial reports of this decree, see Partlow 2010). Faced with the brutal imperatives of politics, the law

13 Afghanistan Analysts Network 2009: 3. For further reports of fraud, see Mackenzie 2009, Partlow and Constable 2009, Gall 2009, Filkins 2009b, Starkey and Swain 2009, Gall and Filkins 2009, and Boone 2009b.

proved a feeble protector for Afghanistan's fragile democratic system, and the future of electoral processes in Afghanistan looks extremely bleak.

Conclusion

The lessons from this case, and from many others one could equally cite, are sobering. Attempts to build the rule of law do not typically involve writing on a *tabula rasa*. They take place, to some extent at least, in the context of pre-existing power structures and relations that not only reflect the history of a particular polity but contribute to its future development, especially if they have been harnessed to legitimate a political transition. Furthermore, new arrangements themselves have implications for how political power can be exercised. Those seeking to promote the rule of law may be powerfully challenged not only by the desire of local actors to exercise power unchecked, but also by the preference of international actors for simple lines of engagement that the emergence of a 'strong leader' can offer. Building the rule of law, in other words, is not a narrowly technical task. It far transcends mere 'justice sector reform', and is inescapably political in its scope and implications.

But the daunting scale of the challenge makes it no less worth pursuing. In the seventeenth century, the supremacy of law was ringingly endorsed by Thomas Fuller: 'Be you never so high, the law is above you' (quoted in Denning 1979: 140). Unconstrained power is a recipe for instability, whether simmering or rampant. Under its shadow, a whole range of evils easily flourish, and ultimately this is likely to be at the expense of political legitimacy, that generalised normative support that in the final analysis underpins durable and institutionalised political structures. From Juvenal in Roman times to Lord Acton in modern times, the tendency of power to corrupt its users has been recognised even as the phenomenon has persisted. In law one can find a device to address this problem. The challenge in Afghanistan is to find ways of deploying this device in what are singularly unpropitious circumstances. The rule of law is a splendid resource for rebuilding a disrupted society, but too many members of the political elite seem to see it as a threat to shorter term and ultimately secondary priorities.

References

Afghanistan Analysts Network (2009). *Polling Day Fraud in the Afghan Elections.* Kabul: AAN Briefing Paper 03/2009

Aristotle (1976). *The Ethics of Aristotle: The Nicomachean Ethics*. Harmondsworth: Penguin Books

Asia Foundation (2004). *Democracy in Afghanistan 2004: A Survey of the Afghan Electorate*. Kabul and San Francisco

Asia Foundation (2009). *Afghanistan in 2009: A Survey of the Afghan People*. Kabul and San Francisco

Avant, Deborah D. (2005). *The Market for Force: The Consequences of Privatising Security*. Cambridge University Press

Barfield, Thomas (2004). 'Problems in establishing legitimacy in Afghanistan', *Iranian Studies*, 37(2), June 2004

Barfield, Thomas (2005). 'An Islamic state is a state run by good Muslims: Religion as a way of life and not an ideology in Afghanistan', in Hefner, Robert W. (ed.), *Remaking Muslim Politics: Pluralism, Contestation, Democratisation*. Princeton University Press

Barfield, Thomas (2008). 'Culture and custom in nation-building: Law in Afghanistan', *Maine Law Review*, 60(2)

Baumol, William J. (2002). *The Free-Market Innovation Machine: Analysing the Growth Miracle of Capitalism*. Princeton University Press

Boone, Jon (2009a). 'Afghanistan: anatomy of an election disaster', *The Guardian*, 20 October 2009

Boone, Jon (2009b). 'Fraud fears grow as Afghan election body defies UN', *The Guardian*, 29 October 2009

Brooking, Stephen and Schmeidl, Susanne (2008). 'When nobody guards the guards: The quest to regulate private security companies in Afghanistan', *Sicherheit und Frieden/Security and Peace*, no. 4

Buchheim, Hans (1968). *Totalitarian Rule: Its Nature and Characteristics*. Middletown: Wesleyan University Press

Bull, Carolyn (2008). *No Entry Without Strategy: Building the Rule of Law under UN Transitional Administration*. Tokyo: United Nations University Press

Butler, W.E. (1983). *Soviet Law*. London: Butterworths

Chayes, Sarah (2006). *The Punishment of Virtue: Inside Afghanistan after the Taliban*. New York: Penguin Press

Constable, Pamela (2009). 'Afghan panel overrides warnings', *Washington Post*, 30 October 2009

Denning, Lord (1979). *The Discipline of Law*. London: Butterworths

De Soto, Hernando (2001). *The Mystery of Capital: Why Capitalism Triumphs in the West and Fails Everywhere Else*. London: Black Swan

Deschamps, Colin and Roe, Alan (2009). *Land Conflict in Afghanistan: Building Capacity to Address Vulnerability*. Kabul: Afghanistan Research and Evaluation Unit

Dicey, A.V. (1952). *Introduction to the Study of the Law of the Constitution*. London: Macmillan

Edwards, David B. (1996). *Heroes of the Age: Moral Fault Lines on the Afghan Frontier*. Berkeley and Los Angeles: University of California Press

Elklit, Jørgen, and Svensson, Palle (1997). 'What makes elections free and fair?', *Journal of Democracy*, 8(3), July 1997

Elster, Jon (1990). 'Norms of revenge', *Ethics*, 100(4), July 1990

European Union Election Observation Mission to Afghanistan (2009). Press statement: 'EU EOM urges immediate action against large-scale fraudulent results', Kabul

Filkins, Dexter (2009a). 'The great American arm-twist in Afghanistan', *New York Times*, 25 October 2009

Filkins, Dexter (2009b). 'Tribal leaders say Karzai team forged 23,900 votes', *New York Times*, 2 September 2009

Fukuyama, Francis (2010). 'Transitions to the rule of law', *Journal of Democracy*, 21(1), January 2010

Gall, Carlotta (2009). 'Increasing accounts of fraud cloud Afghan vote', *New York Times*, 31 August 2009

Gall, Carlotta and Filkins, Dexter (2009). 'Fake Afghan poll sites favored Karzai, official asserts', *New York Times*, 7 September 2009

Ghani, Ashraf (1983). 'Disputes in a court of *Shari'a*, Kunar Valley, Afghanistan, 1885–1890', *International Journal of Middle East Studies*, 15(3), August 1983

Giustozzi, Antonio (2009). *Empires of Mud: Wars and Warlords in Afghanistan*. London: Hurst & Co

Golden, Tim (2005). 'In US report, brutal details of two Afghan inmates' deaths', *New York Times*, 20 May 2005

Goldsmith, Jack (2007). *The Terror Presidency: Law and Justice inside the Bush Administration*. New York: WW Norton

Goodhand, Jonathan (2008). 'Corrupting or consolidating the peace?: The drugs economy and post-conflict peacebuilding in Afghanistan', *International Peacekeeping*, 15(3), June 2008

Haggard, Stephan, Macintyre, Andrew and Tiede, Lydia (2008). 'The rule of law and economic development', *Annual Review of Political Science*, 11

Hallaq, Wael B. (2005). *The Origins and Evolution of Islamic Law*. Cambridge University Press

Hallaq, Wael B. (2009). *Shari'a: Theory, Practice, Transformations*. Cambridge University Press

Hart, H.L.A. (1961). *The Concept of Law*. Oxford University Press

Hayek, F.A. (1948). *Individualism and Economic Order*. Chicago: University of Chicago Press

Hayek, F.A. (1955). *The Political Ideal of the Rule of Law*. Cairo: National Bank of Egypt

Hayek, F.A. (1960). *The Constitution of Liberty*. London: Routledge & Kegan Paul

Hume, David (1985). 'Of civil liberty', in Miller, Eugene F. (ed.), *David Hume: Essays, Moral, Political, and Literary*. Indianapolis: Liberty Classics

International Crisis Group (ICG) (2007). *Reforming Afghanistan's Police*. Kabul and Brussels: ICG

ICG (2008). *Policing in Afghanistan: Still Searching for a Strategy*. Kabul and Brussels: ICG

ICG (2009). *Afghanistan's Election Challenges*, Kabul and Brussels: Asia Report No. 171, ICG

Ioffe, Olimpiad S. (1985). *Soviet Law and Soviet Reality*. The Hague: Martinus Nijhoff

Kamali, Mohammed Hashim (1985). *Law in Afghanistan: A Study of the Constitutions, Matrimonial Law and the Judiciary*. Leiden: EJ Brill

Kippen, Grant (2008). *Elections in 2009 and 2010: Technical and Contextual Challenges to Building Democracy in Afghanistan*. Kabul: Afghanistan Research and Evaluation Unit

Krasner, Stephen D. (1999). *Sovereignty: Organised Hypocrisy*. Princeton University Press

Krasner, Stephen D. (2004), 'Sharing sovereignty: New institutions for collapsed and failing states', *International Security*, 29(2), Fall 2004

Krygier, Martin (1988a). 'Law as tradition', in Panou, Stavros (ed.), *The Philosophy of Law in the History of Human Thought*. Stuttgart: Franz Steiner Verlag

Krygier, Martin (1988b). 'The traditionality of statutes', *Ratio Juris*, 1(1), March 1988

Layton, Robert (2006). *Order and Anarchy: Civil Society, Social Disorder and War*. Cambridge University Press

Lewidge, Frank (2009), 'Justice in Helmand – The challenge of law reform in a society at war', *Asian Affairs*, 40(1), March 2009

Maass, Peter (2002). 'Gul Agha gets his province back', *New York Times Magazine*, 6 January 2002

Mackenzie, Jean (2009). 'Afghanistan's sham vote', *New York Times*, 26 August 2009

Maley, Michael (2003). 'Transplanting election regulation', *Election Law Journal*, 2(4), December 2003

Maley, William (1985). 'Laws and conventions revisited', *Modern Law Review*, 48(2), March 1985

Maley, William (2006a). 'Democratic governance and post-conflict transitions', *Chicago Journal of International Law*, 6(2), Winter 2006

Maley, William (2006b). *Rescuing Afghanistan*. London: Hurst & Co

Maley, William (2008a). 'Human rights in Afghanistan', in Akbarzadeh, Shahram and MacQueen, Benjamin (eds.), *Islam and Human Rights in Practice: Perspectives Across the Ummah*. London: Routledge

Maley, William (2008b). 'Trust, legitimacy and the sharing of sovereignty', in Jacobsen, Trudy, Sampford, Charles and Thakur, Ramesh (eds.), *Re-envisioning Sovereignty: The End of Westphalia?* Aldershot: Ashgate

Maley, William (2009).'Democracy and legitimation: challenges in the reconstruction of political processes in Afghanistan', in Bowden, Brett, Charlesworth, Hilary and Farrall, Jeremy (eds.), *The Role of International Law in Rebuilding Societies after Conflict: Great Expectations.* Cambridge University Press

Mani, Rama (2003). *Ending Impunity and Building Justice in Afghanistan.* Kabul: Afghanistan Research and Evaluation Unit

Marmor, Andrei (2009). *Social Conventions: From Language to Law.* Princeton University Press

Murray, Tonita (2007). 'Police-building in Afghanistan: A case study of civil security reform', *International Peacekeeping*, 14(1), January 2007

Otto, Jan Michiel (2009). 'Rule of law promotion, land tenure and poverty alleviation: Questioning the assumptions of Hernando de Soto', *Hague Journal on the Rule of Law*, 1(1)

Partlow, Joshua (2010). 'Afghanistan's government seeks more control over elections', *Washington Post*, 15 February 2010

Partlow, Joshua and Constable, Pamela (2009). 'Accusations of vote fraud multiply in Afghanistan', *Washington Post*, 28 August 2009

Pemberton, Jo-Anne (2009). *Sovereignty: Interpretations.* New York: Palgrave Macmillan

Raz, Joseph (1979). *The Authority of Law: Essays on Law and Morality.* Oxford University Press

Richburg, Keith B (2010). 'In Afghanistan, US seeks to fix a tattered system of justice', *Washington Post*, 28 February 2010

Risen, James (2009). 'Afghan killing bares Karzai family feud', *New York Times*, 19 December 2009

Sampford, Charles (2006). *Retrospectivity and the Rule of Law.* Oxford University Press

Sartori, Giovanni (1970). 'Concept misformation in comparative politics', *American Political Science Review*, 64(4), December 1970

Schmeidl, Susanne and Maley, William (2008). 'The case of the Afghan refugee population: Finding durable solutions in contested transitions', in Adelman, Howard (ed.), *Protracted Displacement in Asia: No Place to Call Home.* Aldershot: Ashgate

Scott, James C. (1998). *Seeing Like a State: How Certain Schemes to Improve the Human Condition Have Failed.* New Haven: Yale University Press

Singer, P.W. (2003). *Corporate Warriors: The Rise of the Privatised Military Industry.* Ithaca: Cornell University Press

Starkey, Jerome (2009).'UN fears for second Afghan vote after commission refuses to tackle fraud', *The Times*, 30 October 2009

Starkey, Jerome and Swain, Jon (2009). 'President Hamid Karzai takes 100% of votes in opposition stronghold', *Sunday Times*, 6 September 2009

Suhrke, Astri (2008). 'Democratising a dependent state: The case of Afghanistan', *Democratization*, 15(3)

Suhrke, Astri and Borchgrevink, Kaja (2009). 'Negotiating justice sector reform in Afghanistan', *Crime, Law and Social Change*, 51(2), March 2009

Suskind, Ron (2008). *The Way of the World: A Story of Truth and Hope in an Age of Extremism.* New York: HarperCollins

Tapper, Nancy (1991). *Bartered Brides: Politics, Gender and Marriage in an Afghan Tribal Society.* Cambridge University Press

Taylor, Telford (1993). *The Anatomy of the Nuremberg Trials: A Personal Memoir.* New York: Alfred Knopf

Thier, J. Alexander (2007). 'A third branch? (Re)establishing the judicial system in Afghanistan', in Danspeckgruber, Wolfgang with Finn, Robert P. (eds.), *Building State and Security in Afghanistan.* Princeton: Liechtenstein Institute on Self-Determination at Princeton University

Unger, Aryeh L. (1981). *Constitutional Development in the USSR: A Guide to the Soviet Constitutions.* London: Methuen

United Nations Assistance Mission in Afghanistan (2009). *Silence is Violence: End the Abuse of Women in Afghanistan.* Kabul, Geneva: Office of the United Nations High Commissioner for Human Rights

United Nations Development Program (2007). *Afghanistan Human Development Report 2007. Bridging Modernity and Tradition: Rule of Law and the Search for Justice.* Kabul

Uslaner, Eric M. (2008). *Corruption, Inequality, and the Rule of Law.* Cambridge University Press

Walicki, Andrzej (1987). *Legal Philosophies of Russian Liberalism.* Oxford University Press

Wardak, Ali (2004). 'Building a post-war justice system in Afghanistan', *Crime, Law and Social Change*, 41(4), May 2004

Watson, Paul (2006). 'In Afghanistan, money tips the scales of justice', *Los Angeles Times*, 18 December 2006

Weinbaum, Marvin G. (1980). 'Legal elites in Afghan society', *International Journal of Middle East Studies*, 12(1), August 1980

Weingast, Barry R. (1997). 'The political foundations of democracy and the rule of law', *American Political Science Review*, 91(2), June 1997

Wilder, Andrew (2007). *Cops or Robbers?: The Struggle to Reform the Afghan National Police.* Kabul: Afghanistan Research and Evaluation Unit

Wily, Liz Alden (2003). *Land Rights in Crisis: Restoring Tenure Security in Afghanistan.* Kabul: Afghanistan Research and Evaluation Unit

Yassari, Nadjma (2005) (ed.), *The Shari'a in the Constitutions of Afghanistan, Iran and Egypt – Implications for Private Law.* Tübingen: Mohr Siebeck

6

Human security and the rule of law

Afghanistan's experience

SHAHMAHMOOD MIAKHEL

> The United Nations has learned that the rule of law is not a luxury and that
> justice is not a side issue. We have seen people lose faith in the peace process
> when they do not feel safe from crime. We have seen that without a credible
> machinery to enforce the law and resolve disputes, people resorted to violence
> and illegal means. And we have seen that elections held when the rule of law is
> too fragile seldom lead to lasting democratic governance... but one size fits
> all does not work. Local actors must be involved from the start. The aim is to
> leave behind strong local institutions when we depart.

This statement by former UN Secretary-General Kofi Anan to the UN
General Assembly on 25 September 2005 reflects the now widespread
understanding that human security and rule of law are interlinked.
Around the world, the physical security of human beings is most endan-
gered in situations in which violations of national and international law
are most apparent. If the root causes of all conflicts in the world are
examined, we would see that most are associated with or are the result of
social injustice, violation of law and abuse of power by rulers. Afghanistan
exemplifies this nexus between conflict and the abuse of power. The rule
of law, by virtually any account, significantly inhibits the abuse of power.
Afghans' yearning for law and order above all else reflects the capricious
abuse that has characterised life in that country for more than thirty
years.

To the extent that the international community has attempted to foster
the rule of law since intervening in late 2001, it has done so through limited
technical interventions while doing nothing to curb – and in fact often
empowering – the most notoriously abusive individuals and institutions.
To begin to appreciate how Afghans perceive the current pattern of abusive
behaviour by powerful figures backed by the international community,
it will be helpful to consider the heritage of abuse that the West's allies
inherited and on which they are now building.

Afghanistan was maintained as a buffer zone between British India and the Russian empire. It remained underdeveloped and economically isolated from the rest of the world. This lack of investment ensured that its rulers were unable to improve the socio-economic conditions of their subjects. Of sixteen rulers since the year 1901 and the death of King Abdur Rahman (the 'Iron Amir'), six have been killed while in office, and with the exception of President Karzai, who remains in office, the remainder have been deposed one way or another. Democratic transfers of power have to date not occurred in Afghanistan. With their very lives at stake, it is not surprising that the rulers of Afghanistan have used all means possible, including brutally suppressing their opponents and subjects, to stay in power.

Examples of abuse by those in power abound

In 1324 Solar Calendar (1945), the people of Kunar Valley, in particular the Safi tribe, rose up against the government of King Mohammed Zahir because of extremely brutal taxation, oppression and poverty. The demands of the unjust system made it impossible for citizens to respect and adhere to the government's demands. For example, the farmers or landlords were required to forfeit one-third of their harvest to the government, a practice referred to as *sekoti*.[1] The government would then require the farmers or landlords to transport the grain to government warehouses (*godowns*), which were located in Bar Kunar (Asmar) and Kuz Kunar (Khewa) districts. At that time, animals were the only means of transportation. Once at the *godowns*, the government officials would delay acceptance of the deposit and question the quality of their produce. The farmers and landlords would then be obliged to pay bribes to have their crops accepted and be relieved from the government dues. In addition, the *momor malia* (taxman or district financial officer) would seal the crops in the field, and the farmers or landlords would then be prevented from harvesting them at the appropriate time to take it to their homes. In many cases, the sealed harvest would then remain in the field and eventually become unusable due to rain and lack of proper care. Similar unjust taxation schemes were applied to livestock. The government also enforced compulsory conscription, which outraged people.

The people of the Safi tribe[2] eventually rebelled against the government because of its unreasonable demands, and hundreds of people were

1 Discussion with my uncles and elders of Khas Kunar.
2 The Safi tribe is the biggest tribe in Kunar province, and is divided into the main three sub-tribes of Gurbuz, Mosaood and Wadir (known as Kandahari as well).

killed[3] during this revolt, which lasted for six months. Recently, I was discussing the Safi uprising with my mother, who at the time was about seven years old. She told me that government planes bombed her house in Tanar village as well as the village of Pacheyano Banda in the district of Khas Kunar in the Kunar province. During the bombardment, one of her older sisters, Bibi Rabo, was killed, along with two other women named Bibi Ayesha[4] and Khadeja. Several others were wounded. My mother told me that her grandfather, Mirza Mohammed Jan, who was an influential person in Khas Kunar district, was also arrested despite his old age; he eventually died in Jalalabad prison. My mother's father, Lal Mohammed Khan, pleaded to the government to release his father because of his age and health condition, but the government refused. In another such incident in Tanar village, a government plane bombed the house of Mirza Aziz Khan Akhundzada.[5] Eleven members of his family were killed, and due to danger of more bombardments, they were not able to bury the dead in the village graveyard. They were instead buried in front of the family home, where the graves remain to this day.

When the uprising of the Safi tribe was suppressed by the government, most of the elders of Safi and other tribes of Kunar were exiled to Herat and the northern provinces of Afghanistan. Many of them still live in Balkh, particularly in Shulgara district. All the male family members of Mir Zaman Khan of Kunar[6] were arrested and interned in Dehmazang[7]

---

3 Discussion with my father, uncles and elders in the Khas Kunar district. During the Safi uprising, the religious scholars ruled that tribesmen who rebelled against their King or *Ameer* and died should be excluded from being counted as *shahids* (martyrs). Therefore, they were required to select one member as a king, which would inevitably result in two rulers competing for the support of their people. The Safi tribe selected Shahswar as king (*padshah*), Salemai as prime minister (*sadr-e-azam*) and Amanul Mulk as minister of defence (*wazir-e-defa*). I met Amanul Mulk in Peshawar when I was living there as a refugee in the 1980s and 1990s. He died recently in Peshawar, but until his last days he continued to wear his military jacket. All three were exiled to Balkh province and lived in Shulgara districts. Their offspring still live in Shulgara district. My father during the Safi uprising was a student at the teacher training institute of Kabul (*Darul Malemen*). After graduating from the institute, he became a teacher in Shulgara district of Balkh province in 1326 Hijra calendar (1947) just two years after the rebellion, and he himself met in Shulgara with Shahswar and Salemai. The Safi uprising is also known in Kunar as the year of Safi (*Safi kal*).

4 Bibi Ayesha was mother of Judge Esmatullah Rohani, who is currently living in Canada.

5 Mirza Aziz Khan was father-in-law of the author's aunt, Bibi Rafia.

6 Mir Zaman Khan was grandfather of the author's mother.

7 Dehmazang was the notorious main prison in Afghanistan until Pul-e-Charkhi prison was built during the reign of President Mohammed Daud. It was located in Dehmazang area near Kabul zoo.

prison in Kabul, and the women members of the family were interned in their house in Qalacha[8] near Kabul city for thirteen years. Due to extreme hardship in the prison, about thirty members of Mir Zaman Khan's family, including children, women and men,[9] died in the prison. Later, the entire family was exiled to the province of Herat, where they lived a further eight years. The entire family of Mir Zaman Khan, during twenty-six years of their time in prison and exile, were never allowed to return to Kunar. My uncle, Abdul Jalil Malang,[10] who became a member of parliament (1969–73), was in sixth grade when my grandmother sent him to Herat province to enquire about her brothers. On his return to Kunar, my uncle was arrested by the government and jailed for six years. Imagine a child of the sixth grade having to spend six years in jail. In 1964, when the absolute monarchy was changed to a constitutional monarchy, Mir Zaman Khan's family was allowed to return to Kunar and reclaim their land and property. Such examples of injustice are typical of all regimes in Afghanistan, and many tribes have suffered under the oppression of rulers throughout the country.

In 1964, when the absolute monarchy changed to a constitutional monarchy, many Afghans were exposed to the outside world for the first time, and many from the educated elites wanted to play a larger role in the government decision-making process in accordance with the new constitution. The forming of political parties was constitutionally permitted, but the King never endorsed the law. The mainstream moderate elites were not allowed to establish political parties, which could have positively countered left- or right-wing extremist groups, because of the obstruction of the King, who feared mainstream moderate entities could threaten his monarchy.[11] The King was unfortunately wrong. Sardar Mohammed

---

8 Qalacha is located in the south of Kabul about 5 km from the city of Kabul on the road towards Logar province. This house of Mir Zaman Khan's family became known as the women's prison (*Mahbas-e-Zanana*) later on because the government would send women prisoners to the house due to lack of an alternative women's prison in Afghanistan at that time. At present, the daughter of Mir Zaman Khan, who is married to his nephew, lives in that house.

9 Mohammad Hasim Zamani, son of Mir Zaman Khan, wrote a book in the Pashto language entitled *Zandani Khaterat* (memoirs of prison). It is a very tragic memoir of his time in the prison (available at www.zamanifamily.com/Ghazi/ghazi_eng.html, last accessed 24 January 2010).

10 Abul Jalil Malang died on 23 December 2009 in Peshawar and was buried in Tanar village of the Khas Kunar district in his ancestral graveyard.

11 During a meeting in Virginia in the 1990s, I asked Dr Abdul Qayum, former Minister of Education and the Interior during the King's time, why the educated elite of Afghanistan during the reign of King Mohammed Zahir was not able to establish a national mainstream

Daud, the first cousin and brother-in-law of King Mohammed Zahir, who was sacked from the position of prime minister in 1963, joined hands with the leftist Parcham[12] faction of the People's Democratic Party of Afghanistan (PDPA) and overthrew the monarchy in a 1973 coup. President Daud replaced the monarchy with a presidential system, but was unable to strengthen democratic institutions or organise free and fair elections in Afghanistan. President Daud extended his term by convening a *loya jirga* in 1977, but one year later the communist party of the Khalq faction of the PDPA took power in a bloody coup in which President Daud along with his family members were eventually killed. Despite his advanced years, Daud had followed the Afghan tradition of clinging to power, and failed to pave the way for a transition towards greater civil liberties and accountability.

In 1978, the new communist regime of Afghanistan launched a massive 'social justice agenda' which included land reforms and the abolition of the mortgage (*grawe*) system. A similar reform agenda had been launched by King Amanullah Khan (1919–29) but failed because it was too progressive for the rural areas of Afghanistan. The communist regime's attempt to solidify and maintain power backfired because of the perceived injustice of appointing loyalists to government and security institutions, and the removal of trusted and respected public servants. The introduced reforms were not welcomed by the Afghans (Miakhel 2009), especially in the rural areas, and adversely affected all strata of society. Armed struggle or *jihad* against the communist regime began in the rural areas of Afghanistan, and spread until the last regime of Dr Najibullah collapsed in 1992. Over the past thirty years, the people of Afghanistan have suffered enormous injustice due to civil war and at the hand of communist regimes, the Soviet invasion, the mujaheddin groups and Taliban regimes. No one has ever truly listened to or addressed the outstanding grievances or concerns of the Afghan people.

After the collapse of Dr Najibullah's regime in 1992, the mujaheddin groups fought against each other for control in the country, and many

---

moderate political party in the 1960s. He replied that the King was the main obstacle because he thought that if the mainstream elite became organised, it might be a threat to the monarchy. Dr Abdul Qayum was also the brother of former Prime Minister Dr Abdul Zahir (1971–72). He lives in Maryland, US.

12 The pro-Moscow PDPA was divided into two factions: *Khalq* (People or Masses, led by Noor Mohammad Taraki, the first president after the PDPA took power in a bloody coup in April 1978), and *Parcham* (Banner, led by Babrak Karmal who was installed President after the Soviet invasion of Afghanistan in December 1979).

commanders became de facto rulers in their areas. Proxy war, which was supported by the regional powers, continued for several years; tens of thousands of people were killed and millions displaced. As reported by the UN, in Kabul between May and August 1992, 1,800 civilians died in rocket attacks and 500,000 people fled the city.[13] The actual number is not easy to determine, but according to different estimates, just in Kabul city alone, between 1992 and 1996, more than 60,000 people were killed and 80 per cent of the city was razed to the ground (Kolhatkar 2001). In the regions, different warlords who were supported by some of Afghanistan's neighbours took control and acted as mini kings, ruling their area of control with brutality. Life, property and the honour of ordinary Afghans were not safe. Shooting people in the streets, playing with dead bodies for fun, rapes, mass killings, cutting the breasts off women – any crime imaginable was committed (Dorronsoro 2007). In 1994, when I worked for the UN, I sometimes had to travel from Jalalabad city in the east of Afghanistan to Asadabad, the capital of Kunar province, about 75 kilometres distant. In the course of that journey, we would encounter more than 150 checkpoints maintained by different groups. Passing each checkpoint was like crossing into an alien territory without a visa; you were never sure what would be happen to you each time you were stopped. In 1994, when the Taliban movement emerged in the south and took over Kabul in 1996, it was in response to the common aspiration that the people of Afghanistan shared to get rid of these warlords (Dorronsoro 2007). When the Taliban took power, they didn't keep their promises, and instead tried to apply harsh rules, which were contradictory to Islamic values, to punish people on the street without verdict of the courts, close girls' schools, and eventually align with Arab terrorist groups.

After the tragic events of September 11, 2001 and the collapse of the Taliban government, the people of Afghanistan had a new chance to enjoy better government and social justice. The government and the international community raised hopes that the removal of the widely loathed Taliban regime would presage the transformation of Afghanistan into a society in which the most powerful individuals, and even the state itself, would be held to account for abusive behaviour. Nine years later, though, Afghanistan is still at war, and facing an insurgency with both internal and external dimensions. The warlords and criminal kingpins who were defeated by the Taliban have now been returned to power. They

---

13 See http://en.wikipedia.org/wiki/Civil_war_in_Afghanistan_(1992–1996) (last accessed January 2009).

wield executive, political and economic power, and have no opposing force able to counter their injustice in the affected villages, districts and provinces. President Karzai's first term as president technically[14] ended on 22 May 2009, but he used various excuses to delay the election until August 2009, and finally prevailed in elections marred by extensive vote-rigging.

The current insurgency in Afghanistan can only be curtailed and defeated if the government is able to deliver social justice and balanced economic development to ensure improved human security. The single greatest failure of the intervention has been to entrench the culture of impunity for the powerful, and thereby entrench the abuse at the root of the country's long history of conflict. This central failure can be seen in a series of misalignments of purported goals and actual actions.

Inflated expectations and poor follow-through

After the collapse of the Taliban regime at the end of 2001 and the establishment of a new interim government in Afghanistan, the international community promised to launch another Marshall Plan for Afghanistan. The international community vowed not to abandon Afghanistan as it had after the Soviet withdrawal in 1989. It seems clear in hindsight that the main objective of the war in Afghanistan was not state-building or any other process of development requiring a long-term commitment. The Bush administration only focused on hunting down al-Qaeda in Afghanistan, and prematurely announced the defeat of the Taliban as a pretext for diverting attention and resources from Afghanistan to Iraq.

In consequence, Afghanistan has received far less money per capita, at $57, than either Bosnia or East Timor ($679 and $233 per capita respectively); yet the US military has been spending more than $100 million a day in Afghanistan since 2001 (Waldman 2008). This demonstrates that most of the money supposedly allocated to improving the life of Afghanistan's citizens has instead been used to rent security rather than to build it. According to a 2007 NHDR report, Afghanistan is still ranked 174 out of 178 countries in terms of poverty, and 6.6 million people (out of a population of about 28 million) cannot meet their minimum daily food requirements. Only a small fraction of the money spent on the military

---

14 According to art. 61 of the constitution which stipulates that 'the presidential term shall expire 22 May of the fifth year after election. Election for the new president shall be held within 30 to 60 days prior to the end of the presidential term'.

has been devoted to the development and support of Afghan institutions, which lack the quality necessary to win public confidence and support.

Even the military has a short-term focus that undermines its ability to win public confidence. President Obama's commitment of 30,000 more US troops was accompanied by a pledge to begin transferring forces out of Afghanistan in July 2011.[15] However understandable it may be in domestic political terms, Obama's announcement of a timetable for drawing down forces just eighteen months after the surge began sent the wrong signal to the people of Afghanistan and to countries of the region. The perception among Afghans is that the US will abandon them once again, and both Afghans and regional powers feel they have little choice but to hedge their bets on the government of Afghanistan by opening channels to the insurgents.

Short-term political considerations trump longer term development

Since the Bonn agreement of 2001, the main focus of the government and international forces was on legitimisation of President Karzai's government rather than on institution-building. Most of the programmes and reforms were supply-driven and based on ideas and experience cut and pasted from other countries rather than adapted to the context of Afghanistan. The Afghan government also failed to play an effective coordination role, and left this to the international community, especially UNAMA, which also lacked the necessary capacity and leadership. Furthermore, the government was not able to put its own agenda on the table to rally the support of relevant stakeholders. Instead, opportunistic companies and organisations, both Afghan and international, benefited. Billions of dollars were wasted between 2001 and 2010.

An under-resourced, Balkanised international effort

In January 2002, a donors' conference in Tokyo[16] adopted the idea of individual nations taking lead responsibility for reforming the military, police and judicial system, and for DDR (disarmament, demobilisation and rehabilitation) and counter-narcotics. This was a mistake. The lead

---

15 President Obama's speech on Afghanistan at West Point, 1 December 2009.
16 See www.ictj.org/static/Publications/ICTJ_AFG_SSR_pb2009.pdf (last accessed 15 January 2010).

nations were not able to provide necessary resources and build consensus among various government agencies to strengthen relevant institutions. Only the Afghan national army (ANA) had some success, but even its sustainability is questionable. The Afghan government will not be able to fund its army for many years to come. The judicial system and police still remain the weakest institutions, and people are not able to address their grievances or resolve disputes through legal government institutions. Lack of rule of law has been the biggest factor in alienating the people of Afghanistan from their government.

If we only look at police reform in Afghanistan, Germany as lead nation was unable to coordinate with donor countries or with the government of Afghanistan. Germany only supported a police academy, which has produced few graduates. From 2001 until 2003, there was decreasing focus on supporting the police, which should have been the top priority for the government of Afghanistan and the international community. It took a couple more years before the US jumped in to support the Afghan police system; the additional resources were only channelled to them in 2006.[17] The US contracted police reform to MPRI (Military Professional Resource Inc), which didn't have a police background or experience. MPRI imposed a military structure on the reformed police system, which was mostly missing the policing component to maintaining rule of law. The contractor was only concerned to fulfil its contracting obligation rather than to build police institutions. There are different estimates, but due to poor design of police reform and implementation, about 10,000 professional police officers who had educational background and experience lost their jobs or were appointed in passive positions. Instead, about 10,000 incompetent and corrupt police officers who were related to the top leadership, or were able to bribe their way into leadership positions at all levels, were recruited. Just recently, a group of professional MOI generals told me that during 2009, MOI has been restructured three times. Even with more resources and attention to police in the past three years, it seems that it will take many years for better policing to come to Afghanistan.

Conclusion

Human beings tolerate injustices and tyranny to a point, but not forever. If there are no peaceful means through which people can address

---

17 The author of this chapter worked in the Interior Ministry from 2003 to 2005 as senior adviser and Deputy Minister of Interior in charge of local governance.

their grievances, eventually they lose patience and, as history has proven, opt for violence. There is a saying in our language: when water fills a cup, it flows over the sides. People will only tolerate so much injustice; beyond this, people move against the government – it could be through an orange revolution,[18] a rose revolution[19] or, in the case of Afghanistan, perhaps a pomegranate revolution. When you examine the insurgency in Afghanistan, it doesn't seem that the people of Afghanistan like Taliban-style government, but they also do not trust or respect the presiding government, and so remain ambivalent about the contest between them.

The aspirations of Afghanistan's people and the strategic aims of the international community would converge in a state that is widely perceived as legitimate and that is committed to upholding at least a minimal standard of equality before the law so that no one can abuse with impunity.

History has repeated itself in Afghanistan several times. All outsiders and rulers who are installed or selected by the people have made the same mistakes. The Afghan people have been the great losers in the Great Game, the cold war, and now the ongoing war against al-Qaeda.

Reforms to promote individual rights have been pushed from Kabul to the rural areas of Afghanistan, and they have not worked. Afghans, and especially Pashtuns, are always ready to sacrifice individual rights for family and community interests. Therefore, a balanced approach is needed between reforms that promote the rights of individuals and those that strengthen the communities with which Afghans identify their own values and interests.

Most reforms in Afghanistan are introduced by outsiders through their cronies in order to achieve quick fixes. Reform should be a long-term process, not a means to address short-term goals. Most of the reforms introduced in Afghanistan have been cut and pasted from different countries without adjusting to the context of Afghanistan. They have been counterproductive and have largely failed.

The elections in Afghanistan in the past few years have been incomplete and very costly exercises. The constitution of Afghanistan stipulated that village, district, provincial, municipal, parliamentary and presidential elections should take place in specified periods. So far only provincial, parliamentary and presidential elections have taken place, but with a huge price tag that Afghanistan cannot possibly afford over the long term. Yet without an ongoing election schedule, the democratic process is incomplete. If we adapt the current election system to the local context,

18 Reference to orange revolution in Ukraine.   19 Reference to rose revolution in Georgia.

it will cost much less and can be sustained in the long run. In 2002, I was involved in the election process of the emergency *loya jirga* in the four eastern provinces of Kunar, Laghman, Nangarhar and Nooristan. These did not cost more than $100,000. The quality of elections does not depend primarily on how much money you spend, but on the credibility of the process and the level of popular participation from the campaign period to the casting and counting of votes.

Spending money is not a solution in itself; the question is how to spend money so as to do no harm. The money that has been spent in Afghanistan since 2001 can be looked at in two ways. On the one hand, a lot of development has occurred which has no precedent in the history of Afghanistan. On the other hand, it has created animosity among Afghans at all levels, and created tensions in the country and even among government officials. In the urban areas, the gap between rich and poor has widened enormously, and in the rural areas, assistance-enhanced rivalries flourish between those who benefit from the current situation and those who do not. Above all, warlords, drug lords and criminal networks have become very rich, and have control and near monopoly of the lifeline of economic activities in Afghanistan.

Last but not least, in order to enhance security in Afghanistan and improve the rule of law, building professional police should be the top priority for the government of Afghanistan and the international community. If one had to choose between having a capable army or capable police force, police should certainly win out. (Strengthening the judicial system and improving governance should be addressed concurrently.) In Afghanistan, we cannot compete with our neighbours militarily, but they won't attack Afghanistan because it is not in their interest to do so.

The police, on the other hand, are indispensable in upholding the law and order that form the foundation of any functional society. The police are the most visible face of a government's commitment to and capacity to uphold the rule of law.

Unfortunately, Afghanistan's police have received almost no training in actual police work, and have instead been pushed through eight-week courses in small arms and paramilitary operations. Nearly all police recruitment takes place locally, which results in groups that function like militias acting in support of local tyros. The (misleadingly named) Afghan national police is not like ANA, which recruits nationally and mixes soldiers from different ethnic communities in units that can operate in any part of the country. The police should adopt a similar national recruitment and deployment scheme. In order to train good police, commissioned officers need to do a course of three to four years duration. Also important to accountable policing is an independent oversight mechanism to review complaints and accompanying measures to protect whistleblowers.

References

Dorronsoro, Gilles (2007). 'Kabul at war (1992–1996): State, ethnicity and social classes', *South Asia Multidisciplinary Academic Journal*, http://samaj.revues. org/document212.html (accessed 20 January 2009)

Kolhatkar, Sonali (2001). 'By any standard, this is a war against Afghans', www. commondreams.org/views01/1212-01.htm

Miakhel, Shahmahmood (2009). 'Repeating history: Parallels between mujaheddin tactics and Afghanistan's current insurgency', in *Afghanistan 1979–2009: In the Grip of Conflict*. Washington, DC: The Middle East Institute, www.mei.edu/Portals/0/Publications/Afghan%201979-2009.pdf

Waldman, Matt (2008). *Falling Short: Aid Effectiveness in Afghanistan*. ACBAR Advocacy Series, March 2008

PART III

The political economy of opium

The political economic origins

7

The Afghan insurgency and organised crime[1]

GRETCHEN PETERS[2]

Insurgents and counter-insurgents in Afghanistan are evolving in parallel. Both have come to recognise that achieving ultimate success requires winning the support of the people. This realisation has led both sides to try to limit the harm they cause while maximising their perceived benefits. For each this demands difficult trade-offs. For the NATO coalition, it means limiting civilian casualties and other negative impacts inflicted in the course of operations to eliminate insurgents. For the Taliban, it means limiting the violence done in the course of carrying out criminal activities that have become an increasingly important source of financial support.

Militant groups on either side of the frontier function like a broad network of criminal gangs, not just in terms of the activities in which they engage, but in the way they are organised, how funds flow through their command chains, and how they interact with each other. Within this complex adaptive system, criminal profits fund the insurgency, while terrorist violence helps militants to coerce and exert a level of control over local communities. Within a realm of poor governance, widespread state corruption and predation by local powerbrokers, the Taliban and other belligerent groups engage in and protect organised crime – mainly smuggling, extortion and kidnapping. Organised crime helps the insurgents to raise funds, and – whether by design or by accident – has effectively become a key element of their asymmetric warfare campaign, spreading fear and insecurity. Crime slows the pace of development and frustrates attempts to extend the rule of law and establish a sustainable licit economy. Insurgents find ways to justify criminal behaviour as part of their

---

1 This is an abbreviated version of a longer report published by the Combating Terrorism Centre at the US Military Academy at West Point. The paper was first published in April 2010 and is reprinted here with permission from USMA.
2 Peters was supported in her research by ten local researchers who chose not to be named here. Don Rassler, USMA/CTC, edited the original monograph.

jihad, claiming, for example, that they live off the alms of the people, or that they deal in drugs in order to make addicts of infidels. As with Mafia families operating in the West, criminal insurgent behaviour can be simultaneously protective and predatory towards the communities where insurgent entities operate. In 2009, the Taliban promulgated a new code of conduct that seeks to centralise control of illicit revenues while also limiting the harm to civilians caused by criminal activities.

The Taliban's ability to threaten the civilian population through crime, in addition to paramilitary and terrorist activities, broadens the coalition's security challenge. At the same time, though, the insurgency's financial reliance on predation also creates a strategic liability, limiting the group's popular appeal and sparking fierce internal rivalries. The coalition and the wider community trying to stabilise Afghanistan could potentially exploit both these weaknesses. This chapter will examine how the Afghan Taliban, commonly referred to as the Quetta *shura* Taliban (QST), engage in criminal activity in the south and south-west, how their involvement in crime is deepening, how money moves through their command chain, and how they interact with autonomous smuggling organisations.[3] By examining the tensions between financial and political motives behind the Taliban's 2009 code of conduct, this chapter attempts to assess the strength and coherency of the QST leadership, and the group's wider brand strength among the Afghan public.

Organised crime has played an important destabilising role in post-2001 Afghanistan. Protecting and taxing the opium trade helped fund the Taliban resurgence, and has intensified the conflict in Afghanistan's south by bringing both militants and corrupt state actors significant wealth and access to explosives and weapons. Kidnapping, attacks on supply convoys and widespread protection rackets have dramatically increased security and other costs for the coalition, local governments and international organisations working in the region, slowing the pace of development and reconstruction, and spreading the perception that the Afghan government is weak and ineffective. The vicious cycle of development projects and businesses that pay protection to insurgents, who then use the funds to buy explosives and attack coalition troops, creates a moral hazard for the international community and contributes to a self-sustaining war. In districts where local communities earn from the opium trade, Taliban

---

3 Two other factions of the insurgency in Afghanistan are widely referred to as the *Haqqani* network and the *Hizb-i-Islami Gulbuddin*. This chapter focuses only on the Quetta *shura* Taliban.

protection of illicit commerce can elicit various forms of cooperation and support from civilians.

Organised crime fuels corruption, probably the single biggest obstacle to stabilising Afghanistan. Corrupt state actors not only have a perverse disincentive to improve governance; they also rob their governments of critical revenue. According to a January 2010 report by the United Nations Office on Drugs and Crime (UNODC), Afghans paid $2.5 billion in bribes in 2009, equivalent to 23 per cent of that country's GDP (UNODC 2010). Critics of the US-led plan to stabilise the region note that anti-corruption efforts typically must come from within in order to succeed, a vexing consideration for NATO military commanders trying to implement a counter-insurgency strategy with often unreliable local partners (see Heineman 2009).

Western estimates of the QST's annual earnings from narcotics vary by hundreds of millions of dollars. Although most analysts agree it's not possible to determine precisely how much the QST earns from opium, nor estimate what portion of its total budget comes from narcotics, senior US military intelligence officials and members of the Afghan Threat Finance Cell, an interagency body tracking Taliban finance, believe the Afghan insurgency is now self-financed and that narcotics represents the largest portion of QST funding (US Senate Committee on Foreign Relations 2009: 14, and personal interviews by the author). The Taliban profit from the opium trade in four main sectors: by taxing poppy farmers 10 per cent (*ushr*) of their farm output; by charging fees to protect opium shipments and heroin refineries; by taxing and, increasingly, running their own drug labs; and in the form of large cash payments made to the Quetta *majlis* by major trafficking groups. Of these sums, tax collected from the farmers appears to represent the smallest portion of the insurgents' take, and these earnings by and large remain at the village level, where sub-commanders often sell off what they collect to local agents in order to cover operational costs.

Though crime brings financial advantages, the associated levels of violence caused by insurgents have also prompted growing numbers of civilians to question the purported religious, political and ideological motives of the militants. This creates an opportunity that the coalition has barely begun to tap. Belligerents on both sides of the Durand Line have long portrayed themselves as impoverished mujaheddin, battling under the flag of Islam and living off the alms of ordinary civilians who support them. A 2009 statement by the Taliban's number two, Mullah Abdul Ghani Baradar, who was detained in Pakistan in February 2010, expresses the typical rhetoric heard from militants on both sides of the frontier: 'This pious and patriotic people have offered tremendous material and soul sacrifices in the way of their sacred objectives. The mujaheddin have not chosen this path of strife between the truth and the evil to obtain material goals. They have lofty Islamic and nationalist aims' (NEFA Foundation 2009).

Whatever legitimacy such claims may provide, there are growing indications that militant involvement in organised crime and high levels of terrorist violence have undermined public support, particularly since local communities – virtually all of them fellow Muslims – are the main victims. While militants may protect illicit economies – and in doing so gain cooperation from community members who seek to protect their income source – militants also prey on civilians, both through the taxes and protection fees the militants charge and by creating instability that hampers the development of licit alternatives.

Though members of the local community may at times cooperate with the Taliban for economic reasons or out of fear, that cooperation appears not to indicate that the QST has been embraced as a popular force. Rather, recent public surveys indicate that approval ratings for the insurgents are dropping. Some 90 per cent of Afghans surveyed in a January 2010 ABC/BBC News poll preferred the government of President Hamid Karzai to the Taliban – an increase of eight points over a figure provided a year earlier – while 69 per cent, a new high, described the insurgents as the nation's greatest threat (ABC News 2010). Some analysts have questioned the high favourability rates that the Karzai government earned in the survey, but low and declining levels of public support for the insurgents could be tracked across several polls taken in 2009 in both Afghanistan and Pakistan.[4] The shift in perception was particularly apparent on Pakistan's frontier where dozens of civilians interviewed for the project referred to the Taliban using the Urdu term for gangster (goonda) rather than using more reverential terms like Taliban or mujaheddin. Rising levels of public antipathy may account for why the

---

4 MacKenzie 2010. This article notes that there is little empirical evidence of optimism among many ordinary Afghans, suggesting that the numbers could reflect a sense of hope that things will improve, rather than expectations. A 2009 survey by the Asia Foundation also found Afghans to be growing more optimistic, but by a smaller margin. That survey can be seen at http://asiafoundation.org/resources/pdfs/2009AGpollKeyFindingsFINAL.pdf. A 2009 survey by the same ABC/BBC/ARD conglomerate tracked dropping confidence levels. That data is found at http://abcnews.go.com/images/PollingUnit/1083a1Afghanistan2009.pdf

Taliban's 2009 code of conduct attempted to reduce the exploitation of civilians in their control zones, and could indicate that insurgent leaders fear a public backlash.

US forces and the NATO coalition – which also remain unpopular – stand to improve relative levels of community support and capitalise on public disgust towards the militants by developing strategies to protect civilians victimised by organised crime and violence.[5] The Afghan government, widely perceived as corrupt, could also improve its image by making concrete efforts to stamp out crime and reduce corruption. Separately, rivalries over criminal profits create structural weaknesses within and between insurgent and terror groups in the conflict zone. Exploiting those rivalries and breeding distrust could serve to degrade levels of militant cooperation and disrupt funds reaching militant coffers. This strategy is risky, however, to the extent that it could spark internecine violence and contribute to more civilian casualties.

Examining motives: the greed and grievance factors

Over the past decade, a growing body of academic literature has examined the role that organised crime has played in recent cases of insurgency and civil conflict, probing the various ways in which involvement in crime can alter the trajectory of belligerent groups, and considering the most effective counter-measures that governments and military planners can adopt in order to counter the phenomenon. There has been lively debate over the question of whether greed or grievance is more often the predicator of violence in such conflicts (see for example Berdal and Malone 2000; Collier and Hoeffler 1998 and 2004). This chapter does not claim that greed, grievance or some combination thereof sparked the post-2001 rebellion in Afghanistan, as there was clearly a broad range of factors. Rather, it is useful to consider the role that greed and grievance now play in affecting the insurgency's staying power. In a region where a broad range of actors profit from the drug trade and other illicit activities, there is no question that reducing levels of organised crime will be essential to rebuilding the Afghan state, improving governance, reviving licit economies and ensuring tax revenues enter federal coffers in both

5 Six in ten Afghans view the work of the US and the NATO coalition poorly, according to the ABC News poll (ABC News 2010), although that reflects a ten point improvement over last year's (2009) rate. Meanwhile, 64 per cent of the Pakistani public regards the US as an enemy, according to an August 2009 Pew survey, while only 9 per cent describe it as a partner. The Pew survey is available at http://pewglobal.org/reports/display.php?ReportID=265.

Pakistan and Afghanistan. The prevalence of organised crime, and the extent to which militant groups appear to be deepening their involvement in it, also suggest that certain factions of the insurgency may be motivated more by profit – in other words, greed – than the political grievances for which they claim to fight.

The Taliban have capitalised on political, ethnic and economic grievances of members of the local community, and there is scant evidence that rank and file Taliban take up arms simply to enrich themselves or earn much once they do. At the same time, however, there is clear evidence that the continued state of insecurity richly benefits a small number of elites on both sides of the battlefield, giving both corrupt state actors and militant leaders a clear financial incentive to sustain disorder, regardless of whether their wider political and other goals have been achieved. For military planners, troops in the field, diplomats and others engaged in the effort to negotiate solutions to the conflict, it will be useful to assess which actors are motivated primarily or exclusively by profit, and which engage in crime as a means to further their political and ideological goals.

No doubt there will be a blend of motivations in some cases. Understanding them – and their relative weight in each case – will assist in making decisions about how to co-opt powerbrokers, or whether to remove them from the playing field instead. Licit financial alternatives may prompt those Afghans motivated predominantly by avarice to put down their weapons.[6] Crime is not the only source of income for insurgents in Afghanistan, nor is greed the sole motivating factor among a wide range of insurgent and terror groups. People predominantly motivated by grievances about how their society is run or how they are treated will hold out until their political goals are met. Judging how to read key players while simultaneously making efforts to improve the lot of ordinary civilians could support stability operations.

Greed and political grievances often complement one another. Anti-state actors are not the only ones profiting from drugs and other crime; regional powerbrokers, warlords and corrupt state actors also protect and engage in illicit activities. State corruption facilitates and strengthens organised crime generally and vice versa. Afghanistan is not the first

6 See Snyder 2006 for an analysis of how the military regime in Burma co-opted rebels who profited from the opium trade there, investing their narco-profits into legitimate businesses. As Snyder points out, this tactic succeeded in reducing levels of disorder but did nothing to reduce drug trafficking. Within the Afghan conflict, several powerbrokers tied to poppy cultivation and organised crime have agreed to change their ways in return for development aid and other support. There may be significant numbers of cases where co-option is a better alternative than interdiction.

conflict zone where organised crime has become a major destabilising factor, and yet the wider phenomenon has received scant attention among military strategists in this and other recent conflicts. Wartime underground networks in Bosnia, for example, morphed into political criminal networks that were tied to smuggling, tax evasion, and human trafficking, according to a 2000 US government study (US General Accounting Office 2000). Ties between the Kosovo Liberation Army and Balkan smuggling networks also slowed efforts to stabilise Kosovo (see UNODC 2008). In a more recent case, organised crime in post-Ba'athist Iraq became the 'unrecognised joker in the pack', funding al-Qaeda, *Jaish-al-Mahdi* as well as several Sunni tribes that initially fought US forces (Williams 2009). There is good reason to give this issue close attention in Afghanistan: a 2002 Stanford University study (Fearon 2002: 13) that analysed 122 civil wars since 1945 found that conflicts in which the actors depended upon 'valuable contraband' lasted on average five times as long as the rest.

Information presented in this report has been compiled mainly from interviewing Afghans in insurgent-affected areas in order to gauge *their* perceptions of how their communities are victimised by insurgent criminal activity. There are advantages and drawbacks to field-based research in a conflict zone, and there are particular challenges associated with the Afghanistan-Pakistan border areas, many parts of which are inaccessible to foreign and local researchers alike. Members of the community are able to provide a level of immediacy and intimacy that few outsiders would be able to attain on their own, but reliance on their largely anecdotal information also makes the data presented herein harder to corroborate. Complicating matters further, examining illicit activity is a challenging prospect in any environment, since most crime goes unreported and criminal actors tend to lie. There is no way to compensate for these issues entirely, but each case presented in this report has been corroborated by Afghan and Western officials, the media and other open source reporting, or was recounted by enough sources to be considered generally accurate. The US military shared with the author a raft of declassified documents seized in Afghanistan, which also served to corroborate local reporting.

A kinder, gentler Taliban?

In 2009, the QST named new regional commanders and shuffled the lineup of its executive council. The QST also issued a new code of conduct in an apparent attempt to exert control over unruly Taliban subcommanders, make strategic preparations for the surge of US troops, and improve relations with ordinary Afghans by establishing a civilian shadow government at the local level. Under the new structure, the Taliban also established provincial-level commissions where Afghans can present their requests or complaints to a local council of religious scholars, who answer back to the *shura*.[7] 'The reason they changed their tactics is that they want to prepare for a long-term fight, and for that they need support from the people; they need local sources of income', said Wahid Mujda, a former Taliban official who now tracks the insurgency on the internet (Rubin 2010).

In parallel with US-led efforts to reshape NATO strategy in Afghanistan,[8] Mullah Mohammed Omar, the leader of the QST, also altered his tactics, ordering his commanders to avoid victimising locals in what could be seen as a population-centric approach, Taliban style. In 2009, he released a thirteen-chapter code of conduct instructing QST sub-commanders to treat villagers fairly, broadened his shadow government and the Shari'a court system that settles local disputes, and appointed provincial-level commissions where civilians could bring complaints about local commanders. These efforts were undermined by an increase in suicide bombings, improvised explosive device (IED) attacks and targeted killings by insurgents to which the UN attributed 67 per cent of the civilian deaths in Afghanistan in 2009.[9] (Though this is just over twice the number of civilian deaths attributed to the coalition and their Afghan government allies, this quantitative difference is not sufficiently great for most Afghans to view them as qualitatively different from the insurgents.) Although the February and March 2010 arrests of

---

7 The Quetta *shura* is so named because the Taliban leadership is widely believed to operate from the western Pakistani city of Quetta, in Baluchistan province. In recent months, there have been open source reports suggesting that the Taliban leadership has shifted to the southern port city of Karachi out of fear that an intensive US-led drone campaign in the FATA would be extended to Baluchistan to target QST leaders (see for example Ali 2010: 13). The QST number two, Mullah Baradar, was captured in Karachi in February 2010, followed shortly thereafter by as many as four other Taliban officials in other parts of the country.

8 In his sixty-page initial assessment to Defence Secretary Robert Gates, Lieutenant-General Stanley McChrystal wrote that 'our objective must be the population'. A redacted version of the assessment is available online at http://media.washingtonpost.com/wp-srv/politics/documents/Assessment_Redacted_092109.pdf

9 A January 2010 report by the UN Assistance Mission in Afghanistan said the Taliban killed 2.73 times as many civilians in 2009 as pro-government forces. UNAMA blamed Taliban insurgents for 1,630 civilian deaths (67 per cent of the total recorded deaths) in 2009 – a 41 per cent increase on 2008, when 1,160 deaths, or 54 per cent, were attributed to the insurgents. For details, see www.irinnews.org/Report.aspx?ReportId=87716.

key Taliban officials in Pakistan raise the possibility that the shadow government could be significantly disrupted, its influence and reach have spread dramatically in the past twenty-four months, with some 80 per cent of Afghanistan witnessing at least some insurgent activity, and as much as one-third of the country under tight Taliban control for much of 2009 (personal interview by author with David Kilcullen, an adviser to Lieutenant-General McChrystal, 27 October 2009).

In addition to attempting to bring unruly village-level Taliban commanders into line, the strategy embodied in the Taliban's new code of conduct gives lower ranking insurgents fewer opportunities to earn money at the ground level. This makes commanders more dependent on the Taliban's ten-man ruling council, or *shura majlis* (referred to as the Quetta *shura*), for funding. The code of conduct decreed that no one outside the Quetta *shura* had the power to alter the new regulations, and listed the 'provincial, district and central military commissions [as] responsible for the dissemination and implementation of these rules'.[10] Various chapters of the decree appear aimed at limiting local commanders from taking their own decisions or earning funds at the local level, instead ceding all authority to the provincial commissions and the Taliban supreme leadership. The new system streamlines the way in which money raised by the Taliban at the local level is funnelled back to the Pakistan-based QST leadership, in some cases bypassing the local Taliban commander entirely.

Mullah Mohammed Omar, the reclusive one-eyed founder of the movement, remains the supreme leader (*amir-ul-momineen* – literally, 'commander of the faithful') of the Afghan Taliban movement. He named his trusted lieutenant Mullah Baradar, who also chaired the *shura*, to oversee the implementation of its rulings, and to appoint military commanders and provincial shadow governors (personal interviews by research assistant, Kabul, August 2009; see also Moreau 2009). Baradar's February 2010 capture in Pakistan, followed by the arrests of as many as four other QST officials, would appear to corroborate claims that Baradar oversaw the shadow leadership. Another significant capture was that of Mullah Agha Jan Mutassim, a key Taliban strategist who, until his March 2010 arrest, chaired the powerful finance committee (personal interview with Afghan officials by research assistant, Kabul, July 2009). Afghan security and intelligence officials say Mutassim, a native of Panjway, convinced Mullah Omar of the need to reduce the financial exploitation of the local population by Taliban fighters, arguing that the insurgents risked losing

10 A partial translation of the code can be found at www.nefafoundation.org.

their support. Afghan officials and tribal sources close to the Taliban say Mutassim also convinced Mullah Omar that internecine fighting between Taliban sub-commanders, particularly over money and resources, had become detrimental to the overall strength and unity of the movement (personal interview with Afghan officials by research assistants, Kabul and Kandahar, July 2009). Apparently Mutassim feared a return of the kind of violence that occurred in the early 1990s, when rival mujahed-din commanders turned their guns on each other and terrorised local communities across southern Afghanistan after the departure of Soviet forces (personal interview with Afghan officials by research assistants, Kabul and Kandahar, July 2009). Perhaps even more significantly, Mutas-sim implemented a series of reforms (discussed in greater detail below) that streamline how funds collected at the local level reach the Taliban's central coffers. 'He is like the Ashraf Ghani of the Taliban', said an Afghan official who tracks the Taliban leadership, referring to the former Afghan Finance Minister who ran for president on a campaign to stamp out graft and who was instrumental, until he resigned from the Karzai government in 2004, in increasing the amount of tax revenue collected provincially that reached Kabul (personal interview with Afghan officials by research assistant, Kabul, July 2009).

The establishment of the provincial-level commissions represents another way in which the Taliban leadership seemed to be trying to reach out to civilians in 2009, in particular since the commissions were often headed by religious clerics, not just Taliban commanders. Locals could go to the Taliban's shadow Shari'a court system in order to settle local disputes, or could take their complaints to the commissions, which also dispense justice. In particular, the provincial-level commissions have become a venue where ordinary Afghans and local businessmen can come if they have a complaint to file against the Taliban. The Taliban's willing-ness to punish their own is one of the main reasons many Afghans view the QST insurgents as being more fair – even if strict and ruthless – than the notoriously corrupt Afghan government. The new code of conduct decrees that Taliban 'who commit crimes should be referred to the provin-cial commission', which has the right, along with the shadow governor, 'to expel the perpetrator or to accept if the person repents'. As explained by a tribal elder in Ghazni: 'They have been going to people in the mosques and saying any Taliban member who shows a sudden increase in wealth has to explain it.' He gave the example of Qari Wali, a Taliban sub-commander who suddenly showed up with a Toyota Corolla outside Ghazni city. 'The commission took his car. He was suspended, and he had to explain how they got the car', said the elder. It turned out that Wali had agreed to kidnap a member of a rival tribe, using his twenty-man fighting unit to carry out the abduction. The Taliban leadership responded by taking away his command and reassigning him to Helmand province (interview by research assistant, Ghazni, August 2009).

In at least one reported case, the Taliban commission in Helmand even castigated a judge in Musa Qala whom the Taliban had appointed. 'One judge was found taking a bribe and the Taliban put black all over his face and tied him to a tree', recounted businessman Eitadullah Khan. 'When he was released, he was fired' (Gannon 2009). Afghans interviewed for this chapter in various parts of the country described the Taliban courts and commissions as more fair and less corrupt than the state justice system. Others, however, insisted that they used the Taliban justice system partly out of fear, apparently worried about the potential consequences of local Taliban finding they had turned to the local government.

The provincial commissions issue decrees using the stamp of the Islamic Emirate of Afghanistan, the official title of the Taliban government (personal interviews with Afghan officials by research assistant, Kabul, July 2009). They also help the QST maintain control over funds raised and dispatched to the provinces. Each commission has a political and economic committee, according to locals who have dealt with them, and each gets a set budget, decided by and negotiable with the QST. Wardak province, for example, receives a budget of about $36,000, while more active combat zones like Ghazni and Zabul might receive as much as $107,000 monthly.[11] The commission controls how money is earned at the village level in each province, but the Quetta leadership appears to shuffle the commission members on a frequent basis, apparently to prevent any one individual or group from becoming too powerful.

The QST has also attempted to end Taliban sub-commanders routinely bickering among themselves over operational issues. An Afghan national police officer who was abducted within the past year by Taliban fighters in Paghman province recalled three Taliban sub-commanders arguing over his fate. One wanted to ask a ransom from the policeman's family and commander, and pocket the money. A second commander had a

11 Interview with a senior Interior Ministry official by research assistant, Kabul, August 2009. The official has seen intercepted Taliban documents noting the quantities. This information was corroborated in part by an Afghan military intelligence official in Ghazni who confirmed that Taliban commanders in his zone were receiving budgets worth millions of PKR monthly, and by a provincial official of the NDS, who confirmed the PKR3 million budget for Wardak province.

cousin jailed in Pul-e-Charki prison outside Kabul, and he wanted to try to trade the police officer for his relative. A third just wanted to kill the policeman simply because he worked for the Karzai government. In the end, the police official said, the provincial commission decided his fate, and he was eventually freed for a ransom payment (interview by research assistant, Paghman, August 2009).

In terms both of financial matters and political decisions, the Taliban appear to be trying to centralise the decision-making process. While it is too early to draw firm conclusions, there are indications that the effort may have backfired in some areas. Mullah Omar has purged several commanders, most notably Mansoor Dadullah, who were not following orders sent down by the senior leadership, and – according to some sources – for skimming money meant to be sent to Quetta (interview by research assistant, Kabul, August 2009). Several years ago, Omar also disciplined Mansoor Dadullah's notoriously violent elder brother, Mullah Dadullah, for similar transgressions. The elder Dadullah was killed in a 2007 firefight in Helmand, amid rumours that rivalries over money led to his death (see Peters 2009: 27). A spokesman for the Taliban called the media in late 2007 to announce that Mansoor Dadullah, who had assumed many of Mullah Dadullah's responsibilities, had been fired 'because he disobeyed orders of the Islamic Emirate' (Agence France Press 2007). Researchers for this chapter heard of multiple cases where QST commanders across the south were disciplined, demoted and shifted to new regions, or even pushed out of the group entirely. In some zones, the Taliban also distanced themselves from local criminal gangs during 2009, although locals and government officials alike say that insurgents continued to subcontract local criminal gangs as needed in regions where the insurgents were less dominant or where they are attempting to establish wider control.

Efforts to reshuffle Taliban commanders and impose more control over their ability to earn funds independently may have partly backfired for the QST leadership, possibly exposing a strategic weakness in the organisation. Sources close to the movement told researchers that some QST commanders had rebelled against efforts to rein them in, sometimes violently. In a December 2009 Kabul press conference, Afghanistan's National Security Council appeared to corroborate at least one report, saying the Kabul government had received intelligence indicating that Mullah Omar had sacked two more Taliban commanders in the poppy-rich districts of Arghandab in Kandahar and Gereshk in Helmand. Jamil Bahrami, director of strategy at the National Security Council, said some of the command changes 'have triggered differences and oppositions among local Taliban commanders', according to a local news report (Arman-e Melli 2009). The possibility that QST commanders are resisting or even revolting against efforts to cut them off from local funding sources would not only indicate those specific commanders were more driven by profit motives than ideology, but that the new streamlined system could be threatening, rather than strengthening, the *shura*'s control over its network in some areas.

Certain passages in the new code of conduct suggest that Mullah Omar wants to reduce the ways in which fighters under his command victimise ordinary Afghans: 'The mujaheddin should strive to win the hearts and minds of Muslims by treating them with justice and good faith...As representatives of the Islamic Emirates, the mujaheddin should present themselves in such a manner that the whole nation would welcome and cooperate with them.' The code, which has been spottily enforced, bans Taliban soldiers from 'forcefully collecting alms, donations, and *ushr*', an agricultural tithe that the Taliban levy on farmers. It warns its fighters not to enter people's homes without permission, and instructs them to do 'their best to avoid civilian casualties and refrain from inflicting damage on people's vehicles and property'. Only Taliban-appointed judges can settle local disputes, the code dictates, calling their rulings final. It forbids kidnapping for ransom, saying that 'criminals who kidnap in the name of the Islamic Emirate should be disarmed and introduced to the leadership'. Additionally, the decree bans Taliban fighters from smoking and from keeping young boys (traditionally exploited for sex) on their bases.

The release of the code was accompanied by a Taliban propaganda campaign that also appeared to direct insurgent fighters not to victimise the local population. According to Afghans who saw the message on the now defunct Taliban website *Shahamat*, a statement by Mullah Mutassim advised Taliban forces not to attack schools, clinics, bridges and roads. It also directed commanders not to harass people on the highways. Meanwhile, Mullah Abdul Manan Niazi, the Taliban commander along the Kabul-Kandahar highway, reportedly ordered his fighters to stop damaging bridges and collecting 'tolls' on the busy interstate. In one 2009 message, he urged insurgent fighters 'to make sure there was no distance between the people and the Taliban'. According to locals interviewed for this paper who heard the broadcast, his radio message went on to say that if the Taliban accepted bribes, 'then there will be no difference between us and the police' (interview by research assistant, Kabul, August 2009).

Despite such lofty statements, however, it is important to recognise that the Taliban has not been entirely successful in implementing its new code of conduct, nor entirely innocent on the charge of attacking civilians (any more, indeed, than the coalition has been). Many Afghans continue to face – or at least perceive – a tangible level of threat if they do not abide by Taliban decrees. There seems to be no let-up whatsoever, for example, in the vicious punishments handed out by the insurgents, with locals in the south saying QST commanders continue to hold public executions of anyone suspected of 'spying' for the coalition (personal interviews by research assistant, Lashkar Gah, Kandahar, July 2009). 'People cooperate with the Taliban out of fear', said Abdul Ghani, director of the Afghan national police's anti-terrorism department in Ghazni province. 'If the Taliban sense the slightest whiff of espionage by local individuals, they instantly kill those people without any mercy' (personal interview, by research assistant, Ghazni, July 2009). When US marines pushed into Mian Posteh in Helmand province, villagers initially refused to re-enter the bazaar the American troops cleared, saying the Taliban had threatened to chop off their heads if they did. 'There are Taliban everywhere', village elder Haji Fada Mohammed told the marines, 'If I tell you who they are, I will be in danger' (Tyson 2009).

The code of conduct also instructs field commanders on money matters, institutionalising how profits earned from organised crime are to be shared within the command chain. The code specifies that Taliban soldiers are permitted to keep up to 80 per cent of whatever 'booty' they capture from 'an infidel combatant' or coalition base, but one-fifth of the value or property seized must be transferred to the shadow provincial governor, in much the same way mobsters and gang members must kick a portion of their earnings to their boss. The code permits Taliban fighters to attack and destroy coalition vehicles and convoys, but says that capturing and then 'releasing them in exchange for money is forbidden'. It decrees that any cash captured from the NATO coalition or the Karzai government must be transferred in its entirety to the Taliban treasury. The code also regulates shakedowns and extortion fees, banning provincial or district-level Taliban commanders from directly making deals with local businesses and companies. 'Disputes on issues related to businesses and companies should be referred to the leadership', the code states. This would suggest the QST is evolving into an organisation that openly functions like a traditional mafia, with a strict code governing criminal earnings, and where the bosses have the final say in all matters of collecting protection money. It also indicates a much higher level of internal discipline than the government can maintain.

The code of conduct lays down strict new rules concerning the treatment of prisoners, moving to limit Taliban fighters from accepting ransom payments on their own and stating that 'it is strictly forbidden to free coalition prisoners in exchange for money'. The same goes for contractors working with the coalition. The authority to execute foreign prisoners, trade them or set them free in exchange for money now rests entirely with Mullah Omar and his deputy, who must personally approve the circumstances. The code additionally bans Taliban fighters from torturing, beheading or dismembering prisoners, but states that obtaining confession through promises of 'money or position' was acceptable as long as the insurgents were able to deliver on their promises. It bans 'cash payment' as a form of disciplinary punishment, and prevents sub-commanders from killing local government officials who offer to lay down their arms and not support the government. It also forbids Taliban commanders from taking on new fighters without prior consent of the insurgent leadership. The code of conduct thus struggles to reconcile competing priorities. On the one hand, the Taliban claim they want to improve relations with the local community, but the code explicitly permits and regulates violent criminal activities that continue to harm civilians.

Taliban moving up the opium value chain

Declining farm prices apparently motivated Taliban commanders to move up the value chain of the drug trade, shifting their focus from taxing farm output to the more lucrative processing and exporting end of the business. 'To separate the drug smugglers from the insurgency in the south is now almost impossible', says a US officer who closely tracks the opium trade (personal telephone interview by author, September 2009). The three largest smuggling rings collaborating with the insurgency, known collectively as the Quetta Alliance, operate from Pakistan, by and large out of reach of the NATO coalition. The Quetta Alliance has historically included three clan-run smuggling organisations. Haji Juma Khan (HJK) ran the largest, known as the Khan Organisation, until his October 2008 arrest. Haji Bashar Noorzai reportedly commanded another clan-based group until his 2005 arrest. The Notezai clan, based in Dalbandin in western Pakistan, is the third major actor in the Quetta Alliance, according to declassified US Drug Enforcement Agency documents. In addition to their close ties to the Taliban, cartel leaders pay off key government officials in Afghanistan, Pakistan and Iran, greatly complicating efforts to interdict them with the help of local security forces.

HJK's gang was the dominant drug-smuggling organisation in southern Helmand province, where more than half of Afghanistan's poppy crop is cultivated. He ran a major opium market out of Marjah, a town in the Helmand River floodplains just 27 kilometres south-west of the provincial capital Lashkar Ghah where coalition forces in February 2010 launched a major operation to clear out the Taliban. He also maintained multi-tonne storage depots and drug refineries in Baram Chah, a dusty outpost that straddles the Afghanistan-Pakistan border. Despite the kingpin's arrest in October 2008 in Indonesia, from where he was swiftly extradited to the US, the organisation appears to have continued functioning without interruption under the command of Khan's nephew and former chief of operations, Haji Hafiz Akhtar (personal interview by author with US military official, October 2009). The immense scale of the group's operations – and their close ties to the Taliban – became clear in May 2009 when NATO and Afghan troops launched a major offensive to clear militants out of Marjah ahead of a suspected assassination plot being launched from there against the Helmand governor (see US Senate Committee on Foreign Relations 2009 for a detailed account). After three days of intensive fighting, sixty Taliban lay dead and the troops had seized a staggering 92 tonnes of heroin, opium, hashish and poppy seeds, as well as hundreds of litres of precursor chemicals, making it the second-largest drug haul in global history. Indicating how closely opium merchants and insurgents now work, the market also housed a Taliban command centre complete with elaborate communications systems, suicide vests and a large weapons cache (Vogt 2009 and personal interviews by author).

Reliable local media reports have also indicated that due to the declining farm-gate price of raw opium, there has been an explosion of refineries inside Taliban-held regions of Afghanistan capable of refining opium into crystal heroin, the high-value and most potent version of the drug. One lab worker in Marjah claimed there were more than 100 refineries operating in the district before the February 2010 offensive took place (Tassal 2010). Separately, Western counter-narcotics officials told *Time* magazine there was evidence that traffickers operating there had packed up and fled with their goods before the February 2010 NATO operation began. Prior to the offensive, a squad of American and Afghan paramilitary troops raided a major opium bazaar, finding shop after shop stacked to the ceiling with bundles of opium, heroin, hashish, guns and IEDs used in roadside bombings. 'If anybody needed proof that there was a nexus between the Taliban and drug traffickers, this was it', said a Western counter-narcotics agent in Kabul (McGirk 2010). Not only do Taliban commanders increasingly take on the role of running or managing heroin labs, but local and Western official sources say there are indications that Taliban forces are increasingly getting into the business of moving drug shipments across Afghanistan's border into Pakistan and Iran, where the wholesale value of drugs more than doubles (multiple interviews by author and research assistants with US, Afghan and Pakistani officials). The shift in focus from farm-level taxation to the processing and exporting end of the drug trade indicates that the QST is becoming more like a drug cartel, capable of purchasing locally, refining and then exporting narcotics.

Two further seizures in 2009 in southern Afghanistan indicate that the QST and the traffickers have developed and sustain a sophisticated supply chain for both drugs and explosives, despite the increased foreign troop presence and the lack of basic infrastructure in the south. An October 2009 drug raid on another Taliban base, also in Helmand, recovered 45 tonnes of opium, along with a stunning 1.8 tonnes of processed heroin, according to a press release from the Afghan Defence Ministry (Associated Press 2009). The heroin alone would have been worth $4.3 million on the local wholesale market, and more than double that if smuggled across the border into Pakistan or Iran (calculated from data in UNODC 2009). While there appears to be a shortage of military-grade explosives among the insurgents, the militants in the south have increasingly relied on fertiliser products that can be mixed into explosives. Coalition troops in Kandahar in November 2009 seized an astonishing 200,000 kilograms of ammonium nitrate, the fertiliser used in the overwhelming majority of homemade bombs in Afghanistan. About 2,000 bomb-making devices like timers and triggers were also found at the insurgent hideout (Filkins 2009).

A steady increase in heroin seizures, according to coalition officials and the DEA, indicates that more and more drug labs are capable of refining raw opium into crystal heroin, the most potent and high-value grade of the drug. The number of refineries south of the bend in the Helmand River (Garimser and Deshu districts) has reportedly climbed in recent years, although officials say it is hard to determine a precise number since the operations have become smaller and more mobile. Increasingly, according to US and Afghan officials, there are reports of Taliban commanders running their own drug labs, something almost unheard of just three years ago, and controlling drug shipments beyond the Afghan border into western Pakistan (personal interviews by author, Washington DC). Because the labs are increasingly mobile and operate in Taliban-dominated zones, it is difficult to assess how much control the Quetta leadership maintains over taxes collected at the refineries.

Village-level Taliban sub-commanders do not just tax poppy crops. They collect a portion of all farm output, whether licit or illicit, usually in the range of 10 per cent, but negotiable depending on the wealth of the farmer and the level of influence the Taliban commands in a given area. Poor farmers tell of handing the local Taliban sub-commander as little as a bag of fruit from their annual harvest, and there were also reports that large landowners had to pay a significantly higher agricultural tithe – as much as 20 per cent in certain districts of Farah province, for example. In some villages, the Taliban sub-commander has to split what he collects 50:50 with the local mullah, and in most zones, he must send 10 per cent of his take to his provincial-level commander. When village-level sub-commanders collect a commodity for which they and their troops have no use, they will often sell it to a local broker, known as a *jalab* in Pashto. Although this practice is not universal, in some areas the Taliban have begun handing out tax receipts to ensure that villagers and shopkeepers are not charged more than once. This practice has been implemented in northern Kunduz province, where the QST has made significant inroads in the past year (based on information from various researchers across Afghanistan in July and August 2009).

Shopkeepers and other small businesses, including pharmacies, teashops and automotive repair stations, are also required to hand over a portion of their monthly proceeds to the Taliban – usually in the range of 10 per cent, although also dependent on total earnings. In some cases, Taliban will ask the shopkeepers for supplies in place of money. One grocer in Ghazni described having to supply local insurgents with cooking oil and rice in lieu of a monthly payment, and said he received a receipt (personal interview by research assistant, Ghazni, August 2009). Because the Taliban depend on communications, and change their phones regularly to avoid surveillance, the local shopkeeper who sells mobile phone handsets, top-up cards for airtime credit and phone chips is likely to be visited routinely by the local Taliban unit, researchers for this chapter found. Shopkeepers also reported that Taliban who have looted goods or confiscated them from trucks will resell the commodities for money. 'They will call up and say we have some telephones or generators or whatever, if you want to buy them', said a local businessman (telephone interview by author, November 2009). Shopkeepers interviewed for this report also described having to pass on messages for the Taliban as they moved through town. Some claimed they did not want to serve as messengers but feared the consequences of not helping the insurgents.

Although QST sub-commanders continue to 'tax' farmers and small-time businesses at the local level, there is also evidence that the *shura majlis* has moved to regulate how protection money is collected from larger businesses, aid and development projects, as well as the trucking firms that operate on the busy Kandahar-Quetta corridor and other southern highways. A half-dozen truck drivers and the owners of two large trucking firms interviewed for this chapter said that QST forces in the south no longer collect payments on the Quetta-Kandahar highway, for example. Instead, under a system Mutassim developed, trucking firms now must deposit protection payments with specified moneychangers in Quetta and Kandahar. The moneychangers record the licence plate numbers of the trucks and details about what cargo they will carry, and the money is handed over directly to the financial council (personal interviews by research assistants in Kabul and Kandahar, August 2009). Drivers reported receiving a code that they could give to armed men who stop them on the road. 'The tiger is wounded but alive', was a code one driver gave as an example.

Trucks carrying goods for the local market, or transiting across Afghanistan, can expect to pay about 10 per cent of the value of their shipment. Convoys carrying goods for the coalition get charged a higher rate, which can range from 25 to 40 per cent of the total value being carried, according to truckers and officials at trucking firms (personal interview by research assistant, Kandahar, August 2009). A member of the Achakzai tribe, which has long dominated the transport business on the Quetta-Kandahar route, said he paid the Taliban between $95,000 and $130,000 every six months to protect convoys he sends to supply the Kandahar airfield. 'This is very organised between the [Taliban] fighters and the *shura*', he said. 'You give the name of the driver and the licence plate, and your truck is safe.' Low-ranking Taliban who ply the roads between Kandahar and the Pakistan border continue to hit up passenger cars for protection payments, but the large sums now go direct to Quetta.[12]

The Afghan Taliban appear to rely on an elaborate network of informants – the so-called village underground – to help them determine how much they can charge each trucking firm (as well as families, businesses and aid groups) they target. The informants get paid off for the information they provide, and local sources say they believe bus and taxi drivers and merchants who have excuses for leaving the village on a regular basis are routinely part of the information network. Those trucking firms that try to avoid paying the Taliban end up paying a higher price. One trucker

12 So far, this system seems to operate only in Kandahar and Helmand. In other parts of Afghanistan where there is a mix of insurgent factions and criminal gangs, truckers can expect to be hit up for cash on the roads.

in Kandahar recalled the story of a trader who imported spare parts from
Pakistan, and who made the mistake of bragging in a teashop at the border
that he didn't plan to pay off the insurgents. His four vehicles barely made
it outside the government-controlled border town of Spin Boldak before
Taliban gunmen overtook the convoy, and it cost him close to $200,000 to
buy his equipment back (personal interview by research assistant, Kandahar, August 2009). It is not always clear if such tales are actually true.
The important thing is that they are widely believed among the trucking
community, which is therefore persuaded not to take chances. There has
been documented evidence that the Taliban have tried to regularise its
tax collection system. In 2009, the Taliban in Helmand issued its local
representative with a notice 'to all Kajaki shopkeepers and truck drivers':
'The bearer of this letter is our new representative. Please cooperate with
him like ever before.'[13]

The Quetta *shura* also collects protection money from larger businesses, notably the telecoms sector, and construction projects funded
by international aid organisations and the coalition. Sargon Heinrich,
a Kabul-based businessman in construction and service industries, was
quoted in September 2009 as saying that 16 per cent of his gross revenue
went to paying 'facilitation fees', mostly to protect shipments of valuable equipment coming from the border (Baker 2009). The report aptly
describes the circular nature of the problem: the US government provides
money to local contractors to build roads, schools and bridges as part
of the counter-insurgency campaign, but the contractors must pay off
insurgents to avoid having those projects attacked. The insurgents then
spend the money they raise to purchase weapons and explosives, which
in turn get used to kill American soldiers. 'It becomes a self-sustaining
war', says an adviser to the Afghan Ministry of Interior. 'A self-licking ice
cream.' (Baker 2009)

In parts of the country where there is little or no poppy grown, especially
in districts where there is major construction work or central roadways
pass through, extortion is believed to be the largest source of income for
the insurgents. This creates a moral hazard for the international community, which seeks to stabilise Afghanistan but inadvertently ends up
financing the insurgency and the explosives rebels use to kill Western
troops and Afghan civilians. The US Agency for International Development has opened an investigation into allegations that its funds for road

13 This document was given to the author by the US military. A scan of it can be viewed on
the Combating Terrorism Centre's website, www.ctc.usma.edu.

and bridge construction in Afghanistan are ending up in the hands of the Taliban, with Congress set to hold hearings on the issue (MacKenzie 2009). Investigating the problem will be challenging enough, since few contracting firms admit to making security payments. How to stop the phenomenon – and provide adequate protection for development projects around the country – is yet another challenge.

The Taliban has also targeted Afghanistan's mobile phone network. The four main Afghan telecoms firms, which service about two million subscribers between them, must pay monthly protection fees in each province or face having their transmission towers attacked. Payments are usually around $2,000 per tower per month, but it depends on who controls the zone around each tower. 'In the Taliban areas, you have to deal with their commissions', said a local businessman whose firm builds transmission towers, who estimates about a quarter of his company's budget goes to protection fees on the roads and at building sites. 'Most of them, they act just like businessmen in a way. They tell you "we will make sure your people are not kidnapped and your sites are not burned". But they expect regular payments.' However, he said that in Helmand and Kandahar, the QST had established a new system in which payments must go direct to Quetta. The businessman routinely sends a representative to Pakistan to pay off the Taliban leadership, he said, rather than dealing with the district-level commander (personal interview by research assistant, Kandahar, August 2009).

Protecting civilians from crime will enhance rule of law

When US forces first arrived in Afghanistan in 2001 in the wake of the September 11 attacks, few military planners, policymakers and intelligence analysts ever imagined the extent to which organised crime – and specifically the heroin trade – would dramatically aggravate, prolong and reshape the conflict there. The spread of organised crime on both sides of the Afghanistan-Pakistan border, and both sides of the insurgency, highlights the need for a holistic strategy in such environments that works simultaneously to foster security, development and the rule of law. Evidence suggests that the QST is increasingly behaving like a traditional drug cartel, having moved up the value chain of the opium trade to focus on refining and exporting narcotics, rather than just taking a cut for protecting drug shipments and taxing poppy farmers. The fact that the insurgents are becoming increasingly criminalised should come as no surprise. In conflicts around the globe and throughout history, people who have crossed the line of the law for broad political reasons stay there for narrow self-interested ones.

Research for this chapter yields the following more specific observations:

- Militant groups sometimes collaborate with each other and at other times fight among themselves, much like mafia families and criminal gangs in the West. Since mutual trust on some level is a prerequisite for organised crime to occur, practices that breed suspicion among the militant factions, such as disrupting opium convoys in ways that suggest insider betrayal, could undermine mutual trust, and thereby disrupt insurgent networks and diminish their money flow.[14] Indications that there is already a great deal of competition between rival Taliban commanders on both sides of the frontier give this strategy real potential. That said, it is critical to distinguish between strategies that would spark violence between or among the militants, those that could cause civilian casualties, and those that would simply cause them to stop collaborating with each other, in terms of both criminal and terrorist activities.
- The frustration and rage that ordinary civilians feel towards militant crime is palpable. The QST code of conduct indicates the Taliban are sensitive to the widening public rage and see it as a strategic liability. The coalition could take advantage of this liability, which will continue as long as the Taliban remain dependent on profits from criminal activity, but only to the extent that the government's performance is seen as clearly better.
- Military commanders and Western policymakers need to consider the central motivations for insurgent and extremist leaders in this conflict. Amid international efforts to persuade the Taliban to stop fighting, no political concessions will be sufficient for those motivated primarily by greed.

The central implication of this chapter is that as much as drug trafficking and other organised crime have had debilitating effects on NATO's efforts to combat militancy and establish stability, the spread of criminality in Afghanistan has been even more deleterious for ordinary civilians there. Protecting local communities from organised crime represents a still largely untapped opportunity within the wider counter-insurgency strategy. If security providers (including foreign and local troops and

14 I am indebted to Dr Phil Williams for his thoughts on this matter in Williams 2009.

police) were able and willing to provide adequate community-level security, Afghans would suffer far fewer shakedowns, abductions and thefts. Just as NATO soldiers expect relative security from crime for themselves and their families back home, Afghans also long for a safe atmosphere in their communities.

References

ABC News (2010). 'Views improve sharply in Afghanistan, though criticisms of the US remain high', 11 January 2010, conducted with the BBC and ARD German TV, http://abcnews.go.com/PollingUnit/afghanistan-abc-news-national-survey-poll-show-support/story?id=9511961

Agence France Press (2007). 'Taliban sacks key rebel commander', 29 December 2007

Ali, Imtiaz (2010). 'Karachi becoming a Taliban safe haven?', *CTC Sentinel*, January 2010

Arman-e Melli (2009). 'Cracks in Taliban ranks widening', 23 December 2009, available on www.opensource.gov

Associated Press (2009). 'Afghan drug haul nets 50 tons of opium', 9 October 2009

Baker, Aryn (2009). 'How crime pays for the Taliban', *Time*, 7 September 2009

Berdal, Mats and Malone, David M. (eds.) (2000). *Greed and Grievance: Economic Agendas in Civil War*. Boulder: Lynne Rienner

Collier, Paul and Hoeffler, Anke (1998). 'On economic causes of civil war', *Oxford Economic Papers*, 50(4)

Collier, Paul and Hoeffler, Anke (2004). 'Greed and grievance in civil war', *Oxford Economic Papers*, 56(4)

Fearon, James (2002). 'Why do some civil wars last so much longer than the rest?', Stanford University paper, July 2002, www.web.mit.edu/polisci/polecon/www/dur21.pdf

Filkins, Dexter (2009). 'Bomb material cache uncovered in Afghanistan', *New York Times*, 10 November 2009

Gannon, Kathy (2009). 'Taliban's shadow government poses challenge to election, US troops', *Associated Press*, 18 August 2009

Heineman, Ben (2009). 'Corruption – the Afghan wild card', *The Atlantic Monthly*, 2 October 2009

MacKenzie, Jean (2009). 'Are US taxpayers funding the Taliban?', *Global Post*, 2 September 2009

MacKenzie, Jean (2010). 'Are Afghans really happy?', *Global Post*, 23 January 2010, www.globalpost.com/dispatch/afghanistan/100118/afghanistan-opinion-poll

McGirk, Tim (2010). 'Drug trade complicates US task in Marjah', *Time*, 6 March 2010

Moreau, Ron (2009). 'America's new nightmare', *Newsweek*, 25 July 2009

NEFA Foundation (2009). 'Taliban deputy Amir – Obama's new strategy', 30 October 2009, www.nefafoundation.org/miscellaneous/nefaAkhund1109.pdf

Peters, Gretchen (2009). *Seeds of Terror*. New York: St Martin's Press

Rubin, Alissa (2010). 'Taliban overhaul their image in a bid to win allies', *New York Times*, 21 January 2010

Snyder, Richard (2006). 'Does lootable wealth breed disorder?', *Comparative Political Studies*, 39(8)

Tassal, Aziz Ahmad (2010). 'Heroin menace grows', *Institute of War and Peace Reporting*, 4 February 2010

Tyson, Ann Scott (2009). 'In Helmand, caught between US, Taliban', *Washington Post*, 15 August 2009

UNODC (2008). 'Crime and its impact on the Balkans and affected countries', March 2008, www.unodc.org/documents/data-and-analysis/Balkan_study.pdf

UNODC (2009). *World Drug Report*, www.unodc.org/documents/wdr/WDR_2009/WDR2009_Statistical_annex_prices.pdf

UNODC (2010). *Corruption in Afghanistan*, January 2010, http://viewer.zmags.com/publication/8515c039#/8515c039/1

US General Accounting Office (2000). 'Bosnia: Crime and corruption threaten successful implementation of the Dayton peace agreement', testimony before the Committee on International Relations, House of Representatives, 19 July 2000

US Senate Committee on Foreign Relations (2009). 'Afghanistan's narco-war', a report to the committee, 10 August 2009, http://frwebgate.access.gpo.gov/cgi-bin/getdoc.cgi?dbname=111_cong_senate_committee_prints&docid=f:51521.pdf

Vogt, Heidi (2009). 'Troops make large drug seizure in Afghanistan', *Associated Press*, 23 May 2009

Williams, Phil (2009). 'Criminals, militias and insurgents: organised crime in Iraq', *Strategic Studies Institute*, June 2009, www.strategicstudiesinstitute.army.mil/pdffiles/pub930.pdf

8

Afghanistan's opium strategy alternatives – a moment for masterful inactivity?

JOEL HAFVENSTEIN

No examination of the rule of law in Afghanistan can overlook the fact that the country's largest, most mature industry is illegal. The unprecedented surge in opium price and production following the Taliban poppy ban of 2000–01 has exacerbated corruption at every level of government, as well as partly funding the neo-Taliban insurgency. This chapter explores the alternatives for Western governments' response to the Afghan opium economy, taking into account certain under-emphasised trends and the linked but not fully compatible priorities of counter-insurgency, counter-narcotics and strengthening the rule of law.

The Afghan drug economy: two key trends

Policymakers examining opium in Afghanistan are blessed with an abundance of quantitative and analytical studies, based on extensive field research by UN agencies and independent researchers.[1] Yet many policy briefs and media reports overlook key lessons from this body of work, and orient themselves instead around sensational but misleading narratives.

For example, the Taliban are still widely described as the dominant actors in the traffic, with opium called 'the economic engine for the insurgency' (Filkins 2009). Also, many analyses of poppy and alternative livelihoods presuppose opium's overwhelming economic superiority, citing a farm gate price that is unbeatable by anything save (perhaps) a few high-value, exotic crops.

There is some truth to both of these popular narratives, but they miss two larger, more significant trends.

---

1 Quantitative data comes primarily from the annual reports of the UN Office on Drugs and Crime (UNODC) and its predecessor agency, the UNDCP. Key analytical work includes Buddenberg and Byrd 2006; MacDonald 2007; and the studies by Adam Pain and David Mansfield published by the Afghanistan Research and Evaluation Unit (available online at www.areu.org.af).

First, Afghan government actors play a more significant role than insurgents in the narcotics trade.

Given the limitations on gathering evidence about criminal networks, this assertion must be hedged with caveats. It is based on allegations that are not always from credible or objective sources and can rarely be substantiated by attributable data. Journalists who have pursued the story generally find sources who insist on withholding specific details and speak on condition of anonymity. As a former police chief of Kandahar province said in May 2009: 'In this country, if someone really tells the truth, he will have no place to live' (Lasseter 2009). Moreover, the distinction between government and insurgent actors is often ambiguous, especially in contested areas where major economic players may have roles on both sides.

Nonetheless, policymakers would be foolish to ignore the insistence of Afghan sources that the trafficker-state nexus is more significant than the trafficker-insurgency nexus, both in the scale of the rents charged on the drug traffic and in the importance of the facilitating role played by state actors. One cannot review the research literature on the opium economy without being struck by this consistent message from Afghan informants.

For example, David Mansfield found after 2008 fieldwork in Helmand and Kandahar provinces that 'the overall perception in the south is that corrupt government officials are earning more money [than the Taliban] from their direct or indirect involvement in the drug trade' (Mansfield 2008: 48). Gretchen Peters, whose research focuses specifically on the nexus between drug traffickers and insurgents, reminds her readers that 'the Taliban and their allies may be earning hundreds of millions from the drug trade, but one thing almost everyone interviewed for this project agreed on was that crooked members of Hamid Karzai's administration are earning even more' (Peters 2009a and b). Mark Shaw's 2006 study on the structure of organised crime in Afghanistan barely mentions insurgents, while emphasising the indispensability of government connections: 'The nature of the emerging criminal organisations suggests a close linkage with state institutions – indeed, the protection provided by state functionaries is critical for their survival and prosperity' (Shaw 2006: 210).

Media and policy commentary on the opium trade generally overstates the role of the Taliban and underestimates the role of state actors. This is partly due to another common but misleading narrative: a weak Afghan government which struggles to extend authority beyond Kabul. In reality, Afghan national police, border police, counter-narcotics police, customs officials, and provincial, district, and municipal governors all have power within their jurisdictions to significantly impede or facilitate narcotics production and trafficking. The low salaries of most government officials and the common practice of paying a monthly stipend to their superiors to retain office make rent-seeking unavoidable. This affects any lucrative economic activity, but particularly the opium trade. Government figures with the authority to assign offices in provinces with high levels of drug production or trafficking can skim off enormous benefits – a UN researcher found that district police chiefs along major opium transit routes might be expected to pay as much as $40,000 a month to their patrons (Peters 2009a: 136).

The various police branches overseen by the Ministry of Interior have been particularly corrupted by this process. 'The majority of police chiefs are involved [in protection of drug trafficking]', Shaw was informed by a senior officer. 'If you are not, you will be threatened to be killed and replaced' (Shaw 2006: 199). Analyst Jonathan Goodhand (2009: 20) reports that 'the Ministry of Interior in effect operates as a shadow "ministry of opium" by controlling key positions in drug producing and smuggling areas'. Journalist Graeme Smith has published evidence suggesting that General Mohammed Daud, Deputy Minister of Interior for counter-narcotics, uses his position to protect opium shipments (Smith 2009).

From the traffickers' side, insurgent cooperation is unquestionably necessary to move opium through many areas of the country, especially at night or across the Pakistan border (Giustozzi 2007). Giustozzi rightly points out that at many points along the border, drug traffickers can get better help by 'purchasing the collaboration of Afghanistan's border police'. The benefits of government connections are obvious: not only protection for convoys and greater immunity against law enforcement, but the ability to retain private militias in police uniform and deploy state resources against rival traffickers. Drug lords who are associated with government have greater freedom to travel and network than those closely associated with insurgent groups. Shaw's analysis of the 2003–05 consolidation of the drug traffic in southern Afghanistan makes clear that the successful traffickers were those who were able to use government connections against rivals: 'Despite the separation between the political "upperworld" and the criminal "underworld", it must be emphasised that it remains impossible to operate in the latter without support from the former' (Shaw 2006: 198, 205–8).

While it might seem natural that criminals would have an affinity for anti-government groups, many high-level traffickers clearly prefer a friendly and co-opted but minimally functioning state to a very weak or collapsed one. The current nexus between traffickers and government is an adaptation of the 1990s norm, when opium cultivation and trade were carried out openly and payments to the local authorities were taken for granted. The comprehensive state failure of the early 1990s mujaheddin era, epitomised by extortionate armed checkpoints every few kilometres along major highways, was not the ideal for organised crime. There are indications that major narco-traffickers (like other businessmen with an interest in secure transit across southern Afghanistan) were among the earliest financial supporters of Mullah Omar's militia to restore basic law and order. Many of the alleged connections between the Taliban and key drug kingpins (such as Haji Bashir Noorzai of Kandahar or Haji Juma Khan of Nimroz) were consolidated during the time when the Taliban was the state authority in southern Afghanistan (Peters 2009a: 73–5, 149–50).

Geographically, poppy cultivation and heroin processing are now highly concentrated in insecure areas of the south where the Taliban insurgency is strong. It would be facile, however, to assume that this indicates insurgent domination of the narcotics sector. Lawless spaces are useful to state actors, and northern political figures have reportedly 'subcontracted' southern traffickers to handle the dirty end of their drug business (Shaw 2006: 207). Major pro-government figures in the south such as Ahmed Wali Karzai in Kandahar and the Akhundzada brothers in Helmand are still widely reputed to command enormous influence in the opium trade.[2]

As discussed in more detail below, the fact that Afghan state actors are not disinterested parties regarding the opium economy, but are among the most important participants, strongly affects the options available for a Western response.

> Second, opium prices are falling and, in the absence of outside intervention, are likely to continue to fall.

Until late 2009, the high farm-gate price of opium was a staple of reports on the Afghan drug economy. It is commonly compared to the much

---

2 The Karzai and Akhundzada families deny that any of their members are engaged in narcotics trafficking (see Lasseter 2009; Risen and Landler 2009; and Rubin, E. 2009).

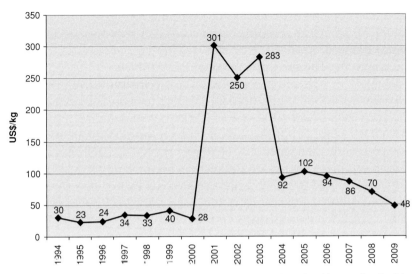

Figure 8.1 Fresh opium farm-gate prices at harvest time (weighted by production) in Afghanistan, 1994–2009
Source: UNODC 2008: 14; UNODC 2009a: 23

lower cash value of wheat (generally grown at the same time of year), with the suggestion that only high-value crops such as saffron, black cumin or rose oil could possibly compete with opium.

Yet the high price of opium in Afghanistan primarily results from a single dramatic constriction of supply: the Taliban ban in the 2000–01 season. As Figure 8.1 shows, even after dropping precipitately in 2004 (the first major supply surge of the Karzai era, and the first year in which poppy was grown in every Afghan province) and steadily receding thereafter, the farm-gate price for fresh opium remained more than double its late 1990s average until the 2008–09 season, when it fell to $48 a kilogram, triggering recognition by UNODC that a major market correction was under way (UNODC 2009a: 25).[3]

The 1990s average is not necessarily a 'natural' floor price for Afghan opium, given the increased costs of trafficking in the 2000s. Whatever its other impact, the shift from legality to illegality under the late Taliban and Karzai regimes increased the number of actors with the ability to

---

3 Previous UNODC reporting had only briefly noted the downward trend of prices, explaining poppy cultivation patterns in terms of political will rather than market forces.

claim rents on opium. In the most opium-intensive areas of the country, insurgents as well as government are now extensively engaged in taxing poppy farmers.

Despite these forces pushing costs upward, however, the enormous oversupply of Afghan opium since 2006 is poised to drive prices further down. UNODC calculates Afghanistan's total opium production in the years 2006–09 at 6,100, 8,200, 7,700 and 6,900 tonnes respectively (UNODC 2009a: 16). If the current UNODC estimate of global annual demand for illegal opiates at 3,700 tonnes (UNODC 2009b: 10)[4] is even close to accurate, opium stockpiling has been taking place on an epic scale. As of late 2009, the UN believes that 'some 12,000 tons of opium are now stockpiled, in unknown locations'. According to UNODC estimates, only a small fraction (perhaps 10 per cent) is kept by Afghan farmers (UNODC 2009B: 70).

This stockpiling strongly suggests that actors at many levels of the opium trade – traffickers both inside and outside Afghanistan, officials, insurgents – are not only hedging against but actively betting on a future constriction in opium supply that would drive prices back towards their early 2000s levels. Significantly, the annual oversupply began following the 2005 plunge in cultivation in Nangarhar province, which demonstrated for the first time since the fall of the Taliban that it was possible dramatically to curtail cultivation in a top poppy-producing province.[5] If there is no major supply constriction, however, the value of these stockpiles will slowly degrade as the opium gum dries out, and their holders will eventually have to sell at a loss. A price crash is likely to result if many actors sell their stockpiled opium all at once.

A continuing fall in price would not automatically cause farmers to abandon poppy. As David Mansfield observes, 'opium cultivation has proven relatively irresponsive to declining prices once they have fallen below a given level' (Mansfield 2006b: 60). Afghan households' cultivation decisions are based on many factors besides income maximisation, such as access to land, credit and agricultural inputs; relative returns on labour and water, as well as land; and household food security, considering especially the expected market availability of staple crops. Even

---

4 Earlier UNODC reports used figures in the range of 4,500 tonnes.
5 Though Sher Mohammed Akhundzada orchestrated a marked decrease in cultivation in Helmand in 2003, it still left Helmand as the second-largest poppy producer that year. By contrast, the 2005 Nangarhar reduction in cultivation (a drop of 96 per cent of the previous year's area) left it barely in the top twenty (see UNODC 2005: 4 and Mansfield 2006a on the effects of the ban).

in a shrinking market, many vulnerable farmers will continue to turn to opium as 'a low-risk crop in a high-risk environment'[6] or to clear opium-denominated debt.

Nonetheless, as the price falls, opium's Achilles heel – high skilled labour costs for weeding and harvesting – impinges on the viability of growing it. Prices for dry opium vary considerably by region across Afghanistan, and already in 2007–08 farmers in northern Afghanistan, where the price dropped much more steeply, were finding the terms of trade for other crops preferable to those for opium. For example, in Badakhshan province after the 2007 harvest, opium prices plunged to less than $50 a kilogram, leaving local farmers earning a greater net profit per hectare from vegetables such as onions and okra.[7] This market trend, rather than improved governance or 'strong leadership' (suggested in UNODC 2008: vii), was primarily responsible for the steep drop in Badakhshan's poppy cultivation in 2007–08. The worldwide surge in the price of staple crops in 2008 has also affected farmers' planting decisions.

Overall, falling prices are likely to accelerate the consolidation of the drug trade in provinces with the best climatic conditions for poppy (for example, plentiful irrigated land without high groundwater levels), the best-protected heroin processing facilities, and the best-established transit routes through neighbouring countries. The Helmand-Kandahar area, already established as the 'central market' influencing opium prices in other regions (Byrd and Jonglez 2006: 141–2), is well situated to supply the entire world demand for illegal opiates. Unless another market disruption causes the price to return to its earlier heights, the concentration of the opium economy in the southern provinces observed since 2006 can be expected to continue.[8]

---

6 A formulation of Mansfield, found in inter alia Ward et al. 2008 and Byrd 2008: 3.
7 For the opium price, see UNODC 2009c: 4. The comparison with vegetables is derived from an unpublished livelihoods survey for the Alternative Development Project-North by PADCO/AECOM, October 2007. It should be noted that local vegetables sell at a premium in Badakhshan due to the difficulty of trucking in other produce. One unintended consequence of major road paving projects (such as the Kishem-Faizabad highway project in Badakhshan) may be the displacement of local licit produce by imports from agricultural surplus areas in the irrigated plains.
8 The concentration of poppy farming in the south is not belied by the 33 per cent reduction of area under cultivation in Helmand in the 2008–09 season. This drop has been hailed as a success for the governor of Helmand's 'food zone' CN programme; the UNODC's 2009 Afghanistan Opium Survey cites a Cranfield University study which found that within the targeted food zone districts, poppy cultivation dropped by 37 per cent, compared to an

Keeping these under-acknowledged trends in mind, how should one evaluate the various strategies proposed for the Afghan government and foreign donor countries to respond to opium?

Alternative opium strategies in Afghanistan

The success of an Afghanistan counter-narcotics campaign can be measured against several criteria:

- sustainable reduction in illicit poppy cultivation through a demonstrable expansion of licit livelihoods for Afghan farmers;
- reduction in export of illicit opiates to consumer countries (primarily Europe, but also significantly to Iran, Russia and Pakistan);[9]
- reduction of the illicit drug trade as a share of Afghanistan's GDP (a gradual process, so as not to shipwreck the economy);
- reduction in drug money going to the insurgency;
- reduction of drug-related corruption in government;
- reduction in the scale and clout of criminal syndicates in Afghanistan.

Taking rule of law and counter-insurgency goals into consideration, any proposed counter-narcotics strategy must also recognise the overarching importance of fostering Afghan government institutions that are perceived as legitimate by the population. It would be all too easy to pursue opium reduction targets in ways that highlight or exacerbate government incapacity and corruption, undermining the overall state-building goal.

The multitude of counter-narcotics strategies proposed for Afghanistan tends to fall into one of five categories.

8 per cent increase outside the zone. However, UNODC's own 2009 district data show a 36 per cent reduction in the zone and a 20 per cent reduction outside the zone – suggesting that the food zone programme benefited greatly from a broader, market-driven contraction across the province. It is not surprising that farmers in districts that were better suited to food crop cultivation (the definition of the food zone) were readier to switch out of poppy than those in less fertile areas. The fact that Helmand still produced 4,085 tonnes of opium in 2009 – compared to estimated global illicit demand of 3,700 tonnes – should caution us against declaring victory for the 'food zone' as a counter-narcotics approach (see UNODC 2009a: 29–30, 140).

9 Drug demand reduction and harm management strategies in consumer countries, while outside the scope of this chapter, must be at the heart of any serious campaign against the drug economy.

Legal cultivation ('poppy for medicine')

Taking successful counter-narcotics strategies in India and Turkey as models, some Western advocacy groups have recommended an Afghan licensing system for growing opium for medicine. This has been most persistently proposed by the Senlis Council (recently rebranded as ICOS, the International Council on Security and Development).[10] ICOS cites the low levels of morphine use in low-income countries as a sign of enormous unmet need among the chronically ill for painkillers, which current global stocks of legal opiates are too small to address. Under the ICOS scheme, Afghan farmers would be licensed to produce the appropriate quantity of medical opiates. Traditional community *shura* councils would be primarily responsible for monitoring the participating farmers and preventing diversion into the illegal market.

This strategy would fit poorly with the existing international infrastructure for managing medical opiates. This market operates under several artificial constraints, with the International Narcotics Control Board (INCB) playing the key management role. The INCB measures demand according to countries' formal requests, and tries to keep prices at a level it considers sustainable. It also restricts trade with countries whose health systems are too weak to prevent diversion of opiates onto illegal markets. Much of the demand identified by ICOS is from people who cannot access opiates within the constraints of the INCB-managed market, often because their governments do not formally request medical opiates from the INCB (see Chouvy 2006 and Felbab-Brown 2007).

On the supply side, most of the INCB-recognised demand is met by developed countries such as Australia, which carry out large-scale mechanised production of opiates from poppy straw. Turkey and India remain (barely) competitive in this market because of an American law which requires US drug companies to buy 80 per cent of their opiate raw materials from those two countries. The entry of even a small portion of Afghanistan's opium into this licit international market would break it, reducing prices below sustainable levels for Turkish or Indian producers.

To meet the need for painkillers highlighted by ICOS, it would in theory be possible to create a separate humanitarian institution to buy Afghan opium and produce massive quantities of medical morphine which could be distributed at below market rates to chronic pain sufferers in the developing world. Setting aside the details of this process, one central

10 The ICOS proposals are collected at www.poppyformedicine.net

challenge at the source would be convincing Afghan farmers that legal poppy – as with any alternative livelihood – offers anything approaching the level of benefits they currently get from illicit traffickers. This does not just include the price (the low $20–$30 a kilogram for medicinal opium could be amplified by subsidies) or the guaranteed market, but the access to credit, land and agricultural expertise that the traffickers offer, as well as their willingness to buy at the farm gate rather than at market centres.

If such a package of subsidy and support could be assembled for legal poppy cultivation, it could surely be assembled for other crops and livestock, which calls into question the purpose of the whole ICOS scheme. Afghan farmers are eminently familiar with other cash crops – some requiring long-term investments like orchard and vine crops, others annual like vegetables, melons, legumes and oilseeds – which would not have the same high risk of illicit diversion, or require the same level of national and international institution-building. It would be better to de-link ICOS's humanitarian concern for providing painkillers from the Afghan poppy issue.

As a side note, the ICOS proposal for enforcement by community *shuras* overestimates the power and impact of such groups. Local Afghan justice institutions are far from a panacea for rule of law efforts, as Susanne Schmeidl documents in her contribution to this volume. In major drug-producing areas, village elders and tribal institutions have been comprehensively undermined by decades of conflict. For example, the Akhundzada family created their narco-fief in Helmand in the 1980s through a campaign of murder and intimidation against the traditional tribal leadership (Hafvenstein 2007: 129). It is implausible that most *shuras* today would be able to keep powerful local landowners from profiting from illegal opium.

Cash for drugs

Along similar lines are the periodic proposals to 'buy up the crop and destroy it' or 'pay farmers not to grow poppy'. Like poppy licensing, the cash-for-drugs approach seeks to influence farmers through subsidies rather than sanctions, and hopes to achieve counter-narcotics goals without violent disruption of the traffic (eradication or interdiction). As a result, it faces similar problems of monitoring and responding to non-compliance. It has the added disadvantage of providing a major perverse incentive.

In 2002–03, the British government promised farmers in Kandahar and Helmand financial compensation for voluntarily destroying their own poppy fields. The budget of $3.5 million ran out, with many irate farmers' claims still outstanding. Many of the farmers who were compensated had increased poppy cultivation in order to have more acreage to destroy: 'In a classic moral hazard scenario, the north of the country, where poppy planting takes place later in the season than in the south, started cultivating more poppies only to collect greater compensation' (Felbab-Brown 2009: 15). Farmers also reported that much of the compensation had been skimmed off by the government officials administering the programme (see IRIN News 2004a).

While this failed experiment is now widely disparaged and unlikely to be repeated, the ongoing alternative livelihood campaigns funded by NATO countries frequently resort to unsustainable activities that scarcely differ from cash handouts. Massive 'cash-for-work' campaigns and one-off distributions of seed and fertiliser – measures originally designed for short-term relief in humanitarian emergencies – have become a staple of alternative development in Afghanistan. Such activities are large, simple and popular, but they do not meaningfully improve farmers' livelihoods beyond a single season. Like 'cash-for-drugs', they constitute a perverse incentive to sustain high poppy cultivation, and are similarly prone to corruption (and to causing distortions in the local agricultural economy) due to their enormous scale. Western aid agencies must reserve such activities for genuine humanitarian emergencies and refocus their counter-narcotics programmes on long-term agricultural development, despite the political pressures to quickly spend large budgets and show conspicuous but ephemeral results.

War on drugs – interdiction plus eradication

The third option is a full-fledged war on drugs: disrupting the opium economy through law enforcement interventions at every point of vulnerability. Since the most vulnerable point is the farmer's field, this approach is generally distinguished by a strong focus on crop eradication.

With the departure of the Bush administration, which pushed hard for extensive aerial spraying along the lines of American policy in Colombia, the argument about poppy eradication in Afghanistan has lost much of its heat and force. While the Afghan and British governments continue to embrace targeted ploughing up of poppy fields (Farmer 2009), eradication has been recognised as counterproductive by the Obama administration, UNODC and most other actors in the country.

From a counter-narcotics perspective, crop eradication has been a symbolic gesture with no discernible impact on poppy cultivation levels. From a rule of law perspective, some have argued that turning a blind eye to a widespread crime, such as farmers' cultivation of illegal crops, further erodes the power of law in Afghanistan.[11] Yet a system that consistently punishes the vulnerable while ignoring the powerful will foster neither respect for the law nor a propensity to follow it. In Afghanistan, the main burden of eradication is inevitably borne by poorer farmers. Wealthy landowners are insulated by the sharecropping system (where sharecroppers absorb much of the risk of eradication),[12] as well as by their ability to bribe police teams.

From a counter-insurgency perspective, poppy eradication in Afghanistan has been even more damaging. It has spotlighted the corruption and hypocrisy of major Afghan government institutions, and damaged the livelihoods of the people whose allegiance NATO is hoping to win away from the insurgents. It has demonstrably boosted the Taliban's political legitimacy, and was never likely to cripple them financially. Finally, had eradication been carried out more effectively and extensively, it would have reversed the declining poppy price, increasing incentives for cultivation and rents to criminals, insurgents and corrupt officials.

This points to a generally overlooked danger. While winning the debate with a handful of Western 'true believers' may remove the spectre of a massive aerial spraying campaign, the real potential for widespread eradication has always been in the hands of the Afghan government. Recall the under-emphasised trends above: the extent of Afghan state officials' financial interest in opium, the general trend of falling prices, the evidence of extraordinary stockpiling. These trends suggest that we can expect eventually to see a startlingly effective, government-led poppy elimination campaign across all the major producer provinces – a more extensive version of the internationally praised campaigns of recent years in Nangarhar and Balkh.[13] This would boost prices back towards their

---

11 This case was previously made by the UNODC director – see IRIN News 2004b.
12 'Even when poppy is eradicated on land belonging to a large landowner, it is likely that the landowner has rented the land to sharecroppers to whom he has advanced *salaam* contracts. The sharecroppers' debts stand even if the crop is eradicated, and they stand to lose more than the landowner, who retains his claim on their assets' (Rubin, B. 2007).
13 As with the Taliban ban, these more recent campaigns have targeted poppy farmers while taking care not to disrupt the opium traffic. For example: '[Pro-government former warlords] Gul Agha Sherzai and Hazrat Ali ... at various times have been in charge of counter-narcotics in Nangarhar and have carried out large-scale suppression of opium poppy there while protecting their drug networks in Kandahar and Afghanistan's north respectively' (Felbab-Brown 2009: 11).

levels from earlier this decade and allow major government-allied figures to profitably tap their opium stockpiles. Such market manipulation is widely alleged to have been the motive for the Taliban ban in
2000, and (regardless of the real mix of motives behind Mullah Omar's
fatwa) is certainly the lesson every Afghan observer took away from the
episode.

Of course, like the Taliban ban,[14] a national poppy eradication campaign would have a disastrous impact on the livelihoods of millions of
Afghan farmers, sharecroppers and labourers. Like the Taliban ban, it
would deal a major blow to the popularity and legitimacy of the government. Yet Afghan political elites are manifestly capable of this sort of
coordinated, self-interested, tactically successful, clumsy and profoundly
counterproductive behaviour – witness the 2009 presidential election
fraud.

As long as Western political actors continue to measure success in
terms of 'poppy-free provinces' (Mansfield 2009), and to reward those
provinces with extra aid, they are providing both cover and incentive for
self-serving eradication by government traffickers. The UN and Western governments in Afghanistan must begin to emphasise consistently
that for the time being – at least the next decade – the key measure of
counter-narcotics success in Afghanistan is *not* reduction in cultivation.
Instead, Western agencies should step up their funding to provinces that
have shown demonstrable improvement in rural livelihoods, and threaten
to reduce or end it if governors adopt wrong-headed policies (including
large-scale poppy eradication) that hurt the livelihoods of the most vulnerable farmers.

Target the traffickers

With eradication shelved by the US government, the conventional wisdom
is now firmly behind a strong interdiction campaign – using law enforcement actors to target traffickers, processing facilities and drug shipments.
In theory, an interdiction-focused strategy has much to recommend it.
Enforcing the law against powerful traffickers offers a potentially significant bonus to the legitimacy of the Afghan state, countering perceptions
of government corruption and criminality. Finding and destroying some
of the stockpiles that UNODC believes exist would hurt organised crime

---

14 The devastating shock of the Taliban ban to rural livelihoods has been documented
   extensively, and is summed up well in MacDonald 2007: 77–85.

and reduce the incentive for another damaging supply shock. Interdiction should in theory raise costs for traffickers while (potentially) further lowering the farm-gate price of opium.

However, interdiction also increases the profitability of trafficking (by removing competition and raising the risk premium that successful traffickers can charge) and markedly increases the incentives for consolidation, mafia-building and state capture by criminal actors. These processes are already well advanced in Afghanistan, especially in the south, where the consolidation in the opium traffic in 2003–05 primarily benefited traffickers who were able to employ strong political connections and state resources against their rivals (Shaw 2006: 203–5).

In this context, if a strong interdiction strategy is not directed *primarily* towards traffickers connected to the Afghan government, it will in effect and perception be merely a state narco-mafia cracking down on its rivals. This can hardly be expected to provide much of a government legitimacy bonus, real improvement to the rule of law or reduction in trafficked opium. It might reduce narcotics money flowing to insurgents, but even that cannot be guaranteed. If state-allied mafias were over-ambitious in their consolidation of power, they could easily drive rival traffickers to step up their financial support to the insurgency. (We can see an analogy in the consolidation of power by certain government-allied Pashtun tribes since 2002, which has pushed other tribes in the south closer to the Taliban.)

Most interdiction advocates accept this warning, and insist that purging drug-related corruption in government is central to their strategy. Many see this as a question of Western political will, as if the main obstacle were foreign governments' willingness to forcefully demand the removal of corrupt Afghan politicians. Despite the reliance of the Afghan state on international financial and military support, it is not clear that foreign governments would have enough leverage to do this even if it were a top priority. Given the massive investment of international credibility and effort in Afghanistan, can Western countries or the UN plausibly threaten to sever support to their Afghan clients? Or does the West need the Afghan government even more than the Afghan government needs the West?

The aftermath of the 2009 presidential election is an unfortunate (if unfinished) lesson in the limits of international leverage. After extensive vote theft turned the August ballot into a confirmation of popular cynicism and Taliban propaganda, dismayed Western countries spent two months applying diplomatic pressure to Hamid Karzai to conduct a clean second round. Karzai finally accepted a runoff, but insisted on keeping the electoral structures that had permitted the first-round fraud. The failure of international leverage to enable a fair vote was epitomised by the pro-Karzai election commission's 29 October decision to marginally *increase* the number of polling stations.[15] According to a foreign diplomat involved in the negotiations between the UN and the Afghan government, 'the Afghan security establishment and the IEC initially wanted to open hundreds more polling centres for the runoff than in the first round, almost all of them in ethnic Pashtun areas that back Mr Karzai. The figure released on Thursday was a compromise between the Afghan authorities' demand for a large increase and the international community's pressure to reduce the number' (Gopal and Trofimov 2009).

As a result of this and other tactical victories by the Karzai camp, his rival withdrew from a second round he could not possibly have won, and Karzai was declared victor by default. Western actors (especially the UN and the US) lost significant political capital through their high-profile, ineffectual response to the election. Notwithstanding Karzai's subsequent mollification of his Western sponsors with anti-corruption promises, the episode clearly demonstrated that he could face down Western demands and survive on the support he has cultivated across the spectrum of the Afghan political elite (Humayoon 2010: 6).[16] The strength of the neo-Taliban insurgency has proven, paradoxically, to be a political asset for Karzai – it simultaneously facilitated election fraud in ethnic Pashtun areas and made it difficult for irate Western governments to respond too forcefully to that fraud.

Interdiction advocates might still argue that because less is at stake in punishing drug-related corruption than in preventing a corrupt election, Western pressure can be more effectively applied there. Yet to date there are few promising examples in the narcotics arena. One rare and partial success was the British government's insistence on the removal of Sher Mohammed Akhundzada as governor of Helmand in 2006. The Akhundzada family had played a key role during the anti-Soviet jihad in turning Helmand into the epicentre of the drug trade.

---

15 Much of the first-round fraud had stemmed from phantom stations in insurgent-dominated areas (see Galbraith 2009).

16 Humayoon makes the under-emphasised point that Karzai's powerful supporters include not only warlords spanning Afghanistan's ethnic groups, but also much of the 'ambitious technocratic political class within the government' beloved of international donors.

After the Taliban government was routed, President Karzai appointed Akhundzada governor of Helmand, from which position he had reputedly re-established himself as a central figure in the Helmand traffic, as evidenced by the discovery of 9 tonnes of raw opium in his offices in June 2005. Though he acceded to the semi-public British demand for Sher Mohammed's removal, President Karzai promptly appointed him as a senator in Kabul, and has said he now regards removing him from Helmand as one of the two key errors of his presidency. The other was dropping Mohammed Qasim Fahim, another alleged opium kingpin, as Vice-President in 2004 – an error Karzai avoided in 2009 by naming Fahim as his running mate in the corruption-plagued presidential elections (Rubin, E. 2009).

In early 2009, Karzai also undid years of work by the internationally sponsored Criminal Justice Task Force when he pardoned five young men convicted of drug trafficking. 'The task force is a model for the justice system that Western officials want for Afghanistan, but the pardon sent a signal that even major drug traffickers with the right connections could escape . . . According to the decree signed by Mr Karzai . . . the men were pardoned "out of respect" for their family members, who dominate politics in a broad section of eastern Afghanistan' (Oppel 2009).[17]

Under the centralised constitution Afghanistan adopted with Western blessing in 2002 (see Vendrell in this volume), a non-cooperative president can easily undermine justice sector reforms. The current Afghan government is highly unlikely to facilitate interdiction against pro-government narco-mafias. It would cut against President Karzai's abundantly demonstrated political instinct to seek conciliation and inclusion, and would immediately hurt many of his key political allies. Despite the government's creeping failure in the struggle to 'out-govern' the neo-Taliban insurgency, Karzai can be expected to keep focusing on his support among the Afghan political elite rather than addressing popular disgust with criminality and corruption in his government.

Masterful inactivity

Given the limited leverage that outside powers can bring to bear in Afghanistan, we must consider a fifth and final option: deliberately doing nothing. This is the posture that Sir John Lawrence, Viceroy of British

---

17 One was the nephew of Karzai's re-election campaign manager, Hajji Din Mohammed (see Oppel 2009 and Humayoon 2010: 16).

India during a period of continuous temptation to act rashly on the Northwest Frontier, described as 'masterful inactivity'.

Today this would mean de-prioritising law enforcement action not only against opium cultivation, but against the opium trade; focusing all Western counter-narcotics efforts on facilitating alternative livelihoods for farmers; and attempting to reduce government corruption without specifically focusing on narcotics. This was in essence the American policy of 2002–04, and is much derided today for facilitating the creation of a narco-state. However, given the weakness of the new Afghan state institutions and the overwhelming economic advantage of poppy in the years immediately following the Taliban ban, it is hard to see that a different outcome was ever likely.

De-prioritising enforcement of narcotics law – a measure often taken in hard-to-police areas such as drugs and prostitution – is no victory for the rule of law. It does not offer a legitimacy boost for the government or provide a strong platform from which to tackle corruption. The most that can be said for it is that it is realistic, given the penetration of the Afghan government by narco-traffickers; that it conserves political will and donor resources for more winnable rule of law battles; and that it does not have the unintended negative consequences of the other alternatives.

Given the current economic context – where market forces are reducing drug income as a share of Afghan GDP and narrowing poppy cultivation to a geographically small, insurgent-ridden area of Afghanistan – the wisest course is probably to refrain from any action that might increase the profitability of either farming or trafficking in opium. As mentioned above, the primary challenge here will be discouraging Afghan government figures with an economic incentive to boost poppy prices by manipulating the market through selective eradication.

The inevitable objection raised to doing nothing to combat the opium trade directly is that it does nothing to weaken the Taliban. While there is no consensus on the proportion of neo-Taliban funding that stems from narcotics,[18] the insurgents clearly derive a substantial income from protecting poppy farmers, taxing the crop, and facilitating drug convoys to and across Afghanistan's borders. How can the West

18 As an example of the huge variance in estimates, in August 2009, America's Defence Intelligence Agency and CIA reported that the Taliban received about $70 million from opium per year, compared to UNODC estimates of $400 million per year (see Miller 2009). Peters (2009a: 14) favourably quotes DEA analysts who claim that 70 per cent of Taliban funding comes from opium. A much more cautious analysis (without any numerical estimates) is offered by Giustozzi (2007: 88–9).

seriously address the insurgency without trying to cut off this source of its funding?

If all Afghanistan's poppy abruptly vanished, the loss of opium income would considerably inconvenience the neo-Taliban but would hardly cripple it. Their operations are financially well-supported from other sources, including donations from the Gulf, sympathetic business cartels in Karachi and, most importantly, taxes and protection money on other economic activity (both licit and illicit) in their areas of control. Without an economic embargo on Kandahar – scarcely a winning counter-insurgency strategy – the insurgents will not be short of funds to carry out their operations. Moreover, funding is rarely if ever the determining factor in an insurgency's staying power. As Vanda Felbab-Brown, an ana-lyst of counter-insurgency and counter-narcotics, asserts: 'There has not been one single case in which an insurgency has been defeated by eco-nomic means – and this includes drugs. It has never worked anywhere' (quoted in Kirschke 2008).

To beat an insurgency, it is crucial to foster a government that serves rather than preys upon its citizens. Narcotics is not the most promis-ing sector in which to begin this campaign. The incentives for criminal behaviour in the opium sector are, obviously, hard to match; even in much richer nations, drug money has enormous power to corrupt law enforcement agencies. As we have seen, both eradication and interdiction campaigns can be expected to exacerbate this corruption by increasing the incentives for state capture. They also exacerbate government illegitimacy by shining a spotlight on some of its most hypocritical, predatory activity.

We need to be strategic in challenging the Afghan state's culture of impunity. Former World Bank development expert and Afghan Minister of Finance Ashraf Ghani, a man not noted for any fear of challenging Afghan power structures, has recommended that any strategy for gov-ernment transformation should 'focus initially on areas where reform is possible and could generate positive momentum for larger, subsequent reform – and where the political will and commitment to change exists' (Ghani 2009). There are rule of law failures that negatively impact a sig-nificant majority of the rural Afghan population: for example, highway bribery, or corruption in land registration and contract disputes. This sort of extortion and rent-seeking serves as a drag on all economic activ-ity, and is more corrosive of the Afghan government's legitimacy than a suspension of counter-narcotics enforcement would be.

In short, instead of quixotically attempting to divorce the Afghan gov-ernment from drug money, Westerners should focus on supporting the tough reform battles that will reduce the risk to farmers and traders of shifting to licit crops.

Beyond opium: facilitating alternative livelihoods

Alternative livelihoods – non-poppy sources of rural jobs and income – are generally acknowledged as the long-term prerequisite for ending Afghanistan's opium dependence. Less frequently recognised is the critical extent to which these livelihoods depend on improvements in the rule of law. Again, this is largely because discussions of opium in Afghanistan focus so much on the farm-gate price. 'Alternatives' are often evaluated simply in terms of crops whose income per hectare matches or exceeds poppy. As noted above, however, farmers' planting decisions take into account not only expected income, but the broader enabling environment created by opium traffickers over the years, which provides them with greater risk mitigation and access to credit, assets and land. Western donors must focus on creating a similar enabling environment for licit crops.

For example, one key risk mitigation advantage for opium farmers is opium traffickers' willingness to buy the crop at the farm gate. Fewer farmers than ever are willing to venture out on the road with their crops – not only because of threats from insurgents and criminals, but because of the yearly increase in official and unofficial checkpoints. A 2006 report on the livestock trade in northern Afghanistan found that after security, the second most mentioned bottleneck restraining business development was corruption, especially for 'traders who have to transport their animals or goods over long distances'. The report suggests that bribes paid in transit can amount to 10 to 15 per cent of the farm-gate price of an animal (Van Engelen 2006: 35).

Similarly, the district of Nawa-e-Barakzai in central Helmand should be ideally suited to licit commercial agriculture, thanks to its extensive irrigation system and proximity to the Kandahar market. Yet Mansfield cites a farmer there who in 2007 discovered that growing onions had become uneconomical. 'After calculating the price of hiring a truck to Kandahar city, the cost of which he reported had increased due to the deteriorating security situation and the rise in the price of diesel, as well as what he estimated to be the cost of bribes for up to 14 checkpoints between Gereshk and Kandahar, he realised that he would incur a financial loss' (Mansfield 2008).

The bribes demanded at checkpoints are often arbitrary and incalculable, adding to the risk of transporting licit crops (and failing to capitalise on one of poppy's weak points – the uncertainty and volatility of the opium price). As a USAID agriculture consultant working in Farah reported in summer 2009 'there are 18 road blocks between Farah City and Herat, and 14 between Farah City and Quetta, where folks (Taliban, ANP, whoever) ask for bribes. The cost for bribes reportedly ranges anywhere from $2 a truck to the entire truck plus the life of the driver. So how does a shipper price his Farah watermelons in Herat (US agriculture consultant in Farah, personal communication with author, August 2009)?'

A serious government campaign against highway bribery would offer major economic and symbolic gains. Ending checkpoint extortion was a key legitimating factor for the Taliban in the 1990s; the Karzai government's backsliding on this point is acutely felt across Afghanistan. A reboot and rebranding of the dissolved (because thoroughly corrupt) Afghan highway police would probably be necessary for any drive against roadside extortion. Though a daunting task, the successful creation of the Afghan civil-order police shows that police reform in Afghanistan is not a lost cause; when starting more or less from scratch, it is possible to build a competent force with defined responsibilities. Since many Afghan political leaders have business interests that are hurt by the increase in checkpoints, it should be possible to enlist a broad coalition of support for a crackdown on highway bribery.

Like keeping the roads extortion-free, critical dispute-resolution is considered by many Afghans to be a core government function. While traditional community justice systems are often rural Afghans' first resort, they want an impartial final arbiter for the most serious land and contract disputes. At the moment, the neo-Taliban provide this much more credibly than the government judicial system. The Shari'a-based judgments of Taliban courts are widely regarded as clear, unbiased and immediately enforced – as opposed to the formal court system, where a culture of ambiguity and delay allows judicial officials at all levels to claim rents from litigants.

Since speedy, fair resolution of land and contract disputes is a precondition for legal agribusiness development, here again we find a major obstacle to both counter-narcotics and counter-insurgency goals. The confusion and conflicts of donor efforts at Afghan judicial reform are covered elsewhere in this volume. For purposes of facilitating alternative development, perhaps the most important area to focus on would be land titling – establishing a complete land survey for Afghanistan, a special court to resolve land disputes, and a competent, honest cadastral office. This has been tried without much success by Western donors already, but it is worth a renewed effort, this time with more of the financial, technical and diplomatic resources that have previously been devoted to efforts that directly target narcotics.

Another important goal would be reforming and resourcing the Ministry of Agriculture, Irrigation, and Livestock (MAIL). At the moment, many MAIL staff are appointed on the basis of their willingness to pay their boss a monthly stipend, rather than their capability or effectiveness. Most MAIL staff rarely visit the districts where they are supposed to provide agricultural extension training; even those who have the inclination often lack the resources (vehicles and fuel) to do so. All this deters qualified staff from joining the ministry in the first place. A senior NGO employee recently declined an offer to become provincial director of agriculture 'because it would not be safe for him and his family if he were to run the department the way it should be run, cleanly and efficiently' (US agriculture consultant in Herat, personal communication with author, August 2009). While anti-corruption campaigns in a major government department are never simple, the MAIL should be an easier target than the Interior Ministry. The Ministry of Rural Rehabilitation and Development (MRRD), Afghanistan's best-resourced ministry, could serve as a model in this process; though hardly perfect, the MRRD has been an effective tool for providing services to rural Afghans, and its image is far better than that of other government departments.

These reform priorities are proposed not because they are *easier* than other counter-narcotics strategies – land titling in particular is as daunting a project as any interdiction campaign – but because they are feasible even under the current government, and because their unintended consequences should not undermine broader international goals in Afghanistan. The continuing fall in the opium price – again, provided it is not artificially boosted with a selective eradication campaign – will prompt many farmers to consider moving into licit crops; international donors should be doing all they can to make that process not only feasible but relatively attractive.

References

Buddenberg, Doris and Byrd, William A. (eds.) (2006). *Afghanistan's Drug Industry: Structure, Functioning, Dynamics, and Implications for Counter-Narcotics Policy.* UNODC/World Bank

Byrd, William (2008). *Afghanistan: Economic Incentives and Development Initiatives to Reduce Opium Production.* World Bank and DFID

Byrd, William and Jonglez, Olivier (2006). 'Prices and market interactions in the opium economy', in Buddenberg and Byrd (eds.)

Chouvy, Pierre-Arnaud (2006). 'Afghan opium: licence to kill', *Asia Times*, 1 February 2006

Farmer, Ben (2009). 'Britain to continue poppy eradication in Afghanistan despite US reversal', *The Telegraph*, 28 June 2009

Felbab-Brown, Vanda (2007). *Opium Licensing in Afghanistan: Its Desirability and Feasibility*, Policy Paper No. 1, Brookings Institution, August 2007

Felbab-Brown, Vanda (2009). 'The drug economy in Afghanistan and Pakistan, and military conflict in the region', in *Narco-Jihad: Drug Trafficking and Security in Afghanistan and Pakistan*, Special Report #20, National Bureau of Asian Research, December 2009

Filkins, Dexter (2009). 'Poppies a target in fight against Taliban', *New York Times*, 29 April 2009

Galbraith, Peter (2009). 'How to rig an election', *Time*, 19 October 2009

Ghani, Ashraf (2009). *A Ten-Year Framework for Afghanistan: Executing the Obama Plan . . . and Beyond*, Atlantic Council of the United States

Giustozzi, Antonio (2007). *Koran, Kalashnikov and Laptop: The Neo-Taliban Insurgency in Afghanistan.* London: Hurst & Company

Goodhand, Jonathan (2009). *Bandits, Borderlands, and Opium Wars: Afghan State-Building Viewed From the Margins*, working paper, Danish Institute for International Studies

Gopal, Anand and Trofimov, Yarolslav (2009). 'Afghanistan adds poll sites despite fraud fears', *Asia News*, 30 October 2009

Hafvenstein, Joel (2007). *Opium Season: A Year on the Afghan Frontier.* Connecticut: The Lyons Press

Humayoon, Haseeb (2010). *The Re-Election of Hamid Karzai*, Afghanistan Report No. 4, Institute for the Study of War, January 2010

IRIN News (2004a). 'Bitter-sweet harvest: Afghanistan's new war', September 2004, www.irinnews.org/InDepthMain.aspx?InDepthId=21&ReportId=63019

IRIN News (2004b). 'Interview with Antonio Maria Costa, executive director of the UN Office on Drugs and Crime', 24 August 2004

Kirschke, Joseph (2008). 'State Department pushing aerial poppy eradication in Afghanistan', *World Politics Review*, 29 February 2008

Lasseter, Tom (2009). 'Afghan drug trade thrives with help, and neglect, of officials', *McClatchy Newspapers*, 10 May 2009

MacDonald, David (2007). *Drugs in Afghanistan.* London: Pluto Press

Mansfield, David (2006a). *Opium Poppy Cultivation in Nangarhar and Ghor*, AREU

Mansfield, David (2006b). 'Responding to the challenge of diversity in opium poppy cultivation in Afghanistan', in Buddenberg and Byrd (eds.)

Mansfield, David (2008). *Responding to Risk and Uncertainty: Understanding the Nature of Change in the Rural Livelihoods of Opium Poppy Growing Households in the 2007/08 Growing Season*, Afghan Drugs Interdepartmental Unit of the UK Government, July 2008

Mansfield, David (2009). *Poppy-Free Provinces: A Measure or a Target?* AREU

Miller, Greg (2009). 'Taliban drug proceeds lower than thought, US report says', *Los Angeles Times*, 12 August 2009

Oppel, Richard Jr (2009). 'Afghan leader courts the warlord vote, but others fear the cost', *New York Times*, 7 August 2009

Peters, Gretchen (2009a). *Seeds of Terror*. New York: St Martin's Press

Peters, Gretchen (2009b). *How Opium Profits the Taliban*. US Institute of Peace

Risen, James (2008). 'Reports link Karzai's brother to Afghanistan heroin trade', *New York Times*, 4 October 2008

Risen, James and Landler, Mark (2009). 'Alleged drug ties of top Afghan official worry US', *New York Times*, 26 August 2009

Rubin, Barnett (2007). 'Counter-narcotics in Afghanistan III: The false promise of crop eradication', *Informed Comment*, www.igca.blogspot.com, 31 August 2007

Rubin, Elizabeth (2009). 'Karzai in his labyrinth', *New York Times Magazine*, 9 August 2009

Shaw, Mark (2006). 'Drug trafficking and the development of organized crime in post-Taliban Afghanistan', in Buddenberg and Byrd (eds.)

Smith, Graeme (2009). 'Afghan officials in drug trade cut deals across enemy lines', *The Globe and Mail*, 21 March 2009

UN Office on Drugs and Crime (UNODC) (2005). *Afghanistan Opium Survey 2005*

UNODC (2008). *Afghanistan Opium Survey 2008: Executive Summary*

UNODC (2009a). *Afghanistan Opium Survey 2009: Summary Findings*

UNODC (2009b). *Addiction, Crime & Insurgency: The Transnational Threat of Afghan Opium*

UNODC (2009c). *Afghanistan Opium Price Monitoring: Monthly Report, June 2009*

Van Engelen, Anton (2006). *Preparing the Commercial Agriculture Development Project: Phase I Report, Vol II, Livestock Agribusiness Report*, Asian Development Bank

Ward, Christopher, Mansfield, David, Oldham, Peter and Byrd, William (2008). *Afghanistan: Economic Incentives and Development Initiatives to Reduce Opium Production*. World Bank and DFID

PART IV

Afghan approaches to security and the rule of law

9

Engaging traditional justice mechanisms in Afghanistan

State-building opportunity or dangerous liaison?

SUSANNE SCHMEIDL

Introduction

Afghanistan, like many post-conflict societies, struggles with not only having to rebuild destroyed infrastructure and institutions, but also to come to terms with a legacy of interrupted and inadequate rule of law and justice. Yet the problem does not lie only with the breakdown of a once-functioning formal justice system, but also with the fact that 'Afghanistan has a rich and layered legal history' influenced by multiple regime changes (including monarchy, communist/socialist and Islamic) and a complex relationship between different justice systems, including statutory/state, religious (Shari'a) and customary law (Barfield, Nojumi and Thier 2006).

Regardless of what formal legal system was favoured by the ruling government, 'Afghanistan has often operated under dual systems of governance' – with formal justice, as much of the Afghan state, never fully reaching into all rural areas, where the majority of the Afghan population reside (Wardak 2004: 326; see also Shahrani 1986, and Wimmer and Schetter 2002). Even before the Afghan wars, the formal legal system, largely restricted to urban areas only, was considered 'elitist, corrupt and involved in long delays', and in many ways irrelevant for the rural and illiterate majority (Wardak 2004: 320).

The customary system, in contrast, has shown remarkable though uneven resilience despite the turmoil of the past decades. It survived disruptions of the Afghan wars, government attempts to introduce a centralised legal system (Jones-Pauly and Nojumi 2004), and direct threats from various actors – a communist government set on destroying it through the 1980s, the mujaheddin resistance introducing the rule of commanders and guns in the early 1990s, and the Taliban emphasising religious Shari'a courts until they were overthrown in 2001.

Ignoring Afghan history and culture, international actors and Afghan urban elites have pushed another top-down reform agenda, which has focused almost exclusively on the formal justice system, so far with little success. This has created a situation where the weak formal system competes with a comparatively strong informal system, with the latter still handling the vast majority (an estimated 80 to 90 per cent) of all disputes in areas not controlled by the Taliban (Barfield, Nojumi and Thier 2006). In areas controlled by the Taliban, they either displace customary mechanisms altogether or assume the right to appeal customary decisions. The absence of any strategy for dealing with this plurality of justice systems (formal, customary and Taliban) has not only encouraged disputants to shop around for the forum in which they feel most likely to get a favourable decision, but also alienated the rural majority, both culturally and politically, who have no reliable access to justice. This justice gap has been increasingly filled by the insurgency, which, as the Taliban regime once before, have been setting up Shari'a courts across Afghanistan, even in areas nominally under government control.

This trend has forced the international community to reconsider its stance against customary justice. The question now, however, is whether the pendulum should swing from one extreme to the other – from ignoring customary mechanisms towards viewing them uncritically as the sole solution to Afghanistan's justice gap. A more constructive approach would be to explore how formal and informal justice mechanisms could be linked in a mutually complementary relationship, as proposed by several authors (Barfield, Nojumi, and Thier 2006; Jones-Pauly and Nojumi 2004; Wardak 2004).

The Afghan government, in the justice sector component of the Afghanistan National Development Strategy (ANDS), has acknowledged the need to engage with customary structures by 'investigating appropriate policies for improved links between formal and informal justice sectors and oversight of the informal by the formal to develop a policy on its relationship with the customary dispute system' (Islamic Republic of Afghanistan 2008: 6). So far, however, despite considerable efforts by the US Institute of Peace, the development of such linkages remains inchoate.

Drawing on qualitative research conducted by The Liaison Office (TLO) for the purpose of evaluating the Commission on Conflict Mediation (CCM) – a hybrid dispute resolution mechanism in Khost province – this chapter assesses the effectiveness and fairness of traditional, informal justice mechanisms and the formal, state-administered justice system, and explores ways to bring aspects of the two systems together in a hybrid

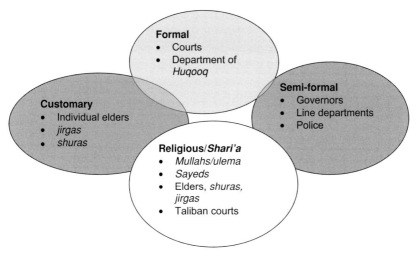

Figure 9.1   Overview of justice providers and systems in Afghanistan

model in which the formal and informal systems enhance and improve one another.[1]

Formal and informal justice in Afghanistan

Figure 9.1 depicts the interactions between the different kinds of justice providers in Afghanistan. In addition to the three main systems (customary, formal/state and religious), there is an array of semi-formal justice providers that deal with disputes due to their position within the Afghan government, even if they are not part of the formal justice mechanism.

---

1 In total, forty-six individuals were interviewed between 6 and 13 January 2009 in five focus group discussions (nineteen participants) and twenty-seven semi-structured interviews. In addition to interviewing five members of the Commission on Conflict Mediation, nine government officials, three traditional *jirga* mediators, a cross-section from the general public, two officers of the United Nations Assistance Mission in Afghanistan (UNAMA) and conflict parties of two conflicts resolved by the Commission on Conflict Mediation (four FGDs), one pending case with the Commission on Conflict Mediation (two FGDs), and one conflict outside the Commission on Conflict Mediation (two FGDs) were interviewed. Due to security concerns in Khost, non-probability sampling was used in order to reduce the risk to the two local surveyors. A mix of purposive/stratified, judgement and convenience sampling was used to select those interviewed. Afghan researchers also relied on a snowballing technique, where they used referrals from initial interview partners to identify additional ones. Only those individuals who had at least heard of the CCM were interviewed (see TLO 2009d).

Some dispense justice based on their personal stature and others because they are linked to one of the three justice systems, with many occupying positions in both. In many districts, for example, disputants may approach the governor or police chief because often these are the most active and only continuously present representatives of the government, while the actual judiciary has no presence.

Formal justice in Afghanistan

Afghanistan's formal justice system has been strongly influenced by Islamic law (Shari'a), and the *Hanafi* school of jurisprudence (alongside traditional customary laws) provided the basis of the Afghan justice system. According to article 31 of Afghanistan's constitution, whenever the civil code does not cover certain issues, judges are directed to refer to *Hanafi* jurisprudence. In addition, a cadre of Islamic judges (*qazi*), linked to the religious class (*ulema*), has made rulings on the basis of *Hanafi* jurisprudence and passed religious orders (*fatwas*) (Barfield, Nojumi and Thier 2006: 12). Many religious leaders (*pirs, mullahs*) and those considered direct descendants of the prophet (*sayyeds*) might also draw on Shari'a in mending conflicts at the request of local communities.[2]

While 'the *ulema* held rural customary law in contempt' (Barfield, Nojumi and Thier 2006: 12), Islamic law is also often referred to in informal procedures, and often converses with customary law. There are, of course, exceptions, such as women's (land) rights and common property, where Islamic law is actually less restrictive than customary law, and thus often overruled in informal settlements (Wily 2003). During the Taliban regime (1996–2001) and in the areas currently controlled by the Taliban, Islamic law and Shari'a courts predominate.

The complex nature of the current formal system is that the Bonn agreement stipulated an integration of existing laws and regulations as long as they did not clash with international law (Barfield , Nojumi and Thier 2006: 19). Thus, it was up to the new Ministry of Justice to muddle through the legal legacy left by previous regimes, a long and drawn-out process which has left many urgent issues, such as passing new land laws, pending.

In addition to the Ministry of Justice, Afghanistan's justice institutions include the office of the Attorney-General, the Ministry of Interior

---

2 The practice of esteemed individuals being asked to mediate disputes in what became the heartland of the Islamic world predates Islam itself.

(police) and the Supreme Court (*Stara Muhkama*). The last, as the highest court, also manages secondary or provincial-level (*morafiya muhkama*) and primary or district-level (*ibtidaya mukhama*) courts. Many primary courts, however, do not exist, though they are sometimes replaced by travelling courts.

The Ministry of Justice includes an independent department of *huqooq* (rights), which is tasked with helping to resolve civil disputes (such as family, debts or properties) without their having to go to court. *Huqooq* offices operate wherever there are Ministry of Justice offices, which includes all provincial capitals. They regularly refer disputants to customary resolution mechanisms, with the reference to the Shari'a principle of *sulh* (peace) (Barfield, Nojumi and Thier 2006: 19), in addition to undertaking mediation themselves. Though it has not yet developed the array of mutually enhancing linkages described below, *huqooq* departments do register cases that are brought to their attention, which creates an official record, and by implication a degree of official recognition, of cases that often end up being resolved in the informal system.

Informal justice in Afghanistan

Customary law (*rawaj*) in Afghanistan is far more complex and calls for greater explanation. It is a set of rules and regulations based on group norms and accepted community practices that are rarely codified and tend to differ between communities and over time (Barfield, Nojumi and Thier 2006; Wily 2003; Wardak 2004). Far from being fixed, customary law has been influenced by the turmoil of the Afghan wars and resulting displacements. It rests largely on the oral history of those using it – the white-bearded elders (*spin giri* or *rishsafid*) of each community. In addition to keeping with existing rules and regulations, these elders have a right to break new ground by ignoring precedents, interpreting them to fit the case or modifying them, although such changes must meet with general agreement.[3]

One of the most elaborate customary laws in Afghanistan is the *pashtunwali* – the oral 'code of ethnic values and norms' of the Pashtun ethnic group (Glatzer 1998: 169). It comprises two parts – an accumulation of rules used for decision-making in *jirgas/shuras* and a traditional code of conduct structuring social behaviour (Steul 1981). Even within *pashtunwali* there are regional variations, and only *spin giri* within a tribe tend to

3 I would like to thank Thomas Barfield for pointing this out to me.

be familiar with their specific *narkh* (set of customary rules, comparable to a civil code). There are, however, some underlying values influencing all interpretations of the *pashtunwali*. In theory, all Pashtun (men) have an equal status (especially in front of the law) and no one should possess more rights and power than others (Schmeidl and Karokhail 2009: 318–42). Furthermore, land ownership and honour (personal – *ghayrat*, and that linked to women – *namus*) play an important role (Barfield, Nojumi and Thier 2006; Glatzer 2002: 265–82), with the former expressing the autonomy of the tribesmen. The majority of disputes are said to be over the three Zs: *zar* (gold), *zamin* (land) and *zan* (women) (Barfield, Nojumi and Thier 2006).

The ethics underlying *pashtunwali* (as many other customary laws) differ from those applied in the Western (and modern) legal system. First, it is a community rights approach where peace between communities is more important than individual rights. According to this ethos, exchanging women in compensation for criminal offences (*bad*), for example, is considered a reasonable and acceptable outcome, as the alternative would be a blood feud that can easily escalate into a full-blown tribal conflict.[4]

This community rights approach strongly emphasises community consensus for any decision (Barfield, Nojumi and Thier 2006). Furthermore, as most Pashtun communities lack executive organs that can enforce decisions made (the *arbakai* in the south-east being an exception) (Schmeidl and Karokhail 2009), *pashtunwali* is based on restorative rather than retributive justice (Barfield, Nojumi and Thier 2006). Similar to customary systems elsewhere, *pashtunwali* 'emphasises restoring harmony and peace in communities by focusing on the needs of victim and the accountability of the offender, while also giving him a way back into the community (Monaghan 2008: 83–105). Thus, '[r]ather than being sent to prison for a wrong committed, the wrongdoer is asked to pay *poar*, or blood money, to the victim and to ask for forgiveness [*nanawati*]' (see International Legal Foundation 2004 and Wardak 2004 for a detailed description of the ritual for requesting *nanawati*).

This egalitarian ethos of *pashtunwali* is embodied in the central decision-making mechanism, the *jirga* (or *maraka* in the south).[5] A *jirga*

4 Since other ethnic groups in Afghanistan do not use *bad* and it is in violation of the religious Shari'a law, Pashtuns have been under some pressure to abandon it (including by the Taliban), so it is an outcome that is justified on a cost-benefit basis.
5 Hence the judges of a *jirga* are called *marakachian* (Barfield, Nojumi and Thier 2006: 9). *Jirga* originates from *jirg*, 'which means a wrestling ring', or 'circle', but is commonly used

is a temporary and ad hoc body created for resolving communal disputes, but in some cases also disagreements between local communities and the government. After a *jirga* reaches a decision on the issue for which it was formed, it is dissolved. The form and composition of a *jirga* depends on the dispute dealt with (as participants are required to hold knowledge about the specific *narkh* to be applied). By and large, however, it includes elders and tribal notables (*rishsafid* or *spin giri*) (Centre for Policy and Human Development 2007: 9), at times also religious figures (especially in the south), and, since the anti-Soviet *jihad*, commanders (Jones-Pauly and Nojumi 2004).

Comprised exclusively of adult males of a certain standing (social status, wealth and leadership qualities) (Wardak 2004: 326), its egalitarian and representative nature is thus limited to *pashtunwali*. Once a *jirga* decision or ruling (*prikra*) is reached, it is binding for the entire community (Wardak 2004: 326). The length of a *jirga* usually depends on how long deliberations take to reach a satisfactory decision and consensus among all participants. Before the proceedings begin, all parties involved must agree on which laws (*narkh*) will be used in the mediation or resolution process. This may even include elements of Shari'a, which is increasingly invoked in the south.

Jirga mediators request three things from disputant parties to ensure a successful outcome and be able to enforce decisions:[6]

- *Wak*: By agreeing to *wak*, disputants give authority to the *jirga* to resolve the conflict on their behalf.[7]
- *Machalga/baramta*, which is collateral (usually money, valuables or commodities such as land) that both conflict parties pay to the *jirga* in order to ensure their cooperation. The *machalga* is only returned to the conflicting parties if they accept the *jirga* decision.
- *Kabargen*, which is an agreement by the communities involved to socially isolate those who violate their *wak* by refusing to accept the final *jirga* decision. Thus it can be considered another enforcement mechanism to ensure compliance with *jirga* or *shura* decisions.

---

to refer to a gathering of people. There is a similar word in Turkish, which makes some scholars believe it originates from there (Wardak 2004: 326).

6 This draws from a presentation in TLO 2008: 32.

7 Due to the variations even within *pashtunwali*, there are two kinds of *wak – toya warai wak* (absolute authority) and *nark wak* (authority limited to apply to the specific subset of laws to be used, usually different for each tribal community).

A second informal body dealing with dispute resolution is the *shura*, a local council or consultative body introduced largely during the Afghan wars by the mujaheddin commanders as a way to influence community decisions (Barfield, Nojumi and Thier 2006). *Shuras* exist for all official gatherings and are not exclusively part of the *pashtunwali*. In contrast to *jirgas*, *shuras* are more permanent; the government has created district and provincial *shuras*. There are also *ulema shuras*, which are councils of religious scholars. *Shuras* can also arbitrate disputes (mostly property, family and business), just as disputing parties can approach individual *spin giri* or religious figures to help them settle a dispute. Disruptions caused by the Afghan wars have started to reduce the number of *jirgas*, with more and more disputes being settled by *shuras* or individual tribal or religious figures.

Even though *jirga* decisions are final, it is possible to appeal a decision to a higher level body, though more typically a case is referred to a higher level due to non-resolution (TLO 2008). For example, if a village-level *jirga* or *shura* is unable to resolve the conflict, conflict parties could request a greater tribal *jirga*, which has more influence and authority. In the case of large-scale and difficult land disputes, it is also possible to call together a provincial *jirga* that can draw on various respected elders from different tribes in the area to ensure there is complete impartiality. According to oral evidence, however, conflicting parties can only appeal twice (TLO 2008), allowing their case to be heard in three *jirgas*, with the last being a *tukhum*, a tribal assembly in which representatives of other lineages and even other Pashtun clans are called in (Barfield, Nojumi and Thier 2006: 10).

Technically, dispute parties under *pashtunwali* are not allowed to reject such a final grand decision, but practically, as noted earlier, even a high-level *jirga* cannot impose or reinforce its decision, albeit associated costs and visibility may be enough pressure for the final *prikra* to stick. Even though it is not looked upon well in a community, conflicting parties at this point can still approach the formal court system (Jones-Pauly and Nojumi 2004; TLO interview, member of CCM, Khost, 12 January 2009). Referring a case back to the formal court system is often seen as a measure of last resort (McEwen and Nolan 2007) before taking up arms (TLO 2008). Unfortunately, such 'forum-shopping' has been on the rise in Afghanistan, especially as the informal system has also been weakened in certain areas due to the Afghan wars, allowing powerful individuals to buy or coerce the decision they want from the justice system they feel they can influence most.

Within the customary mechanism of *pashtunwali*, it is worth briefly exploring the tribal police or *arbakai*. Even though the word *arbakai* has been, and still is, used interchangeably with irregular militia in the Afghan context,[8] its original meaning in Pashto is 'guardian', which refers to the unique mechanism of a 'community-based customary policing structure with a central focus on keeping law and order and stopping fighting within tribal communities' (Schmeidl and Karokhail 2009). The *arbakai* in this traditional form are associated with the south-eastern provinces of Afghanistan (Paktia, Khost, Paktika and some districts of Ghazni). They can be considered the executive arm of the *jirga* (and *shura*), which functions as both the legislative and judicial authority among the Pashtuns.

Their size and mandate are usually very limited. They serve specific purposes linked to protecting community interests and resources, such as 'to enforce and implement the decisions of a *jirga* or *shura*' (Schmeidl and Karokhail 2009: 322), to 'maintain law and order' (general policing) and 'to protect borders and boundaries of the tribe or community' (Tariq 2008). The *arbakai* is never a permanent standing policing structure, but more an ad hoc mechanism that serves as long as it takes to enforce a *jirga* or *shura* decision – often mere days – and as such can be compared to a gendarmerie. The size is stipulated by the *jirga* or *shura*, and varies greatly, as it depends on the task to be accomplished. The upper limit, however, is the number of eligible male members of the community raising the *arbakai*. As their jurisdiction is strictly limited to the jurisdiction (sub-national geographic spaces such as *quam*, *wanda*, *mantegas*) of the *jirga* or *shura* that calls it into life, *arbakai* in general tend to be small in size. While in more recent times *arbakai* have received support from the Afghan government, traditionally they are funded by the community with which they are associated.

Perceptions of justice systems in Afghanistan

At present the informal justice system is widely judged to be dealing with the great majority (an estimated 80 to 90 per cent) of disputes across Afghanistan (Barfield, Nojumi and Thier 2006: 9). Land and property disputes in rural areas, including water rights, boundaries and right of way, inheritance or mortgage disputes, are especially likely to be handled

8 The fact that *arbakai* means army in Arabic possibly explains this (Schmeidl and Karokhail 2009).

either by local elders or the *jirga* or *shura* system (McEwen and Witty 2006; Wily 2004: 41). This is often interpreted as a preference for the informal over the formal system – yet often it may simply be that the informal system is the only mechanism accessible to the rural majority. A mediator in a hybrid dispute-resolution system captured the situation with a proverb: 'When water is available, you do not need to use *tayamum* [using anything related to earth for cleaning prior to prayer]; if we had a proper court system and able law enforcement agencies, we would not have to use the *jirga* or *shura*' (TLO interview, member of CCM, Khost, 7 January 2009).

Perceptions of the formal justice system

There are some fundamental barriers between the majority of the Afghan population and the formal justice system. As noted earlier, even histori-cally courts were largely restricted to urban areas only, hence in many ways irrelevant for the rural majority. Furthermore, in comparison to shifting Afghan regimes, it has stayed more or less constant in the minds of people, who therefore feel more familiar with it (TLO 2008; TLO interview, mem-ber of CCM, Khost, 13 January 2009). There is also a stigma associated with dragging 'embarrassing' cases, especially those involving honour and women, into the public arena. This creates an immense social pressure on individuals to keep it within the bounds of whatever mechanism is used by the extended family (Jones-Pauly and Nojumi 2004).

The focus on rights and retribution over reconciliation and restoration is also to the disadvantage of the formal court system. Though it might be able to speak for justice and punish the individual offender, it cannot address the associated animosity between the conflicting parties and the need for forgiveness and reconciliation (TLO interview, *jirga* mediator, Khost, 12 January 2009; TLO interview, members of CCM, Khost, 9 and 12 January 2009). Especially in rural areas, the punitive focus of the formal legal system is criticised as 'of little use in a social environment in which peace cannot be enforced by a strong state, but has to be achieved through consent to a compromise (even though in the negotiation of this compromise, a wide variety of power relations come to bear)' (TLO 2009b).

This sometimes leads to interesting choices as to when to approach the formal justice system. For example, when a murderer is unknown, com-munities may ask the formal system for assistance to find the murderer.

Yet if the guilty person is known and comes from the community, communities prefer to use the informal system in order to reconcile victim and offender families and communities.

There are also conflicts where the 'right' issue is less important than the maintenance of peace, such as when it comes to the sharing of communal or government land. Here a court would have difficulty in achieving a lasting agreement, while the informal system may be able to broker a compromise (TLO 2008; TLO interview, members of CCM, Khost, 8 and 9 January 2009). Similarly, when disputants in a land conflict hold only customary documents, a court may be unable to hear their case or may discriminate against the party with weaker documentation. Again, in such circumstances the customary system can assist to broker an agreement suiting both parties (TLO 2008; TLO interview, members of CCM, Khost, 8 and 9 January 2009). In contrast, in cases where formal papers exist, people are likely to go to the court system (TLO interview, member of CCM, Khost, 9 January 2009).

Yet the courts also clearly suffer from a capacity problem. In many rural districts there are no primary courts, and people have to either go to the provincial centre or wait for mobile judges to arrive. Only about 50 per cent of all judges estimated to be needed by the Ministry of Justice are actually in place, with two-thirds of those not having university-level training (TLO 2008: 20). The situation is no better among legal prosecutors and legal professionals, and there are not nearly enough defence attorneys to honour the constitutional requirement that all criminal defendants be represented by counsel. The police, too, have been criticised repeatedly for their lack of professionalism (ICG 2007; ICG 2008; Wilder 2007).

The deteriorating security situation has further reduced the presence of judges at the district level, and mobile judges functioning from the provincial centre often do not reach deep into rural areas. Thus, many rural communities, especially remote ones, still do not have much contact with the legal justice mechanism in their everyday lives. Furthermore, overwhelmed courts are often only too happy to refer cases back to the informal system for settlement, or to have them prevented from reaching the courts through mediation by the Justice Ministry's *huqooq* department (TLO interview, *jirga* mediator, Khost, 12 January 2009).

Last, experience with the justice system that does exist is usually bad. It is seen as corrupt, easy to manipulate, self-serving, very costly, and above all an extremely lengthy process to go through (ILF 2004; TLO interview, members of CCM, Khost, 7, 8 and 13 January 2009; TLO interview, head of executive and director of administration, office of the Governor, Khost,

13 January 2009; many other interviewees, both governmental and non-governmental, agreed). In the words of a member of the CCM in Khost: 'Nobody is against the court or its decisions, but it takes a very long time (sometimes years) until a decision is final' (TLO interview, member of CCM, Khost, 12 January 2009, also noted in other interviews). In one case that was eventually handed over to the CCM for resolution, the court system had actually ruled in favour of *both* parties in a land dispute, rather than resolving ownership rights – leaving the conflicting parties at square one (TLO focus group discussion, conflict party of case resolved by CCM, 8 January 2009). In another case, an offender was able to bribe his way out of a jail sentence, which left the case unresolved (TLO interview, conflict party, pending case, 7 January 2009). With a weak, understaffed and corrupt police, the courts' ability to enforce their decisions is also frequently questioned (TLO interview, members of CCM, 7 and 13 January 2009; see also TLO 2009b).

Perceptions of the informal justice system

In contrast to the formal justice system, the customary system is often considered more accessible, efficient and respected by local communities, and also far less costly. It would be wrong, however, to assume that customary structures don't have problems of their own.

As noted earlier, the informal system is often favoured in cases where people feel social pressure to avoid going to the court because that would entail airing dirty laundry in public and thereby losing face (TLO focus group discussion, conflict party pending case, 7 January 2009). This is especially the case involving women. As the customary mechanisms are linked to a belief system that favours male elites of a certain age and standing, it tends to exclude, and by extension discriminate against, all women and younger males (McEwen and Nolan 2007: 21; see also Barfield, Nojumi and Thier 2006). Thus women may actually stand a better chance in the court system if laws are applied justly. The Afghan constitution clearly states that laws should not contradict international law,[9] and there

---

9 Islamic Republic of Afghanistan 2004:

> *Article 7:* The state shall observe the United Nations Charter, inter-state agreements, as well as international treaties to which Afghanistan has joined, and the Universal Declaration of Human Rights.
>
> *Article 57:* The state shall guarantee the rights and liberties of foreign citizens in Afghanistan in accordance with the law. These people shall be obliged to respect the laws of the state of Afghanistan within the limits of the provisions of international law.

is some concern that '[s]ome traditional practices violate Afghan and international law, including honour killings, forced and underage marriage, and payment of blood money in lieu of punishment' (Barfield, Nojumi and Thier 2006: 3).

Though in principle, traditional structures stress the independence of disputants to select their own representation in the *jirga*, and their ability to voluntarily and on a case-by-case basis accept a *jirga* and their decisions, reality often proves otherwise (TLO 2009b).[10] The effectiveness of the informal system, which rests on community cohesion and the sharing of common values and attitudes, tends to disintegrate when communities are fragmented and power imbalances are created (as occurred during decades of war). In such circumstances, strongmen and mujaheddin commanders 'tend to subvert the principles of equity upon which the system relies for its popular legitimacy' (Barfield, Nojumi and Thier 2006: 3), and *jirga* mediators no longer function independently but as puppets of strongmen, for either patronage or financial interests (TLO 2008; TLO interview, director of *huqooq* department, Khost, 6 January 2009). While this can lead to the collapse of the *jirga* process, often disputants are well aware of the consequences of not accepting a *jirga* decision, however unfair it may appear. The more likely scenario is that in such a situation, the weaker party to the conflict will not seek a *jirga* in the first place.

The customary system is also weak in cases where strong communal interests are involved (Wily 2004), especially if there are power imbalances between disputant parties. In such circumstances, a *jirga* might be judged to be too weak to pass a just decision against strong conflicting parties (TLO 2008). Local legal aid counsellors of the Norwegian Refugee Council who participated in *jirgas* adjudicating between returning Pashtun internally displaced populations (IDPs) and non-Pashtun residents in northern Afghanistan, for example, observed that most cases tended 'to be resolved in favour of the latter because local power-holders and government officials support them instead of the returnees' (Schmeidl, Mundt and Miszak 2009).

While the customary system may be considered on average less costly than the formal system, there are certain cost-benefit assessments that disputants nevertheless have to make. The cost of the *machalga* or *baramta* (guarantee fee) and the need to pay for the fee for *jirga* mediators (*khalat*),

---

10 This is analogous to the regular violation of the precept 'there is no compulsion in Islam', which does not include, inter alia, severe sentences in many Islamic jurisdictions for apostasy and violations of Shari'a.

including *jirga* costs (such as food and transportation) (TLO interview, director of *huqooq* department, Khost, 6 January 2009), also restrict access to justice by the poor. Poorer disputants may simply accept a *jirga* outcome they are unhappy with as they cannot afford to lose the *machalga* paid (TLO focus group discussion, conflict party resolved case, 8 January 2009). In turn, much as in the formal justice system, richer disputants may be able to simply 'buy' a decision, even though it is more difficult and costly to bribe a dozen or more *jirga* members than the three judges who normally preside in a trial. Corruption and bribery have also made inroads into the *jirga* system (even if less prevalent than among state judges). While in the past tribal notables saw resolving conflicts as a community service, in recent years *tijaraati* elders (commercial elders) have set up shop in district centres rendering their services purely for financial benefit (TLO 2009b: 16).

There are also frequent reports of customary structures being abused to grab government land. According to a government official: 'The local tribes are normally claiming the ownership of state lands, and then they give money to the *jirga* mediators to pass the decision in their favour. Then the government registers the decision of the *jirga* as a deed; this is the common procedure nowadays in the area. It is indeed a trick of the tribes to gain more land though *jirgas*' (TLO 2008: 33).

Last but not least: 'Large-scale problems often defy resolution by exist-ing means, as community-based justice mechanisms are often unable to deal with inter-community problems – especially between communities from different ethnic or sectarian groups' (Barfield, Nojumi and Thier 2006: 3). This has left disputes between nomadic Kuchi and sedentary populations, for example, unresolved over many years (TLO 2009c).

Overcoming shortcomings through linking informal and formal justice mechanisms

The above discussion illustrates the strengths and weaknesses of both the formal and the informal systems. Furthermore, the dual nature of justice has created a situation where those with power and funds will 'forum-shop' around for the system where they can apply the most influ-ence on the final decision or outcome (TLO interviews, CCM member, 12 January 2009; head of UNAMA and political officer, Khost, 6 January 2009). Justice providers of both the formal and informal systems may also force disputants to accept a decision by threatening to transfer their case to 'the other' system where their chance of getting a fair decision may be worse. *Jirga* mediators have used this to enforce a decision unfairly favouring one of the conflicting parties (Jones-Pauly and Nojumi 2004).

While the informal and formal justice mechanisms compete against each other, the Taliban have once again filled the void, setting up Shari'a courts that deliver, in the eyes of the people, speedy and fair justice. While there have been calls to strengthen informal justice mechanisms in order to counter Taliban courts until the formal justice system has come up to speed, a better solution may be to create a hybrid system that utilises elements from both formal and customary mechanisms, and ameliorates their respective weaknesses.

Barfield, Nojumi and Thier (2006: 25), for example, suggest a complementary approach in three areas: referral of disputes between the entities; courts' recording of decisions by informal mechanisms; and enforcement of informal decisions. Wardak (2004: 335–6) proposes an actual hybrid or integrated model wherein a customary system exists next to a court of justice which would 'mainly deal with minor criminal, and all types of civil, incidents at the district level'.[11]

While scholars speak about linking customary mechanisms to the formal justice system, and call for more research (Jones-Pauly and Nojumi 2004), numerous linkages and considerable cooperation already exist. Many judicial professionals come from influential tribal families, which are frequently called to mediate in *jirgas* while also serving as judges or prosecutors in the formal legal system (Jones-Pauly and Nojumi 2004). Informal justice providers often register either with the district government or in some cases the provincial governor as well (TLO 2009b: 18). However, such linkages are often still ad hoc, personalised, incomplete and lacking formalisation, which limits the influence and oversight of the state. The public widely desire such oversight by the state system, despite their criticism of the government's performance (TLO 2009d).

Courts or individual judges are often only too happy to refer civil cases to the informal system in order to reduce their own caseload. This acceptance derives from the Shari'a principles distinguishing between *haq-ullah* and *haq-ul abd*. The former is the law of God or society – any issue which might potentially disrupt the peace within a community for which the state has a duty to intervene, calling for punishment. The latter is the law of the individual (civil cases), the priority of which is allowing for reconciliation between perpetrator and victim. Often formal justice providers see no problem with *haq-ul abd* cases being judged by customary

11 Wardak refines and costs this 'hybrid model' in CPHD 2007.

mechanisms, while strongly arguing for the role of formal courts in the case of *haq-ullah* cases (TLO 2009b; TLO 2010). Both the state's and the Taliban's interpretation of Shari'a prohibit the customary mechanisms' use of the exchange of women for crimes committed (*bad*).

The Commission on Conflict Mediation in Khost

In addition to the Ministry of Justice's department of *huqooq*, described above, there are a few other concrete examples where an integration of both systems has been tried. One is the Information and Legal Assistance Centres of the NRC (Barfield, Nojumi and Thier 2006); another is the CCM that was established in Khost in 2007[12] on the initiative of its visionary Governor at the time, Arsala Jamal.

'Feeling that the capacity of the formal court was not able to deal with conflicts in a speedy and efficient way, and fearing that unresolved conflict had a great potential to destabilise the province and region', Governor Jamal sought an alternative to the court system that did not involve handing full authority to the informal system (TLO 2009d: 6). While the CCM uses the methods of the traditional customary mechanism, the *jirga*, it differs in three key regards: it is free of charge and does not request guarantees from conflict parties; it does not require dispute parties to accept the final decision made; and it deals with cases referred or authorised[13] by the office of the Governor – in return, its decisions receive the stamp of approval of the Afghan government (TLO 2009a). As such, the CCM tends to deal with high-profile cases, as smaller cases rarely come to the attention of the Governor's office. Indeed, many of the cases the CCM deals with are ones in which either violence is about to escalate or a ceasefire needs to be brokered to de-escalate conflict (TLO 2009d).

Assessing the CCM[14]

The CCM experience yields some useful lessons for future attempts to harness the advantages of working with informal justice mechanisms.

---

12 A similar mechanism was established in neighbouring Paktia in 2009.
13 Initially the CCM was supposed to deal only with cases that came via the office of the Governor. This, however, proved impractical, as often disputants directly approached the CCM, or other traditional mediators referred cases to the CCM. The CCM, however, tended to discuss these cases with the office of the Governor, seeking approval for litigation (TLO 2009d).
14 This section draws from TLO 2009d, which was drafted by the author.

Offering a familiar customary mechanism that bears the Afghan govern-ment's stamp of approval has been a great advantage to rural commu-nities. Providing conflict resolution free of charge decreases the scope for corruption and increases access to justice for the poor. At least in the eyes of Afghan government officials in Khost, the CCM has made a lasting contribution to peace and security in the province – and possibly helped to prevent further destabilisation. While the success of the CCM greatly depends on the people inside the mechanisms, there are also some procedural considerations worth highlighting.

Choosing the right people

'The *legitimacy* of "modern" governance systems in tribal societies depends on the *credibility* of those who institute and operate these systems' (TLO 2009a: 6). The CCM mechanism exemplifies this, benefiting greatly from the perceived impartiality and neutrality of commission members (TLO interviews, general public (4), 9–13 January 2009) and also from the 'clean' reputation of the Khost director of The Liaison Office (TLO) that facilitated its establishment. A representative of IDPs and returnees summed this up: 'When the water is clean at the top of the stream, it will remain clean to the end' (TLO interview, general public (commander and representative of returnee/IDP camp), 9 January 2009). Given the allega-tions of corruption against both informal and formal justice providers, this should come as no surprise. Still, '[t]he fact that personal credibility is a prerequisite for institutional legitimacy is a reality that continues to beguile state-building efforts' (TLO 2009a: 6).

There are, however, clear criteria that need to apply in staffing such bodies. The following were highlighted:

- Family background: The fact that most CCM commissioners came from known Khan or Malik families was seen as beneficial, as it was understood that individuals of standing would not want to lose face through a poor decision or taking bribes (TLO interviews, general public (tribal elder), 8 January 2008).
- Financial background: Most commissioners were also considered to be sufficiently well off that they would not be tempted by bribes.
- Diversity of the commission: The diversity of the entire CCM body, socially, politically and tribally, was also highlighted as an important point for a trust in fair decision-making. Here the credit goes to TLO, which worked jointly with communities and the Governor to pick a representative body. The diversity is further increased through the

practice of including other mediators or elders on the CCM on a case-by-case basis if their knowledge in a specific area is seen as beneficial.

- Technical know-how: Commissioners are considered knowledgeable and qualified individuals, who are able to speak justice, rather than being awarded their seat on the CCM due to personal connections. Furthermore, the CCM tended to call on additional elders in cases where they felt their expertise was lacking.

The importance of bringing the right individuals to the table was re-emphasised by concerns raised that the CCM should only then be expanded if individuals of equal quality, knowlege and standing could be found (TLO interview, head of executive and director of administration, office of the Governor, 13 January 2009).

Devising the right procedures

There are some factors associated with the mechanism and its procedure that are worth highlighting. In many cases, the CCM has added some of the positive elements of the criminal justice system to its procedures while still using customary laws to settle disputes. Most of them, however, are not formally noted down, but rather seem to derive from best judgement and experience.

- *Impartiality clause*: CCM members agreed to excuse themselves from any case that involved their own tribe or individuals with whom they had relationships, a protection worth replicating elsewhere (TLO interviews, head of executive and director of administration, office of the Governor, 13 January 2009; former CCM member and Deputy Governor, 13 January 2009 (but it was echoed throughout the interviews)).
- *Offer services free of charge*: at present the CCM is completely free, which increases access to justice by the poor and at the same time decreases the option of more well-off disputants to manipulate outcomes through financial means (TLO interview, director of *huqooq* department, Khost, 6 January 2009; director of tribal affairs, Khost, 6 January 2009 (but it was raised in most interviews)). Furthermore, as the guarantee is returned to disputants at the end of the process, this also decreases the risk of going along with a decision out of financial necessity.
- *Ability to reject decisions made*: unlike in the customary system, and more similar to the formal justice system, disputants are allowed to reject the decision put forth by the CCM. While commissioners spend

a lot of time explaining to disputants that their decision was the most just they could make (TLO interview, prosecutor, 12 January 2009), the social pressure of having to accept decisions is diminished. As no decision has been rejected so far, it is unclear if there are still some remnants of social pressure at play.

- *Thorough assessment of evidence*: commissioners were credited with applying a thorough array of investigation techniques, including fact-finding through site visits and listening to the claims of conflicting parties. Outside experts (other mediators or elders) were called upon when needed, sometimes in a greater *jirga*, which could be compared to a trial by jury.

- *Government oversight*: as much as customary structures have functioned outside the state, and as much as communities may criticise the Afghan government, there have nonetheless been recommendations for official supervision. While this is provided to some extent through the link to the office of the Governor, who refers cases to the CCM and provides a stamp of approval for the decision reached, there are still calls for 'proper supervision of their work by a reliable official branch of the government' – that 'the government should observe the commission, and they should not be allowed to adopt any automatism – they should work under the government' (TLO interviews, general public, 8, 9 January 2009).

Outstanding issues

This chapter has attempted to shed light on the justice landscape in Afghanistan, especially the call for an increasing use of customary mechanisms to bridge the justice gap until Afghanistan's court system is fully reformed and resourced. The strengths and weaknesses of both systems need to be understood and addressed before supporting any effort to integrate or link the formal and customary systems. The experience of the CCM in Khost, which was facilitated by the Afghan NGO, TLO, provides some concrete lessons as to how possible 'terms of reference' for a hybrid structure might look. However, it is also important to appreciate the features of the context in Khost that could make replication of the CCM in other provinces difficult.

First, the CCM emerged organically and was set up according to the best knowledge and judgement of the TLO Khost office director, commissioners, and the then Governor of Khost. Most selection criteria and procedures remain ad hoc and oral, much in the tradition of customary mechanisms. For them to succeed, however, they need to be written down in order to allow an institutionalisation process.

Second, while the CCM is attached to the office of the Governor, a frequently criticised factor is that it has not yet been able to establish a formal link to the Ministry of Justice as well as the office of the Attorney-General and the court systems (TLO 2009d; TLO 2010). This has already created legitimacy issues and complaints from the office of the prosecutor, but also other government officials (TLO 2009d; TLO 2010). Feelings of competition especially need to be addressed by emphasising how a hybrid structure such as the CCM can complement rather than transplant formal justice mechanisms. Thus, if the CCM is to survive in the long term, it needs to evolve from being a 'pet project' of the Governor to an independent integrated structure of Afghanistan's justice landscape. This is also crucial in order to avoid the risk of a governor using such an institution to his personal advantage.

Third, to date it is not officially decided or noted as to which cases the CCM should or should not work with. So far they have dealt with a wide array of cases, and the newly established Paktia CCM is dealing with an even broader range of cases than their Khost counterpart (TLO 2010). Most formal justice providers, such as prosecutors, are adamant that the CCM, as any mechanism using customary law, should stay away from criminal cases, especially murder (TLO interview, prosecutor, 12 January 2009). Thus, as the CCM finds its formal place in the Afghan justice system, it might be well worthwhile to define the cases it should or should not deal with, such as out-of-court mediation services in the West that tend to deal *en gros* with civil cases only. However, this does not exclude exploring the use of the CCM or other customary mechanisms for victim–offender reconciliation parallel to a formal court sentence.

Fourth, if the CCM or similar bodies are to be integrated with the formal justice system, they also need to reconsider the utilisation of settlements that violate international and Afghan laws, such as the exchange of girls for crimes committed (*bad*). Thus, an agreement is needed among customary mechanisms as to which parts of their laws are in line with the formal and international systems and which are not.

Fifth, there is a greater need for record-keeping and the registration of decisions with the formal justice system, or a greater database that can be accessed by courts and litigators in case a dispute is reopened. While the CCM in theory has agreed to this, so far decisions are only recorded with the office of the Governor, and case files are rudimentary. Assistance to customary justice providers in this element, who function within the oral tradition, is important.

Sixth, as the current CCM follows the traditional practice of only allowing men to litigate traditional justice, a new hybrid model could increase its diversity and access to justice for all by allowing women into its ranks. Such a suggestion, including considering an all-female CCM in order to ensure fairer treatment of cases involving women, was offered by the Department of Women's Affairs and the Afghanistan Independent Human Rights Commission in Paktia (TLO 2010).

Last but not least, the sustainability of the CCM and similar mechanisms needs to be addressed. Currently the CCM is able to provide its services free of charge because many commissioners have agreed to provide pro bono services and pay for their own expenses, and TLO and supporting donors[15] have contributed financial support. While commissioners have said that the issue was less with working for free as it is considered a community service, a solution for litigation expenses (phone, travel, research costs and so on) needs to be found.

It is unlikely that a cash-strapped Afghan government would be able to fund such mechanisms. Thus, efforts need to go into finding a transparent fee structure that avoids reliance on financial support from the central government but does not reduce access to justice by the poor or allow the rich to manipulate outcomes. The provision of services free of charge is the least sustainable aspect of this model, but this does not set the hybrid model apart from any other mechanism of justice in Afghanistan.

This said, there are already enough lessons to suggest that an integration of customary mechanisms into the formal justice apparatus is not only possible but also desirable, so long as certain standards and criteria are applied. The Afghan state needs to understand the benefit of such cooperation rather than fearing competition from traditional structures. Customary structures, in turn, need to accept a certain amount of government oversight, checks and balances, the need for a minimum paper trail, and to dispense with tools, such as *bad*, that contradict Afghan and international law. Such integration, if done properly, could be a winwin solution for multiple parties – the Afghan government, customary structures and, above all, the Afghan people. The only winners from the current lack of cooperation and the parlous state of all the non-Taliban justice systems are the insurgents.

15 During 2009 this was the US Institute for Peace.

References

Barfield, T., Nojumi, N. and Thier, J.A. (2006). *The Clash of Two Goods: State and Non-State Dispute Resolution in Afghanistan*. Washington DC: United States Institute of Peace, www.usip.org/ruleoflaw/projects/clash_two_goods.pdf (accessed 23 September 2008)

Centre for Policy and Human Development (CPHD) (2007). *Afghanistan Human Development Report 2007*. Kabul University: CPHD

Glatzer, B. (1998). 'Is Afghanistan on the brink of ethnic and tribal disintegration?' in Maley, William (ed.), *Fundamentalism Reborn? Afghanistan and the Taliban*. Lahore: Vanguard Books, pp. 167–82

Glatzer, B. (2002). 'The Pashtun tribal system' in Pfeffer, G. and Behera, D.K. (eds.), *Concept of Tribal Society*. New Delhi: Concept Publisher

International Crisis Group (ICG) (2008). *Policing in Afghanistan: Still Searching for a Strategy*. Brussels: ICG, Asia Briefing 85

ICG (2007). *Reforming Afghanistan's Police*. Brussels: ICG, Asia Report No. 138

International Legal Foundation (ILF) (2004). *The Customary Laws of Afghanistan*. Kabul, ILF Report, www.TheILF.org (accessed 21 April 2008)

Islamic Republic of Afghanistan (2008). *Draft Summary of ANDS Justice Sector Strategy*. Kabul, Afghanistan: Afghanistan National Development Strategy (ANDS), www.ands.gov.af/ands/jcmb/site/src/Meeting%20and%20Documents/seventh%20JCMB/files/IV.%20ANDS%20Documents/Justic%20Sector%20Strategy,%20Draft%20Summary%20-%20English.pdf (accessed 9 February 2009)

Islamic Republic of Afghanistan (2004). *The Constitution of Afghanistan*. Kabul, www.supremecourt.gov.af/PDFiles/constitution2004_english.pdf (accessed 30 April 2010)

Jones-Pauly, C. and Nojumi, N. (2004). 'Balancing relations between society and state: Legal steps towards national reconciliation and reconstruction of Afghanistan', *American Journal of Comparative Law*, 52(4): 825–57

McEwen, A. and Nolan, S. (2007). *Water Management, Livestock and the Opium Economy: Options for Land Registration*. Kabul: Afghanistan Research and Evaluation Unit, Working Paper Series

McEwen, A. and Witty, B. (2006). *Water Management, Livestock and the Opium Economy: Land Tenure*. Kabul: Afghanistan Research and Evaluation Unit, Case Study Series

Monaghan, R. (2008). 'Community-based justice in Northern Ireland and South Africa', *International Criminal Justice Review*, 18(1)

Nojumi, N., Mazurana, D. and Stites, E. (2004). *Afghanistan's Systems of Justice: Formal, Traditional, and Customary*. Boston: Feinstein International Famine Centre, Youth and Community Program, Tufts University, www.gmu.edu/departments/crdc/neamat1.pdf (accessed 9 February 2009)

Schmeidl, S. and Karokhail, M. (2009). 'The role of non-state actors in "community-based policing" – an exploration of the arbakai (tribal police) in south-eastern Afghanistan', *Contemporary Security Policy*, 30(2): 318–42

Schmeidl, S., Mundt, A.D, and Miszak, N. (2009). *Beyond the Blanket: Towards more Effective Protection for Internally Displaced Persons in Southern Afghanistan*. Washington DC: The Brookings Institution, Joint Report of the Brookings/Bern Project on Internal Displacement and The Liaison Office

Shahrani, M.N. (1986). 'State building and social fragmentation in Afghanistan: A historical perspective', in Banuazizi, A. and Weiner, M. (eds.), *The State, Religion, and Ethnic Politics: Afghanistan, Iran, and Pakistan*. Syracuse University Press

Steul, W. (1981). *Pashtunwali: Ein Ehrenkodex und seine rechtliche Relevanz*. Wiesbaden: Franz Steiner Verlag

Tariq, M.O. (2008). *Tribal Security System (Arbakai) in Southeast Afghanistan*. London: Crisis States Research Centre, LSE, occasional paper 6

The Liaison Office (TLO) (2008). *Land Based Conflict in Afghanistan: The Case of Paktia*. Kabul: TLO, unpublished working paper

TLO (2009a). *Between the Jirga and the Judge: Alternative Dispute Resolution in Southeastern Afghanistan*. Kabul: TLO, programme brief

TLO (2009b). *Linkages Between State and Non-state Justice Systems in Eastern Afghanistan: Evidence from Jalalabad, Nangarhar and Ahmad Aba, Paktia*. Kabul: TLO, unpublished working paper

TLO (2009c). *The Kuchi Nomads of Khost and Paktia Provinces*. Kabul: TLO

TLO (2009d). *An Evaluation of the Khost Commission on Conflict Mediation*. Kabul: TLO

TLO (2010). *An Evaluation of the Paktia Commission on Conflict Mediation*. Kabul: TLO

Wardak, A. (2004). 'Building a post-war justice system in Afghanistan', *Crime, Law & Social Change*, 41

Wilder, A. (2007). *Cops or Robbers: The Struggle to Reform the Afghan National Police*. Kabul: Afghan Research and Evaluation Unit

Wily, L.A. (2003). *Land Rights in Crisis: Restoring Tenure Insecurity in Afghanistan*. Kabul: Afghanistan Research and Evaluation Unit, Issues Paper Series

Wily, L.A. (2004). *Looking for Peace on the Pastures: Rural Land Relations in Afghanistan*. Kabul: Afghanistan Research and Evaluation Unit, Synthesis Reports

Wimmer, A. and Schetter, C. (2002). *Staatsbildung zuerst: Empfehlungen zum Wiederaufbau und zur Befriedung Afghanistans*. Bonn: Zentrum für Entwicklungsforschung, ZEF – discussion papers on development policy

10

Casualties of myopia

MICHAEL E. HARTMANN[1]

Since 2002, the international community has launched a series of initiatives aimed at fostering the rule of law in Afghanistan. The Bonn agreement and its follow-up and conference created roles for 'lead nations' in various sectors of development: Italy was assigned the justice system, while Germany was assigned police and the UK counter-narcotics. The London compact in January 2006 attempted to create an Afghan-owned national development strategy, the Rome conference in July 2007 framed an Afghan-managed national justice sector project, and since October 2009 the international community has intensely escalated its pressure on the Afghan government to tackle the crippling corruption. In 2010, the US, as the highest spending justice donor, has added to its strategy significant assistance to customary (non-state) justice mechanisms.

At the technical level, international influence has been distorted by bureaucratic inefficiency and self-interested policies and implementation, an emergency rather than sustainable development mindset, and a lack of coordination and collaboration both within the international community and between foreign donors and Afghanistan's justice institutions and stakeholders. Still worse, the international community has failed to help establish the necessary preconditions for the long-term legal and political development necessary to make the justice system a source of legitimacy, predictability and protection for the wider society. Among these, none is more fundamental, as has belatedly been recognised, than checking corruption and ending the impunity of the powerful.

Corruption feeds on itself and vitiates progress in other areas. Lack of capacity and, more important, political will on the part of both Afghan and international institutions have translated into impunity for those who are corrupt and those who committed crimes against humanity

---

1 This chapter expresses the personal views of the author, and does not represent the views of UNODC, nor of the US State Department/INL or its JSSP-Afghanistan programme.

in Afghanistan's recent past. The resulting growth of corruption and impunity, gross and pervasive, throughout Afghan state institutions including the judiciary, prosecution and police, is both a major symptom of the absence of the rule of law and a serious impediment to establishing it.

Afghanistan cannot establish the rule of law without confronting corruption, narcotics and security, ending impunity, and adopting a farsighted view towards capacity-building. This chapter argues that self-interest and disorganisation of the international community, which resulted in uncoordinated and zigzag strategies for reforming Afghan institutions and a plethora of uncoordinated and ill-monitored projects for assistance, could not solve the inherent problems preventing establishment of rule of law. It also highlights the symbiosis in four areas that worked to prevent establishment of the rule of law, each contributing to and nurturing the others: corruption, narcotics, insecurity, and the publicly visible failure to end impunity. The result was an increase, not decrease, in all these ills since 2002, accompanied by a rising public distrust of the justice institutions compared to traditional non-state dispute resolution (*shuras* and *jirgas*).

As long as the formal legal system is considered crucial for the rule of law, law reform should be done in such a way as to ensure that the law is accessible, understandable, and resonant with the realities of the society it is meant to regulate.

What is the state of rule of law in 2010 in Afghanistan?

After nine years of intensive international involvement in Afghanistan, the state of the rule of law is extremely disappointing. Since the author's arrival in 2005, Afghanistan has seen increased insecurity, corruption and trafficking in narcotics, which has emboldened those flaunting their impunity, and resulted in the formal justice institutions losing credibility among the public. These trends feed off one another.

Insecurity

Civilian deaths due to the conflict between insurgents and ISAF/US coalition forces increase each year, surpassing in 2008 and 2009 the number of deaths in 2001. In 2007, 1,523 civilians killed; in 2008, 2,118 civilians killed; in 2009, 2,412 civilians killed – and with the 'surge', a further increase is expected in 2010. While the anti-government elements or militants (insurgents) were responsible for the majority of deaths, the ISAF/US coalition forces were found responsible for a sizeable minority (UNAMA 2010). But these numbers tell only part of the story. What is important is the perception of Afghans, and that too has worsened.

As for the civilian population, the increase in insecurity has been exemplified by an increased number of abductions for ransom and other organised criminal acts against Afghans. The increased threats of the insurgency are illustrated not only by attacks by the insurgents' improvised explosive devices (IEDs), but also by increased casualties caused by the 'collateral damage' of NATO and US coalition attacks on insurgents, including deaths of women and children, wedding party guests and others. Complex suicide bomber and small arms attacks on Kabul central government institution headquarters and landmarks, including the Ministry of Justice, Central Bank, Ministry of Interior, Central Prison Directorate, Serena and Safi Landmark hotels, and Indian Embassy (twice), demonstrate to the public as well as to the government and internationals that nowhere can be considered safe.

For the international and national armed forces, and the national police, the body counts have risen dramatically since the 'end' of hostilities in 2002, and the 'surge' by US forces and increased NATO troops are expected to increase the number of combat deaths still further.

The regrowth of the insurgency since 2002 has resulted in swathes of territory, indeed entire provinces apart from a few fortified enclaves, falling under the strong influence or outright control of the Taliban. The road trips in normal SUVs taken in 2005 from Kabul to nearby provinces have now been replaced by helicopter flights or convoys of armoured vehicles. The UN agencies have gone from a few armoured vehicles for top officials to armoured vehicles for all international (and some national) staff, even within Kabul. With the plunge in security, UN staff are forbidden from going to even the most heavily fortified restaurants. The fatal attack on the UN guesthouse in October 2009 resulted in these restrictions, and closed down almost 90 guesthouses previously occupied by UN staff to concentrate staff and security.

Corruption

When Afghanistan first appeared in Transparency International's annual corruption perception index in 2005, it was ranked 117th out of 159 countries, tied for the 35th most corrupt, with a score of 2.5 (out of 10).

In 2007 Afghanistan was ranked 172nd out of 179 countries, being tied for the eighth most corrupt, with a score of 1.8. In 2008, Afghanistan moved to 176th place out of 180, tying for the fifth most corrupt, with a score of 1.5. The trend continued through 2009, with Afghanistan ranking 179th out of 180, beating Myanmar, Sudan and Uzbekistan as the runner-up for most corrupt, outstripped only by Somalia (www.transparency.org).

At the beginning of 2010, the UN Office on Drugs and Crime (UNODC) released a perception survey study (UNODC 2010a), based on the experiences of over 7,000 rural and urban Afghans. The results, according to the report: 'In 2009, Afghan citizens had to pay approximately $2.5 billion in bribes, which is equivalent to 23 per cent of the country's GDP.' This tracks closely with the revenue accrued by the opium trade in 2009, which UNODC estimates at $2.8 billion. UNODC executive director Antonio Maria Costa said: 'Drugs and bribes are the two largest income generators in Afghanistan: together they correspond to about half the country's (licit) GDP' (UNODC 2010a). The report showed that one Afghan out of two had to pay at least one kickback to a public official. In more than half the cases (56 per cent), the request for illicit payment was an explicit demand by the service provider. In three-quarters of the cases, *baksheesh* (bribes) were paid in cash. The average bribe is $160, where GDP per capita is a mere $425 per year. The average bribe to prosecutors and judges was well over $200. Between 10 and 20 per cent had to pay bribes either to judges, prosecutors or members of the government. 'Corruption is the biggest impediment to improving security, development and governance in Afghanistan', said Costa, warning 'it is also enabling other forms of crime, like drug trafficking and terrorism' (UNODC 2010a).

No paper discussing Afghan corruption would be complete without mentioning the August 2009 presidential election 'ballot-box stuffing' fraud, in which the international majority Electoral Complaints Commission (ECC) declared the equivalent of 1.2 million ballots cast as fraudulent.[2] The election fed the public perception of government corruption on a grand scale. With most of the fraudulent ballots being cast for Hamid Karzai, the Independent Electoral Commission (IEC) reluctantly reduced his preliminary uncertified 54.6 per cent victory down to a 49 per cent vote in his favour, a figure that independent observers believed was still too high.

---

2 The Karzai-appointed IEC reluctantly announced it was excluding almost 1 million (995,802), leaving 4.5 million valid votes.

Narcotics trafficking

While Afghanistan's post-2001 rise to its current status as the world's leading opium producer by far – over 90 per cent of the world total – is well known, UNODC announced in March 2010 that it is now the leading hashish producer as well (UNODC 2010b). While implementation of the counter-narcotics (CN) law and related central counter-narcotics tribunal (CNT) has been heavily supported by UK and US mentors and funding since 2006, its cases to date have not resulted in convictions of the 'drug kingpins' that were proclaimed as the targets of the CNT.[3] Indeed, in 2009, the plight of the lower level 'mules', the poor with few other options available, moved the parliament to amend the 2005 counter-narcotics law to remove heavy fines, which were being disproportionately imposed on these low-level couriers.[4]

The US and NATO have said they would consider some narcotics traffickers as combatants, due to their knowingly providing substantial funding assistance to the Taliban, and thus not rule out targeting them through direct military. This deserves a full airing within the Afghan and international community, with legal discussion under international humanitarian law (see Koelbl 2009 and US Senate Committee on Foreign Relations 2009: 1 ('. . . [under] the new policy, major drug traffickers who help finance the insurgency are likely to find themselves in the crosshairs of the military. Some 50 of them are now officially on the target list to be killed or captured')). An ISAF/NATO officer said in November 2009: 'That's the major ones – it is closer to 300' (conversation with the author).

Symbiosis

Like the shark and the pilot fish or the tickbird and the rhino, there is a continuing symbiotic relationship between insecurity, corruption and narcotics trafficking. Each feeds and is fed by the others. Most would agree with Afghanistan's Attorney General's conclusion that corruption is related to the problems of narcotics and insecurity,[5] and UNODC that 'corruption has been a major lubricant of the very prosperous drug

---

3 'So far, the special drug court has not handled any cases against major figures because none has been arrested' (US Senate Committee on Foreign Relations 2009: 16).
4 See discussion on the counter-narcotics law and how the legislative decree process under article 79 of the constitution works in Hartmann and Klonowiecka-Milart in this volume.
5 *Daily Outlook Afghanistan* (English language newspaper), 15 November 2009, citing Attorney General Mohammed Ishaq Aloko.

industry . . . it's throughout the system' (Owen 2010, citing UNODC executive director Antonio Maria Costa). How? 'Corruption is the biggest
impediment to improving security, development and governance in
Afghanistan. It is also enabling other forms of crime, like drug trafficking and terrorism (UNODC 2010a).' Narcotics trafficking requires
and enables corruption, and corruption of the police and justice system
are just a cost of doing business for the traffickers. Both corruption and
narcotics trafficking help the insurgency create insecurity by providing it
with money and a widely valued role as protector.

The public perception of the large-scale and pervasive government
corruption that is enabled by drug money catastrophically undercuts
the perceived legitimacy of and popular support for the Afghan state.
Presidential candidate Ramazan Bashardost, who came in an unexpected
high of third in the voting, campaigned on the argument that without
a real crackdown on officials stealing aid money or profiting from drug
deals, Afghanistan would never have a proper government that people
can trust and support (Pugliese 2010a). The US rule of law strategy for
2010 has added significant support to the heretofore official and aid-
marginalised non-state traditional justice mechanisms (*shuras* and *jirgas*)
as part of NATO's counter-insurgency strategy, which is meant to provide
'security and space' for these traditional dispute resolution mechanisms
to 're-emerge organically in areas cleared of the Taliban'.[6] The strategy
envisages formal state justice sector institutions following later.

This is problematic because the legitimacy of the state depends on
repairing the integrity and professionalism of formal justice and government. The state must be an 'appealing alternative to the Taliban' in both
justice and overall governance. 'The myth is that the absence of governance in Afghanistan creates a vacuum in which the Taliban thrive. But
the truth is the opposite. Karzai governs everywhere in the . . . south and
east of the country: the Taliban succeed in these very places not because of
no governance but because of corrupt and abusive government (Kaplan
2010: 65, quoting Sara Chayes, former special adviser to ISAF (NATO),
who also chaired several international agency conferences and meetings
on corruption and rule of law).'

Bribes and influence trading in government have resulted in impunity
for high-level government officials and other powerful figures. This fuels

6 Quotes from page 1 of a nine-page handout of the draft US 'rule of law strategy for
  Afghanistan', as provided to international institutions in December 2009 at a strategy
  conference.

support for the Taliban system of justice, which is perceived to be significantly less corrupt and more effective in holding individuals accountable
for crimes than the state system. In Kandahar province, the Taliban courts
resolve civil disputes, and Taliban ombudsmen take not only complaints
but action against commanders, including dismissing and even executing
offending Taliban commanders. As when the Taliban first emerged as vig-
ilantes combating vicious and undisciplined militias in 1996, today the
Taliban system appeals to Afghans whose top priority is justice.[7] The issue
is not whether Taliban justice is fair, but whether it is perceived as more
fair and less corrupt than the formal Afghan government justice system
and politicians. Kilcullen (2009) argues, along with other Afghanistan-
experienced soldiers, that 'in a battle for hearts and minds, corruption
and aid ineffectiveness are still the biggest issues'. Ineffective aid to the
justice system manages to combine the two.

To these factors of corruption and narcotics trafficking decreasing state
legitimacy must be added the delegitimising effect of massive fraud in
the 2009 presidential election. After denying for months that the scale
of fraud had been significant, on 1 April 2010 Karzai told a conference
of IEC officials that there had been massive fraud, but that it had been
carried out by foreigners, in particular by the UN and EU.[8]

What is obvious to most in Afghanistan, including the UN, US, UK
and other major donors to and implementers in the justice sector, is
that the factors of corruption, fraud, narcotics trafficking and insecurity
are symbiotic, and have a synergy that undermines the credibility and
legitimacy of the Afghan state, possibly fatally.

Corruption and other systemic forms of crime, in turn, are all underpinned by a culture of impunity. Andrew Wilder of the Afghanistan
Research and Evaluation Unit believes the people at the top of the country's opium trade enjoy impunity: 'Arresting top-level traffickers would
send out a signal that if you are important, you are not untouchable. Even

---

7 See Peters in this volume and Nicholson 2009.
8 'The truth, brothers, is this, and is why I am here today... There was fraud in the presidential and provincial council elections – there is no doubt that there was very massive
fraud, very massive, but not by Afghans. Foreigners carried out the fraud; [UNAMA deputy
SRSG Peter] Galbraith did it, [EU head of mission Phillippe] Morillon did it, and embassies
here did it... The United Nations, the office of the deputy [SRSG Galbraith] had become
centres for fraud. Fraud was carried out there, organised there, and then made available
to... all their media, which were at their service to publish the fraud and accuse us of fraud
(text of recording of Karzai's speech, as broadcast by Afghanistan TV on 1 April 2010,
1610 hours GMT, translated, and then obtained by the author).'

putting one government official on trial would send out an important message' (Meo 2004).

Gross violations of human rights, war crimes and crimes against humanity

The twenty-three years of war and conflict before 2001 can be divided into three phases: the period of the Soviet invasion and communist rule (1978–92), the period of the rule of the mujaheddin (1992–96), and the era of the Taliban regime (1996–2001) (Afghan Independent Human Rights Commission 2004). All these periods were marked by large-scale atrocities, crimes against humanity, war crimes, extrajudicial executions, and rape as a weapon of war, committed by combatants on all sides. Members of all of Afghanistan's major ethnic and political groups were implicated.[9] Mass graves have been discovered belonging to all three periods of conflict.[10]

Some argue that the civilian deaths caused by the 2001 and subsequent military acts of the US coalition and NATO and their Northern Alliance allies, as well as the Taliban's post-2001 acts including suicide bombings, should also be reviewed for war crimes and crimes against humanity. These issues are beyond the scope of this chapter, which will focus on the failure of the Afghan government and the international community to properly address the crimes outlined above, including those from 1978 through 2001, and the post-2001 corruption, fraud, organised crime and narcotics trafficking.

A culture of impunity: getting away with murder

Impunity is defined as 'not being punished for a crime or misdemeanour committed'. Experience around the world confirms the truth of the Latin

---

9 Starting in 2002, reports documenting these crimes, including victims and perpetrators, were published, with perhaps the most comprehensive in 2004 from the Afghan Independent Human Rights Commission, a constitutional body, and in 2005 from an international NGO, Human Rights Watch.

10 See Reuters AlertNet 2006: '2,000 bodies are believed to have been dumped in a recently unearthed mass grave . . . in Kabul . . . [from a communist government] massacre [that] took place between 1978 and 1986 . . . a mass grave in south-eastern Paktika province [was found] containing some 500 bodies of the communist government's soldiers, which were allegedly killed by the mujaheddin . . . in 2002 . . . [and] the bodies of thousands of Taliban fighters were found in a grave in northern Afghanistan. Human rights groups blamed the killings on Abdul Rashid Dostum . . . now an adviser' to Karzai.

maxim, *Impunitas continuum affectum tribuit delinquent* – 'the impunity of crimes is one of the most prolific sources [from] whence they arise' (Bouvier 1856). The value of ending impunity for corruption, narcotics trafficking and other organised crime, mass atrocities and gross human rights violations goes beyond the value of 'general deterrence from committing future crimes'; it is essential to demonstrate to Afghans that in their reconstituted state, it is the law, rather than power, wealth and connections, that rules. Punishment not only deters criminal conduct; it establishes the rule of law rather than personal power, and with it, credibility of the justice system and legitimacy of the state.

The post-2001 culture of impunity was born with the failure of the newly established Afghan state to start preliminary discussions with the Afghan public about options for transitional justice; nor did the interim government ever seriously consider the use of various mechanisms that would be less potentially divisive than initiating criminal investigations.

The post-2001 culture of impunity began with the CIA and other covert agencies funnelling tens of millions of dollars to regional warlords outside the central Kabul interim government, and using influence to protect them and what they had done in the past, while the US and NATO were concerned more with security than transitional justice issues (see Rashid 2008 and US Senate Committee on Foreign Relations 2009: 4–5). As a US Senate report concluded: 'Despite alliances with the opium trade, many of these [US-paid] warlords later traded on their stature as US allies to take senior positions in the new Afghan government, laying the groundwork for the corrupt nexus between drugs and authority that pervades the power structure today' (US Senate Committee on Foreign Relations 2009: 4). At the same time, the new UN mission and central government did not have the political capital or mandate to ensure justice, but were focused on establishing the government and its ability to control the provinces, which led to the strategy of co-opting the warlords into being regional governors. In part this is due to the UN deciding it would have a 'light footprint' as an assistance mission (UNAMA) rather than have a stronger mandate such as executive or enforceable monitoring powers as did UNMIK, UNTAET and UNMIBH, which would have made an emphasis on transitional justice possible. (See Vendrell's chapter in this volume.)

Once the presidential election of 2004 and later parliamentary election of 2005 took place, pressure built for justice for the gross human rights violations and atrocities during the pre-2001 years of war and conflict. Yet the corruption and narcotics trafficking continued, and there was no accountability for these crimes, nor for the pre-2001 war crimes and atrocities. The warlords continued to gain power, so that 'former muja-heddin commanders' became 'gangster-oligarchs'. 'Warlords like Rabbani, Fahim, Sayyaf, and Dostum have all been empowered by Karzai and the US government' (Kaplan 2010: 64). Indeed, many have been not merely empowered but adopted: 'Most of those warlords (accused by Human Rights Watch and other reports of war crimes) – Sayyaf, Dostom, Fahim, Khalili, Mohaqiq – went on to join President Karzai's presidential re-election campaign' (Rubin 2009).

Over the past five years, Afghan prosecutors and police and Ministry of Justice officials have recounted to the author in detail about being 'unable' or 'not allowed' to go after such individuals for violent, organised narcotics and corruption crimes. Indeed, the increase in insecurity in 2009–10, with the 'withdrawal' deadline in 2011 set by President Obama, encouraged those who believe negotiations with warlords and regional powerbrokers trump any accountability.

> The rogues' gallery of warlords and war criminals being courted by the Karzai government and its Western backers [Hekmatyar, Sayyaf and Dos-tum] betrays just how desperate the dilemma of Afghanistan has become, and how treacherous the road to peace and stability that lies ahead. President Hamid Karzai's much vaunted new strategy of reconciliation with the militants has found his government doing deals with the same cast of villains who helped tear Afghanistan to shreds during the past 30 years of war. Most notorious of all is the veteran jihad commander Gulbuddin Hekmatyar, an accused terrorist, war criminal and protector of Osama bin Laden.
>
> (Neighbour 2010)

Former Attorney General Abdul Jabar Sabit told the author that during the period he was first attempting to order the arrest of Dostum, and then to summons him for investigation, higher-ups and others in the government discouraged or actually forbade it.

The 'peace before justice' argument prevailed even during the relatively favourable security conditions in 2002–06, as it continues to be used now. Justice Minister Assadulah Ghalib argued (7 April 2010) against repealing the 2007 general amnesty law, reasoning that scrapping the law would create 'more instability' and could undermine current efforts to reach out to insurgent factions'. He contended that 'in such an atmosphere [that is, the upcoming peace *jirga*], it is not necessary to raise this issue [of repeal] and go after those people who are in government positions, have accepted the system and the constitution and are not [now] involved in any violence'. "'The state has left victims and criminals to solve their problem without its intervention", said Shukria Barakzai, a member of parliament, adding that most victims were too weak to challenge the alleged culprits who wielded extensive power in government, and "what about the hundreds of thousands of victims who do not [now] exist?"' (UNAMA Morning Media Monitoring, 8 April 2010). Moreover, neither the 1974 CPC nor the ICPC allow private prosecutions or investigations of such crimes.

In contrast, the author's conviction, based as well on experience in Bosnia and Kosovo, echoes that of the Canadian Ambassador to Kabul: 'Any possible peace deal with insurgents will be almost impossible to achieve in Afghanistan until the country comes to grips with the war crimes that have bloodied its recent past' (CTV News 2010, citing Ambassador William Crosbie).

Impunity for war crimes and mass atrocities

Even before insecurity spiked and negotiated settlement with the Taliban became a mainstream priority, accountability for war crimes and atrocities had never been seriously contemplated. President Karzai's original response to the AIHRC report, 'A call for justice' (Afghan Independent Human Rights Commission 2004), created hope that accountability would result. He told the UN High Commissioner for Human Rights that 'justice is very important. Human beings are prisoners of their memories. If you don't deal with them properly, you cannot get rid of them' (Rubin 2009). He went on to appoint a committee to work with the UN on a transitional justice action plan, which was approved by Karzai in late 2006.

The 'peace, reconciliation and justice action plan in Afghanistan' contained five key actions, of which action five involved criminal justice: 'Establishment of effective and reasonable accountability mechanisms: In order to end impunity... and ensure that there will be no amnesty for war crimes [and] crimes against humanity... the conditions for fair and effective justice procedures are established in accordance with the principles of the sacred religion of Islam, international law and transitional justice.' Specifically, it required by December 2005 a presidentially decreed five-member task force 'to provide recommendations... for a legal, procedural and institutional framework necessary for Afghanistan's implementation of its international legal obligations' and that 'the perpetrators of war crimes, crimes against humanity and other serious human rights violations... not be ignored'.[11] As an implied comment on the credibility of Afghan courts, a survey of citizens found that a large majority preferred the inclusion of international judges in a specialised judicial chamber (Afghan Independent Human Rights Commission 2004: 24–6 and 50–2; see also US Institute of Peace 2003). The AIHRC concluded that there was widespread support for accountability and for the removal of perpetrators from power. The AIHRC proposed an independent and permanent special prosecutor's office for the investigations and prosecutions, and a special chamber to be created to hear the cases. Interestingly, of thousands of Afghans surveyed, a majority wanted trials of war criminals, and of them, 49 per cent wanted mixed tribunals of international and local judges on the tribunal, an additional 27 per cent wanted only international judges, with only 21 per cent desiring solely Afghan judges. This is consistent with a public perception of corruption and influence controlling some court outcomes.[12] Prosecution for genocide, war crimes and crimes against humanity would be impeded, in any case, by their not being criminal offences according to the 1976 penal code or elsewhere in Afghanistan's criminal law. They are absent from Afghanistan's law despite the ICC's Rome statute, which Afghanistan has ratified, requiring such laws to be enacted.[13]

Instead, the national assembly did the opposite. On 20 February 2007, less than two months after the President had announced his support and approval of the transitional justice action plan with great fanfare, the year-old national assembly institutionalised impunity (UK Border Agency 2008: 4.01). Parliamentarians, including many of those – among them 'a group led by Abdul Rabb al Rasul Sayyaf, Burhanuddin Rabbani, and Taj Mohammed, all of whom have been implicated in war crimes and other serious human rights abuses' (Human Rights Watch 2007) – who had been named in the AIHRC and Human Rights Watch reports as potential subjects of prosecution or other transitional justice accountability modalities, enacted a law granting blanket immunity to all.[14]

11 The plan is at www.aihrc.org.af/actionplan_af.htm.
12 For mixed national/international judging, in addition to the Bosnia and Herzegovina and Sierra Leone war crimes chamber models, another alternative is the Regulation 1999/64 panels used in Kosovo.
13 The AIHRC and its legal adviser, Professor Mohammed Mohsin Farid, have drafted proposed ICC amendments to the penal code; Farid has been unsuccessful so far in his request to the Ministry of Justice *Taqnin* to begin work on incorporating it into the penal code (discussions with author; see also www.iccnow.org/?mod=country&iduct=1).
14 The national reconciliation, general amnesty, and national stability law (amnesty law), at *Official Gazette* 965, 13 Qaus 1387 (December 2009).

The amnesty law provides general amnesty, without limitation, to 'all political factions and hostile parties' who were involved in hostilities before the post-2001 interim administration, ensuring that they 'shall not be legally and judicially prosecuted'.[15] The law also provided for amnesty for any current opposition 'individuals and groups' who 'cease enmity after the enforcement of this resolution' if they 'join the process of national reconciliation, and respect the constitution and other laws'.[16] There was no limitation as to the nature of the crime, nor how far back the amnesty applied, so that it immunised against all war crimes, crimes against humanity and mass atrocities. The only exception, inserted on national and international condemnation of the scope of the amnesty as it was being considered, was that the victims of these crimes could themselves go forward on an individual basis, but there was no procedure or modality of investigation provided.

The law violates article 7 of the constitution, which mandates obser-vance of international obligations, including Afghanistan's obligations under the ICC Rome statute, as well as the ICCPR and customary inter-national law, which require accountability for war crimes and crimes against humanity.[17] The ICC Rome statute does not allow circumven-tion of a state's obligations by the granting of amnesty. In addition,

15 Article 3(1) of the amnesty law, quoted at http://aan-afghanistan.com/index.asp?id=665, is the most comprehensive legal analysis and translation publicly available and known to the author.

16 Article 3(2) of the amnesty law. Article 4(1) did provide that those who 'are under prosecution due to crimes against internal and external security' shall not enjoy the benefits of this law. However, at article 4(2) the law softened this limitation: 'Those people who are sentenced to crimes against internal and external security of the country shall be forgiven or their punishment mitigated by separate decrees, according to the situation and based on recommendations and guarantee of the Commission for Consolidation of Peace ... [if] they commit ... not to resume their activities against the Islamic Republic of Afghanistan.'

17 Moreover, customary international law requires prosecution, and thus prevents any such amnesties; the 'principles for the protection and promotion of human rights through action to combat impunity' (the Joinet/Orrentlicher principles), as already incorporated in international law, state that, even when intended to establish conditions conducive to a peace agreement or to foster national reconciliation, amnesty may not benefit perpe-trators of serious crimes under international law until states have undertaken prompt and independent investigations and prosecutions. Amnesties shall never prejudice the right of victims to truth and reparation (E/CN.4/2005/102/Add.1, principle 24). The UN Secretary-General in his report on the establishment of the Special Court for Sierra Leone of October 2000 also reiterated that 'the UN has consistently maintained the position that amnesty cannot be granted in respect of international crimes, such as genocide, crimes against humanity or other serious violations of international humanitarian law' (UN Doc. S/2000/915, 4 October 2000, paragraph 22).

article 6(1) of the ICCPR establishes 'the inherent right to life. This right shall be protected by law.' This has been interpreted by the UN Human Rights Committee to require investigation by the state.

What was President's Karzai's reaction? He promised the international community he would not sign it.[18] But Karzai in 2002 had also pledged to set up a truth commission that would seek to uncover the atrocities committed over two decades of war, and to seek accountability for perpetrators of past abuses of human rights; he has taken no steps to fulfil this pledge. Indeed, the action plan Karzai had approved only months before forbade any amnesty. Ironically, the preamble to the plan's action number four requires the President to 'submit a scheme to the parliament . . . so that it [parliament] can make the necessary decisions and end the state of impunity in Afghanistan. In making such a decision, attention should be paid to this reality that considering the clear Koranic verses and international law, no amnesty should be provided for war crimes, crimes against humanity and other gross violations of human rights.' The President submitted nothing to parliament, which then approved the amnesty law. 'After the amnesty law was passed by parliament in 2007, President Karzai said he would not sign it. The chairperson of the AIHRC, Dr Sima Samar, stated that "the President himself promised me twice that he would not sign the law"' (Human Rights Watch 2010). In 2007 and 2008 it was forgotten as it was thus not published in the *Official Gazette*, a requirement for any laws or legislative decrees to take effect.[19] However, the amnesty law was quietly, and without any warning from the government, published in the *Official Gazette* in December 2009,[20] just before the January 2010 London conference, where reconciliation and peaceful resolution by negotiation were emphasised. Karzai later stated that he would not extend the original four-year timeline of the not yet implemented action plan (IRIN Humanitarian News and Analysis 2010).

Even worse, there have been attempts by the government to discourage even AIHRC documentation and investigation of the war crimes and mass

---

18 See statement by Mary Robinson, United Nations High Commissioner for Human Rights, at opening of 58th session of Commission on Human Rights, Geneva, 18 March 2002.

19 Article 79 of the constitution requires that if the President 'rejects' what parliament sends to him, he is to send it back within fifteen days. While some reports state he approved it, others explain he simply took no action, and thus by operation of law he approved it.

20 ' . . . some sources say it was not published until January 2010, when printed copies of the law were received by organisations that monitor the gazette' (Human Rights Watch 2010).

atrocities covered by the action plan, which appears to be yet another civilian casualty of the conflict. 'The director (rais) of the *Taqnin* has stated, in contradiction to principles of penal law and constitution article 27, that "the human rights commission cannot investigate or document evidence for legal or judicial processes against the provisions of this law," warned Yusouf Haleem . . . "As with other laws, a violation of this [amnesty] law is a punishable crime," he said' (Human Rights Watch 2010). Unfortunately, this pronouncement seems to ratchet higher the government's apparent support for peace and reconciliation over the need for justice as a foundation for a lasting peace, and thus is consistent with that of the newly appointed Minister of Justice's security justification against repealing the amnesty law.

Thus, if the amnesty law remains in effect, Afghanistan will not see any attempt by the police to detect and discover, and by the prosecutors to investigate and indict, those who committed war crimes, crimes against humanity and other mass atrocities. In sum, no one identified or brought to justice. "'It was a total disaster," said Ahmal Samadi of Afghanistan Rights Monitor, a human-rights group. "No single criminal was identified; no one brought to justice." There was no political will among the Karzai government, nor the international community, which did not provide the support and expertise to carry out proper forensic investigations, he said' (CTV News 2010).

Sadly, this may leave as Afghanistan's transitional justice war crimes prosecution legacy only the flawed and unfair 'war crimes' trial against Assadullah Sarwari, head of the communist Afghan secret police[21] in 1979 before the Soviet invasion, who then returned with the Soviets to Afghanistan in 1980. He was arrested in 1992 after the communist-backed Afghan regime collapsed, and was kept in pre-trial detention until early 2006. There was general agreement among Afghans, and the AIHRC, Human Rights Watch and NGO reports, that Sarwari was guilty of crimes against humanity, torture and mass atrocities. Then Deputy Attorney General Muhammad Ishaq Aloko, who is now the Attorney General, explained to the author that the AGSA and KhAD were Afghanistan's equivalent to the Gestapo, and that Sarwari was its Himmler, and had murdered and ordered the extra-judicial murder and torture of 50,000 or more (see also Afghan Independent Human Rights Commission 2004 and Human Rights Watch 2010).

---

21 The Afghanistan Gattho Satunkai Aidara (AGSA), the predecessor to the KhAD, the secret police set up in 1980 to suppress internal opponents.

However, while some optimistically saw the Sarwari trial as a sign that 'a culture of impunity may be ending in Afghanistan' (Nadery 2005), in the end there was unanimous consensus among international observers that the trial was not fair, and rife with blatant and gross violations of the rights of an accused as protected by the constitution and ICPC. The UN and NGO (including Amnesty International) reports are shocking. During the two trial days, no witnesses were summoned, but rather it appeared that the court had volunteers from the spectators come up and testify to the court without any examination by prosecution or defence attorneys. None of those that testified had been eyewitnesses, and repeated what they 'knew' or guessed. For example, one witness had been an infant and somehow knew that the police that came to his house and took his father away were under Sarwari's orders. The indictment presented as 'grounds for liability' inter alia that Sarwari had been 'deliberately avoiding answering questions during the investigation', notwithstanding his right to silence and advisement of that right under article 5(6–7) of the ICPC, and that Sarwari had 'for the purpose of hiding the truth by asking for a defence lawyer . . . this is another reason of proof for his liability'.

The trial started on 26 December 2005, then was continued to allow appointment of an attorney (who was not Sarwari's choice), and then continued again to allow the defence to prepare. The trial then resumed and concluded on 12 February 2006 (Nardery 2005).

The court's short one-paragraph judgment referred to Sarwari being 'the head of the AKSA' and referred only to article 130 in sentencing him to death.

The trial, consisting of one day of so-called 'proof', concluded with Sarwari being found guilty of murdering 'hundreds of Muslims and mujaheddin in secret prisons' and sentenced to death.[22] Ironically, the conviction of this communist totalitarian secret police chief came after what must be characterised as a 'show trial'. On appeal, his sentence was 'secretly' reduced to twenty years, and he remains imprisoned in Kabul. There was no public announcement, but from senior officials of the Attorney General's Office's national security unit and Kabul district court, the author confirmed that Sarwari's sentence was reduced to eighteen years, the maximum imprisonment allowable under the penal code, and he remains imprisoned within a high-security National Directorate of Security prison (which, per the 2005 prisons' law, should be, but is not,

---

22 See Hartmann and Klonwiecka-Milart in this volume for discussion of constitution article 130 upon which the verdict of guilt was based, rather than the original charges of multiple murder based on the Penal Code. The author has an English translation of the court's verdict, as well as the original and final indictments.

administered by the Ministry of Justice). Sources involved in the original trial stated that the presiding judge had been first offered bribes, then threatened, and lastly told to reduce the sentence to eighteen years. When the presiding judge refused, the military courts were used to obtain the same result (conversations with author in April 2010).

Impunity for corruption and electoral fraud

The action in 2007–08 by the international organisations to provide 'mentors' to the Attorney General's office to assist in the development of a unit to investigate and prosecute corruption resulted in the creation in early 2009 of the office's anti-corruption unit, twelve prosecutors vetted by polygraph and interviews, provided with 'top-ups' to multiply their salaries by a factor of six, and trained and mentored by the international community. The impact on the culture of impunity and the endemic corruption discussed above? None is apparent yet, and the impatience of the international community may prompt the mentors to push the unit's prosecutors faster than they can grow into their new roles.

The impunity for corruption is illustrated by the government's attempt to blame it on the international community rather than assuming responsibility and indicting those at the top. Yasmin Osmani, director-general of the government's High Office of Oversight and Anti-Corruption, stated to the *Meshrano Jirga* that '80 per cent of corruption in foreign funds was being done by the foreigners, and that the Afghan government was unable to question the corruption of foreigners'. Osmani did, however, admit that the Afghan corruption was facilitated by 'warlords and powerful men' (*Daily Outlook Afghanistan*, 5 April 2010).

In fact, although the government, with assistance from the international community, has been issuing anti-corruption proclamations, declarations and paper strategies since the January 2006 Afghanistan compact and the July 2007 Rome conference, there is so far little sign of any real willingness to take down the 'big fish'. The huge mansions in the Sharpur neighbourhood of Kabul, known in local parlance as 'narcotecture', still stand as testament to financial resources far exceeding their owners' ministerial salaries. As of this writing, the asset declaration forms of over 1,400 high government officials, collected by the High Office of Oversight, have been entered into a database. However, at the time of writing these have not yet been investigated or verified. Plans do exist to provide technical support and funding to the government to carry this project out, but again at the time of writing have yet to come online. USAID in May 2010 announced the winner of an over $25 million tender for an anti-corruption project focused on the High Office. The UN Development Programme, UNODC and USAID have provided aid and technical support to the High Office since its autumn 2008 start-up.

The Afghan national development strategy programme resulted in the government's 2007 promulgation of a 'cross-cutting' anti-corruption strategy, as well as separate strategies from the Attorney General's office, Supreme Court and Ministry of Justice, each with (theoretically) its own separate anti-corruption strategy. The justice sector consolidated strategy of October 2007 also included an element of anti-corruption, as did the national justice programme (NJP) that was approved and launched in February 2008. Unfortunately, at the time of writing, the NJP had just started, slowly, to build national justice capacity. In any event, anti-corruption activities are not the central focus of the NJP.

In August 2006, the government appointed a commission, chaired by Chief Justice Azimi, to investigate and report on administrative corruption, its modalities and solutions. In early 2008, the commission released its 200-page 'strategy and policy for anti-corruption and administrative reform'. However, by the end of 2009, there had still been no significant discernible results.

More recently, there have been renewed signs of effort – including the 2009 establishment of the anti-corruption unit, the major crimes taskforce of the Ministry of Interior, and the 2010 formation of an additional court *diwan* or division in Kabul for anti-corruption. Because of the government's and Supreme Court's rush to start up the anti-corruption court quickly, there is no law establishing this court's territorial or subject-matter jurisdiction. This results in the Supreme Court using its change of venue power in an opaque and ad hoc manner, as of yet without any written standards or criteria. This will result in a lack of credibility due to a perception of bias and favouritism. Based on the experience of UNMIK's international judge programme, which had the same issue of an undefined jurisdiction, legally established subject and territorial jurisdiction is essential for objectivity, transparency and legitimacy.

These, and the High Office of Oversight of Corruption (and anti-corruption strategies), will receive more technical assistance, funding and attention from the international community in 2010. At present, however, impunity still reigns. As of early 2010, not a single minister, deputy minister or provincial governor has even been indicted for corruption. While the 2004 constitution mandated in articles 78 and 127 that any criminal trial of a minister or Supreme Court judge required a special court, which awaited legislation for its organisation and structure, it was not until April 2010, six years later, that the draft of a special court law was finally being reviewed by the Ministry of Justice *Taqnin*. The *Taqnin* has asked the criminal law reform working group (CLRWG) to analyse it and propose revision.

Late in 2009, the Attorney General's office did announce that it was investigating several current and former ministers. Deputy Attorney General Fazil Ahmad Faqiryar announced the AGO was investigating two ministers, whom he properly refused to name during the investigative phase. Later the AGO raised that number to fifteen sitting or former ministers. Two days later, Deputy Attorney General Faqiryar said 'We are investigating allegations against fifteen ministers – three of them in the current cabinet and the rest of them former ministers'. He admitted that 'none of them have been questioned yet' (*Daily Outlook*, 25 November 2009). President Karzai's office added that no arrest warrants had been issued. Nonetheless, as of June 2010, no arrests had been made of any former ministers, their deputies or any governors. The constitution requires that any trial of a minister requires a 'special court' that is to be established by legislation,[23] and as of June 2010, neither the government nor the parliament had submitted such law to the other, granting all ministers effective immunity from criminal trial for the past decade. The reluctance to subject ministers to any accountability is exemplified by the *Taqnin*'s draft law on special courts[24] studiously omitting any mention of the word 'minister'; clumsy circumlocutions referring to 'persons as defined in article 78 of the constitution' are used to avoid any 'loss of respect' for a minister,[25] notwithstanding the need to inform citizens that finally ministers are accountable.

The case of former Minister of *Hajj* Sediq Chakari, who lost his position in December 2009 during a cabinet reshuffle, can be seen as illustrative of

---

23 There cannot be any trial of a minister until a law forms a 'special court', as required by article 78 of the constitution. The draft law also includes former ministers within the protection of a special court, an interpretation arguably not within the plain language of 'minister' at article 78. The phrase 'If a minister is accused of crimes against humanity, national treason or other crimes' is more intended to protect the functioning of government and thus sitting ministers from the vicissitudes of politics while allowing trials of former ministers to proceed in regular courts.

24 The Ministry of Justice *Taqnin* as of April 2010 had prepared a draft law on special courts that would fulfil the requirements of articles 78 and 127 of the constitution regarding ministers, former ministers and the nine Supreme Court justices.

25 On 25 April 2010, when the *Taqnin* declined to use 'ministers' in many places as proposed by the CLRWG. Later a further reason was given as not wanting to give offence to the ministers. This indeed demonstrates the reluctance of many in the government to attempt even theoretical accountability.

the continuing impunity that high-ranking officials enjoy. It was reported that Chakari was a high-value Attorney General's office anti-corruption unit target, and that two of his staff were arrested in 2009 carrying approximately $400,000 in cash back from Saudi Arabia, money believed by anti-corruption unit prosecutors to have come from bribes. It was reported that the unit instructed the police to arrest Chakari, but that the presidential office blocked the arrest because of Chakari's close links with former warlords Mohammed Qasim Fahim, who is now the Vice-President, and Burhanuddin Rabbani. A few weeks afterwards, Chakari was allowed to leave Afghanistan, and is currently suspected to be residing in the UK. The Attorney General's office denied receiving any pressure to let Chakari go (Farmer 2010). However, this story is consistent with other lower level examples of 'off-limits' instructions given to the Attorney General's office that have been circulated within the international rule of law community.[26]

Chakari is not alone in impunity. There have been hundreds of millions of dollars smuggled or carried openly out of Afghanistan through Kabul and Kandahar airports, yet there has not yet been one minister, former minister, deputy minister, governor or powerful warlord arrested for money laundering or corruption. Chakari's ministry officials were caught at Kabul airport attempting to smuggle $360,000 in cash, and later convicted, illustrating the funds being siphoned off and channelled out of the country (Pugliese 2010b). Second runner-up presidential candidate Ramazan Bashardost stated: 'Much of the estimated $75 billion sent to Afghanistan . . . has been funnelled off to warlords, corrupt government officials, Karzai cronies . . . Much of the cash allegedly comes from drug cartels eager to get the money to Dubai . . . The rest may be from corrupt officials, or otherwise law-abiding businesses that wish to dodge taxes' (Perry 2009, citing Afghanistan Finance Minister Omar Zakhilwal). Perhaps the most visible example of impunity is the complete lack of any criminal accountability for the million-plus fraudulent ballots in the 2009 election. While the top two IEC officials have lost their jobs, as discussed above, there have been no significant investigations into the fraud. The ECC referred only ten cases to the Attorney General's office, but could not provide identities due to confidentiality requirements of the elections law. However, the police and Attorney General's office have the

---

26 The author was present when Attorney General Abdul Jabar Sabit would complain angrily that he was being told to stop and did not have a free hand in making arrests and summoning in the powerful for investigations.

power independently to detect and investigate any reported crime, and an attempt to steal a million votes through ballot stuffing is a crime worthy of major resources. Yet the only election crimes currently being investigated by the Attorney General's office acting on its own mandate are minor cases relating to 'whether some presidential candidates manufactured the 10,000 signatures of support... needed to stand in election [because] they did not actually win 10,000 votes on election day' (Khadhouri 2010: 47–8).

Why has there been no attempt to determine who masterminded and implemented the election fraud? The author suggests that the international community's 'tiptoeing around' the fraud in order to gain a result negotiated with Karzai in advance, coupled with the lack of international insistence on accountability, led Karzai to believe he could get away with blaming the fraud on the UN and EU. In fact, he has got away with it; following a face-saving spate of meetings and calls, and the resignations of the two 'patriotic' election chiefs (who have since been promised other 'good jobs'), the international community agreed to fund the parliamentary elections. In fact, Karzai was so emboldened that he decided to strike while the iron was hot by sending a legislative decree to the parliament that removed the internationals from the EEC, among other changes that will make hiding fraud easier next time.

Short-sighted bilateral technical assistance

Corruption and narcotics trafficking, as well as organised crime, can only be successfully reduced through long-term organic and sustainable capacity-building of the Afghan justice institutions, with true collaboration, cooperation and a unity of action and purpose within the international community, and between international and national institutions. This will require accountability on the part of both Afghan and international institutions, including independent monitoring and evaluation of the effectiveness of rule of law development aid. Aiming for quick results will not work.

Consistency of principle: 'practise what you preach'

Judicial independence and transparency

If the international community expects the Afghan government to respect the rule of law, the international community must cease flaunting and undermining it. This means, first of all, that internationals must heed the idiom 'practise what you preach'. The international rule of law community in Afghanistan refers to the need for 'judicial independence', 'transparency in fair and uniform application of the law' and 'sustainable development and capacity-building'. Yet when it serves foreign states' domestic political interests and values, these rules are broken. There are many such examples supporting this contention, of which a few follow.

First, judicial independence and public understanding of the law are involved in a series of cases invoking article 130 of the constitution. The international community uses pressure to ensure its interpretation prevails, but once the desired result is reached, no frank discussion of differences is enabled; opaqueness rather than transparency is desired to allow the international and Afghan governments to tell their respective constituencies opposite views. The opposing views of freedom of choice of religion and apostasy are not publicly debated or even acknowledged. One could also refer to the international actions as embodying a 'don't ask, don't tell' philosophy.

The Sarwari case, where the court based its judgment on 'article 130' rather than any section in the penal code, warned of things to come. The lower courts routinely convict women for 'running away', especially from an arranged marriage or with an intended husband opposed by her family. But it was not until the Abdul Rahman case (see below) that the international media revealed that there was indeed a clash between the human rights instilled in the constitution and the Afghan application of article 130. After the case was resolved to Western satisfaction, however, there was no attempt to engage.

Article 130 means completely different things to the internationals and to many Afghans. To the foreigners (including moderate Muslims from Egypt, where *Hanafi* jurisprudence is also practised) and some Afghans, article 130 allows judges to interpret the meaning of already promulgated laws much the same way common law lawyers might look at case precedent or legislative history. To many Afghans, the phrase 'the courts shall in pursuance of *Hanafi* jurisprudence' rule in a way that attains justice allows Islamic crimes to be punished even if not in the penal code. The West, however, notes the immediately following phrase of 'within the limits set by this constitution', and states that it refers to, inter alia, article 27, which mandates that 'no one shall be punished without the decision' that is 'taken in accordance with the provision of the [written] law, promulgated prior to commitment of the offence'. The Afghans may reply, however, that article 130 must be read with article 3's language that 'no law shall contravene the tenets and provisions of the holy religion of Islam'. This is perhaps the most significant disagreement between internationals and nationals in the constitution, raising as it does a clash between prosecution for apostasy and the human rights freedom of religion, including changing one's religion, that is incorporated into article 7 of the constitution.[27]

What is most disturbing, however, is that neither side wants to debate the merits, and perhaps even agree to disagree, in a public setting, as some cases have shown. Politically, how can some Western nations justify to their Christian majority their military and financial support to Afghanistan when a fundamental freedom is denied to a minority religion? Does Afghanistan want to risk losing international support over a case or two, and does the West (and the US in particular) want to emphasise that as well? However, one could also say this of other conservative or fundamentalist Muslim countries that are also supported by the West. In a rare admission, former presidential candidate Dr Abdullah Abdullah noted that 'every time we have a case, it is like an alarm. These contradictions [freedom of religion and apostasy] will not go away with one or two cases' (Constable 2006).

Consider the cases of Abdul Rahman, Sayed Pervez Kambaksh and Ahmed Ghous Zalmai.

Rahman, born in Panjshir Valley, had converted to Christianity after working for a Catholic NGO in Peshawar. Upon his return to Afghanistan, he was disowned by his parents. In February 2006, they reported him to the police as an apostate, and he was arrested (Cooney 2006; Morarjee 2006; Wafa 2006a). Prosecutors charged him with apostasy;[28] among the prosecutors, the new parliament and clerics, there were frenzied calls for the death penalty (Wafa 2006b). He was indicted under article 130, from which came the Islamic crime of apostasy, and his trial started on

---

27 Article 2 of the Afghan constitution states: 'The sacred religion of Islam is the religion of the Islamic Republic of Afghanistan. Followers of other faiths shall be free within the bounds of law in the exercise and performance of their religious rituals.' However, conversion is not protected, especially since the free exercise of other faiths must be 'within the bounds of law', and according to many Afghans, apostasy is to be punished by Islamic law. However, article 7 of the constitution expressly incorporates the Universal Declaration of Human Rights, which at article 18 mandates 'everyone has the right to freedom of thought, conscience and religion; this right includes freedom to change his religion'.

28 Informed Afghan prosecutor sources told the author that then Chief Justice Fazl Hadi Shinwari had heard of this 'convert' and personally gone to Rahman's cell, interviewed him, and then told the prosecutors that the case would not be physical abuse of Rahman's family but apostasy.

16 March 2006. The pressure was intense from the international side, with in camera meetings with the Attorney General, the court, and even the President's office (MacKay 2006; Radio Free Europe 2006a). The President met with his cabinet to find a solution that would free Rahman without angering Afghanistan's Muslim clerics (BBC News 2006a; this was also common knowledge on the ground). The result avoided any discussion or confrontation of the actual disagreement, and instead the court discharged Rahman's case and referred it back to the Attorney General's office due to undefined legal flaws (Salahuddin 2006). A judge and prosecutor involved in the case took the position that since Rahman refused to repent, his mental state must be examined (Al Jazeera 2006; Constable 2006; Radio Free Europe 2006b). This creative solution resulted in his release on 28 March 2006, after which he was flown out via an Italian military transport and granted asylum in Italy (BBC News 2006b). Thus both international and national institutions were thrilled that this serious conflict could disappear, and both avoided any conference or lessons learned on article 130.

Sayed Pervez Kambaksh was a 23-year-old student of journalism at Balkh University in Mazar-i-Sharif when on 27 October 2007 he was arrested for downloading from the internet and showing others an article commenting on the Koranic verses about women's rights. He was originally indicted for damaging symbols of religion, in his case the Koran, under article 347 of the 1976 penal code, which had a maximum sentence of five years. At his first court appearance on 17 December 2007, the presiding judge directed the prosecutor to add as a crime blasphemy, under constitutional article 130. Before the trial it was reported that Balkh Governor Ustad Atta Mohammed Noor, one of the most powerful men in Afghanistan, had stated that 'he has been accused of blasphemy . . . there is no way for him to be acquitted', and the influential council of *Ulema* recommended the death sentence. Other international NGOs and the EU parliament appealed to President Karzai to spare Kambaksh's life.[29]

On 22 January 2008, after less than two hours in session, the primary court convicted the accused under article 130, found blasphemy, and sentenced him to death. The court of appeals on 21 October 2008 affirmed his conviction under article 130 but reduced the sentence to the maximum allowed for imprisonment, twenty years. After the presidential election

---

29 The author's sources for this account include unofficial memoranda from the UN and EU, the appellate brief of the Legal Aid Organisation of Afghanistan that through attorney Mohammed Afzal Nooristani represented the accused, his own discussions with principals, and a large number of articles in *The Independent* (UK) in 2008 and 2009, and the International Federation for Human Rights (FIDH) at www.fidh.org.

in August 2009, President Karzai, under the political fallout due to the election fraud, granted Kambaksh a pardon, and he left Afghanistan. From the international community there were intense discussions, suggestions, and pressure during 2008 and 2009, upon the President, Attorney General and courts, which more than offset similar pressures by conservative Islamic authorities calling for the death penalty. These meetings involved diplomatic negotiations as well as express statements on what should be done (Sengupt 2009).

Ahmed Ghows Zelmay was the chief of the Attorney General's office's publications department who had arranged for a Dari translation of the Koran when he was arrested, on the orders of the Attorney General, for blasphemy under article 130 while at the border trying to escape to Pakistan on 4 November 2007. The day before, the *Wolesi Jirga* had presented a draft declaration condemning his actions and voted to make it stronger. On 10 September 2008, a Kabul court convicted both Zelmay and Mullah Qari Mushtaq Ahmad, who had approved the translation, for blasphemy under article 130 and sentenced them to twenty years' imprisonment. The court of appeals affirmed the sentences on 15 February 2009. They were both pardoned on 20 March 2010 in honour of Nawruz (Persian New Year). Similar to the Kambaksh case, there was intense pressure and lobbying of the courts, prosecution and President, including diplomatic negotiations.[30]

Judicial independence principles would have properly allowed for pardon discussions with the President after the final conviction, amicus curiae briefs to the courts, technical advice to the defence attorneys, and technical-level discussions with Attorney General's office prosecutors. But these cases involved much more: ironically, the modalities used by Afghan officials and conservative religious elements that the international community rule of law training decried.

> The issue is a delicate one, given the international community's support for an independent judiciary as a cornerstone of a democratic regime. Millions of foreign dollars have gone into training and reforming the legal sector, and asking Karzai to overrule a lower court is not an attractive option, no matter how flawed the decision. The President, for his part, is caught between a desire to please his foreign backers and his need to placate the increasingly powerful mullahs.
>
> (Ibrahami and MacKenzie 2008)

---

30 *Ibid.* See also Ibrahami and MacKenzie 2008, and websites of NGOs such as Reporters Sans Frontieres (www.rsf.org).

> Their release is believed to have been the result of diplomatic pressure. 'The Afghan authorities are being pressured from many sides,' [John] Macleod [director for Central Asia, Institute for War and Peace Reporting] said. 'On the one side, there are the kind of conservative forces who pushed this case. On the other is the international community . . . For the latter, it isn't great to be seen to be backing a system that locks people up using the same kind of reasoning the Taliban employ.'
>
> (All Headline News 2010)

Moreover, once resolved through pressure and diplomacy, there was no effort by the international community to attempt to bring together for discussions the disparate views of article 130's interpretation and whether article 27 limited it, including the legal bases of the judiciary's reasoning. Without this, the 'catch and release' pattern will continue. 'The release follows previous patterns where Afghan civil rights activists and journalists who speak up, for example on an alternative interpretation of women's rights in Islam, are first convicted and only released after pressure from national and international activists (All Headline News 2010).'

Sustainable development and capacity-building

National politics of course influences all donor-country policies and practices. But the international focus is on grinding out short-term results, with results being defined by metrics of 'case convictions', emphasising the speed of implementation. This approach is accelerated by the continually changing rule of law strategies and priorities of the international community.

Such a short-term view may still result in a successful strategy if paired with a bifocal long-term view requiring sustainable, structural changes resulting in a transparent permanent process that will function without constant intervening international oversight. However, this author has witnessed, especially in the past nine months, in various meetings, conferences and emails, the triumph of the short term over the long, of myopia over hyperopia. What is needed is a combination of both – progressive bifocals.

Two illustrative examples are the law on special courts (for ministers and justices) and the establishment of the anti-corruption tribunal.

The law on special courts demonstrates best the philosophy of 'wait, and hurry up'. For over six years, the government chose not to have a special court for ministers and justices, providing them with immunity for any criminal act committed. Once political considerations required the government to come forward with such a law, the rushed drafting and review process provided less than a week for discussion with the criminal law reform working group, and no time for a careful comparative study of the workability and success of differing modalities, processes and compositions.

A wait of one-and-a-half years occurred before the establishment of the anti-corruption tribunal. The tribunal as it existed in May 2010 uses opaque case-by-case selection criteria to take corruption cases from the provinces to Kabul, and each change of venue depends upon the ad hoc decision of the Supreme Court rather than operation of law. In June 2008, the President legislatively decreed (article 19(2), *Official Gazette* no. 957, 29 June 2008) that 'the Supreme Court . . . shall establish anti-corruption *diwans* [divisions or tribunals] in the capital [Kabul] and provinces in order to deal with crimes of corruption'. After waiting for over a year without taking any action, the Supreme Court created an anti-corruption tribunal by its administrative decree, which started hearing cases in January 2010. In contrast to the counter-narcotics tribunal, the anti-corruption tribunal has no statutory basis or publicly defined subject matter and territorial jurisdiction. The high judicial salaries are 'topped up' directly and not within the Afghan budget by the international community, as they are for Attorney General's office anti-corruption unit prosecutors and counter-narcotics tribunal judges and prosecutors. For each case before the anti-corruption tribunal, the anti-corruption unit, closely monitored by international mentors, requests that the Supreme Court change venue to Kabul.

For long-term sustainability, it would have been best to define by law a subject matter (such as 'over 5 million afghanis [$100,000] or any government official of rank 2 or higher') and national territorial jurisdiction, and to publicise the uniform application and fairness of and allowing adjudication by the tribunal without any guarantee of uniform treatment. The need for a 'statutory basis' in order to guarantee long-term independence is stated by the London conference communiqué of January 2010.[31] However, the 'wait, and hurry up' philosophy requires the immediate gratification of case results by February 2010, and rejected even the short delay required by a suggested stop-gap measure of the Supreme Court announcing objective and mandatory selection criteria

---

31 Paragraph 23(2) requires establishment of a statutory basis to so guarantee independence.

so that all cases would be treated equally. When urged by this author to suggest to the judges to publicise and then follow selection criteria, one of the international embassy officials stated: 'We don't have time for that now; we need to get the court taking cases, then we can deal with the legal framework.' However, one suspects that the lack of a mandatory standard is welcomed by the tribunal and anti-corruption unit international mentors to allow cases to be chosen for a variety of reasons that could not be written into mandatory criteria. Unfortunately, the result will be the appearance of a lack of objectivity and the related loss of credibility and legitimacy.

Instead of the legitimacy this step could have gained, the tribunal continued at the time of writing, in May 2010, using its ad hoc exercise of change of venue power, so that cases large and small are taken without any announced rhyme or reason. An example is the case of William Shaw, a UK citizen, who was convicted by the tribunal on 26 April 2010 and sentenced to two years imprisonment for paying $25,000 with the intent to bribe a National Security Directorate officer in order to gain the release of two impounded armoured vehicles (BBC News 2010; see also Boone 2010b). Moreover, since change of venue depends upon the Supreme Court using a discretionary power, it depends upon the will of individual justices.

The rush to results, without first establishing a sustainable, permanent, objective, transparent and thus legitimate process, will result in illusory success. At a rule of law conference in April 2010, a representative of an embassy was asked whether the current anti-corruption reforms, including the tribunal, were sustainable and likely to be permanent in light of the salary 'top-ups' and other international sweeteners and assistance. The UN and EU rule of law experts, among others, were stunned to hear the representative state that 'we are not in development mode; we are in emergency mode', and that while 'sustainability is important . . . we were not at that point yet' because first the emergency had to be 'solved'. This view was said to be 'shared by our ambassador'.

That view, however, is certainly not shared by the author, nor by the expressed view in support of sustainability made by UNAMA, UNODC, UNDP, EU, or many others with years and decades of experience in rule of law development. Rule of law assistance as measured by short-term 'results' may support political support for an 'exit strategy' and 'disengagement'. But to have true success, any changes must be sustainable, structural, objective and legitimate.

Conclusion

Based on this experience, this chapter offers five conclusions.

First, the most important preconditions required for the establishment of a lasting rule of law in Afghanistan were less in evidence in 2010 than in 2002. During this period, corruption and narcotics trafficking flourished while security deteriorated. Meanwhile, the public's early hopes for the end of impunity of the powerful and influential have been crushed by the reality of almost a decade of immunity from punishment.

Second, only a determined and public battle against impunity, in the form of successful prosecution of high-level figures, can catalyse a transformation to the desired state of rule of law. This can only be accomplished through the establishment of accountability and credibility through national action that is successful in the preventative, administrative and criminal spheres. This should include the international community applying appropriate diplomatic means to pressure the Afghan government to discover, investigate and prosecute those national officials who are corrupt, who are involved in drug trafficking, or who were responsible for the massive presidential election fraud of 2009, as well as those responsible for war crimes and mass atrocities from over three decades of conflict.

Third, consistency of principle: 'practise what you preach'. The international community must itself respect the rule of law and cease any inappropriate interference with judicial decision-making. This requires transparency, respecting national justice institutions' independence and procedures regardless of disagreements with the result, and facilitating constructive public dialogue on the interpretation of constitutional provisions such as article 130, rather than ex parte/in camera discussions and pressure by internationals on national justice institutions.

Fourth, corruption and narcotics trafficking, as well as organised crime, can only be successfully reduced through long-term organic and sustainable capacity-building of the Afghan justice institutions, with true collaboration, cooperation and a unity of action and purpose, both within the international community and between international and national institutions. This will require accountability on the part of both Afghan and international institutions, which in turn will require independent monitoring and evaluation of the effectiveness of rule of law development aid. It also requires rejecting false metrics in favour of local-need-driven assistance in mentoring, training, and human and physical infrastructure, based on transparent and objective criteria. Results that are based

upon ad hoc programs and processes depending upon case-by-case decisions by individual national authorities and international mentors are not
consistent with sustainable development.

Thus, and finally, the legitimacy necessary for the consent and acceptance of the formal justice system by the governed, which is critical if
strides in improving security and battling corruption are to be made, will
only be possible if the government can demonstrate effectiveness against
impunity and corruption, using sustainable development to build Afghan
justice institutions with integrity and professionalism.

References

Afghan Independent Human Rights Commission (2004). *A Call for Justice: A
    National Consultation on Past Human Rights Violations in Afghanistan*, www.
    aihrc.org.af/Rep_29_Eng/rep29_1_05call4justice.pdf

Al Jazeera (2006). 'Afghan convert's trial put in doubt', 22 March 2006, http://
    english.aljazeera.net/archive/2006/03/200849163746825405.html

All Headline News (2010). 'Released in translation: Afghanistan frees jailed
    journalists', 31 March 2010, www.allheadlinenews.com/articles/7018269298?
    Releasedper cent20inper cent20Translation:per cent20Afghanistanper
    cent20Freesper cent20Jailedper cent20Journalists

BBC News (2006a). 'Afghan convert "may be released"', 25 March 2006, http://
    news.bbc.co.uk/2/hi/south_asia/4841812.stm

BBC News (2006b). 'Afghan convert "arrives in Italy"', 29 March 2006, http://news.
    bbc.co.uk/2/hi/south_asia/4856748.stm

BBC News (2010). 'Afghan court jails Briton on bribery charges', 27 April 2010,
    http://news.bbc.co.uk/go/pr/fr/-/2/hi/south_asia/8645778.stm

Boone, Jon (2010a). 'Afghanistan quietly brings into force Taliban amnesty law',
    The Guardian, 11 February 2010, www.guardian.co.uk/world/2010/feb/11/
    taliban-amnesty-law-enacted

Boone, Jon (2010b). 'Afghan anti-corruption court tries Briton on bribe charge',
    The Guardian, 25 March 2010, www.guardian.co.uk/world/2010/mar/25/
    afghanistan-anti-corruption-court-briton

Bouvier, John (1856). *A Law Dictionary, Adapted to the Constitution and Laws of
    the United States*, sixth revision, www.constitution.org/bouv/bouvier_i.htm

Constable, Pamela (2006). 'For Afghans, allies, a clash of values', *Washington Post*,
    23 March 2006, www.washingtonpost.com/wp-dyn/content/article/2006/03/
    22/AR2006032201113.html

Cooney, Daniel (2006). 'Afghan convert may be unfit for trial', *Associated Press*,
    22 March 2006

CTV News (2010). 'No peace without justice, says envoy to Afghanistan', 19 April 2010, www.ctv.ca/servlet/ArticleNews/story/CTVNews/20100419/afghan_envoy_100419/20100419

Farmer, Ben (2010). 'Hamid Karzai accused of blocking arrest of official', *The Telegraph*, 28 March 2010, www.telegraph.co.uk/news/worldnews/asia/afghanistan/7532867/Hamid-Karzai-accused-of-blocking-arrest-of-official.html

Human Rights Watch (2007). *Afghanistan Country Summary for 2007*, 31 January 2008, http://hrw.org/englishwr2k8/docs/2008/01/31/afghan17600.htm

Human Rights Watch (2010). 'Measure brought into force by Karzai means atrocities will go unpunished', 10 March 2010, www.hrw.org/en/news/2010/03/10/afghanistan-repeal-amnesty-law

Ibrahimi, Sayed Yaqub and MacKenzie, Jean (2008). 'Fears over "Islamicisation" of judiciary', *RAWA News*, 30 September 2008, www.rawa.org/temp/runews/2008/09/30/fears-over-and-8220-islamicisationand-8221-of-judiciary_9847.html

IRIN Humanitarian News and Analysis (2010). 'Afghanistan: Justice action plan heading for oblivion', 14 April 2010, http://irinnews.org/PrintReport.aspx?ReportId=88807

Kaplan, Robert D. (2010). 'Man against Afghanistan', *The Atlantic*, April 2010 (quoting Afghan analyst Walid Tamim)

Khadhouri, S. (2010). *Consensus recommendations for electoral reform in Afghanistan*, April 2010, in possession of author; an edited summary version is available at http://democracyinternational.com/afghanistan/wp-content/uploads/2010/04/CONSENSUS-RECOMMENDATIONS-Eng-PDF.pdf

Kilcullen, David (2009). 'If we lose hearts and minds, we will lose the war', *Military World*, 21 May 2009, www.military-world.net/Afghanistan/1413.html

Koelbl, Susanne (2009). 'NATO high commander issues illegitimate order to kill', *Spiegel Online International*, 28 January 2009, www.spiegel.de/international/world/0,1518,604183,00.html

MacKay, Maria (2006). 'Kirk moderator appeals to government over Afghan Christian', *Christian Today*, 25 March 2006, www.christiantoday.co.uk/article/kirk.moderator.appeals.to.government.over.afghan.christian/5790.htm

Meo, Nick (2004). 'Corruption gives impunity to Afghanistan's drug lords', *The Independent*, 26 August 2004, www.independent.co.uk/news/world/asia/corruption-gives-impunity-to-afghanistans-drug-lords-557825.html

Morarjee, Rachel (2006). 'Abdul Rahman's family values', *Time*, 29 March 2006

Nadery, Nader (2005). 'Afghanistan: First war crimes trial in 25 years begins', Radio Free Europe/Radio Liberty, 27 December 2005, www.rferl.org/articleprintview/1064214.html

Neighbour, Sally (2010). 'Peace in Afghanistan is unlikely to be brought by the thugs and murderers being wooed by the Karzai government', *The Australian*, 27 February 2010

Nicholson, Brendan (2009). 'Taliban "laying down the law"', *The Age*, 1 September 2009, www.theage.com.au/world/taliban-laying-down-the-law-20090831-f59y.html

Owen, Jonathan (2010). 'Afghan farmers reap cannabis harvest worth £61m', *The Independent*, 11 April 2010, www.independent.co.uk/news/world/asia/afghan-farmers-reap-cannabis-harvest-worth-16361m-1941431.html

Perry, Tony (2009). '$10 million is smuggled out of Afghanistan daily, official says', *Los Angeles Times*, 7 December 2009, http://articles.latimes.com/2009/dec/07/world/la-fg-afghanistan-cash7-2009dec07/2

Pugliese, David (2010a). 'Former Afghan minister not surprised by widespread fraud allegations', *The Gazette*, 11 April 2010, www.montrealgazette.com/news/Former+Afghan+minister+surprised+widespread+fraud+allegations/2789965/story.html

Pugliese, David (2010b). 'A lonely war against corruption in Afghanistan', *Ottowa Citizen*, 12 April 2010, www.ottawacitizen.com/story print.html?id=2790803&sponsor= (US government study of $190 million out of Kabul International Airport over nineteen days)

Radio Free Europe (2006a). 'Germany wants Karzai to intervene in conversion case', 21 March 2006, www.rferl.org/content/article/1066929.html

Radio Free Europe (2006b). 'Pressure mounts over Afghan conversion case', 23 March 2006, www.rferl.org/content/article/1067028.html

Rashid, Ahmed (2008). *Descent into Chaos: The United States and the Failure of Nation Building in Pakistan, Afghanistan, and Central Asia*. New York: Viking Adult

Reuters AlertNet (2006). 'Communist era mass grave discovered highlights need for post-war justice', 22 December 2006, www.alertnet.org/thenews/newsdesk/IRIN/0e42c3938dbabb718723d31d3f58a239.html

Rubin, Elizabeth (2009). 'Karzai in his labyrinth', *New York Times Magazine*, 4 August 2009, www.nytimes.com/2009/08/09/magazine/09Karzai-t.html

Salahuddin, Sayed (2006). 'Afghan judge says Christian convert case has flaws', *Reuters Canada*, 26 March 2006

Sengupt, Kim (2009). 'Free at last: Student in hiding after Karzai's intervention', *The Independent*, 7 September 2009, www.independent.co.uk/news/world/asia/free-at-last-student-in-hiding-after-karzais-intervention-1782909.html

UK Border Agency (2008). *Country of Origin Information Report: Afghanistan*, 29 August 2008, www.statewatch.org/news/2009/mar/afghanistan-ukba-c-of-origin-report.pdf

UNAMA (2010). *Annual Report on Protection of Civilians in Armed Conflict, 2009* (January 2010), http://unama.unmissions.org/Portals/UNAMA/human%20rights/Protection%20of%20Civilian%202009%20report%20English.pdf

UNODC (2010a). *Corruption in Afghanistan* (January 2010), www.unodc.org/documents/data-and-analysis/Afghanistan/Afghanistan-corruption-survey2010-Eng.pdf

UNODC (2010b). 'Afghanistan leads in hashish production', www.unodc.org/unodc/en/frontpage/2010/March/afghanistan-leads-in-hashish-production-says-unodc.html

US Institute of Peace (2003). 'International judges and prosecutors in Kosovo', USIP Special Report No. 112, US Institute of Peace Press, October 2003, www.usip.org/files/resources/sr112.pdf

US Senate Committee on Foreign Relations (2009). 'Afghanistan's narco war: breaking the link between drug traffickers and insurgents', report to the committee, 10 August 2009, www.gpoaccess.gov/congress/index.html

Wafa, Abdul Waheed (2006a). 'Afghan judge in convert case vows to resist foreign pressure', *New York Times*, 23 March 2006, www.nytimes.com/2006/03/23/international/asia/23cnd-convert.html

Wafa, Abdul Waheed (2006b). 'Preachers in Kabul urge execution of convert to Christianity', *New York Times*, 26 March 2006

11

Land conflict in Afghanistan[1]

COLIN DESCHAMPS AND ALAN ROE

For as long as anyone can remember, the main sources of conflict among Pashtuns, the ethnic group that constitutes over half of Afghanistan's population of more than 20 million, have been 'zan, zar and zameen' – women, treasure and land. Of these, disputes over land have come to overshadow the rest. Decades of chronic conflict, political turmoil and other civil disturbances in Afghanistan have left land administration in disarray, with the entitlements to large areas of land – and complementary water resources – subject to dispute between individuals, communities, and political, sectarian and ethnic groups.

In the politically fragile rural Afghan landscape, conflict over land and water resources has become a driver of instability. It is closely related to the persistence of insecurity and corruption, the vulnerability of the rural poor and the tenacity of the opium economy. Continuing land conflict not only threatens efforts to alleviate poverty and rehabilitate the rural economy, but also undermines the attempts of the Afghan state to stabilise insecure districts and decrease farmer participation in the opium economy. Land conflict is a symptom of the weakness of the rule of law and is itself a driver of political instability, civil unrest and corruption, so further eroding citizens' incentives to act within the law.

The first part of this discussion considers the conditions giving rise to conflict over land in Afghanistan and establishes a general typology for understanding land disputes. Using this framework, five case-study disputes are identified to test conflict resolution techniques. The second part of the discussion sets out the lessons learned from these pilot conflict resolution exercises. It suggests practical steps and guidelines for

---

1 This chapter draws upon the findings of a World Bank-funded study undertaken by the Afghanistan Research and Evaluation Unit between 2006 and 2008 entitled *Land conflict in Afghanistan: Building capacity to address vulnerability.*

addressing land conflict and thereby strengthening the rule of law in rural Afghanistan.

At the outset, it is useful to highlight that land in Afghanistan is commonly held under one or both of two different systems of law: the formal and the customary.

The legal framework for land ownership

The constitution of 2004 established a hierarchy for the application of law in Afghanistan. First, constitutional provisions are to be applied; second, statutory law; and third, jurisprudence (Shari'a) from the *Hanafi* school.[2] As few constitutional provisions apply with respect to land tenure, the principal sources of law are statutory and the Afghan civil code (Ministry of Justice 1977), which itself draws upon *Hanafi* jurisprudence.

Land law has been one of the most contentious and politicised areas of government policy in recent Afghan history, with successive regimes embarking upon large-scale programmes of land reform, either overturning the legislation of previous governments wholesale or introducing new legislation piecemeal. Policy initiatives have included contentious programmes of Pashtun resettlement and communist land redistribution. Consequently, the gazettes are littered with diverse statutes enacting often contradictory, overlapping and otherwise incongruous laws which have been legislated successively by the monarchy, the communist regime, the mujaheddin interregnum, the Taliban, and finally the post-Taliban governments (Alden Wily 2003). As a result, there is no clear body of law providing unambiguous legal guidance and precedents; instead, the judiciary and ordinary people are confronted by a bewildering mosaic of inconsistent provisions (McEwen and Whitty 2006).

Although current Afghan statutes do not clearly define all types of land, broadly speaking there are five types: irrigated cultivable; built up; rain-fed cultivable; pasture; and wilderness (or barren) land. Within law, five types of land ownership, each deriving from a different part of the legal code, can be identified. These are summarised in Table 11.1. The Afghan civil code further recognises other 'subordinate' rights to land, namely lease, sharecropping and mortgage. With this multiplicity of bases

---

2 The *Hanafi* school is the oldest of the four main schools of Islamic jurisprudence in Sunni Islam. It has a reputation for putting a greater emphasis on reasoning and being slightly more liberal than the other schools.

Table 11.1 *Summary of land ownership in Afghan law*

Form of ownership	Description	Applicable to	Relevant provisions
Private ownership	Exclusive rights to property	All types of land	Civil code (articles 1035–1215, 1900–1984, 1993–2102, 2293–2323)
Government ownership	Exclusive government rights to property	All types of land	Decree 99 of April 2002 froze all distribution of government lands
Public ownership	Land held by government for public usage (*mawaat*)	Rain-fed cultivable, pasture, wilderness	Law on land 795, 2000 (article 9)
Common ownership	Rights of grazing access to commonly owned village pasture (*maraha*)	Built-up, rain-fed cultivable, pasture	Civil code (article 1935–1950); law on land 795, 2000 (article 3 [1])
Waqf ownership	Land covenanted in perpetuity for a charitable or religious purpose	All types of land	Law on land 795, 2000 (article 86 [1])

for claims of ownership and usage rights, identifying the relevant law has been a challenge, and has contributed to the proliferation of conflicts over land ownership and rights of access (Alden Wily 2003).

Government policy on land has been further revised several times since 2001 through the 'Securing Afghanistan's future' policy paper (2004), the 'Afghanistan national development strategy' process (2008) and a new land policy, adopted by the cabinet in September 2007. Several new edicts issued between 2002 and 2005 have attempted to consolidate government holdings of land so as to counter unlawful appropriations by warlords and others (see Norwegian Refugee Council 2006). While these measures struck at powerful 'land grabbers', they also threatened the position of many who held land under customary or informal entitlements. The new

Afghan land policy is a largely aspirational document, setting out basic political and legal principles upon which a future land administration should be established. Thus far the policy is little understood within government agencies, and legislative and other implementation tools are not yet in place (Roe 2009).

Although there are historical precedents for keeping land records in Afghanistan, there exists no comprehensive cadastre, and land records (such as exist) are today dispersed throughout a range of institutions, including the lands department (*Amlak*), the geodesy and cartography head office, and deeds lodged in the archives of provincial courts. These are often stored in very poor conditions, and in many cases are physically degrading (Stanfield 2006). Even if were it possible to collate available land records, these take many disparate forms that are difficult to reconcile.

The current reality

The effective management of land is critical to Afghanistan's stability and development. The rule of law, defined here as a set of rules consistently applied equally to all, whether this be through government or community systems, is a critical aspect in ensuring the security of land tenure. The security of land, a farmer's most important asset, has a great influence on an owner's or user's commitment to the broader framework of rules, of which land tenure is a part. Secure land tenure also has a significant influence on the agricultural sector, which in turn will be the cornerstone of rural development for the foreseeable future. With the rural population experiencing a higher poverty rate and significantly outnumbering the urban population, the Afghanistan national development strategy makes developing the agricultural sector a top priority.

The Afghan government's lack of capacity to manage land tenure, a situation most visibly demonstrated by the prevalence and intensity of conflict over land, hinders its ability to effectively plan for rural development. In Afghanistan, several decades of conflict have resulted in a governmental legal system that is severely challenged by a pervasive lack of resources, qualified staff and, in many cases, legitimacy in the eyes of the people. The government court system generally requires more time and resources of the plaintiff than community-based mechanisms. In many instances, cases in the government system remain undecided or in a continual state of referral to other courts or offices.

Ambiguity around land tenure creates many problems for farmers even if they never end up in court. For example, as poppy production and the opium economy continue to flourish, many farmers find themselves with insufficient land, or insufficient water for their land, to sustain their families with legal agricultural activities. It is well understood that if they do choose to grow opium poppies, this may have the knock-on effect of funding the insurgency and perpetuating conflict. Similarly, many of the causes of land conflict also underlie other dimensions of Afghanistan's development context: population growth; repeated intergenerational division of family resources; returnees and internally displaced persons; climate change and its impact on meteorological anomalies such as drought; and corruption, at both a government and community level. Better understanding these causal factors can also help mitigate land conflict.

Despite the enormous impact of insecure land tenure on the great majority of Afghans who remain tied to agriculture, establishing consistent and predictable mechanisms to prevent and resolve land conflicts continues to take a back seat to other priorities. Management of land conflict is mostly ad hoc, with disputants trying to navigate a confusing congeries of community-based and government systems, which are themselves often circumvented by influential people or the officials responsible for them. The large demonstrations in Kabul in mid-2008 between settled farmers and migratory kuchis served as yet another reminder of the need to invest more resources and attention in clarifying claims of land tenure and developing consistent, predictable and accessible means for resolving land disputes. Steps have already been taken in the right direction; owing to the influx of donor assistance since the overthrow of the Taliban and, to a more limited degree, a realignment of policy by the post-Taliban government, efforts to manage land conflict in Afghanistan are now better resourced than at any time in recent memory. However, although progress has been made, the results remain tenuous and accomplishments incomplete, and there are many reasons to invest in further continued refinement in the sector.

At the time of writing, property claimants' options range from the most casual of community-based mechanisms all the way to judicial review at the Supreme Court level. Choices of dispute resolution methodology are highly dependent on the circumstances of each case, such as the identity of the parties and their ability and willingness to access the government court system (financially, physically and socially).

A dearth of land titles – necessary for many land transactions and dispute resolution mechanisms administered by the government – leads most rural landholders to utilise community-based resolution mechanisms. Community-based or customary mechanisms for adjudicating disputes predate the formal system and were used in an estimated 90 per cent of property cases in 2010. The informal system is generally perceived to be more efficient, less expensive and at less risk of corruption than the government system. In some communities, decisions made through a traditional mechanism, such as a *jirga* or *shura*, are considered to be more legitimate as they are based on community mores. At times, they may also be more enforceable than decisions by government courts. Customary processes are also well suited to illiterate claimants or those with no legal documentation, which is exceedingly common in rural areas.

With sustained attention from the government and international partners, the government court system will continue to improve, and with expanded government control of territory, its writ will run further. With these improvements, the caseload of the formal system will continue to increase. Already, the government system is an attractive option for certain types of disputants, particularly those returning from extended periods of displacement or who have strong documentation and financial resources. The government system is increasingly popular in the peri-urban and urban areas where the writ of the Afghan government is most enforceable.

Nonetheless, in rural areas, land claims and disputes rely primarily on customary law and mechanisms. The reliance on this system, which lies outside the writ of the government, undermines both the government's legitimacy and its ability to effectively plan for rural development. Moreover, customary mechanisms are generally unable to provide or are barred from providing parties with documentation acceptable to the government. Currently, the government system refuses to support the customary system, but is unable to replace it. This is counterproductive. For the foreseeable future, customary mechanisms will be rural Afghans' primary means for resolving disputes over the resource on which their very lives depend. This being the case, the government should seek ways to interact with customary mechanisms to improve their effectiveness and legitimacy.

In some areas, cooperation already occurs. *Jirgas* and *shuras* may, for instance, resolve certain types of cases and register their decisions in the official court records to give them legal status. When an attempt is made to resolve a case through a *shura* or *jirga* and the case then goes to the government court, findings from the customary mechanism are often incorporated into the brief.

Types of land conflict

Conflicts over land take myriad forms and result from diverse circumstances. For example, siblings may have a non-violent dispute over inheritance, much as in the West; rival ethnic groups may clash physically, causing casualties and significant damage to property and livestock; or one group may appropriate land claimed by another without eliciting an immediate violent response but perpetuating inter-community tensions. In short, each conflict is unique.

However, the unique nature of each case does not preclude the useful recognition of different categories of conflict. With this in mind, the Afghanistan Research and Evaluation Unit project used data from the Norwegian Refugee Council's information and legal aid centres to create a typology of land conflicts. The key findings were as follows:

- The highest frequency of disputes concern property ownership rights (inheritance and occupation are the most common causes).
- The majority of disputes concern less than 10 *jeribs* of land (20,000m^{2}); however, disputes over the largest areas usually concern common property.
- Most disputes are in 'bad faith' (where one party appears to be challenging another party with the aim of illegally acquiring the land); these appear to be more intractable than 'good faith' disputes (where both parties feel they are genuinely entitled to the land).
- Some resources are predisposed to certain types of dispute: non-mortgaged private land has the highest value and is most frequently subject to occupation or inheritance disputes; a high proportion of access and boundary disputes concern mortgaged and common property; and a relatively high proportion of water disputes concern mortgaged land.
- Disputes that challenge land ownership rights generally endure longer.
- It is the most vulnerable who tend to pursue disputes collectively; a high proportion of group cases address power asymmetries and are against commanders, the government and other powerful groups.
- In most respects, group cases differ from individually led cases.

Based on the information from the land conflict typology and other sources, we determined that the majority of land disputes in Afghanistan fall into one or more of five principal categories:

- conflicts involving the illegal occupation of land by powerful people;
- conflicts involving inheritance rights to private property;
- conflicts involving the return of people to land they previously owned;
- conflicts over private property between established villagers (not returnees, refugees or internally displaced people); and
- conflicts involving common property resources managed through common property regimes – for instance, certain pastures, forests and water for irrigation.

Research and evidence from the early stages of the land conflict project and other projects suggest that it is useful to distinguish between two general categories of land conflict: conflicts over land managed by common property regimes, where the conflict tends to be structural and inter-community; and conflicts over private property, typically triggered by outside challenges (such as displaced persons or even the Afghan government itself) to village institutions.

Summary of pilot cases

Five pilot cases were selected to cover each principal category of rural land-related conflict, with some of the pilot cases involving aspects of conflict from more than one category. Three cases relating to private property conflicts and two to conflicts over resources previously managed through a common property regime[3] were selected. The cases comprised:

- a land appropriation dispute between two private parties (farming families) over 20 *jeribs* (1 *jerib* = 2,000m^2) of irrigated land in Kunduz province;
- an inheritance dispute between a female claimant and two of her brothers over 7 *jeribs* of irrigated land and a shop in Herat province;
- a group displacement dispute in Baghlan province between communities of different ethnicities (Ismaili and Pashtun) over 630 *jeribs* of rain-fed land suitable for irrigation and with family dwellings in Baghlan province (the land is currently mostly left fallow due to the conflict);
- a dispute over canal water allocation for irrigation between two village groups of different ethnicity in Parwan province; and

---

3 Common property regimes operate on a local level to prevent the over-exploitation of a resource and to avoid diminishing the benefits of the resource by dividing it into inefficiently small units.

- a pasture access dispute between settled villagers and transhumant pastoralists over approximately 2,000 *jeribs* of what has traditionally been pastureland, which is increasingly being cultivated by the villagers, in Panjshir province.

The pilot cases are summarised in Table 11.2 below:

Challenges and opportunities for clarifying and securing tenure

Throughout the research process for this chapter, interlocutors have identified what they regard as the main challenges to pursuing effective and durable resolution to land conflicts in Afghanistan. Many of these challenges have also been encountered by other institutions and individuals active in the prevention and resolution of land conflicts.

The main challenges identified include:

- limited capacity of the justice sector, particularly the government court system;
- limited capacity at the Ministry of Agriculture, Irrigation and Livestock and its cadastre department;
- variation among community-based dispute resolution mechanisms;
- lack of awareness among disputants as to their legal rights and required steps to formalise or claim those rights, including limited literacy;
- weak communication between the Afghan government, the government court system and those active in community-based mechanisms such as *shuras* and *jirgas;*
- delays in resolution, due to beliefs by one or multiple parties that delaying the proceedings will be advantageous or due to the failure of officials to impose procedure as instructed by law;
- corruption of government officials;
- lack of coordination among government entities;
- lack of rule of law and widespread insecurity.

Alongside these challenges, we call attention to the following opportunities and imperatives:

> Clear indicators can be identified to determine whether a land dispute may be more appropriately resolved through the government court system, a customary system or political advocacy.

The project team found in all cases that indicators of varying complexity can be employed to decide which conflict resolution mechanism is

Table 11.2 *Key characteristics of the pilot land conflict cases*

Characteristics	Features and issues
Land appropriation – returnee land rights • 20 *jeribs* of irrigated land • two male farmers with families • government court system initially; finally resolved by community-based mechanisms	• Advantages of community-based conflict resolution mechanisms versus the government court system, including efficiency and legitimacy in the eyes of the community • Duplicate land ownership documents, possibly both legitimate, frequently because they have been issued by different Afghan government regimes • Corruption in the government court system; in this case, a party to the conflict was perceived to command an influence that could have an extraneous influence on the judgment • Challenge of keeping cases moving through a government court system that is often inefficient and backlogged with cases • Formalisation of decisions reached through community-based mechanisms
Land inheritance rights (females) – returnee land rights • 7 *jeribs* of irrigated land and a shop on the property • a married woman and her two elder brothers • community-based mechanisms	• Advantages of community-based conflict resolution mechanisms versus the government court system, including efficiency and legitimacy in the eyes of the community, as well as retaining honour • Women's inheritance rights according to Shari'a and the government court system, including discrepancies between these • Returnee rights and the difficulty of proceeding with a case when not all stakeholders have returned to Afghanistan • Formalisation of decisions reached through *shura*

Table 11.2 *(cont.)*

Characteristics	Features and issues
Group displacement and possible land appropriation • 630 *jeribs* of rain-fed land (suitable for irrigation and residential use) • Ismaili and Pashtun families • community-based mechanisms and government court system failed • resolution through political advocacy ongoing	• Need to prioritise issues impacting large numbers of people and/or that threaten to destabilise an area • Partiality of Afghan government officials based on ethnicity, religion, history and other factors, and a corresponding biased application of law • Refugee and internally displaced person returnee rights • Large numbers of disputants with no one authorised to represent all plaintiffs or defendants • Duplicate land ownership documents, possibly both legitimate, frequently because they have been issued by different Afghan government regimes
Common property resource • water in an irrigation canal • twenty-three villages largely split into two groups • community-based mechanisms with requirement for external rehabilitation of canal	• Common-property resources • Ethnic underpinnings of land dispute • Ability of communities to access assistance from the Afghan government, international organisations or others • Breakdown of traditional maintenance agreements, such as that for the canal • Strain on natural resources caused by population growth from returnees and birth-to-death rates
Common property resource • 2,000 *jeribs* of pastureland, increasingly being cultivated • a small number of transhumant pastoralists and approximately 210 village households • community-based mechanisms with a component of local political advocacy	• How individual personalities may have been or are able to quell or inflame the situation • Risk of outside intervention in conflating or politicising a dispute by bringing in new expectations

most appropriate for a specific dispute. When the five pilot disputes were initially selected, there was a presumption, based upon previous experience, regarding how each would most likely be resolved. In practice, once the dispute was investigated or methods tried, it often became clear that these assumptions were incorrect due to a range of circumstantial factors. A good example of this is the female inheritance dispute, which initially was thought to be suitable for advancing through the government court system, but in fact was rapidly resolved through a *shura*.

> *Dispute resolution must remain adaptive and flexible to setbacks or changes. As circumstances (or stakeholders) change, it may be advantageous to switch dispute resolution approaches completely.*

The project team observed an impasse at two pilot sites that necessitated a change in approach to an alternative resolution mechanism. In the first, concerning the group displacement case in Baghlan, a lack of progress through the courts led to an examination of the case at the political level. In the second, the dispute over private land in Kunduz, questions about the legitimacy of a court ruling led to both parties accepting that the case be heard by a *jirga*.

> *Preparation, advocacy and oversight are essential to improve the performance of the government court system.*

The government court system in Afghanistan is under pressure from lack of capacity, lack of resources, heavy caseloads and endemic corruption. Courts in Afghanistan have traditionally been subject to the influence of powerful parties, including government officials. Even in areas where the courts have been significantly improved, many Afghans continue to doubt the legitimacy or independence of the courts. The experience of the pilot project in Kunduz has shown that with effective support from independent legal aid,[4] such as in the preparation of witnesses and documents, collation of the relevant points of law, and advocacy for adherence to procedure, courts can operate with increased efficiency, although they may still lack legitimacy in the eyes of the community. More significantly, the team also found that the presence of independent counsel in

---

4 The provision of defence counsel to defendants in criminal trials is constitutionally mandated, but in practice there are very few defence lawyers practising outside Kabul. Hence, the great majority of trials are conducted by prosecutors arguing before judges with no one to represent the defendant.

judicial proceedings greatly improves transparency and accountability while reducing the risk of corrupt practices.

> *Preparation, information and oversight can build the capacity and effectiveness of community-based adjudication mechanisms.*

The performance of *jirga* and *shura* proceedings may also be enhanced through preparation and facilitation. Team members have found that participants generally welcome briefings on applicable civil and Shari'a legal standards, as they are seeking to reach well-informed and durable solutions. Participants also welcome the participation of an objective third party to ensure that proceedings remain focused and balanced, and that all parties are equally heard throughout. In the case of the inheritance dispute in Herat, the project team helped the parties to facilitate an organised process by gathering available testimony and documentation, and briefed the parties throughout the preparation phase on relevant provisions of Shari'a law on inheritance. Participation of an objective external actor in the mediation enabled the parties to discuss the issues calmly, as both felt more secure that their interests were being protected equally. The team further facilitated the drafting of an inheritance distribution document, which was signed by all parties to ensure durability.

> *All stakeholders should be given ownership of the dispute resolution process to help legitimate the outcome.*

Dispute resolution efforts should include all stakeholders to achieve a successful and legitimate outcome. Perhaps the best example of this is the Herat inheritance mediation, which involved the entire group of heirs, not just the immediate disputants. This wider group brought social legitimacy to the proceedings and peer pressure to ensure an equitable division of the inheritance. The dispute in Kunduz also shows that where a resolution is delivered as a decree without wider community participation or acceptance, it might not enjoy social legitimacy; it may need to be taken to a more participatory forum such as a *jirga* to win wider community support.

> *Some disputes may not be resolvable through the existing government court system or community-based mechanisms, and so require an ad hoc approach, which may include administrative action, executive attention and political advocacy up to the national level*

Some disputes may be so politically divisive that it is virtually impossible to ensure a fair and equitable resolution within a reasonable timeframe through either the official court system or *jirgas* or *shuras*. This is evident where large power asymmetries exist, including those in which Afghan government authorities themselves hold a strong vested interest in the outcome of a dispute, such as in the Baghlan group displacement dispute. Under these circumstances, the likelihood of reaching a durable solution through provincial-level mechanisms is remote, and thus the team must move to its position of last resort, that of national-level political advocacy. The dispute is then brought to the attention of senior members of the national Afghan government and judiciary, as well as the media and international donors.

> *Community-based agreements are best sustained by some form of official endorsement to guarantee them, especially where rule of law is weak.*

Community-based agreements may only be considered credible where endorsed by provincial authorities, particularly where asymmetries exist between disputants. Official endorsement serves as an incentive for participation, and is also viewed as a guarantee that the authorities are prepared to uphold the agreement. This was evident in Parwan, where some stakeholders only agreed to come to the table if the authorities consented to act as a guarantor of any agreement. Interestingly, the reluctance of one party in the Panjsher dispute to involve the provincial authorities seems to reflect that this may change the power relations between the disputants.

> *Parties may require some form of incentive to participate in a mediated settlement.*

In negotiated settlements, where outcomes cannot be enforced by the state, participants need to see some form of incentive for engaging with the process. This may be something as straightforward as the opportunity for a fair hearing, or it may be something more substantive. In the Parwan dispute, the possibility that a donor could be found to undertake canal repairs was sufficient to draw both disputant parties into negotiation. In Panjsher, the pastureland is officially state land, and so both parties had only common rights of access. They may have perceived a certified access and use agreement as strengthening their respective entitlements in some way, which was seen as a potential outcome of the mediation.

Government stakeholders should be engaged from the outset of any conflict resolution initiative.

Partnering with a range of government stakeholders served to increase local acceptance of the projects and legitimise their activity by association with government. Evidence from USAID's rebuilding agricultural markets programme suggests that where central government support is withdrawn, projects are prone to fail. There is therefore a clear need to engage with government stakeholders from the outset of any conflict resolution initiative, convincing them of the value of the action and the appropriateness of the methods utilised. Government stakeholders should ideally be drawn into the resolution process itself, and their participation should be engaged throughout the process.

Supporting both village-level institutions and local government is important to achieving lasting resolutions to land conflict and better quality land management in general.

Local community and village-level governance institutions are key actors in the management of land rights and the resolution of community conflict. Evidence indicates that with the degradation of the formal state system of land rights and dispute resolution, communities have come to rely increasingly on customary adjudication practices. Several interventions supported by international donors (UNHCR, UNAMA, RLAP and the Afghan conservation corps) have all successfully harnessed the capacity of *jirgas* and *shuras* to mediate disputes.

In addition, local institutions often help to enforce settlements after they are agreed. In recognition of this important role, village-level institutions are being increasingly identified in the draft national land policy and pasture and forestry laws as valued partners in the management of common-property land.

The rural land administration project has shown that village councils are willing and able to contribute to land administration and management, but need government recognition and support to be effective. One way to institutionalise such support may be to work through community development councils, charged with administering donor funds under the national solidarity programme, which together form a body that is equally recognised by the village, the government and the international community.

Another recommendation emerging from the land conflict project is the need for clearly defined roles for land use management and the planning of common property resources that facilitates partnerships with formal and informal land institutions. In principle, it appears that the Ministry of Agriculture, Irrigation and Livestock is open to a community-led approach as a way to establish a land information system for common and privately owned land. With support, it seems likely that other parts of government would also be open to participating in community-based approaches to land management and dispute resolution.

> *Recognition of shared 'rights of use' rather than 'ownership' of common property diminishes scope for conflict.*

The work of regional initiatives such as 'sustainable agricultural livelihoods in eastern Hazarajat' and the rural land administration project on common property draws particular emphasis to the need to address rights of use rather than ownership over common property, such as pastures. Disputes over the ownership of pasture have proven to be intractable and inflammatory in the past, often leading to violence.

Experience indicates that the resolution of community disputes needs to be managed at the community level, which has been shown to be more flexible in its recognition of land entitlements. Both of the above projects supported community-level institutions in successful negotiations of access rights based on traditional entitlements. The rural land administration project succeeded in registering pasture agreements largely because of support from customary *shura* rather than the government's land administration offices.

> *National NGOs can help legitimise and support the implementation of agreements.*

For the rural land administration project, the facilitation of land agreements in partnership with a national NGO proved to be a workable option. Both UNAMA and UNHCR approaches also involve integrated activities with other national NGOs and international agencies.

Particularly where they have strong local credibility within communities, NGOs can help legitimise and support the implementation of agreements in much the same way as local governance structures. Some NGOs are able to bring specific expertise to conflict resolution efforts that may not be available to government or other actors.

Careful criteria applied to the selection of disputes improve chances of a successful resolution.

Experience suggests the importance of applying careful criteria in the selection of disputes so that there can be a reasonable expectation of successful resolution. It has been demonstrated that where disputes are accentuated by ethnic tensions, longstanding animosity between communities or irreconcilable power asymmetries, the likelihood of achieving successful resolution on land issues alone is diminished.

The importance of well-planned timing has also been highlighted by the experiences of the rural land administration project. The activities and interests of rural communities are linked to the seasonal calendar and the local agricultural schedule. Consequently, in certain seasons, stakeholders will have more time to participate and contribute to resolution actions. This is particularly important when land use involves nomadic pastoralists, who may be physically absent from the land during certain times of the year.

Conclusion

The prominence of conflicts over land among the pathologies afflicting rural Afghan society today makes the improvement of mechanisms for establishing land ownership and usage rights, and for more effectively resolving disputes, urgently important. The formal court system and customary mechanisms both have their weaknesses. But empirical research reveals several steps that can be taken to ameliorate the weaknesses of both, largely by putting the formal and customary systems in a complementary relationship with each other.

Establishing security of land tenure would greatly reinforce the perceived legitimacy of the legal order as a whole. The legal order will not be playing its proper role until it can secure the asset on which most rural Afghans' lives depend.

References

Alden Wily, L. (2003). 'Land rights in crisis: Restoring tenure security in Afghanistan', *Issues Paper* series. Kabul: Afghanistan Research and Evaluation Unit

McEwen, A. and Whitty, B. (2006). 'Water management, livestock and the opium economy: Land tenure', *Case-Study* series. Kabul, Afghanistan Research and Evaluation Unit

Ministry of Justice (1977). 'Civil law of the Republic of Afghanistan', *Official Gazette* No. 353. Kabul Ministry of Justice, www.worldlii.org/af/legis/laws/clotroacogn353p1977010513551015a650/ (accessed February 2010)

Norwegian Refugee Council (2006). *A Guide to Property Law in Afghanistan.* Kabul

Roe, A. (2009). 'Water management, livestock and the opium economy: Challenges and opportunities for strengthening licit agricultural livelihoods'. Afghanistan Research and Evaluation Unit, *Synthesis Paper* series

Stanfield, J. D. (2006). 'Reconstruction of land administration in post-conflict conditions', paper given at the Wisconsin Land Information Association annual conference, www.terrainstitute.org/pdf/Reconstruction_of_Land_Administration.pdf (accessed February 2010)

PART V

International interventions

12

Exogenous state-building

*The contradictions of the international project
in Afghanistan*

ASTRI SUHRKE

In the contemporary writing on state-building in post-conflict situations, remarkably little attention is paid to what it takes to build a state. There is much advice on policy priorities and sequencing – security, rule of law, humanitarian assistance, fast pay-out of a peace dividend, demobilisation, elections, and so on – but much less attention to the basic ingredients that are required for the enterprise.

Historical experience and the political science literature suggest four necessary components: coercion, capital, legitimacy and leadership. In Europe, as Charles Tilly (1990) tells us, the modern state developed as local rulers marshalled revenues to pay for armies to fight other rulers; protection and increasingly other services were provided to their subjects to ensure continued flows of resources, and the state became a going concern.

Time is commonly also added in recognition of the fact that most contemporary states are the product of a long historical process of state-*formation*. Yet even these cases typically have some periods of more active state-*building*, when leaders mobilise arms, capital and legitimacy in ways that decisively strengthen the state. Given the internationalised nature of current state-building, arguably the most central, but also the least addressed, question is therefore to what extent the four components of state-building can be effectively provided by international actors, as opposed to being mobilised through an endogenous process. The present chapter explores this question with reference to post-2001 Afghanistan, first by reviewing the features of successful non-European state-building processes, and then by contrasting these with the tension-filled experience in Afghanistan.

The four components of state-building

As one of the most internationalised cases of state-building since the 1990s, Afghanistan is a good place to start, and an article by Barnett R. Rubin (2005) is of particular relevance. Rubin, a close observer of Afghan affairs, discusses the role of coercion, capital and legitimacy in UN-assisted state-building with special reference to Afghanistan after 2001. Overall, Rubin advocates a prominent international role in what he calls 'constructing sovereignty for security'. International peacekeepers can assist in the critical task of managing violence by providing initial security, he notes. Robust mandates are necessary in situations where many well-armed local groups operate, as in Afghanistan. International donors can provide capital for reconstruction and critical state functions. As for legitimacy, international recognition and a UN operation help to legitimate the post-conflict government at the outset. 'Legitimacy begins with that of the international operation . . . International legitimacy of such operations appears to increase domestic legitimacy' (Rubin 2005: 103). Standard UN-supported procedures of constitution-writing and elections will further legitimise the government.

However, Rubin (2005: 100) notes some caveats. The international actors must coordinate their actions, aid should be channelled through the host government so as to permit national decisions about its use, and international economic support should be transitional. This is particularly important for the coercive element of state-building. 'States must eventually develop an economic and fiscal capacity to pay for their security forces.'

Rubin's analysis merits reflection in several respects. First, there is no consideration of the well-known tendency of deeply entrenched support structures to create a self-sustaining momentum towards continuous dependence. In part, it comes down to an incentives problem. In Afghanistan, the post-2001 government was installed by the international community, and has been economically and militarily maintained by the same external powers since. In this situation, what incentives do national leaders have to create state structures that can effectively mobilise local revenues to pay for a national army and other state functions? What incentives do factional leaders have to eliminate the coercive potential of other leaders and create a state with a monopoly of legitimate force? As a recent study prepared for the OECD (NORAD 2009) concluded, regimes in so-called fragile states may find that preservation of their power depends not on strengthening the state, but on maintaining existing patronage structures; the result is to undermine the institutionalisation of state in society. International actors, for their part, can only compel local leaders to take on state-building tasks that conflict with existing sources of revenue if they pay more (thus deepening dependence) or threaten to pay less (and thus risk loss of influence over local developments).

Second, Rubin flags the concept of 'dual legitimacy' – a state or government can be legitimate by virtue of servicing 'nationally determined goals', as distinct from gaining international legitimacy 'as agents of externally defined interests' (2005: 97). In his analysis, the two kinds of legitimacy form a seamless whole, where international operations and UN presence provide both international and domestic legitimacy to a government. Rubin does not acknowledge that the two forms of legitimacy can be deeply contradictory, although this is a well-known historical phenomenon. Recent analysis of intrusive international peace operations emphasises the problem of weak domestic legitimacy of externally imposed structures (Caplan 2002; Chesterman 2004). The history of state-formation in Europe, and later of the anti-colonial struggle, shows that internal legitimacy is typically forged in opposition to 'the other', whether that is a foreign state, a different nation or an external agent. In the case of Afghanistan, the fact that the transitional government was installed by an international military intervention, which favoured the losing side in a long-running civil war, suggested at the outset that dual legitimacy might be a problem rather than a seamless entity.

Third, there is no discussion at all in the article of the fourth component of state-building – national leadership. Strong leaders or distinct national leadership have figured in all the major cases of state-building in modern history, as in Germany and Italy in the late nineteenth century, Japan and Thailand about the same time, and Turkey after World War I. National leaders who seek to strengthen central state structures face an array of opponents, hostility from vested interests, and often a wall of inertia. Moving ahead therefore requires mobilisation of the other components of state-building – revenues, force and legitimacy. National leaders who are installed and heavily dependent on foreign forces and international aid – as were many Afghan leaders after the US intervention removed the Taliban – typically have to walk a tightrope. External support provides leverage for national action, but uncertain legitimacy and heavy dependence on foreign resources beyond their control also limits their capacity to undertake reform.

Its limitations notwithstanding, Rubin's article is of interest for several reasons. As a recognised scholar of Afghan affairs, Rubin has been much cited; he has also been deeply involved in post-2001 policymaking towards Afghanistan on both the UN and the US sides. His views at the time of writing were broadly consonant with the prevailing perspectives on state-building and peace-building in policy and academic circles concerned with these issues. Yet the underlying problems with the analysis have become all the more evident over time. There are many reasons why the internationally supported state-building project in Afghanistan after 2001 has floundered to the point that by 2010 the ambitions were being scaled back. A unifying theme of the process, however, is the extreme internationalisation of the process. A heavy foreign hand has been visibly present in the provision of all the main ingredients – coercion, capital, legitimacy and leadership.

The central argument of this chapter is that the heavy internationali-sation of the state-building process has generated its own contradictions. Four main tensions are discussed below related to control versus own-ership; dependency versus sustainability; effective versus legitimate state; and cross-cutting tensions associated with the rapid build-up of coercive forces (the Afghan police and national army). The greater the interna-tional role, the stronger these internal tensions in the project are likely to be. This casts the current effort to recreate Afghan political life in a very different light from what international and Afghan supporters of the state-building enterprise envisaged in the early years after the regime change in 2001.

Lessons from national state-building projects

The recent emphasis on internationally assisted state-building reversed the dominant assumption of the post-1945 period that 'state-building could *not* be accomplished by external powers, but depended on state sovereignty and political solutions decided by local actors', as David Chandler (2007: 71, italics added) writes. That assumption rested on the antithetical legacy of colonialism and the force of the nationalism it provoked. State-building of a limited kind had occurred in some of the areas colonised by the Western powers, even if mainly to serve colonial purposes of maintaining social order and an extractive economic struc-ture, and some colonial powers left very little when they had to withdraw. At independence in ex-Belgian Congo there were reportedly fewer than a dozen Congolese with secondary education. However, by the end of the twentieth century, after the cold war, the international environment favoured the recasting of assumptions. Northern interests in political stability and an open and globalised economy seemed to require more direct intervention in conflicted areas in the South. The result was a growing number of interventions to create stable and effective states in the South, especially in 'failed states' – recently and more diplomatically renamed 'states in fragile situations' (NORAD 2009) – or in the form of a peace-building operation in a 'post-conflict' situation.

As the growing literature on contemporary state-building shows (Call and Wyeth 2008; Chandler 2006; Chesterman, Ignatieff and Thakur 2005; Paris and Sisk 2009), the task is extraordinarily difficult. In this context, it is useful to consider some of the earlier, endogenously driven non-European state-building efforts that were successful in terms of their stated objective, that is, to reform a relatively weak or fragmented central authority so as to create a stronger and more effective state capable of taking on the functions associated at the time with 'the modern state'. Outside Europe, some of the most successful cases of state-building of this kind, that resonated among the peoples of Asia as well as beyond, were the Meiji Restoration in Japan (1867), the Kemalist 'revolution' in Turkey after World War I, and, another world war later, the revolution in China. Less well known and more modest were the achievements of Abdul Rahman Khan in Afghanistan in the late nineteenth century. As nationally driven state-building projects in what the Europeans, Russians and North Americans at the time considered weak or backward states, or subject to semi-colonial systems of unequal rights, these cases form a counterpoint to contemporary projects of internationally driven state-building in weak states. Leaving aside China, which is particularly complicated and *sui generis*, let us look at these other early cases of state-building. What incentives made the leaders embark on radical change? How did they marshal the necessary coercive force and capital? How did they address the problems of legitimacy – both external and internal?

The Meiji Restoration

The Meiji Restoration marked the transition of weak, isolated feudal Japan into an industrialised, modern state under the slogan of 'strong army, rich country'. The transformation took place under the legitimising banner of the restoration of the young emperor to his rightful place, out from the shadow of the Tokugawa shogunate that had ruled for generations in the emperor's name. The young emperor took the name of Meiji, which means 'enlightened rule'. The main forces of the transformation, however, lay elsewhere. Interpretations that stress internal factors point to the developing stress in the feudalist structures during the first half of the nineteenth century. After a series of civil wars, a period of relative peace had led to increasing trade and production, and an emerging capitalism. Capital had accumulated in the hands of merchants, who nevertheless lacked social standing. '[S]ocial and political power came to be divorced from wealth' (Ike 1963: 160). At the same time, increasingly frequent peasant uprisings created schisms among feudal officials and fear among landlords. From the sea, different threats to the existing order appeared. The Western powers had shown their ambitions and capacity to penetrate China, and were pressuring Japan to open up. In this situation, the most direct threat from the West in the form of Commodore Perry's grey ships was 'more a catalyst than cause' of what became known as the Meiji Restoration (Beasley 1972: 6). In this perspective, Japan was primed for change before Perry made his appearance.

Other interpretations give more weight to incentives for change produced by the shocks and humiliation which the 'sudden, rude intrusion of Commodore Perry' (Gibney 1985: 113) created among the samurai class and led them to seize power. Whatever the precise balance between external and internal forces, the weakness of the Tokugawa shogunate was exposed on all fronts, inviting rebellion. Smaller rulers in the south-west region that traditionally were hostile to the Tokugawa clan led the rebellion, which was financed by some of the wealthy merchant families in the cities. The rebels overthrew the Tokugawa in the name of restoring the emperor to his rightful place, and proceeded to rule as an oligarchy.

The defining features of the radical change that the new rulers introduced was 'modernisation' designed to strengthen Japan in the face of Western imperialism by borrowing technology, tools and ideas from the West. The oligarchy set in motion a rapid-pace and top-down revolution that hastened the demise of feudal, isolated Japan. Abolition of the feudal domains and land tax reform enabled the state to collect revenues for the modernisation projects and increased its independence from the pre-Meiji social structure. A conscript army was raised, which was useful for suppressing unrest and rivals, and involved the people in the national project. Educational reforms were introduced to instil civic virtues and provide technical skills required by the state. There were a range of other reforms familiar from contemporary state-building: the administration was centralised (with prefectures replacing feudal principalities), a unified currency and a modern banking system were established, the internal market was liberalised to facilitate trade, a civil service based largely on a merit system was introduced, and the justice sector was reformed. The reform process sparked demands for political inclusion as well, leading to the rapid introduction of a parliament (1881) and a constitution (1889).

Many of these reforms were inspired by Western systems and practices. Western advisers were invited to Japan, and Japanese students were sent abroad to study. This was in line with the underlying premise of the state-building project that Japan needed to import from the West in order to stand up to the West. But the importing agent, in Bertrand Badie's (2000) term, was the Japanese state and Japanese elites. The indisputably national agency in the reform process created what in contemporary state-building jargon would be called 'local ownership'.

The Meiji state-builders were remarkably successful. The rising power of Japan was demonstrated in the Japanese victory over China in the 1894–95 war, and more dramatically in the victory over Russia in the 1904–05 war, when the rising nation defeated an established and at least semi-Western empire. The impact in the Muslim world, where the onslaught of Russian imperial expansion had been directly felt, was particularly dramatic. 'Egyptian, Turkish and Persian poets wrote odes to the Japanese nation and the emperor' (Esenbel 2004: 1). But it was not only Japan's military might that inspired. The model of state-building by modernisation was keenly followed, and became a reference point for reformers in much of the Muslim world, including constitutionalists in the Middle East and Afghanistan. The leading Afghan reformer in the early nineteenth century, Mahmud Tarzi, the mentor of Afghanistan's modernising King Amanullah, asked the Afghans to look to Japan as well as Persia and the Ottoman empire.

The Ottoman empire and the successor state

Further west, reforms had started somewhat earlier in the Ottoman empire under Sultan Mahmud II in the first half of the nineteenth century, culminating after World War I in the transformation of the rump empire into the modern Turkish state under the leadership of Kemal Ataturk.

The Kemalist state-building venture was preceded by two previous but in many ways similar phases of state-building and reform in what was then the Ottoman empire. In the middle of the nineteenth century, Sultan Abdülmecid introduced sweeping reforms that gave their name to the period (*tanzimat*, or 'reorganisation'). The process officially began in 1839 with the Imperial Rescript of the Rose Chamber declaring Muslim and non-Muslim citizens equal before the law. The evident purpose, as Bernard Lewis (1968: 106) writes, was to 'demonstrate to Europe that the Sultan's government . . . could produce a liberal and modern regime'. The Sultan modernised the army and revenue collection system, built railroads and a telegraph that enabled him to collect taxes and conscript his army more effectively, and introduced changes in the legal and educational system. Tax reforms were introduced. The administrative apparatus of the state was reformed in the spirit of Weberian rationality and specialisation, 'whereby a complete set of ministries and boards on the European pattern was gradually established' (Zurcher 1994: 60). European expertise was enlisted in other areas as well. French advisers were invited to help with educational reforms and a new commercial code, in both cases introducing elements of secularisation. There was nothing mysterious about the reasons for these changes. Foreign powers – Russia, Great Britain and France in particular – were pressing the Sultan to give equal rights and treatment to the Christian minorities living in the empire (mainly Greeks and Armenians), and the Sultan rightly feared that the empire was vulnerable to the kind of colonial economic and political penetration that characterised the period. As in Japan a little later, reforms patterned on Western 'modern' models were introduced to strengthen the state, or in this case empire, so as to ward off Western intrusions. It was not, it should be stressed, a policy of isolation or introspection. The reforms entailed a deliberate and selective importation of Western ideas, but the Sultan and his advisers defined the terms and sent out the invitations.

The second wave of modernisation took place in the early twentieth century. Mostly led by a group of constitutionalists (the Unionists) serving in the cabinet of a much weakened sultan, the reforms were undertaken in the same spirit and followed the same pattern. By now, the Ottoman empire had been reduced to a semi-colonial status. Most crippling was the right of foreign powers to determine tariff policy, establish trading monopolies and administer revenue collection to ensure that the empire's foreign debt was serviced. Foreign wars (especially with Russia) and modernisation had been costly, and when the Sultan in 1875 defaulted on the external debt, the foreign creditors established a debt collection administration (*Caisse de la Dette Publique Ottoman*) where they dominated the board. The *Caisse* created a modern bureaucracy that administered important sources of revenue (such as salt and tobacco monopolies) and collected taxes that it used to pay off foreign creditors. At one point, the *Caisse* had 5,000 employees and controlled roughly a third of the regular state income (Zurcher 1994: 88). In the present age of internationally assisted state-building, it would have been called 'shared sovereignty' (Krasner 2004). In the weakened Ottoman empire at the time, the economic rights of the foreign powers were known, tellingly, as 'the capitulations'; they were the principal impetus for the early twentieth century reforms that sought to modernise and strengthen the state so as to secure for itself a measure of independence.

The reforms covered all major public policy areas. The army was reorganised and strengthened under the leadership of General Enver Pasha with German assistance. Secularisation of the educational and the legal system was accelerated. The Shari'a courts were brought under the jurisdiction of the (secular) Ministry of Justice, and *madrasa* were placed under the Ministry of Education. The provincial administration was reorganised and decentralised. Addressing the underlying economic weaknesses of the state was more difficult. The Unionists liberalised foreign trade and balanced the budget in the hope that it would generate economic surplus and also impress the European powers sufficiently to induce them to modify the system of unequal economic rights. When this did not happen, the government took advantage of the outbreak of World War I to unilaterally renounce 'the capitulations'. It was a late and token victory. Four years later, the Ottoman empire was dismembered by the victorious Entente powers. The rump state was subsequently occupied in parts by the victors or their client, Greece, which led to renewed war (1920–22).

The main task of the nationalists who came to power in the early 1920s was to create a new state out of the ashes. In this respect, the state-building project of the Kemalists differed fundamentally from the reforms of the imperial period. Moreover, the disastrous defeat that topped the gradual weakening of the Ottoman empire now invited a near total rejection of the past that was associated with the Islamic and Ottoman cultures. History was rewritten, secularisation was brought forward, Westernisation was required on a broad scale (from dress to the calendar and Latinisation of the language). In other respects, there were similarities with previous reforms, above all in the recognition that a strong, modern state apparatus, centralised leadership and economic independence were necessary to ensure the existence of the community, now redefined as the Turkish nation.

The transformation undertaken by the Kemalists over the next two decades stands out as one of the most remarkable state-building projects in modern history. The project had five interlocking components, as Necla Tschirgi (2009) writes: first, establishing national sovereignty by renegotiating the punitive Treaty of Sèvres (1920) imposed after the defeat in World War I; second, achieving internal security; third, consolidating political authority; fourth, implementing educational, legal and cultural reforms; and fifth, economic development. As in earlier European state-building processes, the task required coercion, capital, legitimacy and leadership. A strong army succeeded in restoring sovereignty and squashing internal rebels. Strong personal leadership and a one-party state were critical instruments throughout.

Kemal Ataturk established and led a one-party state that brooked no dissent, eliminated political opposition, and imposed draconian punishments on opponents and rebels. Firm party control was established over the state administration (for example, the party provincial leader was appointed provincial governor), and over the range of social, economic and cultural reforms. Capital was required to finance the infrastructure of the new nation-state, above all the ambitious educational expansion and legal reforms, and to erase the Ottoman and quasi-colonial legacies in the economic sector. The state bought out the foreign-owned railroad companies and trading monopolies, and gave the state a significant role in economic development through banking, state enterprises and the like. Determined to avoid foreign borrowing, the Kemalist state secured enough capital through economic *étatism*, a cautious fiscal policy and tax reform to finance the reforms and encourage economic growth, despite the very unhelpful impact of the Great Depression. A strident, state-promoted nationalism gave legitimacy to the transformation. The Kemalist nationalism was a mixture – a total rejection of the Ottoman past was coupled with the reconstruction of a near mythological distant past where the Turkish people and language appeared as the source of all ancient civilisations. As for the West, the Kemalists defied anything that looked like Western controls and *diktat*, but eagerly embraced European models in matters of state and society.

A nationally owned state-building process does not guarantee success. Elsewhere in Asia, Thailand's reforms led by King Rama V in the late nineteenth century succeeded, but similar efforts in neighbouring Burma were overtaken by British colonialism. Afghanistan's own experience includes both successes and failures.

Early Afghan state-builders

The success story is that of Abdul Rahman Khan, who in the late nine-teenth century appears as the country's first serious state-builder. The 'Iron Emir' came to power at a time when Afghanistan was organised in semi-feudal fiefdoms, divided by tribal wars and weakened by foreign invasions. He established a markedly stronger central state framework than any previous ruler, and is credited with creating a nascent modern Afghan state. As elsewhere in Asia, Russian and British imperialism pro-vided the incentives. The Russian empire was pressing down from the North and the British in India were pushing his eastern borders. Abdul Rahman exploited the Anglo-Russian rivalry, but also recognised that he had to strengthen the Afghan state. His skilful political tactics and demon-stration of coercive power at home enabled him to mobilise resources and armed men. By creating a standing Afghan army, modelled after the Anglo-Indian army and paid in cash, the emir was the first Afghan ruler to reduce his dependence on tribal *lashkars*, although he still had to tap tribal resources to raise militias and a cavalry. To finance the expanding state structure, he established small state industries, built infrastructure to promote trade, and introduced tax and currency reforms. Revenue col-lection was a continuous problem, however: 'One quarter of the money, which is rightly mine, I get without trouble; one quarter I get by fight-ing for it; one quarter I do not get at all; and those who ought to pay the fourth quarter do not know into whose hands they should place it' (cited in Gregorian 1969: 142). Limited revenue collection forced him to accept liberal subventions from the arch enemy, the British, who twice had invaded Afghanistan earlier in the nineteenth century.

Importantly, Abdul Rahman invoked Islam not only as a source of legitimacy, but – unlike previous Pasthun rulers whose authority had been conferred by tribal assemblies (*jirga*) – he claimed a divine right to rule and deftly combined this with nationalism against foreign threats:

> As God wished to relieve Afghanistan from foreign aggression and internal disturbances, He honoured this, His humble servant, by placing him in this responsible position, and He caused him to become absorbed in thoughts of the welfare of the nation and inspired him to be devoted to the progress of this people ... for the welfare and true faith of the Holy Prophet Mohammed.
>
> (cited in Gregorian 1969: 129–30)

In terms of early Islamic understanding of the relationship between the ruler and the law, Abdul Rahman's pronouncement harmonised with the idea of the ruler as the upholder of sacred law (Olesen 1995). In this understanding, the ruler is granted the right to issue decrees that are in the public good, provided the laws are not in violation of Islamic principles. The power to interpret these principles and resolve disputes arising from the meaning of the law rests with the *ulema* – the clergy. In this tradition, the *ulema* and the ruler are mutually dependent but also rivals. The state needs the guidance and legitimising force of the *ulema*, but the role of the latter is circumscribed by the power of the state. Recognising the legitimising force of Islam and the *ulema*, Abdul Rahman moved cautiously. While trying to alter the competitive balance in his favour by establishing a centralised, state-controlled Shari'a-based legal system, he did not interfere with the informal justice system represented by the *ulema* and the tribal elders, and encouraged the *ulema* to believe that they, rather than the state, were the ultimate earthly authority of Islamic legal principles. The *ulema* consequently welcomed Abdul Rahman's legal reforms as an affirmation of the Shari'a (Tarzi 2006: 10).

The next great reformer, Amir Amanullah (reigned 1919–29), was inspired by Turkey's Kemal Ataturk in his efforts to strengthen and modernise the Afghan state so as to ward off the pressures from British India. Amanullah adopted the standard programme – secularisation reforms in the educational and legal sector, Westernisation of dress and behaviour codes, reform of the army and the national administration. This state-building process was endogenous and driven by nationalism, key ingredients in successful processes elsewhere, yet failed. Amanullah's nationalist defiance of British imperial demands, and his victory over British forces in the third Anglo-Afghan war, were insufficient to stem the tide of internal opposition to his reformist programme. His reforms alienated a wide range of 'religious, ethnic-tribal, military, administrative and professional notables, who grasped the reforms' objectives and found them threatening to their individual interests in one way or another', Amin Saikal writes (2004: 80). With limited experience and patience, the King failed to build a political coalition to sustain his ambitious programme. Deprived of religious legitimacy when the *ulema* turned against him, the King was dependent on a small army, which he had failed to reorganise and strengthen, and a dwindling coalition of modernists. The British were smarting from the defeat in 1919, and possibly helped deliver the *coup de grace* by aiding eastern tribes that rose in revolt four years later and marked the beginning of the end of Amanullah's brief rule.

What common features can we identify in these early cases of reform? First, the cases constitute state-*building* that is concentrated in time and radical in design. While occurring in a particular historical period that can be more or less favourable to innovation, at the core is a policy process that in theory could be imitated elsewhere. As such, it can contribute to, but is distinct from, a longer historical process of state-*formation*. Second, the state-building cases examined here were nationalist processes, driven endogenously in response to foreign threats or demonstrations of advanced power. This situation provided the principal incentives to change. The state-builders certainly imported foreign ideas and advisers – the importation of change was at the heart of all these state-building ventures – but national agencies and individuals made the selection and set the terms. Foreign intrusions or demonstrations of power provided the incentives to change, and also helped legitimise the state-building project as a whole.

The introduction of radical and concentrated change places strong demands on the project's legitimacy, leadership, coercive power and capital, something all the state-builders experienced. In Japan, the continuity of the legitimising institution of the emperor was important. The Kemalists developed a new nationalism on the back of successfully repelling an international effort to dismember their country. In Afghanistan, the Iron Emir invoked the legitimising power of both nationalism and Islam. The failure of Amanullah was a failure partly of legitimacy, and partly to mobilise sufficient coercive force to compensate for his flagging authority when his enemies mobilised in the name of Islam. Coercive force was in all cases central to the project. As Kemal Ataturk had advised Amanullah (cited in Saikal 2004: 86): 'First, build an army.' Capital was critical as well and mostly raised locally, which helps explain why state-builders typically are desperately short of funds. Finally, all cases demonstrated the importance of effective national leadership.

Afghanistan post-2001

This endogenous process stands in sharp contrast to events in Afghanistan after 2001, which is an extreme case of internationalised state-building. Foreign aid has become the principal source of capital to build the post-Taliban Afghan state and finance its operations. The coercive capacity of the state – the Afghan national army, police and auxiliary armed forces – is totally dependent on foreign training, funding and weapons. Legitimacy claims have shifted from traditional Afghan criteria rooted in Islam to criteria central to Western liberal thought that stress utilitarian functions and a social contract whereby popular support is rendered in return for good governance and provision of basic social services. National leadership has been undermined by extreme dependence on external support. Hamid Karzai was selected by the intervening powers to lead the post-2001 transitional administration, and anointed by the Western coalition as their preferred candidate in the 2004 presidential elections. While the relationship has since deteriorated, the result was the development of a rentier state with uncertain legitimacy, where national leaders had few incentives to undertake major reforms for state-building purposes.

We can now turn to some of the quandaries and contradictions that this internationalisation has created.

Control versus ownership

The first principal contradiction is between ownership and control: 'we' (the international aid community as loosely constituted) want to exercise control over the reconstruction process, yet 'they' (the Afghans generally speaking) want to determine the direction of the process and the distribution of benefits – in a word, they want ownership.

The imperative of foreign control permeates the international engagement in Afghanistan. It is expressed in the creation of a web of consultative mechanisms that oversee the reconstruction agenda, procurement and accountability procedures, and the assignment of technical consultants to the central ministries as well as the sub-national administration. Major donors exercise control over funding and related policy agendas by channelling their assistance through international organisations or national subcontractors rather than through the Afghan government or the multilateral Afghanistan reconstruction trust fund. Foreign donors seek to influence appointments on the sub-national level, including appointment of governors and police chiefs. For example, key donors established a joint process for vetting police appointments in 2006, and were instrumental in the establishment the next year of an independent directorate of local governance that was given responsibility for sub-national administration from the Ministry of Interior.

Likewise, British and Dutch authorities demanded change of provincial governors as a condition for deploying their forces respectively to

Helmand and Uruzgan to fight insurgents. In the military sector, NATO and the US decide on strategy and operations, a not unreasonable practice given that their forces have taken main responsibility for both anti-terrorist operations and more recently counter-insurgency operations. The US has been the principal actor in changing policies and assessments with regard to establishing auxiliary police and militias. The donors also decide on the size and training of the Afghan armed forces and police insofar as they provided the funds and the trainers.

The Afghans, of course, have reacted to the growing international presence in myriad ways, depending on collective and individual fortunes, solidarity ties, experience and normative stance. When disagreements arise, as inevitably happens, the Afghans have a ready and unassailable framework for presenting their demands, that is, 'local ownership'. Local ownership has become a central principle in the international development discourse, and is widely invoked by the aid community in Afghanistan as elsewhere. It is in line with the democratic ideology of a post-colonial era based on the principle of national self-determination, as well as the understanding of the impact of aid, which holds that development must be locally owned in order to be effective and sustainable. Whatever the nature of Afghan demands – whether for participation, influence, benefits or protection – they can legitimately be expressed in terms of one form or other of local ownership, thus sharpening the tension between control and ownership. While coalitions often form across nationality lines, all coalitions have to deal with the potential tension between the principle of local ownership and the reality of foreign concern to exert control. In a symbolic but pointed reminder of the ownership principle, the first major international gathering of donors on Afghanistan was scheduled to be held within the country, in Kabul, in late 2010. The Afghan organiser, ex-Foreign Minister Ashraf Ghani, announced that the working language of the conference would be Pasthto and Dari, with English translators for those who did not command the locally spoken languages.

The control versus ownership contradiction has been expressed in a militant way in the insurgency, and has generated continual tension and friction within the sphere of non-violent political competition as well. Examples are legion, ranging from the early tug of war in 2003–04 between the Ministry of Finance and donors over the channelling of aid funds, to the near-continuous tension over sub-national administration, legal reforms, the role of Shari'a, the electoral process, corruption issues, military strategy and civilian casualties (Suhrke 2007; Suhrke and

Borchgrevink 2009). The level of tension and conflict rose when the initial euphoria that in many parts followed the fall of the Taliban in 2001 was replaced by the messy reality of state- and peace-building, and again when the growing insurgency undermined both processes. The growing recognition that the NATO presence had a limited time horizon, and that some accommodation with the insurgents was probable, further deepened the division between the Afghans and the internationals. The internationals had the option of leaving, while most Afghans do not and had to make the best of the situation. The steadily deteriorating relationship between President Karzai and his major Western backers from 2008 onwards seemed symptomatic of the difficult situation.

Given the enormous stakes that the Afghans have in the attempted transformation of their state and society after 2001, the demands for ownership have been sweeping and persistent. They are promoted openly or through evasion, opposition, manipulation or resistance to the international agenda. The consequent tension with parallel demands for international control has worked like sand in the machinery of the state-building project. By early 2010, major donors, including the US, were expressing doubts about its level of ambition and feasibility.

Dependence versus sustainability

External aid has totally overwhelmed national revenues. By 2009, foreign assistance accounted for some 90 to 95 per cent of the entire state budget and development expenditures, and nearly 70 per cent of all recurrent state expenditures (2007–08). This extreme dependence on foreign aid is unprecedented in Afghan history, including the communist period and the presidential rule of Daoud, which are usually considered periods of extreme foreign dependence. As shown in the table below, domestic revenues, which accounted for just over 60 per cent of the total state budget under Daoud (1973–77) and about half during the first year after the communist coup (1979), had risen to 70 per cent in the middle three years after the Soviet invasion. By comparison, domestic revenues three years after the American intervention accounted for only 31 per cent of the budget. That does not include an additional, fully foreign-financed and controlled 'external budget' that was established in 2004 to channel more funds for development purposes. Nor does it include the budget lines of NATO military commanders for 'force protection' and local development. US commanders alone collectively disposed of around $1.4 billion for this purpose in 2010.

Domestic revenues and national expenditure, Afghanistan, 1973 to 2004–05

Year	Total (m afs)	Domestic revenues (% of total expenditure)	External budget (m afs)	Domestic revenues (% of total budget)
1973	11,318	63	n/a	
1977	24,326	61	n/a	
1979	30,173	52	n/a	
1982	42,112	71	n/a	
2004–05	41,952	31	120,144	8

Note: For 2004–05, converted from $US at rate of 1:48. The additional 'external budget' controlled by the donors was established in 2004.
Source: Rubin 1995; World Bank 2005

External assistance of this magnitude is clearly unsustainable, as the international financial institutions have repeatedly stressed. Consequent efforts to raise national revenues have produced some results. Domestic revenue as a ratio of GDP nearly doubled between 2002–03 and 2006–07, from 3.2 to 7.7 per cent, and enabled Afghanistan to cover the government civilian payroll from its own revenues. Yet the progress was fragile and limited. Revenue collection remained 'substantially lower' than other low-income countries, and increased military expenditures required by the security situation put additional pressure on the budget (World Bank 2009: 6).

The enormous inflow of foreign capital relative to domestic legal resources and structures has turned post-Taliban Afghanistan into a classic rentier state. Rentier states based on natural resources such as oil and diamonds or foreign aid are inherently fragile. Arguably, rentier states based on foreign aid are more fragile than those dependent on natural resources insofar as foreign assistance is shaped by strategic and therefore inherently shifting interests. Recognising this as a recurrent feature of their history, Afghans naturally have sought to maximise aid in the short run, and have extracted pledges at international conferences that exceed the country's absorptive capacity, particularly in relation to project and fiscal management. Donors have responded by channelling money outside the Afghan government through the 'external budget'. When first introduced in 2004–05, the external budget was an estimated three times as large as the state budget; by 2008–09, it had more than doubled in size. It was a 'routing of assistance that...fails to strengthen the role of the state or assure public monitoring and accountability' (World Bank 2009: 2). A vicious cycle was established that undermined local capacity-building required for sustainable state-building.

Dependence versus democratisation

The rentier state also inhibits the development of a democratic polity, a point demonstrated by authors working in different scholarly traditions and with reference to diverse cases (Bates 2001; North 1990; Ross 2001). The main argument is that accountability follows the direction of resource flows. With the national budget mostly financed by foreign governments and institutions, the Afghan government's major responsibility in accounting for the use of these funds was towards the donors rather than its own people. The same observation has been made of earlier Afghan regimes that were heavily dependent on external funding. In his seminal study of Afghan political development, Rubin concludes that Daoud's rentier income from foreign aid and revenue from sales of natural gas had dysfunctional political effects. 'Renewed external revenues relieved Daoud of whatever incentives he might have had to make his government accountable [to the population]' (Rubin 1995: 75).

When starting to rebuild Afghanistan after the Taliban, most donors included democratic reforms. Promoting democracy was also part of the UN mandate. Democratic accountability was expected to contribute to stability, legitimacy and order in the long run. To this end, both the Bonn agreement and the new constitution (2004) provided for a parliament. The parliament elected in 2005 started immediately to flex its muscles. Yet it lacked the principal power of most parliaments – the power of the purse. With foreign aid flows accounting for some 80 to 90 per cent of official expenditures, the donors had a much more important voice than the elected parliamentarians, both in the formulation of policy priorities and in holding the government accountable for its spending. The power of the donors in this respect was underlined by their contract-like provisions with the Afghan government in the compact agreed to at the London conference in 2006. Given these financial structures, the relationship between the Afghan executive branch and the foreign donors became the central element in the state-building process. This might well produce results in regard to improving the reach and effectiveness of the Afghan state, and some progress was indeed recorded (such as in the provision of health and education, and reform of some ministries). It was unlikely, however, to produce the kind of good governance and accountability that is the hoped-for result of democratisation, and by early 2010, the growing concern over maladministration on both the central and sub-national level indicated that it had not.

Effective versus legitimate state

The main justification for the heavy external hand was that international security considerations called for the quick creation of a minimally effective state, at least, from the apparent chaos caused by nearly twenty-five years of internal strife, revolution, invasion and civil war. An effective state that provided a measure of security, justice and basic social services was believed to create its own legitimacy. Afghan reformers joined the Western aid community and the UN in invoking the concept of the 'social contract' familiar from Western liberal thinking. The importance assigned to 'good governance' in explaining the subsequent growing popular disaffection with the government and the growing insurgency reflects a similar thinking.

This logic may well be correct. It is extraordinarily difficult to know what a population affected by decades of internal strife and in the midst of a new internationalised conflict really think, let alone are prepared to express in opinion polls. We do know, however, that Islam and nationalism have been traditional sources of government legitimacy in Afghanistan, and were particularly important to national leaders who tried to strengthen the state or bring about radical reform. Afghan statebuilders and reformers in the past – Abdul Rahman Khan, Daoud, Amanullah – all invoked nationalism to support their policies. Abdul Rahman, as we have seen, prominently invoked Islam and Shari'a as well. Among those that failed, the experience of the Afghan communists is perhaps most significant for the present situation. The People's Democratic Party of Afghanistan that seized power in 1978 and worked with the Soviet Union after the 1979 invasion violated the principles of both nationalism and Islam. The multiple resistance movements to the communists were united at least in one respect – the need to restore to prominence precisely these two principles.

In post-Taliban Afghanistan, Islam was again accorded a central place in the constitution (Afghanistan is an 'Islamic Republic' and 'no law can be contrary to the sacred religion of Islam') as well as in the country's

public and social institutions. Yet the constitution also recognises potentially competing legal principles in its references to the UN Charter and
the Universal Declaration of Human Rights. The uneasy balance between
state and religion that has existed in most of Afghanistan's history since
the early twentieth century surfaced again after the overthrow of the
Taliban regime, and has been sharpened by the presence of numerous
Western agencies with an implicit or explicit modernisation agenda, as
well as a small but articulate group of Afghan reformers. The tension has
played out over issues involving conflicts between Shari'a jurisprudence
and human rights principles, including the contentious Shia personal
status law (Oates 2009), over much-publicised cases of individual transgressions of Islamic law (apostasy and blasphemy), and more generally in
justice sector reforms that require negotiating among multiple sources of
legal traditions. An international review in 2007, led by the noted international legal expert Cherif Bassiouni, commented on the slow progress
and criticised Western legal experts for not engaging sufficiently with
the substantive principles of Islamic law. To be legitimate and effective,
legal reform has to relate to the normative basis of justice in Afghanistan,
that is, Islamic law, the report concluded (Bassiouni and Rothenberg
2007).

In post-Taliban Afghanistan – with a strong Western presence, a government allied to the West, and engaged in a war against other Afghans
who have declared *jihad* to rid the country of the infidel foreign presence – Islam can hardly serve as the principal source of legitimacy for
either the government or the state-building venture. The same applies
to nationalism. A state heavily dependent on international capital and
foreign military forces must develop an alternative legitimising ideology,
and 'good governance' has been moved to the fore as the putative central
source of legitimacy. Unlike Islam and nationalism, however, 'good governance' exerts no force merely by virtue of its ideational existence; it has
to deliver, and hence is a more demanding source of legitimacy.

Building national armed forces

The government's five-year plan for 2006–10, the Afghanistan national
development strategy, is prefaced by a poem by the ninth-century Islamic
scholar Ibn Qutayba. It begins: 'There can be no government without an
army . . . ' The military indeed had critical state-building functions in the
early post-Taliban period, although the troops were international rather
than national. The new Afghan national army (ANA) was built up slowly,

reaching only 22,000 men by mid-2005. In the meantime, both the US-led combat forces and the UN-authorised and NATO-commanded stabilisation force sought to achieve three central objectives of state-building: disarming opponents, deterring rivals, and defeating the militant opposition to the central state.

By early 2010, international forces, now numbering over 100,000 and growing, still took primary responsibility for fighting the insurgents and other militant Islamists. The Afghan security forces were taking a more active role, however, and the training programme was accelerated. In terms of numbers, the expansion of the Afghan armed forces had been extraordinarily fast. The early targets of a force of 70,000 in 2005 had quickly been met. By January 2010, ANA strength stood at 92,000 and the paramilitary police (ANP) at 84,000. The London 2010 international conference on Afghanistan still deemed this insufficient, and settled for a total target of 300,000, with 171,000 in the ANA and 134,000 in the ANP by the end of 2011. American military leaders recommended even higher figures. In his report to the President in August 2009, the US/NATO commander in Afghanistan, Lieutenant-General Stanley McChrystal, had called for a total force level of 400,000 (McChrystal 2009).

The rapid expansion of the armed forces had several implications for the state-building project. First, it drained the budget and increased dependence on foreign aid. The World Bank had already in 2004–05 warned that an Afghan army of 70,000 was not financially viable (World Bank 2005). Subsequent expansions were severely criticised by Bank experts on the same grounds – the armed forces would either bankrupt the country or become a wholly foreign-owned subsidiary (Byrd and Guimbert 2009). Second, to the extent that the armed forces became a strong, professional institution, it would create severe imbalance in relations between the military and civilian authorities. Given the weakness of civilian political institutions, civilian oversight would be difficult. Afghanistan's armed forces have twice staged a coup in recent history, in 1973 and 1978, both times with calamitous consequences. In principle, military leadership could boost the state-building project, as was the case in the classic state-building projects in Japan and Turkey discussed above. These models may have been one reason for the rapid expansion of Afghan armed forces. Yet the result would hardly be a state-building project legitimised by democracy. Third, the near-complete dependence on foreign, mainly US and EU, funds for salaries, training and equipment raises questions about who commands the Afghan armed forces and whose interests it serves. In this situation, the armed forces can serve as a tool of Afghan state-building only when Afghan interests coincide with the interests of the foreign patrons, but not as an instrument of autonomy.

Conclusion

The tensions in the Afghan state-building process are not static. The international community has generally responded to problems and setbacks in the state-building projects by tightening efforts at control and increasing international presence in the form of capital, technical assistance and military forces. These are critical ingredients for state-building, but their external origins give the process an exogenous character that reduces the incentives of the national leaders to undertake change, weakens the legitimacy of the changes attempted, and intensifies the contradictions discussed above. The internationals can provide coercion and capital, but cannot provide national leadership or legitimacy. Weaknesses in both respects have troubled the Afghan venture from the beginning, in large part because of the heavy external footprint.

What are the policy implications of this analysis? There are basically two courses of action. One is to add sufficient foreign capital, expertise and forces to, in effect, overcome the contradictions. The foreign presence would be there for the very long haul and take an overtly direct role in decision-making; in effect, institute 'shared sovereignty'. This course of action has been tried, albeit on a modest scale, for the past eight years of gradually deepening involvement, culminating in the military and civilian surge announced by President Barack Obama in December 2009. The results have not been convincing. A more radical version of the same policy, entailing resources on a scale that might bring the achievement of the intervention's stated objectives within reach, is likely to meet political resistance in the Western countries as well as in Afghanistan.

The logical alternative is to reduce the tensions and contradictions through a reduction in international presence and greater reliance on the Afghan government to provide the four – apparently essential – ingredients of state-building. By early 2010, this seemed to be the way developments were going. This course of action also entails difficulties and conflicts. The idea of 'fixing failed states' is absurdly simplistic even as the title of a book (Ghani and Lockhart 2008). Apart from the problems inherent in any state-building project, the Afghan situation poses problems related to the mounting insurgency, its fragmented society and the deeply complex regional context. Nevertheless, a gradual reduction in the prominent Western presence may give space for national and regional forces to explore compromises and a regional balance of power that will permit the development of a more autonomous and stronger Afghan state.

References

Badie, B. (2000). *The Imported State: The Westernization of the Political Order.* Stanford, CA: Stanford University Press

Bassiouni, C. and Rothenberg, D. (2007). 'An assessment of justice sector and rule of law reform in Afghanistan and the need for a comprehensive plan', paper prepared for the Rome conference, 'The rule of law in Afghanistan', 2–3 July 2007

Bates, R.H. (2001). *Prosperity and Violence: the Political Economy of Development.* New York, WW Norton

Beasley, W.G. (1972). *The Meiji Restoration.* Stanford, California: Stanford University Press

Byrd, W. and Guimbert, S. (2009). *Public Finance, Security, and Development. A Framework and an Application to Afghanistan,* Policy Research Working Paper. Washington DC: World Bank

Call, C. and Wyeth, V. (eds.) (2008). *Building States to Build Peace.* Boulder, CO: Lynne Rienner Publishers

Caplan, R. (2002). *A New Trusteeship? The International Administration of War-Torn Territories.* Oxford University Press for the International Institute for Strategic Studies

Chandler, D. (2006). *Empire in Denial : The Politics of State-building.* London; Ann Arbor, MI: Pluto

Chandler, D. (2007). 'The state-building dilemma: Good governance or democratic government?' in Robinson, A.H. and Robinson, N., *Building States in International Politics.* London: Routledge, pp. 70–88

Chesterman, S. (2004). *You, the People: The United Nations, Transitional Administration, and State-building.* Oxford; New York: Oxford University Press

Chesterman, S., Ignatieff, M. and Thakur, R. (eds.) (2005). *Making States Work: State Failure and the Crisis of Governance.* Tokyo; New York: United Nations University Press

Esenbel, S. (2004). 'Japan's global claim to Asia and the world of Islam: Transnational nationalism and world power, 1900–1945', *American Historical Review,* 109(4)

Ghani, A. and Lockhart, C. (2008). *Fixing Failed States: A Framework For Rebuilding a Fractured World.* Oxford; New York: Oxford University Press

Gibney, F.B. (1985). 'Meiji: A cultural revolution', in Michio, N. and Urrutia, M., *Meiji Ishin: Restoration and Revolution.* Tokyo: The United Nations University

Gregorian, V. (1969). *The Emergence of Modern Afghanistan. Politics of Reform and Modernisation, 1880–1946.* Stanford: Stanford University Press

Ike, N. (1963). *Japan. Major Governments of Asia.* New York: Cornell University Press

Krasner, S.D. (2004). 'Sharing sovereignty: New institutions for collapsed and failing states', *International Security*, 29: 85–120

Lewis, B. (1968). *The Emergence of Modern Turkey.* London: Oxford University Press, 2nd edition

McChrystal, S. (2009). *Commander's Initial Assessment.* Kabul: International Security Assistance Force (ISAF)

NORAD (2009). 'The legitimacy of the state in fragile situations', report for the OECD DAC International Network on Conflict and Fragility, Oslo

North, D.C. (1990). *Institutions, Institutional Change, and Economic Performance.* Cambridge; New York: Cambridge University Press

Oates, L. (2009). *A Closer Look. The Policy and Law-Making Behind the Shiite Personal Status Law.* Kabul: AREU

Olesen, A. (1995). *Islam and Politics in Afghanistan.* Richmond: Curzon

Paris, R. and Sisk, T.D. (2009). *The Dilemmas of State-Building: Confronting the Contradictions of Postwar Peace Operations.* London; New York: Routledge

Ross, M. (2001). 'Does oil hinder democracy?', *World Politics*, 53(3)

Rubin, B.R. (1995). *The Fragmentation of Afghanistan: State Formation and Collapse in the International System.* New Haven, CT: Yale University Press

Rubin, B.R. (2005). 'Constructing sovereignty for security', *Survival*, 47(4)

Saikal, A. (2004). *Modern Afghanistan: A History of Struggle and Survival.* London: IB Tauris

Suhrke, A. (2007). 'Reconstruction as modernisation: The "post-conflict" project in Afghanistan', *Third World Quarterly*, 28(7)

Suhrke, A. and Borchgrevink, K. (2009). 'Negotiating justice sector reform in Afghanistan', *Crime, Law and Social Change*, 51(2)

Tarzi, A. (2006). 'Historical relationship between the state and non-state judicial sector in Afghanistan', Briefing Paper. Washington DC: United States Institute of Peace

Tilly, C. (1990). *Coercion, Capital, and European States, AD 990–1990.* Cambridge, MA: B Blackwell

Tschirgi, N. (2009). 'Constructing the modern Turkish state, 1918–1938: Lessons for contemporary state-building', paper prepared for the Institute for State Effectiveness

World Bank (2005). *Managing Public Finances for Development.* Washington DC

World Bank (2009). *Interim Strategy Note for Islamic Republic of Afghanistan.* Washington DC

Zurcher, E.J. (1994). *Turkey. A Modern History.* London, IB Tauris

13

Grasping the nettle

Facilitating change or more of the same?

BARBARA J. STAPLETON[1]

'Mullah sahib, where are you going?', someone asked Mullah Nasruddin, the stock hero of Afghan folklore, as he trotted past on a donkey. Nasruddin replied: 'I don't know – ask the donkey.'

The London conference and the process of transition

The scale of organised electoral fraud in the 2009 presidential elections substantiated public perceptions within Western countries of Afghan government corruption that had been consistently reported in the international media over recent years. By the time the London conference brought together the Afghan government and its main international backers in January 2010, this image of systemic official corruption, along with deteriorating security, had significantly eroded public support among voters in key donor countries for continued military engagement in Afghanistan.

International political priorities, informed by a mixture of donor exhaustion and the disillusionment of domestic constituents, underpinned the declaration of a much heralded process of transition in the conference communiqué, which presented what appeared to be a clear plan on the part of the Afghan government and international community to overcome the existing security and political impasse.

Despite all the political messaging, the direction set by this plan essentially pointed to more of the same, albeit over a defined and demanding timeframe. The conference outcomes included agreement to the NATO security transition plan, which involves the transfer to Afghan-led security countrywide within five years and a drawdown of international military forces from mid-2011; the reintegration of mid to lower level armed

---

1 This chapter expresses the personal views of the author, and does not represent the views of the EU or the office of its special representative to Afghanistan.

opponents to the Afghan government; a political reconciliation process with the senior leadership of the various insurgent groups; a further increase in Afghan national police and national army numbers (134,000 and 170,000 respectively); and Afghan promises of greater government commitment to tackle corruption.[2]

Changing Afghan and international perceptions regarding the authority and legitimacy of the Afghan government depends, however, on grasping the nettle of meaningful reform, so that the state becomes associated with justice and security rather than the opposite. If not, the London conference outcomes will be subject to a mixture of inaction and manipulation by the powerful actors within and outside the government whose interests are served by instability and the continuation of a war economy. In this regard, the government's commitment to building effective institutions remains very much under question. Grasping the nettle also entails the will, both national and international, to deal with the 'malign actors' who so far have remained supremely capable of sabotaging or outmanoeuvring reforms where they count.

The myth of 'Afghanisation'

The international concept of 'Afghanisation', rather than a renewed and more honest partnership between the Afghan government and the international community aimed at regaining the trust and confidence of the Afghan people, is central to the move into a transitional phase. Among other things, this entails all actors being viewed from the perspective of their actual or potential contribution to the counter-insurgency under the command of US General David Petraeus (at the time of writing under the command of US General Stanley McChrystal). In the London conference communiqué, the former compact between the Afghan government, people and international community was not renewed, though past agreements from the 2001 Bonn agreement were referenced. Instead, it stressed that 'a new phase on the way to full Afghan ownership' had started, while renewing 'mutual commitment' towards helping Afghanistan emerge as 'a secure, prosperous and democratic nation'. The communiqué outcomes further underlined the fundamental paradox between an international strategy that sought to boost responsible Afghan leadership and Afghan

---

2 To date, government action on corruption has been minimal, with continuing questions over the executive powers of the High Office for Oversight. Higgins (2010) indicates the scale of the challenge. Potential Afghan whistleblowers within government do so at risk to their and their families' lives.

power realities that enabled the continuing exploitation of the West's engagement virtually unimpeded. In this regard, 'Afghanisation' can be interpreted somewhat ironically given that the post-Taliban international engagement has been, in effect, Afghanised from the outset. Within a context of a much more extensively resourced effort by the Obama administration to change the nature of the international engagement, the need to bridge the 'justice gap' finally moved up the agenda, driven also by the realisation that complex insurgencies are impelled by injustice (Ledwidge 2009).

The quandaries faced by the international community have in part been arrived at by the relinquishment of international influence over entry points that could have provided the necessary traction for setting the conditions for improving the rule of law, governance and security. This is exemplified by the moribund state of the 'disbandment of illegal armed groups' process and the failure to keep transitional justice – another lost cause – on the agenda. This has seriously reduced if not neutered chances for success in police reform, counter-narcotics and judicial reform – security strategies that were supposed to stabilise the country and enable an international exit strategy. That the possibility of the latter has continued to recede is partly due to the pursuit of policies based on assumptions divorced from Afghan power realities – realities that we either fail to understand or view as too daunting to change.

Afghan official reluctance to address the core issue of transitional justice has been exemplified most recently by the so-called amnesty law, which gives immunity from prosecution for serious violations of human rights, including war crimes and crimes against humanity, committed in the past thirty years. The Afghan Independent Human Rights Commission only discovered in January 2010 that the Ministry of Justice had gazetted this law, officially bringing it into force on 3 December 2008 (Reuters 2010). The May 2009 report by the Ministry of Foreign affairs to the UN Human Rights Council explicitly stated that the bill had not been signed by the President, and had therefore not been implemented.

The Taliban, whose claims to legitimacy are based on fostering perceptions of their claimed moral superiority, exploit most Afghans' lack of any non-violent means to redress wrongs, much less the access to justice in any broader sense. As British barrister Frank Ledwidge, who worked as the first justice adviser to the UK-led provincial reconstruction team in Helmand province, noted:

> One of the flaws of Western counterinsurgency doctrine is a failure to identify the causes for which people fight. First among them, surely, are the

> basics – one's family home and personal possessions. Hence the importance
> of the critical problem of land theft throughout the country... Warlords
> have been engaged in grabbing land often belonging to people who had
> left during the last 30 years.

(Ledwidge 2009)

Ledwidge cites the example of Muktar, a part of Lashkar Gah, where President Karzai had given personal assurances that Afghan refugees in Pakistan would have their land in the district restored to them. However, when the refugees returned to Muktar, they found their properties had been appropriated by local cronies of Helmand's notoriously corrupt governor, Sher Mohammed Akhundzadar, considered a loyal political ally by President Karzai. Unsurprisingly, Muktar is now one of the more pro-Taliban parts of the city. While predators have been empowered, protectors are enfeebled. As Ledwidge says, the rickety but basically functional formal legal system that had existed until the 1970s has collapsed. It now exists mainly on paper, and is chronically corrupt.

The international response to this challenge has been ineffectual. In addition to the very slow outcomes in judicial reform under the Italian lead,[3] the US opposed until 2009 the exploration and adaptation of informal legal structures, perhaps the only viable means of rapidly opening up access to justice. Lessons learned from building bridges between formal and customary systems of justice in post-conflict states in Africa were not applied in Afghanistan. However, more recently, engaging with tribal structures has become of ever greater interest, including in the legal field – the first pilot project in the informal justice sector to provide an alternative to Taliban-delivered dispute resolution is under way in the south-west. But such engagement poses its own risks, not least because of international actors' poor understanding of how tribal structures, and the values they embody, have been distorted during the past thirty years of Afghanistan's turbulent history.

The lack of international comprehension of Afghanistan's complex and multi-layered environment resulted in a tendency (in a context where the international community has been increasingly desperate for a way forward) to grasp at perceived solutions which too often turned into straws. As one anthropologist with decades of experience in Afghanistan

---

3 The five pillars of security sector reform agreed at the 2002 Tokyo meeting of international donors to Afghanistan established Italy as lead country over judicial reform, Germany as lead over police reform, the US as lead over the development of the Afghan army, Japan as lead over demobilisation and reintegration, and the UK as lead over counter-narcotics.

put it to me: 'You can know the rules of the game, but can you play it?' In Helmand, not only is the state system dysfunctional, but the traditional Pashtun system of dispute resolution, *pashtunwali*, based on mediation, honour and consensus, had many of its presumptions shattered by the new political order that surfaced (following the 1973 coup against Zahir Shah and the 1978 Saur revolution), ending the traditional balance of power between the monarchy, khans and *ulema* (see Saikal 2004).

The Soviet Union's destruction of the agrarian economy removed the independent economic basis of the old order while significantly enlarging the rentier state which has been an increasingly central aspect of Afghanistan's economic existence. The rentier state has reached unprecedented heights following the 2001 Bonn agreement. One consequence of this has been to diminish incentives for the Afghan government to create the basis for taxable economic activity by establishing accountability and transparency, providing services and developing public confidence.[4] Instead of working to earn public respect and trust, the Karzai government has relied on the restoration and maintenance of political allegiances that in the eyes of its critics, including many Afghans, amounts to the restoration of the status quo before the Taliban took power, and to colluding in the re-establishment of a war economy based on the control of land and water as well as the trade in narcotics, gems and timber. The ability of the powerful to extract from the enormous sums of development funds intended for the (re)construction of Afghanistan's infrastructure is revealed by the most cursory examination of the kin relationships between the main Afghan contractors at provincial and central levels and prominent political actors and powerbrokers.

Civil-military engagement

The international civilian and military missions in Afghanistan have tended to categorise Afghans as being either pro- or anti-government, as if being on the side of the government meant uniformly being a security asset and being against it meant being a liability. This dualistic picture has obscured the complexity and fluidity (see for example Institute for War and Peace Reporting 2010) of the security environment, and in particular the pivotal role of the criminal 'shadow state', which commands

---

4 See Astri Suhrke's presentation on the rentier state in Wilton Park Conference 1022 2010.

sufficient resources to penetrate and co-opt most state structures.[5] Powerful individuals and groups – who are often directly linked to or part of local state structures, including the judiciary – can with impunity strip from the powerless any assets they choose to take over. The same is true of serious criminal cases, where only those who cannot pay are imprisoned. The development of organised crime has evolved rapidly from 2002 onwards. Law enforcement (including any international presence) may be slow in adjusting to new trends, whereas organised criminal groups can swiftly adjust to changing social, economic and political contexts (Shaw 2006).

The objective of building up a government capable of asserting and expanding its authority over the entire country has been central to the expanding civil-military engagement since 2002. The NATO coalition has pursued this goal mainly through provincial reconstruction teams (PRTs) – small numbers of civilian development officials and diplomats co-located with much larger numbers of soldiers in nearly all of Afghanistan's thirty-four provinces. The military element in PRTs is meant to facilitate the delivery of development aid in conditions that would otherwise be prohibitively dangerous. PRTs were the primary vehicle for NATO's International Security Assistance Force (ISAF) countrywide expansion, completed in 2006, and have continued to function as delivery platforms for international governance-related efforts.

A host of factors have crippled PRTs' contributions to improving justice and human security. First, they were based on the wishful premise that reforms blocked at the central level could be achieved in the provinces. This ignored the fact that Afghanistan has a centralised, non-federalist system in which the president appoints governors and the provinces have no legal way of raising revenue. Where PRTs did attempt to effect progressive change at the provincial level that might threaten the status quo, they have at times been circumvented by the central government (Stapleton 2007).

Second, the PRTs' concept assumed that the provincial powerbrokers would support law and order, and only lacked the technical skill to achieve it by themselves. On the contrary, those who maintained power under conditions of impunity understandably perceived steps towards establishing law and order as a threat. The means to offset the ability of former and new powerbrokers to re-establish their networks was drastically limited by the shift of the US's focus towards Iraq, resulting in the movement

5 UNODC's 2009 estimate of drug-trafficking profits in Afghanistan amounts to $1.9 billion, of which only $1.25 million went to the insurgents, with the bulk of profits going elsewhere.

of key air assets out of the country by mid-2002. It was decided not to expand the UN-mandated international peacekeeping forces throughout Afghanistan by the autumn of 2002, and to launch the de facto compromise that the PRTs plan represented instead. This resulted in a widening security gap that could not be filled by the embryonic Afghan security forces.[6] By 2006, when NATO/ISAF's command had been finally established throughout Afghanistan through a handful of regional bases and smaller PRTs in nearly every province, the vicious circle, involving armed opposition groups, between criminal networks and official elements within the security and governing administrations at all levels had developed to the point that there was little international appetite for challenging them.

Confronting and defeating these vested interests would have required a coherent international strategy involving several steps that were never seriously attempted, perhaps due to fears that the boat would be too profoundly rocked. Necessary steps included the implementation (backed up by international force if necessary) of disarmament, demobilisation and reintegration programmes; substantial political reforms of the (still) heavily factionalised Ministry of Interior; a focus on quality of training rather than merely accelerating an increase in police numbers; and the formation of an ethnically representative army, not one in which one ethnic group dominated the officer class to the point where the existence of a national army or police could be brought into question. The provision of justice needed to be closely linked to police, prison and judicial reform efforts – as it had been before the Afghanistan compact and the Afghan national development strategy moved it out of the security sector reform process. Increasing access to justice should have been made a priority from the outset, and justice in the widest sense, including transitional justice, should have been viewed as fundamental to the stabilisation process.

In Afghanistan, elaborate plans usually drafted by foreigners have often substituted for necessary actions, and nowhere was this more apparent than in seemingly endless reformulations aimed at improving governance and the implementation of the Afghan national development strategy. A prominent feature of these plans was the fiction that reform efforts were being led by Afghans. As with the parallel universe of official reports in the Soviet Union, the claims of Afghan leadership reflected political and

6 The compromise made instead was the announcement by US-led coalition representatives of the PRT plan in Kabul in November 2002.

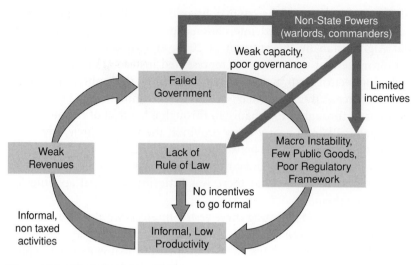

Figure 13.1　The informal equilibrium

ideological imperatives, not reality.[7] Even where mentoring and training succeeded in building capacity at central and local levels, placing trained individuals back into dysfunctional and often highly corrupt systems tended to defeat the object of the exercise.

Figures 13.1 and 13.2 illustrate the vicious circles that have continually frustrated international and national attempts to improve governance.

Vicious circles

Having an Afghan wield authority is often presented as *ipso facto* progress. But the politically unpalatable truth is that until the vicious circle illustrated above is addressed, even the best Afghan official will be unable to deliver real improvements in governance and the rule of law. The failure to implement thorough reforms to the factionalised Ministry of Interior even under minister Hanif Atmar, widely seen by the international community in Kabul as one of the most capable Afghan officials, is a case in point, and illustrates that a far more incisive policy, with strong political backing from the government and its international supporters, was required. The EU office in Kabul long argued – to no discernible effect – that the full implementation of the disbandment of illegal armed

7 On parallels between the post-2001 US-led state-building efforts in Afghanistan and those of the Soviet period of engagement during the Cold War, see Karlinovsky 2010.

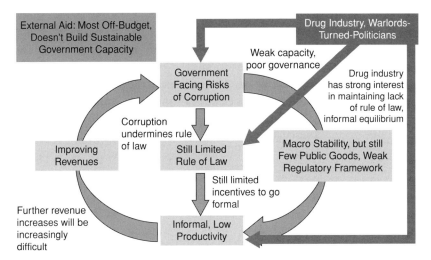

Figure 13.2   The evolving informal equilibrium. Source: Byrd, William (2007). 'Responding to Afghanistan's development challenge (an assessment of experience during 2002–2007 and issues and priorities for the future)'. World Bank South Asia Region PREM Working Paper Series, No. SASPR-11, October 2007.

groups (DIAG) and its predecessor (disarmament, demobilisation and reintegration) programme were a fundamental precondition for police reform, an effective counter-narcotics strategy and the establishment of the rule of law. International and national engagement in DIAG has, with the exception of continuous funding support from Japan, been anaemic.

Only when illegally armed groups were identified as a key component in the 2009 electoral vetting process was focused international action – for example, ISAF's and the UN Assistance Mission in Afghanistan's (UNAMA) verification and updating of the illegal armed group and commanders list – forthcoming, though late in the day. The marked ambivalence demonstrated by ISAF, and to a lesser extent UNAMA, towards DIAG[8] derives from their respective mandates to support the

---

8 The weak engagement of ISAF and UNAMA in the prosecution of DIAG objectives has been diluted further with the transfer of the DIAG unit to the full management of the Ministry of Interior and the disarmament and reintegration commission. By early 2010, DIAG was assessed by security sector analysts to be largely ineffective, especially in the absence of any real interest from the Afghan side actively to target the Afghan powerbrokers with which the government (and to some extent ISAF for tactical purposes) is aligned. The ramifications for the 2010 parliamentary elections – due to the relevance of linkages to illegal armed groups to the vetting process and the fact that security experts estimate that a majority of parliamentarians have links to, or command, illegal armed groups – are serious.

Afghan government of the day rather than government institutions per se.

The threat of the strengthening insurgency also fed into a general unwillingness to take actions that could be potentially destabilising to the fragile status quo. Despite doctrinal definition of counter-insurgency as a long-term process, the importance of long-term state-building and security processes – such as the development of a reliable civilian police force – has been trumped by short-term security requirements in the form of prioritising the boosting of paramilitary police numbers or creating yet more armed militias. Like governance and economic development, the civil-military dimension has moved to the centre of a counter-insurgency strategy that in the immediate term dominates everything else.

Past civil-military initiatives

It is therefore of interest to outline the past civil-military initiatives that predated the most ambitious plan to date: the US government's integrated civilian-military campaign plan.

Provincial stabilisation strategy/regional development zones

One of the earliest civil-military attempts to square the security circle was announced by UN and coalition representatives at a meeting with UN and NGO representatives in Kandahar in 2004 that had been called in the wake of a series of major security incidents targeting UNHCR and UNAMA. The objective of the new plan, termed the provincial stabilisation strategy (PSS), was to provide urgently needed reconstruction in the form of roads and water to dangerous areas that had become inaccessible to UN agencies and NGOs. With their ability to call in coalition airpower, the PRTs were at the core of a security package tailored to facilitate leadership by properly trained Afghan police (as opposed to the militia forces labelled as police in Kandahar), augmented by local authorities loyal to the central government. The inclusion for the first time of good governance indicated growing international concern in this regard. The plan was tested in two areas of Kandahar province with a view to implementation in other areas of the south where the government was already losing control. One year later, there was little to show for the plan. The root causes of failure were identified to this author by a USAID representative who had been directly involved as 'an inability to include a viable security plan or to commit sufficient resources of the right kind fast enough'. Nevertheless, in Kabul, the plan, relabelled 'regional development zones', was widely referred to in military briefings given by the coalition commander, General Barno, and informed policy discussions for many months after the concept had ceased to have any relevance on the ground.

Afghan development zones

Similar ingredients to the PSS were incorporated in 2006 in Afghan development zones (ADZs) that were to be set up around provincial capitals in the south. In theory, as development and governance blossomed within them, these zones would expand like inkblots and gradually join up. ISAF hoped and expected that in the process of establishing such zones, civilian development actors would join in the endeavour. Once more the military failed to understand that it was the Afghan communities themselves who determined whether or not locally recruited NGO staff could continue to work with them. Given the control the insurgent groups had established in large areas of the south and southeast by 2006, experienced NGOs would head away from rather than towards the nearest ADZ, precisely because it would endanger their locally recruited staff to be visibly associated with such an enterprise. A key difference from the earlier PSS approach was that the ADZs followed in the wake of major military operations to clear insurgents from targeted areas. However, the inability of the Afghan security forces and particularly the police to hold the cleared ground meant military gains were transient. A year later, the zones had made no significant headway, and were thus rarely referred to.

The Uruzgan approach

The Uruzgan approach, developed by the Dutch with Australian involvement from 2006 onwards, provides an example of a civil-military intervention that has been under a civilian lead throughout, supported by Afghanistan experts of long standing with the requisite language skills and detailed knowledge of existing tribal and sub-tribal structures. This expertise, built up in some instances over decades, resulted in an engagement predicated more on Afghan than foreign terms. The approach taken by the Dutch in Tirin Kot, the provincial capital of Uruzgan, is an example of civil-military best practice that, uniquely in the south-west, succeeded in increasing the number of international and national development partners working in parts of Uruzgan – from thirteen in 2006 to fifty-four in 2009. By way of contrast, in Helmand and Kandahar, the number of development partners (outside of contractors) declined sharply during this period. Key results included the Dutch military deploying at the request of local populations to clear outside insurgent groups that had penetrated their area (the population tolerate the locally derived insurgent groups). Though Uruzgan province (homeland to Mullah Omar and other insurgent leaders, and one of the most economically backward areas of Afghanistan) is largely under insurgent control, the situation has not deteriorated since 2006 to the same extent as in many other provinces. However, the Dutch have been criticised for not taking the fight to the Taliban.

According to Dutch sources at the Netherlands embassy, interviewed by this author, the Uruzgan approach aims to facilitate local stability rather than trying to create it by imposing solutions. This means attempting to understand what is actually creating instability, and employing the resources to address the causes. Development agencies were not required to associate themselves with the PRT or the military, and were not integrated into a counter-insurgency strategy. Nor has the local population been forced to engage with PRTs or the international community. Outside standard civil-military cooperation activities, development funds were under the control of the embassy, not the PRT. This was done specifically to protect development agencies from the perception of any direct association with the PRT in Tirin Kot. According to the Dutch sources, development partners have said they will depart should the Netherlands hand over to the US in 2010 – their expectation is that such nuanced approaches would not be maintained under US oversight. Though aspects of the Dutch approach – notably its preparedness to miss Taliban targets in order to minimise civilian casualties – exemplify the people-centric style of counter-insurgency advocated by the ISAF and US forces commander General McChrystal, the Uruzgan approach requires a heavy investment of time and expertise. Even experienced Afghan analysts of tribal structures can take a long time to identify who the key tribal leaders really are. Unfortunately, neither time nor expertise would appear, at the time of writing, to be available. Instead, powerful political imperatives linked to the US electoral timetable have cast 2010 as a defining year for reversing security trends in Afghanistan.

Despite indications of some limited success,[9] the Dutch, in common with the British in Helmand province and the Canadians in Kandahar

9 For example, though the voter turnout was low in Uruzgan province, unlike in other parts of the south-west, virtually all planned polling stations for the 2009 presidential elections opened.

province, have not been able to deal decisively with 'malign actors' often linked to the Afghan government at the highest levels. These de facto power-holders are deeply involved in the cultivation and control of the trade in narcotics and other aspects of the black economy (including gems and timber), with allegedly close links to militia groups often constituted as Afghan private security companies used by ISAF and development contractors for day-to-day security. This phenomenon, which has been noted in many other parts of the country, includes the provision of security for guarding forward operating bases and PRT outer perimeters to enable ISAF to resupply via roads controlled or vulnerable to attack by armed opposition groups.[10]

Little is what it appears to be. This was brought home to me during a 2010 visit to Tirin Kot, when an Australian officer in the PRT told me that the Uruzgan chief of police is an enthusiastic supporter of the US-led paramilitary police training programme. This is hardly surprising given the rivalry between the police chief and the local militia commander, Matiullah, over the control of local narcotics routes. Perhaps the fact that there was so little to choose between a militia-dominated police force and the main local illegal armed group had partly informed the PRT decision to accommodate rather than challenge Matiullah, whose forces provided the security for the resupply of ISAF forces in Uruzgan at the time of visiting.

The US government's integrated civilian-military campaign plan

The integrated civilian-military campaign plan was completed in August 2009. It is hugely ambitious in scope and objectives. It aims to achieve eleven counter-insurgency 'transformative effects', starting with population security, and including expansion of accountable and transparent governance, access to justice, and countering the nexus of criminality, corruption, narcotics and insurgency.

Unfortunately, the attainment of these objectives is not rooted in recognisable Afghan realities, such as the extant limited capacity for absorption, the risk of further fuelling corruption via the vicious circles existing

---

10 The growing nexus between armed opposition groups and criminal groups was the subject of a paper presented by the author in November 2007 (Liechtenstein Institute on Self-Determination 2008).

between contractors (international as well as national), local administrations and line ministries, the US government's prioritisation of the 'burn rate', which requires massive amounts of money to be spent in a very short period of time (although that is not expected to continue), and the absence of independent oversight due to the level of security constraints affecting the implementation of projects and programmes in the districts deemed a priority under the counter-insurgency strategy where resources are being focused. All these factors dictate outcomes that analysts fear will prove to be counterproductive (see Wilton Park Conference 1022 2010). Given Afghan perceptions that the international engagement is drawing to a close, the 'grab what you can while you can' mentality is expected to reach new heights.

An extensive civilian command and control structure has been set up to circumvent the longstanding problems with the attenuated chain of military command between ISAF HQ and PRTs at the periphery. However, the most obvious constraint is that this regional integrated plan is to be pushed down the chain of command in coordination with the appropriate Afghan authorities. At local levels in much of the south, these authorities tend, if they exist at all,[11] to be part of the problem rather than the solution. Serious doubt must surround fast-track solutions of this level of ambition in the Afghan context, particularly as the American civilians who form the civilian surge (recruited from 2009 to implement and oversee this plan) have no experience whatsoever of the complex Afghan operating environment. They are unlikely to prove any match for Afghans long experienced in extracting the maximum personal advantage from such cash-rich plans. Moreover, there is growing and well-founded concern that despite pledges to the contrary, the surge and the imperative for quick results emanating from the capitals of lead donors will result in yet more parallel structures being established. Attempts to accelerate the development of Afghan administrative capacity through mentoring and training may also result in another cycle of failure.

Conclusion: no foundation to build on?

The breakdown of the old order and the revolutionary war troubles turned the country into an arena of new political actors, war profiteers, mafia

---

11 The weakness of administrative structures at the sub-national level in some areas of the country was summed up by one US embassy official to the author as: 'There's no "there" there.'

networks, terrorist organisations, parties manipulated from abroad and agents of all kinds of countries . . . with few institutions that bound together the conflictive forces.

(Dr Bernt Glatzer, 2008, cited in Doering 2008)

The counter-insurgency strategy under General McChrystal, which plans to target forty-nine districts in 2010 and a further forty in 2011, was launched in Marjah, located in the centre of the opium-growing Helmand valley, in mid-February 2010. It has been massively resourced in comparison to the earlier civil-military approaches outlined above. Marjah, unlike Kandahar, is not of critical strategic importance, making it possible for ISAF to test the civil-military approaches at the heart of its counter-insurgency strategy.

According to sources in ISAF HQ, initial reports on lessons learned identified the critical role of the better trained Afghan national civil order police (ANCOP) in building local acceptance of a government presence following the operational stage. The problem is that the total number of ANCOP is small (currently around 10,000) and the necessary training takes time. Subsequent reports have, however, linked ANCOP forces to abuse of power including stealing from locals and their alleged involvement in the disappearance of opium stashes that had been located following kinetic operations in the area. Plans to use locally trained police under officers from outside the locality are in the offing, but it remains to be seen whether this shortcut works. Meanwhile, the local people have emphasised that the return of the local police (viewed as predatory and corrupt) is unacceptable (see Miller, Hosenball and Moreau 2010). With serious questions over the availability of acceptable Afghan national security resources (especially police) in consolidating the gains, limited capacity may also affect chances of success for the Afghan government's delivery of (re)construction and services. For ISAF, government service delivery is considered (along with the ability of the ANSF to maintain the 'hold') the most crucial part of the overall objective: the emergence of a legitimate state, enabling the withdrawal of its forces and the handover of security to the government in the near future.

This counter-insurgency effort is intended to generate popular support for the Afghan government. Notwithstanding the pivotal regional dimension to the Afghan insurgency, domestic factors are widely recognised to have powered the insurgency. This has finally brought the role of governance and the rule of law to the centre of what may well be a final attempt by the coalition to reverse negative trends.

When governance is defined as the extension of an administrative presence capable of delivering basic services and justice, but may in practice
amount merely to bringing a district governor to a district hitherto lacking one, the risk is that there will be no impact. What counts is whether
the Afghan experience of that district judge is one of neutral redress and
fairness rather than the usual experience of corrupt practice. The additional injection of massive amounts of funding for stabilisation over the
short term merely adds to the growing sense of the construction of an
end game against all the odds.

The challenges are clearly immense and, to a greater extent than before,
the future of the political process engendered by the Bonn agreement is
in Afghan hands. In American football, when nearly all is lost and time
is running out, the losing side will often throw a 'Hail Mary pass', hurling
the ball as far downfield as possible in the hope that some teammate will
catch it. At the time of writing (2010), the analogy to the international
engagement in Afghanistan as it enters its ninth, possibly decisive, year is
unsettling.

References

Doering, Martina (2008). Interview with Bernt Glatzer, *Berliner Zeitung*, 12 April
2008, translated by Thomas Ruttig as 'How do Afghans tick?', Afghan Analysts
Network, 16 December 2009, http://aan-afghanistan.com/index.asp?id=506
(accessed 20 April 2010)

Higgins, Andrew (2010). 'In Afghanistan, signs of crony capitalism', *Washington
Post*, 22 February 2010

Institute for War and Peace Reporting (2010). 'Taleban buying guns from former warlords', 22 March 2010, www.iwpr.net/report-news/taleban-buying-
guns-former-warlords (accessed 20 April 2010)

Karlinovsky, A. (2010). *The Blind Leading the Blind*, Cold War International History
Project, Working Paper No. 60, January 2010

Ledwidge, Frank (2009). 'Justice and counterinsurgency in Afghanistan: A missing
link', *RUSI Journal*, 154(1), February 2009

Liechtenstein Institute on Self-Determination (2008). 'State, security and economy in Afghanistan: Current challenges, possible solutions', conference,
Brussels, 16–18 November 2007, www.princeton.edu/lisd/projects/afghan_
region/afghan_region_conf_02.html (accessed 20 April 2010)

Miller, T. Christian, Hosenball, M, and Moreau, Ron (2010). 'The gang that couldn't
shoot straight', *Newsweek*, 29 March 2010

Saikal, Amin (2004). *Modern Afghanistan A History of Struggle and Survival*. London: IB Tauris

Shaw, Mark (2006). 'Drug trafficking and the development of organised crime in post-Taliban Afghanistan' in UNODC, *Afghanistan's Drug Industry: Structure, Functioning, Dynamics and Implications For Counternarcotics Policy*, edited by Doris Buddenberg and William A. Byrd, *UN Office on Drugs and Crime and The World Bank, November 2006*

Stapleton, B.J. (2007). 'A means to what end? Why provincial reconstruction teams are peripheral to the bigger political challenges in Afghanistan', *Journal of Military and Strategic Studies*, 10(1), Fall 2007

Wilton Park Conference 1022 (2010). 'Winning "hearts and minds" in Afghanistan: assessing the effectiveness of development aid in COIN [counterinsurgency] operations', conference report, 11–14 March 2010, www.wiltonpark.org.uk/documents/conferences/WP1022/pdfs/WP1022.pdf (accessed 20 April 2010)

14

Lost in translation

Legal transplants without consensus-based adaptation

MICHAEL E. HARTMANN AND AGNIESZKA
KLONOWIECKA-MILART

Since 2004, Afghan law has been extensively revised and amended, with heavy input from foreign jurists, including whole laws being drafted by foreigners and adopted by Afghanistan. Belatedly, the government of Afghanistan and its international partners have developed a sound mechanism for facilitating Afghan-international consultation and consensus, but most new laws are still not subjected to this process, and do not reflect Afghanistan's cultural, political and legal traditions and conditions.

Based on this experience, this chapter argues that:

- foreigners cannot properly draft and revise Afghan laws by themselves, and thus even if Afghan authorities ask the foreigners to do so, any such exercise is doomed to fail;
- however, foreigners can, in partnership with Afghan authorities and experts, contribute to the creation of good law, provided the procedures for drafting and review are viable and transparent, allow full representation of different expert groups, and are adhered to consistently;
- only such a technical and quasi-political law reform process, which engenders consensus, may result in laws that that will be considered legitimate, and thus internalised and applied by Afghans.

Introduction

Most experts agree that the criminal justice codes and laws are now a melange of conflicting and confusing provisions, contained in various legislative pieces of disparate provenance. Conflict and confusion arise from two overlays, one horizontal and the other vertical. Horizontal conflict results from contemporaneously drafted laws whose individual ambit appears clear and non-derogative but whose provisions, when viewed systemically, actually impinge on other laws because of drafting errors. When laws are drafted hurriedly and in pursuit of a narrow agenda, the existing legal context is often disregarded. This disregard creates lacunae, overlaps or, at best, ambiguity about how the newer law relates to those already in force.

Vertical overlays are the result of presidential decrees and parliamentary bills that are meant to regulate the same area that is already subject to existing laws. Foreign development projects use political leverage to push for fast-track legislation in the form of a presidential decree, which, under the law, must then be reviewed by the parliament and either replaced with a statute or rejected. After a complex and non-transparent process of review, the draft statute finds its way back to the presidency for approval. Thus the same area, in relatively short chronological sequence, is subjected to three different regimes: the old statute, the presidential decree and the new law. Clearly, such rapid change undermines legal certainty in that situations that should be clear and straightforward become opaque and tortuous.

The ambiguity of the formal legal framework makes it difficult for Afghan attorneys, prosecutors and judges to learn, interpret and apply. Ordinary citizens – the intended addressees of proscriptions, authorisations and protections offered by the new legislation – may not be able to access and comprehend the state law at all, especially given the dearth of attorneys and their being prohibitively expensive for the poor majority. When this ambiguity is added to the challenges already posed by customary law, state-made law stands even less of a chance to become the basis of an effective regulatory system. The pervasive ambiguities also create abundant opportunities for prosecutorial and judicial discretion that may be guided by corrupt or political purposes, as well as opportunities for intervention by the Supreme Court, which has never hesitated to claim the authority based on Shari'a to make law through their judgments on appeals of individual cases.

For all these reasons, the hectic pace of remaking Afghanistan's law may have been counterproductive to the broader goal of fostering the rule of law. Instead of constructing an edifice that allows Afghans to plan their lives with confidence in how the state or other powers may impinge on their prerogatives, the bewildering speed and lack of coordination of the reform process have only bred resentment of the law, and created incentives and opportunities to operate in a large grey area, if not entirely outside it. Providers of aid in the justice sector themselves struggle to determine the status quo in any sphere of the law, which greatly complicates development of their strategies. Indeed, bearing in mind the Hippocratic injunction to 'first do no harm', one must consider whether the benefits of law reform efforts outweigh their disruptive effect on a system whose effectiveness depends on transparency and predictability.

This chapter will first outline the recent history of the criminal justice laws in Afghanistan from the overthrow of the Taliban regime in late 2001 to early 2010. Second, it will discuss flawed processes and problematic results of several specific cases of lawmaking or remaking. Drawing on these object lessons, it will propose several substantive and procedural changes.

This chapter is based on the authors' experience in Afghanistan working for the UN and for UN and US rule of law and criminal justice projects from 2005 to 2010.[1] The facts discussed are drawn from direct participation in the processes concerned, as well as discussions with former and current Afghan justice officials and jurists, some of whom desire confidentiality. The authors' experience and expertise concern the technical aspect of law reform, and they are viewing the subject through this narrow lens; but they argue that, as long as the formal legal system is considered crucial for the rule of law, law reform should be done in such a way as to ensure that the law is accessible, understandable, and resonant with the realities of the society they are meant to regulate.

The legal background of criminal law reform

Notwithstanding a common belief among foreigners that Afghan law has long been based on Shari'a, the formal justice system and its laws and codes from the 1960s and afterwards were not Shari'a but codified *taziri* laws that draw on Shari'a precepts,[2] which judges are expected to apply as state-made laws, similar to those in Muslim civil law jurisdictions such as Egypt.[3] In terms of criminal procedure, it was inquisitorial and civil law,

---

1 The views expressed here are the authors' own and do not necessarily reflect those of the United Nations Office on Drugs and Crime (UNODC) or the US State/INL's JSSP-Afghanistan programme.

2 See, for example, article 1 to the 1976 penal code: 'The law regulates only the *taziri* crime and penalties. Those committing crimes of *hudood* [fixed punishments], *qessass* [retaliation] and *diat* [compensation to victim's family] shall be punished in accordance with the provisions of Islamic religious law (the *Hanafi* religious jurisprudence).' Thus, for example, neither blasphemy nor the *hadd* (*hadood*) crimes of false accusations against chastity are in the penal code, and while *zina* (adultery) and theft are in the code, they are punished with only imprisonment and fines rather than Shari'a punishment.

3 Both the 1976 penal code and 1965 criminal procedure code, before it was amended in 1974, were closely based on the Egyptian codes, according to members of the Ministry

but there were clearly shared elements with the adversarial system such as where three professional judges presided over trials with submissions by the prosecutor and defence attorney. However, an investigating prosecutor, rather than an investigating judge, conducted the formal inquisition or investigation that provided the dossier of statements to be considered at trial with oral evidence. Other civil law systems, including those of Germany and Egypt, have the same arrangement.

The Taliban regime ignored the criminal procedure code, including eliminating the function of public prosecution (the Office of the Attorney General, or *Saranwali*), and to great degree ignored many provisions of the penal code. When the nascent Afghan government reformed after 2002, with its new constitution of early 2004, these laws and institutions from the 1970s to the 1990s returned. Those of the resurfacing and newly minted prosecutors, defence attorneys and judges who had attended a law faculty had been trained in those laws and codes, and were familiar with their overall structure and philosophy, if not substance.

The criminal procedure code of 1965 (as amended in 1974[4]) was applied in conjunction with the law on discovery and investigation of crime of 1978 (7 Sawr 1358), the law on the structure and authority of the Office of the Attorney General of 1991 (*Official Gazette* No. 738 of April 1991) and the law on organisation and jurisdiction of the courts of 1991.[5] The 1976 penal code was amended by and applied in conjunction with the law on crimes against internal and external security from 1987.[6]

In January 2004, the new constitution took effect, and was characterised by its framers as a meld of the best of international standards as applied to an Islamic republic. This constitution provides a framework for criminal justice that is consistent with internationally embraced principles. In the process of drafting and compromise, however, areas of ambiguity were left in order to gain consensus among conservative Muslims and those who wanted to adopt international human rights standards and norms. Yet by 2010 there was not even a consensus among Afghan leaders that

of Justice legislative department (*Taqnin*) in discussions with the authors, the last being 7 April 2010.

4 The code was enacted and effective in 1965 (5 Jawza 1344), with articles 1–144 on discovery and investigation of crimes amended in 1974 (15 Hamal 1353).

5 *Official Gazette* no. 739, 11 Hamal 1370 (1991), which has been superseded by the post-2001 law with the same title at 31 Sawar 1384, *Official Gazette* no. 851, 21 May 2005.

6 Approved by the Revolutionary Council of the Democratic Republic of Afghanistan by decree 153 dated October 1987.

it was the Supreme Court, rather than parliament, that had the right to interpret the constitution.[7]

The constitution establishes an Islamic republic, proscribing at article 3 that 'no law shall contravene the tenets and provisions of the holy religion of Islam in Afghanistan'. It then requires (at article 7) that the newly formed Islamic 'state shall observe the United Nations Charter, inter-state agreements, as well as international treaties to which Afghanistan has joined, and the Universal Declaration of Human Rights'. From the law reform, rule of law, criminal justice and human rights perspective, the most important treaties to which Afghanistan is a party and which provide specific enforceable standards and norms include the International Covenant on Civil and Political Rights, the Convention against Torture, the UN Transnational Organised Crime Convention, the UN Convention against Corruption,[8] the Convention on the Elimination of All Forms of Discrimination Against Women (CEDAW) and several narcotics trafficking conventions. The constitution also includes concrete provisions on human rights protections, some of them (for example, articles 24–32, 37–38 and 40) specific for criminal law and procedure, which meet international standards and norms.

The constitution sets up an independent judiciary (articles 117–133), headed by a supreme court. The constitution goes on to declare that the Attorney General's Office will be part of the executive but shall be 'independent in its function', which includes not just prosecution but also 'investigation' of crimes, while the police mandate is limited to 'discovery' or 'detection' of crimes. This strict division of responsibilities between police detection of crimes and prosecution investigation originated in the 1964 and 1976 constitutions,[9] and was adopted in 2004 to

7 Leaders in the parliament in particular have argued that article 121, by not being explicit on the judiciary's power to interpret the constitution itself, implies the judiciary has no such power: 'the Supreme Court shall review the laws, legislative decrees, international treaties as well as international covenants for their compliance with the constitution and their interpretation in accordance with the law'. This argument assumes that interpretation of the constitution is done by the article 157 commission: 'The independent commission for supervision of the implementation of the constitution shall be established in accordance with the provisions of the law. Members of this commission shall be appointed by the president with the endorsement of the house of people.' The authors disagree with this argument, and the Supreme Court itself has asserted its own authority to so interpret the constitution in its decision regarding Foreign Minister Spanta.
8 The UN Convention against Corruption was signed by President Karzai in 2004, but not ratified by parliament and lodged with the UN until August 2008.
9 Article 103 of the constitution of 1964: 'Investigation of crimes shall be conducted, in accordance with the provisions of the law, by the Attorney General...' This language was incorporated and the police mandate added in article 106 of the constitution of 1976: 'the

limit the police power after abuses in the previous years. Foreign donors, especially those with common law and adversarial traditions, generally opposed this division of roles, and would have preferred the police to be allowed to investigate and gather evidence and to cooperate more with the prosecutor's office, which some believe should have the power to instruct and direct police during the discovery phase.

Article 28 expresses the principle of *nullum crimen sine lege*: 'No deed shall be considered a crime unless ruled by a law promulgated prior to commitment of the offence . . . No one shall be punished without the decision of an authoritative court taken in accordance with the provisions of the law, promulgated prior to commitment of the offence.' In addition, article 27 of the constitution uses the word *qanun*, meaning a written law. The courts of appeals and Supreme Court have, however, shown a willingness to find guilt and order capital punishment based not on the penal code, but on Shari'a law as applied in the courts through article 130 of the constitution, which states: 'In cases under consideration, the courts shall apply provisions of this constitution as well as other laws. If there is no provision in the constitution or other laws about a case, the courts shall, in pursuance of *Hanafi* jurisprudence, and, within the limits set by this constitution, rule in a way that attains justice in the best manner.' Foreign jurists believe that article 27 forbids applying penal laws that are not promulgated under the aegis of the constitution, even if they are based on Shari'a interpretation. Afghanistan's Supreme Court and courts of appeal, however, have judged otherwise, and allowed the courts to convict for crimes that were not defined in laws enacted or promulgated under Afghanistan's lawmaking procedure, nor decreed by the executive, nor published in the *Official Gazette*. The most famous of these cases was the Assadullah Sharwari 'war crimes' case of 2006, in which a multiple murder indictment based on penal code articles 394 *et seq* was replaced by a reference to 'article 130'. In addition are the publicised criminal cases initially resulting in a death sentence due to blasphemy of Sayed Parvez (aka Parweiz) Kambaksh (Kambash or Kambakhsh), Ahmed Ghous Zalmai (Ghaws Zelmay) and Mullah Qari Mushtaq, and apostasy of Abdul Rahman. These cases were the subject of outcry and lobbying by the international community, but while the latter was resolved through a release from detention by the executive and a quick flight to Italy, the

detection of crimes by the police, and the investigation, pursuit and prosecution thereof by the Attorney General, [both of whom] are part of the executive organ, shall be conducted in accordance with the provisions of the law'. This language of article 106 tracks closely with article 134 of the 2004 constitution.

courts' decisions of guilt in the former cases were never withdrawn, and indeed affirmatively cite article 130 of the constitution rather than any law or penal code provision, and President Karzai issued pardons for them. (For more detail, see Hartmann's chapter in this volume, pp. 194–7.)

As for lawmaking, while the constitution (see, for example, articles 64, 79, 90, 94–97 and 100) outlines the role of the president and the parliament, the procedure of lawmaking has been based on a law enacted by the Taliban regime in 1999. It sets out the process from originating agency through the Ministry of Justice's *Taqnin* (drafting department) through the council of ministers to the president. It has remained in use throughout the post-Taliban period.[10]

While a few criminal justice decrees with the force of law were issued by Hamid Karzai in 2003 in his capacity as transitional president,[11] most were decreed after the constitution was promulgated in January 2004. Within this Afghan legal framework, in 2004, foreigners came to offer their versions of superior law. Rather than accept the 1974 criminal procedure code[12] and 1976 penal code[13] and then gradually amend them, the international community opted for quick solutions to specific problems. For this purpose, foreign lawyers drafted substantive penal laws that incorporated alien concepts and legal syntax, and entailed their own distinctive procedures.

Lessons that should have been learned

The case studies discussed below illustrate generic problems with Afghanistan's internationally driven law reform process – and, one might argue, with the state-building process as a whole.

Various players in the complex mix of powers shaping Afghanistan's political development have often decided to push some legislative change without sufficiently understanding the purposes, limitations and current

10 Law on the publication and enforcement of legislative documents in the Islamic Republic of Afghanistan, 1999, *Official Gazette* No. 787. However, at the Rome conference of July 2007, the Afghanistan national development strategy law reform technical working group called for laws and procedures, including the statutorily defined lawmaking and revision processes (stated in this 1999 law) to be updated to meet Afghanistan's current needs.

11 For example, the law on campaign against narcotics, *Official Gazette* No. 813, 13 Aqrab 1382, was drafted by Afghans with the assistance of UNODC and decreed by President Karzai in late 2003, but within two years replaced by the US/UK-drafted counter-narcotics law, discussed below.

12 The code was enacted and effective in 1965 (5 Jawza 1344), with articles 1–144 amended in 1974 (15 Hamal 1353).

13 The penal code was enacted and effective in 1976 (15 Mizan 1355).

implementation of the law in question. Laws are drafted and implementation planned by foreigners as if in a vacuum, inevitably setting the new law on a collision course with the old law, the legal culture and Afghan legal circumstances, creating mounting confusion and resentment among the Afghan professionals who are expected to implement it. Ideally, the laws would be rewritten after extensive study of their sociological, cultural and political context to understand how state law really functions and to pre-empt dissonance with the non-state normative systems. But even if this is unrealistically ambitious, a legal redrafting exercise must at a minimum identify, translate and analyse relevant written laws already in place. Without this background, how could the would-be reformer assess the need for the change in the first place? Few foreign projects, however, will expend their resources on something as mundane and time-consuming as translating all existing laws relating to the law that will be their project output. Rather, as illustrated below, international donors and projects prefer ad hoc solutions and quick outputs so that they can claim credit for putative progress. This orientation naturally discourages extensive collaboration and consensus with Afghan and even other international experts, and leads to quick-fix laws that lack full legitimacy, workability, clarity and longevity.

Even in cases where an actual legislative gap or niche is correctly identified, transplants of alien concepts or insertions of international standards require sufficient effort to be put into adapting them to the existing legal landscape. Foreigners have generally shown scant consideration for the traditions of the Afghan justice institutions, legal syntax and culture, and drafting style, in addition to frequently ignoring purely technical principles of legal drafting. Especially striking is the omission of provisions to repeal or delineate existing laws that new laws are meant to supersede or complement, which follows almost inevitably from the lack of a proper inventory of all laws affected by the change. The triad of 2004 laws on money laundering, terrorism financing, and bribery and corruption are a clear example of neglecting the relationship of ad hoc laws to existing Afghan criminal law codes.

Because the process is rushed and redrafters have little understanding of the broader context within which they are working, internationally drafted laws as a rule are never explained or defended through any commentary, either during the drafting stage or after they are promulgated as laws. A laudable exception was the ICPC, whose commentary was prepared by the drafter, but it has never been published or even translated into Dari or Pashto. Drafters forgo an opportunity to explain the rationale, provenance and probable challenges of implementation to those Afghan law professionals who are open to legal argument and who are critical of the law gaining broader acceptance and ultimately being used.

The patchwork of special criminal laws enacted in Afghanistan since 2004 rather alarmingly indicates the need for a comprehensive review and revision of the now thirty-five-year-old criminal law and procedure codes. Yet law reform programmes, with one exception,[14] are oriented toward delivering quick results, which precludes a time-consuming code-writing endeavour. The international community's focus on anti-corruption in 2009–10 will likely inject a new congeries of quick anti-corruption decrees into the legal system, which will complicate the criminal law even further. Also, the extensive effort required for publication and training, especially in the provinces, calls into question the reasonability of any law reform, which, by definition and intention, has only an interim character. While difficulties in distribution, popularisation and training have their objective bases, especially security concerns, they do not justify legislative reforms that cannot feasibly be explained to those who are meant to implement them.

The biggest shadow over the law reform process in Afghanistan is cast, of course, by the question of legitimacy. Four-and-a-half years after the inauguration of the parliament, 100 per cent of the criminal justice laws enacted were presidential decrees. Foreign authorship and the overtly foreign content of draft laws naturally breed mistrust and resentment. With no attempt made to explain, to educate and convince stakeholders, the law reform process has all the hallmarks of short-term politics rather than long-term political development. The use of executive power to decree legislation in parliamentary recesses strengthens the perception that the law reform process is antidemocratic. Such top-down, foreign-driven judicial reform projects must also contribute to reigniting the centre versus provinces conflict that has plagued Afghanistan's history throughout the twentieth century.

As Faiz Ahmed eloquently argues:

> Current designs to institute uniform legal codes in Afghanistan suffer from a failure to contextualise the initiative with Afghanistan's history of turbulent centre versus provinces conflict, its extremely complex politics and

---

14 Canadian funding through UNODC enabled a one-year revision drafting process in 2008–09 for the new code of criminal procedure by the mixed national and international group of jurists under the umbrella of the legislative department or *Taqnin* of the Ministry of Justice (see below). US State/INL and US Institute of Peace also provided some directed funding to this process.

ethnically diverse societies, and multiple adjudicatory mechanisms that govern, de facto, in rural areas. The decision to implement highly centralised state-based codes, however, reflects an even broader problem with judicial reform in Afghanistan: a tendency to impose Western legal models in the name of 'development' or 'legal reform', goals which are skewed from the start by the lack of sociocultural awareness of Afghanistan's legal history, principles of Islamic law, and Afghan customary law systems. In a country that has long resisted foreign intervention, authenticity of law and participatory involvement on the local level are all the more important. If judicial reform initiatives are to take firm root in Afghanistan, they must spring from an authentic base of Afghan history and socio-legal cultures, of which both Afghan customary law and Islamic jurisprudence play integral roles. Otherwise, judicial reform will follow the path of previous state-driven reforms in Afghanistan: at the local level they will be at best ignored, and most probably resented, poisoning an already bitter relationship between Kabul and the provinces.

(Ahmed 2007)

The alienation begins with the drafting process. Almost all the new laws have been drafted ad hoc with no formalised, transparent consultative and consensus-building process at the drafting stage. Draft presidential decrees prepared by foreign embassies or agencies find their way to the president's office, often through an Afghan but foreign-paid adviser to the *Taqnin*, without any meaningful Afghan participation in the drafting, any form of public debate, or even discussion and sharing among international agencies. At best, Afghan participation is limited to the formality of passing the draft decree between the Ministry of Justice and the council of ministers for comments. Lacking preparation, expertise and time, the Afghan institutions can contribute little.

Below are several examples of the legislative interventions that resulted from this largely unconscious conspiracy of neglect.

The interim criminal (procedure) code for courts (ICPC), February 2004 – a cure for what does not ail you

The Italian government was given the 'lead nation' role for judicial reform in the January 2002 reconstruction assistance conference (that implemented the agreement of 2001, with Germany given policing, the UK counter-narcotics, and the US the armed forces). Italy set up the Italian justice project office, with an ambassador as head, and brought in an eminent justice and senior criminal law reform expert, Hon. Dr Giuseppe di Gennaro, who had experience working with reform and revision of criminal procedure and criminal codes in Bosnia and Albania, among other countries. Following this commitment, however, this senior Italian expert was not provided with legal assistants and a proper assessment of the Afghan laws, justice institutions and their capacity, traditions and legal culture.[15] Rather, after carrying out meetings with usually higher level Afghan justice officials and jurists, he was asked by the Italian government to draft a new criminal procedure code. As a result, the expert worked in isolation to draft what was envisaged as an interim code, to be used for basic investigation, prosecution and adjudication of serious crimes, until the justice system capacity allowed for a new and more sophisticated code.

As a result, the 2004 interim criminal procedure code (ICPC) was flawed in several ways, both in principle, as a development endeavour, and as a technical matter.

First, the ICPC was seen as a foreign imposition. The ICPC appears made honestly as *su misura* for Afghanistan. Its few transplants introducing Italian procedures, such as prosecutor ratification of police acts, and institutions, such as judicial police, are explicable upon the specific experience and knowledge of the Italian drafting expert. However, Afghanistan's first post-2001 Attorney General, Abdulmahmood Daqiq, told the co-authors that he was informed by an Italian authority that if he did not support the ICPC, Italy would consider withholding millions in aid. This was confirmed by other senior prosecutors. Senior staff of the Ministry of Justice and other prosecutors also confirmed that the vast majority of Afghan policymaking legal professionals and police opposed the ICPC as a replacement of the then existing criminal procedure code of 1974.

Second, that imposition was done without evaluating whether there was actual need for the new code and how it would fit into the existing legal framework. In particular, it is unclear upon what technical assessment, if any, the decision had been made in favor of writing an interim code rather than reforming the old one. Not only did the ICPC ignore the 1974 criminal procedure code, but later others still ignored it; the sparse literature on the ICPC[16] is silent about the 1974 code and its import in the Afghan legal system. The decision on moving forward with the ICPC

15 Hartmann started worked closely with Giuseppe di Gennaro, a former President at the Italian Corte Suprema di Cassazione, in Bosnia in 1997 as part of the Council of Europe's team of experts to assist the Federation of BiH in revising its criminal procedure. He has the highest regard for di Gennaro's professionalism, expertise and gravitas. The issues discussed here are his instructions and lack of legal support.
16 For example, Ahmed 2005, Ahmed 2007 and Nader 2007. Not only do these articles fail to mention the 1974 CPC, but the first two also use the same words in error when they state that Italy presented 'a complete criminal procedure code' to Afghanistan. As discussed in the text and footnotes, the ICPC, due to article 98(3), allowed large portions of the 1974

may have had such trivial bases as the lack of access to the translated legal text by the expert drafter, where translating the 500 articles of the 1974 code in force from Dari into English then to analyse and revise had been found more cumbersome than drafting the ninety-eight articles of the ICPC. The disdain with which the agents of the rule of law approached the local legal system is illustrated by the fact that until 2006, when the JSSP Afghan/American team took the effort to convert the scanned .pdf graphics file into an MSWord document and roughly reviewed the translation, the only copy of the 1974 CPC available for the international community was one hard copy, replete with obvious translation mistakes.

Other drafters and commentators continued to ignore the 1974 code. The unpublished di Gennaro commentary to the ICPC only refers once, in eighty-five pages, to the 1974 CPC: 'The Afghan criminal procedure code in force is structured according to that type of inquisitorial model in which the prosecutor conducts the investigations.' This may indicate the ICPC drafter was unaware of any specifics of the 1974 ICPC. The authors have a copy of this commentary, obtained from the Italian justice project office in 2005. It is unknown as to whether the 1974 criminal procedure code was even translated for di Gennaro's reference.

The 1974 criminal procedure code had three advantages that were lost with the decreeing of the ICPC. First, the 1974 code was a structured, comprehensive and detailed piece of legislation. Second, while it was a legal transplant, it had been voluntarily adopted by and adapted to Afghanistan. The 1965 code came from Egypt, a country close to Afghanistan's Islamic culture as well as with similarities especially in the rural areas of each country, and there was no perception of outside pressure to adopt it. In 1974 the *Taqnin*, in consultation with the national justice institutions, amended the 1965 code to adapt it to Afghan circumstances. Third, and above all, by 2004 the Afghan jurists had been educated on the 1974 code and had decades of experience applying it.

Thus amending the 1974 criminal procedure code in selected areas addressed by the ICPC, such as the explicit statement of certain legal principles, including the rights of the accused or the import of early conditional release, would have been a better option from the point of view of acceptance, ease of implementation and sustainability. Moreover, post-2001 reformers should not have so lightly discarded the 1974 code. Against the historically and culturally entrenched reluctance of different groups, including rural and urban warlords, tribal councils and Islamic

---

CPC (for example, bail, search and seizure procedures) to continue to apply, and it was so applied by Afghan jurists.

legal scholars, to accept any codification,[17] the 1974 code had been the legal landscape's one fixed reference point.

In any event, the process of drafting of the ICPC by Italy, with only minor revisions based upon ad hoc feedback provided orally by the national experts, resulted in a lack of legitimacy of the new code – both the lack of Afghan authorship and the lack of knowledge about the drafting process, the rationale of the changes and the intended result. It took several years to enforce the ICPC upon national jurists: in 2006 and 2007, it was still not being applied at all in parts of Afghanistan, and applied improperly or piecemeal where it was used by prosecutors and judges.

Last, the ICPC, once in effect by law, did not have a planned, coherently designed release or a coordinated training plan. It took three years to distribute the code in Dari and Pashto to all judges, prosecutors and attorneys, which readily violated the traditional rule of law postulates of clarity, accessibility and ascertainable procedures. The training materials devised and taught by foreigners were not made consistent through consensus, neither with the national experts nor with the internationals. Indeed, while the Italian drafter wrote a commentary to the ICPC, it was never translated into Dari or Pashto, nor released among the international community for discussion and to build a consensus. Indeed, some development programmes showed their ignorance as to the ICPC's application within the Afghan justice sector framework by bringing in internationals without any Afghan experience for as little as two weeks, putting them into classes immediately to teach the ICPC and 1976 penal code to Afghan jurists.

Attorney General Abdul Jabar Sabit said: 'I will not have my prosecutors taught their criminal procedure and penal codes by [an IGO's] lawyers from Australia and Argentina who fly in for six weeks and then fly out!' The lack of consistency in training on the ICPC was compounded by a lack of independent monitoring of the content and efficacy of the training, and a lack of sharing and discussion of training materials by various international organisations and NGOs that were doing the training. There was also no coordination, so that there was duplication in who was trained, as well as areas where no one was trained.[18]

On a technical level as well, the ICPC was flawed

Above all, the ICPC's purport to serve as codification of criminal procedure was overly ambitious. Correct as it was as a skeleton of a code,

---

17 For more about traditional opponents to codification in the Afghanistan context, see Ahmed 2007: 6.
18 Personal communication from Sabit to Hartmann.

it was, however, neither exhaustive nor specific enough to comprehensively regulate the field. It failed to legislate in detail on areas of crucial importance for investigation, such as the criteria to justify, and procedures of, detention, search, seizure, forfeiture and confiscation. It left out of scope of legislation non-custodial measures for securing the presence of the defendant at court, which under the constitution must be statute-based and which had been addressed in the old code. Even for well-established justice institutions, staffed with experienced professionals used to interpreting and construing, and having a reliable system of recourses – a system of established rule of law – the ICPC would be difficult to implement, and would make prosecution of complex crimes nigh on impossible. Under the conditions prevailing in Afghanistan, its brevity meant that it manifestly did not meet the demand by jurists for explicit and detailed guidance.

Regrettably, the ICPC introduced what later has become a generic flaw of all newly drafted laws and codes. using as transitional provision an omnibus clause that declared as abrogated any laws that were 'contrary', without listing the laws and provisions that it abrogated. This meant leaving the superseding nature of the new laws and codes up to individual interpretation. The ICPC did not abrogate the 1974 criminal procedure code, which should have been expected of the new code, but left it for the newly formed Afghan judiciary to decide whether the code of 1974 was simply inapplicable as the *lex priori*, or inapplicable as 'contrary' to the new code. Or perhaps, insofar as the new code was only *lex generalis*, the old code still applied as *lex specialis*, that is, in areas where it was more specific. Which logically would bring a jurist to the initial question of why the need for the ICPC at all if it results in a dichotomy, with blanket reference to the old code. Eventually, Afghan jurists adopted the approach of subsidiary application of bits and pieces of the old code, which is a practical solution, yet idiosyncratic and raising concerns about legality, especially with respect to measures of compulsion,[19] and general concerns of certainty and accessibility of the law.

Other flaws are less serious but could have been avoided had the drafter of the ICPC been sufficiently advised on related laws and given more time. The ICPC in parts even contradicts provisions in the new January 2004 constitution that was effective a month before the ICPC was

---

19 Particularly problematic is the statutory authorisation for bail and other measures for compulsion, which should be based in explicit authorisation in the statute. If a statute in force does not foresee bail, the question arises whether it is permissible to apply the old statute or whether the legislative decision was that there should be no bail, and where premises for detention are not present, what follows is release without bail.

decreed by President Karzai.[20] As another example, the law on structure and organisation of the Attorney General's office of 1991, in effect through present times, had not even been translated, and thus its provisions were unknown to the ICPC drafter, who nonetheless, without knowing the Afghan law controlling the area, provided duties and mandates for the prosecutors. In 2005, the law on the structure and organisation of the Attorney General's Office, also known as the law on prosecutors, enacted in 1991 (1370, *Official Gazette* No. 738), had not been translated into English or any other Western language, and the IJPO when asked stated it was not available. A further error was retaining, in violation of the International Covenant on Civil and Political Rights standards, the authorisation for the prosecutor to apply detention for a period up to fifteen days – probably resulting from an oversight of the fact that prosecutors in Afghanistan, unlike in Italy, are not part of the judiciary.[21]

Further, the ICPC was not consistent with general Afghan tradition as to legal institutions. While it kept the civil law tradition and investigating prosecutor of the 1974 code, it also attempted to establish the Italian model of 'judicial police' (articles 28–32), which was never accepted or used, and, according to the three attorneys general to date and the legal advisers to the Minister of Interior, contradicted the separate mandates created by the constitution at article 134. The disregard for the separate mandates was especially visible in the ICPC provisions granting the investigative prosecutor the power and duty to confirm, nullify or modify police actions and decisions during their detection (pre-investigation) phase within the first twenty-four (later seventy-two) hours after arrest.[22] Likewise, a foreign transplant of the abstract idea of *ex lege* nullity of judicial

---

20 For example, the constitution requires at article 38 a judge's permission for searches except for exigent circumstances (*flagrante delicto*), but the ICPC does not state this expressly, and at article 37 only requires an order by the prosecutor.

21 Article 36 of the ICPC requires the suspect to be released if the prosecution does not file the indictment within fifteen days of the arrest unless 'the court, at the timely request of the *saranwal*, has authorised the extension of the term for not more than 15 additional days'. Unfortunately, the prevailing Afghan interpretation is to apply this 15+15 day limit only after the police deliver the suspect to the prosecution per article 31. Moreover, it violates article 9 of the International Covenant on Civil and Political Rights in that it does not provide any standards or criteria for the judicial decision of extension.

22 ICPC, article 33: after receiving the police report on police actions required within twenty-four hours, the prosecutor 'either sanctions [ratifies] the deeds of the judicial police's activities or adopts decisions to revoke or modify them'. Neither the police nor prosecutors believe the prosecutor has any control over the police during the (since 2005 September) first seventy-two hours after an arrest, based on article 134 of the constitution and legal tradition since the 1970s.

decisions was never accepted by Afghan jurists, who were familiar with the less refined but practically equally sound concept of absolute and relative reasons for quashing of a judgment from the code of 1974.[23]

On the linguistic plane, when introducing novel institutions, the ICPC did not attempt to provide clear definitions of novel language,[24] so that those notions were suspended in a contextual vacuum. This shortage of explanation could have been remedied by the publication of a commentary, which was planned but never happened. The di Gennaro commentary, which was never published, was not done in consultation with Afghans and merely described the Italian author's legislative intent. Last, it did not adequately take into account the factual circumstances and legal environment of Afghanistan, so that deadlines were set to meet Western standards of human rights, and were in some cases even more restrictive, while communication, transportation, and detection or investigation of arrested suspects and the facts surrounding their cases were far slower in Afghanistan.

For example, article 31 of the ICPC only allowed the police twenty-four hours to interrogate an arrestee before providing the investigative prosecutor with the case file and legal custody of the suspect; the police were so incensed by this limitation of what had been ten days under the 1974 code and 1978 law on discovery and investigation that the Ministry of Justice insisted upon amending *sub silentio* article 31 by providing seventy-two hours in the 2005 police law, article 25. A second example, decried by the prosecutors, was articles 36 and 6 of the ICPC, which limited detention of a suspect for an investigation (by the investigative prosecutor) to only thirty days before an indictment was required to be filed. The Attorney General's office asserted with some good cause that this prevented any complex or compound investigation or multi-suspect investigation, and ignored the realities of slow or non-existent transportation during winter.

---

23 Afghan members of the criminal law reform working group, comprising, among others, representatives of the Supreme Court, Attorney General's Office, Ministry of Interior and Afghan Independent Human Rights Commission, informed the authors that they had never understood the reason for replacing the familiar concept of absolute and relative reasons of invalidation with the notion of nullity.

24 There are no definitions in the ICPC with the exception of article 5, defining suspect and accused, and article 13, defining *flagrante delicto* crimes. So 'judicial police' is never defined, nor are specific procedures for routine law enforcement activities such as search and seizure. Compare this with the explicit procedures for search and seizure in the 1974 CPC at articles 32 *et seq.*

On the other hand, the ICPC was a lost opportunity, as it did not attempt to implement a balance of the sometimes competing objectives of human rights protections of a suspect or accused versus the efficiency and efficacy of investigation and prosecution of organised crime and corruption. This could have been done through provision for judicially supervised covert and technical means of surveillance, procedures for witness and victim protection, and establishment of procedures to grant reduced punishment for cooperation in testifying in court. Failure to address the organised crime problems in the code created a demand for special investigative measures. They were to be provided soon, scattered around in special-target criminal legislation, laws that were even more obscure in the drafting process and less accessible as laws in force than the ICPC.

As a result, by 2008, there was both a national and international consensus that the ICPC should be replaced with a new code.

Under the 2004 constitution, if the parliament (the *Wolesi* and *Meshrano Jirgas*) is not in session (it did not have its first session until late December 2005), the President may decree non-budgetary laws, which then take immediate effect. As for other criminal justice laws, after the President legislatively decreed the ICPC and it came into effect, laws were quickly drafted by foreigners using standard templates, each to address a specific need or area. This became an institutional imperative, as many foreign rule of law projects found it easier to draft and pressure the executive to decree a law, and thus claim credit for capacity-building, than to actually assess the legal landscape and capacity-build institutions through working as partners with Afghan experts to mentor and advise structural, organisational, professional reform of the justice institutions. Where foreigners were often in the country for a year or less, this became known as 'resumé law reform' or 'summer project lawmaking'.

The 2004 laws on money laundering, terrorism financing, and bribery and corruption – taking credit when credit is not due

While the Italian government focused on the ICPC, USAID and US Department of Justice prosecutors, seconded to the US embassy, worked on specific criminal laws that would help fulfil national priorities whilst bringing recognition to their drafters. Within a half year after the ICPC and the banking laws were decreed, the foreigners drafted laws relating to the campaigns against bribery and corruption (20 Mizan 1383, *Official Gazette* no. 838, 2004), financing of terrorism (30 Mizan 1383, *Official Gazette* no. 839, 2004), and money laundering and the proceeds of crime

(10 Aqrab (the next month in the Afghan solar calendar) 1383, *Official Gazette* no. 840, 2004). These three laws were decreed within a three-week period in September and October of 2004.

The drafters of these laws failed to conduct a formalised, transparent consultative and consensus-building process with Afghan stakeholders while drafting these laws. In fact, USAID and World Bank-financed contractors wrote the last two drafts without any real attempt to fit them within the existing legal framework; all three were freestanding substantive and procedural laws, neither rooted in existing Afghan law nor conceptually compatible with codes and laws that had already been drafted by other foreign consultants.

The fate of the general independent Afghanistan anti-corruption commission (GIAAC), a body created by the law against bribery and corruption, is instructive. The GIAAC, which was given a mandate to create and administer the government's anti-corruption policy, failed primarily because the drafters ignored the pre-existing legal framework. First, it was tasked with 'investigating the affairs related to bribery and corruption in offices' (GIAAC law, article 5(6) – see also articles 1.1 ('principal source for investigation' of corruption) and 3(5)), whereas article 134 of the constitution clearly provided that 'investigation . . . shall be the duty of the Attorney General's Office'. The conflict over jurisdiction that resulted from this overlap in responsibilities prevented any cooperation between the two institutions.[25] Second, while this law (article 3, paragraph 2) referred to penal code articles 254–267 in defining bribery, it also created a list of fifteen additional actions, each of which constituted the crime of 'official corruption'.[26] Many of these additional offences overlapped with other crimes defined in the penal code. The law failed to articulate any

25 Article 134 of the constitution. While the GIAAC law had a provision to prevent overlapping of mandates (for example, article 14 stating 'not intervene with the duties and authorities provided in the legislative documents of other offices'), and also used language that attempted to pose GIAAC providing cases to the prosecution (for example, article 6, paragraph 1 stating 'taking urgent decisions to introduce suspects of bribery and official corruption crimes provided in this law to face judicial prosecution)', the GIAAC position was that it could indeed investigate. Moreover, pre-investigation would also be considered 'discovery or detection', thus in conflict with the duties of the police mandated by constitution article 134 and with the pre-existing 1978 law on detection/discovery and investigation of crime. The GIAAC law also ignored the ICPC-created relationships between the police and prosecution, which did not leave a gap for the GIAAC.

26 Article 3, paragraph 3 – for example: 'Official corruption: It is an illegal act committed by government employees and other public servants to attain to personal or group aims in the following manners: embezzlement, deception and stealing documents; wastage of official records; transgressing the legal scope of authorities . . . [another 12 acts listed].'

specific penalty for these new crimes, stating instead that 'the court has the authority to punish the perpetrators according to circumstances'[27] and thus violating article 27 of the constitution[28] as well as international human rights standards and norms.

The GIAAC's subservience to the President also contributed to its failure. To the dismay of the international community, President Karzai appointed as head of GIAAC Izzatullah Wasifi, who had been convicted of a narcotics trafficking felony and had served three years and eight months in a US federal prison, and thus did not have credibility with many Afghans to lead an anti-corruption battle (see Huggler 2007). GIAAC is now acknowledged as a failure, and was replaced by the President by legislative decree with the 2008 Office of Oversight and Anti-corruption.

The financing of terrorism and the money laundering and proceeds of crime laws were drafted as stand-alone laws, ignoring the existing legal framework, including the ICPC as well as the criminal justice substantive and procedural legislation civil law system already in place. These two laws were based on transplanted foreign concepts, and no serious attempt was made to explain them to Afghan jurists and police, much less to train these stakeholders in how to implement them. As a result, the Afghans effectively ignored both of these special laws.

The law against financing of terrorism set up both procedures and penalties that differed from those existing in Afghanistan without amending, or even referring to, the relevant provisions of the ICPC, 1974 criminal procedure code or 1976 penal code. These provisions and penalties included confiscation, 'freezing' (articles 13–14 of the campaign against financing of terrorism) – itself a novel concept not defined – and seizure of assets (articles 8–16); an aggravated punishment of fifteen years to 'life imprisonment';[29] changes to the jurisdiction of courts, ignoring the penal code's more than adequate existing provisions on jurisdiction (compare article 17 with penal code articles 14–20); and the creation of an entire procedure for mutual legal assistance (just for this law, and ignoring

---

27 Article 12, paragraph 2: 'In case there is not a punishment foreseen for one of the violations defined in this law, the penal code or other laws, the court has the authority to punish the perpetrators according to circumstances.'

28 Article 27, paragraph 3 of the constitution: 'No one shall be punished without the decision of an authoritative court taken in accordance with the provisions of the law, promulgated prior to commitment of the offence.'

29 The penal code has categories of short, medium, long-term and continuing imprisonment, and capital punishment. Continuing imprisonment is 16–20 years; there is no life imprisonment (1976 penal code, articles 97 and 99).

the lack of any mutual legal assistance and extradition procedure in the Afghan legal framework[30]). This law was thus the first of many foreign-written laws to institute criminal procedures in a substantive law, rather than attempting to amend the existing 1974 criminal procedure code to ensure one consistent and uniform procedure for all penal violations.

Similarly, the law against money laundering and proceeds of crime (AML), apparently drafted by the same or related foreign experts, transplants a foreign law without reference to the Afghan criminal justice legislative framework. Again, the AML law does not refer to the 1976 penal code or 1974 CPC general requirements and procedures for confiscation,[31] seizure,[32] or telecommunications 'tapping' or monitoring, and recording.[33] It thus amends *sub silencio* the relevant articles in those laws, causing confusion. Further, the constitutional protection against searches in the home, requiring court approval, is violated by AML law article 44, which allows police to order and implement covert and technical surveillance in the home.[34] The AML law refers to 'judicial officers', a role created in the 1974 criminal procedure code but abolished by the ICPC, compounding confusion about which state organ is entrusted with investigative powers.

As with the terrorism financing law, the AML law creates a new and novel regime covering covert and technical surveillance (article 44), undercover (plain clothes) police operations and 'controlled delivery' (article 45), and extradition and mutual legal assistance (articles 51–73). At the time of writing (2010), these procedures have not been

---

30 Articles 18–24. There are no mutual legal assistance or extradition procedures in the 1974 CPC or ICPC, nor the penal code.

31 For confiscation law and procedures, see for example 1976 penal code articles 117, 119 and 132; ICPC articles 8(4), 88 and 95; and 1974 CPC articles 9 and 106.

32 For seizure law and procedures, see ICPC articles 32, 35, 37, 39(6), 43 and 95; and 1974 CPC articles 32–44, 54–60, 106–116 and 128. Note that due to ICPC article 98(3), most if not all of these 1974 CPC seizure articles apply because they do not contradict any part of the ICPC with the exception of the 1974 requirement of judicial (not prosecutorial) assistance.

33 Article 57 of the 1974 CPC allows this under court order if 'they relate to the accused or the crime under investigation and be considered useful for revealing the truth', a different standard than the AML law, article 44, which allows it if there are 'strong grounds for suspecting that such accounts, telephone lines, computer systems and networks are or may be used by persons suspected of participating in offences'.

34 Constitution articles 37 and 38, which require judicial approval either before or after such residential searches and violations of privacy, are contravened by AML law article 44(1)(b)–(d) and (2), which allows this to be ordered and implemented solely by 'judicial officers', which can only be police.

implemented by the Afghan justice sector authorities due to the lack of mentoring and training, and to the alien nature of the procedures. Moreover, the novel terms of covert and technical surveillance and undercover operations are not appropriately explained by the law, nor are the courts provided with authority or specific standards[35] to prevent invasion of privacy and entrapment, which violate constitutional provisions, including the international standards and norms for law enforcement and human rights incorporated by reference under article 7 of the constitution.[36] Finally, the AML law, while its language sometimes tracks the terrorism-financing law, also contains language and definitions inconsistent with that law. For example, AML law article 30 on 'freezing' allows it to be done solely by the financial intelligence unit of Da Afghanistan Bank, for up to seven days, with an additional seven days authorised by a prosecutor, and an additional fourteen days after that by a court. In comparison, article 15 of the terrorism financing law requires both a prosecution request and court authorisation for any freezing of assets. There is no rationale for the difference.

The police law of September 2005 – the Ministry of Interior strikes back

The police law of September 2005 (31 Sumbula 1384, *Official Gazette* no. 862, 2005) exemplified in its text disagreements between national institutions, and disagreements among international projects and programmes. It is also another example of a *lex specialis* creating its own procedural as well as substantive rights and protections without even referring to the codified criminal procedure in the ICPC.

The police law was drafted by both the Ministry of Interior legal adviser and the international adviser – mentors from international agencies that had Afghan policing within their mandates.[37] While it purported to

---

35 Compare the standard for implementing telephone 'tapping'/monitoring and recording in the 1974 CPC – 'they [must] relate to the accused or the crime under investigation and be considered useful for revealing the truth' – with that from the AML law, requiring 'strong grounds for suspecting that such accounts, telephone lines, computer systems and networks or documents are or may be used by persons suspected of participating in offences'.

36 Thus the International Covenant on Civil and Political Rights (for example, article 17 on home and privacy) should be directly applied by judicial authorities as well as controlling drafting of procedural provisions.

37 Most significant were the German police project office (whose mandate was later assumed by the EUPOL mission), due to the January 2002 Tokyo reconstruction assistance

be a revision of the 2000 Taliban-enacted police law based on the new constitution,[38] it also was used to settle scores and alter power relationships between the Ministry of Interior and Attorney General's Office, and within the national security and justice sectors. Article 4 stated: 'The police shall perform their duties under the leadership of the Minister of Interior in the capital, and under the guidance of the governors and district chiefs in the provinces and districts respectively.' The ill-defined compromise language regarding 'leadership' of the Minister of Interior from Kabul and 'guidance' of governors resulted in significant disagreements between the Minister of Interior and governors, allegedly due to governors issuing orders and influencing the hiring, promotion and assignments of police in their provinces, and the utilisation of police human and financial resources for personal and political gains – for example, police used as bodyguards, drivers and a personal militia of the governor. The governors argued, however, that if they could not control and express an implied or patent threat of force and coercion by the police, they did not have sufficient power to properly govern their provinces. Because the President had used his power under article 79 of the constitution to issue this law as a legislative decree several months before the Afghan parliament had its first session, the national assembly in 2008 and 2009 had extensive debate primarily on article 4, and language as to the balance between the Ministry of Interior and the governors. The national split in opinion was also mirrored among the internationals: those international advisers and mentors with a mandate for either policing or the justice sector supported the Ministry of Interior position, while at the UNODC-organised internationals' presentation to the *Wolesi Jirga*, the speaker for UNDP's sub-national governance programme, along with the national experts of the independent directorate of local governance, supported the governors' positions.

The police law also added to the power of the police vis-à-vis the prosecutors and the courts by broadening existing police power to stop, detain and search individuals, vehicles and residences. These exceptions were added without referring to the applicable provisions on detention

---

conference's assigning of policing to Germany as the lead nation for development, and the US-led military formation, Combined Security Transitional Command Afghanistan (CSTC-A), along with US mentors financed by US State Department/INL and contracted out to DynCorp and MSI among others.

38 Article 1: 'This law has been enacted on the basis of the provisions of article 56, article 75(3) and article 134 of the constitution of Afghanistan to govern the duties and powers of the police in order to ensure public order and security.'

and search in the ICPC.[39] These are examples of *sub silentio* amend-ments of a code by contradictory or expansionist provisions of a later specialised law. In addition, the amount of time that the police could detain an individual before turning the subject and the file over to AGO prosecutors was similarly amended *sub silentio* from the ICPC's (admit-tedly short) twenty-four-hour limit to seventy-two hours under the new law.

The one positive technical drafting provision in the police law was the last and promulgation article that expressly abolished the entirety of the previous police law of 2000.[40]

The counter-narcotics law of 17 December 2005 – in the nick of time

The counter-narcotics law (15 Dalw 1384, *Official Gazette* no. 875, leg-islatively decreed 17 December 2005, *Official Gazette* published 4 Febru-ary 2006) demonstrated the influence and power of the international community to ensure that another target-area regulation, in the form of a presidential legislative decree, with its own unique criminal proce-dures that ignored the ICPC and 1976 penal code, quickly became law. The US and UK (the UK being the 'lead nation' for counter-narcotics) in particular were anxious to have a new law take effect that would improve on the existing 2003 drug law and the relevant 1976 penal code provisions.[41]

The Afghan government, in light of its mandate, under article 7 of the constitution, to comply with its international treaty and convention obligations, legislatively decreed a simple drug law (13 Aqrab 1382, *Official Gazette* no. 813, 2003) in 2003 with UNODC support. Even the Afghan

---

39 Many articles of the police law concerning the police's right to stop, search, arrest and so forth differ from those of the ICPC, which, for instance, provide human rights-based limitations on the justifications of arrests without the order of the prosecutor. The police law does not mention the power of the prosecutor in ICPC article 33 to ratify or revoke such police actions.

40 Article 34 states 'the provisions of the previous police law published in the *Official Gazette* issue 793 dated 20 August 2000 shall be abolished'.

41 The 1976 penal code in article 515 punished sale, transport and storage for sale of narcotics with 'long-term imprisonment', which was five to fifteen years. The code had some progressive provisions, for while article 349 punished use by three to six months' imprisonment, and article 352(2) punished repeat offenders by 'short imprisonment' – a maximum of one year with a minimum of six months – article 352(3) allowed the court to sentence an 'addict' to be confined to a hospital for (inpatient) treatment for up to one year.

government's new counter-narcotics judicial reform action plan admitted that the new 2003 law on counter-narcotics was in effect a quick fix to comply 'with the relevant UN drug conventions, but more detailed implementation regulations are required. Many judges . . . particularly in the provinces, are not aware of it.' Problems with bribery of witnesses, law enforcement and the judiciary, and intimidation of the same, were admitted. Areas for 'future work' included 'amendment to the 1382 (2003) drug law to define serious offences with central jurisdiction and lesser offences with provincial jurisdiction, and review of evidentiary rules' (UNODC 2004).

The US and UK were interested in the new law having significant penalties for trafficking and related corruption offences, in establishment of the Ministry of Counter-Narcotics as the leading body to monitor, evaluate and coordinate all counter-narcotics activities, and in providing for new criminal procedures, including covert and technical surveillance, and undercover 'controlled purchases'. In order to ensure quick passage, staff from the UK and US embassies had numerous meetings with the heads of the Afghan justice sector institutions, as well as with the Italians (lead for 'judicial reform') and members of various UN agencies working in the law reform and rule of law fields. In the course of these meetings, all opposition to their proposals was silenced.

Moreover, the technical experts of the UN agencies in Kabul, from UNODC, UNAMA and UNDP, all had concerns about various provisions of the 2005 counter-narcotics law draft, and vocally and in writing opposed the draft for numerous reasons, including the novel criminal procedures imported into Afghan law for these crimes alone, and penalties that were written in a vernacular and syntax foreign to Afghanistan's legal culture and penal code categories of indeterminate imprisonment. The 2005 draft also set penalties and fines much greater than any in the penal code. After a particularly acrimonious meeting with the US Embassy (seconded US Department of Justice prosecutor) and the Afghan legal adviser to the Minister of Interior who was working closely with the US and UK embassies, and whose salary from the Afghan government was 'topped up' by the UK by $3,000 a month, all three UN agency experts received instructions in December 2005 from their superiors to cease vocal opposition to the draft 2005 law. In addition, Hartmann received instructions in November 2005 from his US Embassy/INL superiors that he should not distribute a legal discussion paper comparing the counter-narcotics law draft provisions to current Afghan law and civil law principles, and was told to cease any oral or written questioning of the counter-narcotics law draft. US Department of Justice representatives in the embassy requested this. It must be noted that the desire of those who opposed the draft counter-narcotics law was to discuss it with Afghan experts and adapt it to conform more closely to Afghan circumstances and drafting. However, the rush to decree the law did not allow this process to occur.

This new law, promulgated as a legislative decree a mere two days before the parliament began its first session on 19 December 2005, was the first obvious and successful attempt to pre-empt the national assembly's lawmaking powers.[42] While previous laws had been decreed out of necessity, the counter-narcotics law was the first of a sequence of laws that were decreed for speed – to avoid the delay of parliamentary debate and voting.

It is also important to note how article 79 of the constitution, which allows the president to create law by decree when the parliament is in recess, became the loophole that would later allow the President to strategically time his decrees of laws on terrorism, abduction and human trafficking, the high office of oversight of anti-corruption strategy, and the elimination of violence against women law. Clearly, bypassing the legislative branch decreases the legitimacy of laws thus enacted.

The terrorism draft law of 2004–08 – born in the USA

In 2004, after meeting with UNODC's terrorism prevention branch in Vienna, the Ministry of Justice *Taqnin* and the legal adviser to the Ministry of Interior (Abdul Jabar Sabit, who was later to be appointed and confirmed as the Afghanistan Islamic Republic's second Attorney General) drafted a new terrorism law that attempted to meet the requirements of the UN terrorism conventions. On 15 February 2005, Afghanistan transmitted to UNODC for review and advice an eleven-page, twenty-two-article draft terrorism law. The draft was a modest start, but did incorporate what the Afghan drafters considered the most important requirements of the UN terrorism conventions. However, the Department of Justice prosecutor stationed at the US Embassy in Kabul was not satisfied with it, and he presented the Afghan ministry officials with his own draft, one that took much of its language directly from the US Patriot Act, which effectively became the draft submitted to the *Taqnin*. That US-drafted terrorism law had forty-six pages and fifty-three articles, with a substantially

42 The national assembly, also known as parliament, was inaugurated on 19 December 2005 (www.nationalassembly.af/index.php?id=430).

more complex structure (for example, article 15 was 3.5 pages in itself, with sub-sub-sub paragraphs such as 15(g)(6)(A)(ii)). Thus, a law that had the legal syntax and organisation of dense, complex US federal criminal laws was simply translated into Dari for use by Afghan prosecutors and judges. This fault alone would have doomed any attempt to properly apply the law.

In addition to imposing a law with an unfamiliar mode of organisation on the Afghan legal system, the drafter went further, importing substantive legal concepts not found in Afghan penal law, such as the designation of terrorist organisations by the government, and then punishment of anyone who provided 'material support' to such organisations. Article 6 of the drafts of 6 August 2006, urged by the US Embassy's Department of Justice representative, allowed the director of the Afghan National Security Council (NSC) to designate any organisation or group, with the president's consent. While there was a reference to judicial review, there were no standards of review in the draft, and in violation of separation of powers principles, the draft provided that 'procedures for judicial review of a designation shall be established by regulations issued by the director of the NSC'. This is in violation of international human rights standards and norms, as well as accepted principles of judicial review. In the October 2006 draft, the designation power of the NSC director is given to the Attorney General, but the human rights violations remain. A 2006 version of the US draft included even religious materials and medical supplies in the definition of material support that could lead to prosecution.[43] In the 6 August 2006 draft, the definition of material support at article 3(5) follows the language of the Patriot Act in the definition of material support and resources, excluding 'medicine or religious materials'. Yet the October 2005 draft, approved by 'Washington', removed the exclusion of 'except medicine or religious materials' (article 3(3) (renumbered)). Other pro-law-enforcement variations on the theme of the US Patriot Act in Washington's draft for Afghanistan included proposals that were contrary to established international or Afghan standards: authorising detentions of suspects on an order of a prosecutor (not a judge) for up

---

43 Co-author Hartmann was present during all of these discussions and received the drafts, as the drafts were being discussed by the criminal law reform working group (CLRWG), discussed below, and Hartmann (then of US State/INL's JSSP), along with co-secretariat UNODC (through criminal law expert Matteo Pasquali), were the moderators of the discussions. This draft language had caused great concern to the ICRC representative, who addressed the CLRWG on this and other issues.

to 120 days (6 August 2006 US draft, at article 43) was a clear violation of human rights standards, as well as of articles 24 and 25 of the Afghan constitution, and article 9(3) of the International Covenant on Civil and Political Rights as applied through article 7 of the constitution,[44] whereas an expansion of the US Patriot Act's definition of a terrorist act from acts that are 'dangerous to human life' also to include 'violent acts' contradicted legal tradition of criminal laws of Afghanistan. Both US drafts include the expansive definition in article 3(1)(a) of an illegal 'violent act', which could be characterised as a person throwing rocks at or pushing armoured police officers. This was also a concern on the part of the criminal law reform working group (CLRWG) and a senior UNAMA lawyer.

After months of discussion by the CLRWG, a mixed national/international expert drafting group discussed below, with a substantial majority consistently in opposition to the US Department of Justice position, the director of the Ministry of Justice *Taqnin* decided to abandon the complex US draft as inappropriate for Afghanistan, and the simpler terrorism law was decreed by the President in June 2008. *Taqnin* director Syed Yousuf Halim, who stated that they had preferred but been pressured into replacing the 'old' (Afghan-written) draft, and that they 'had concerns about the ability of the courts and prosecutors to correctly apply the very long and complex' US draft. The *Taqnin*, he said, had agreed with the Afghan draft and believed it fit Afghanistan and had the best of new ideas put into that older draft, and that it would be 'applicable to the people of Afghanistan'. As a result, per the instructions of director Halim and with the support of a substantial majority on the CLRWG, as well as that of the US Embassy's rule of law coordinator, the CLRWG dropped consideration of the US Department of Justice draft, and after further work, submitted revisions to the original draft terror law to the *Taqnin*. The *Taqnin* accepted the majority of suggestions and approved it, after

---

44 Constitution articles 24 and 25 state the rights to liberty and the presumption of innocence, which require detentions to be an exception that is justified by an ascertainable standard to be decided by an independent judge. Article 7 incorporates the ICCPR's article 9(3), which requires that 'anyone arrested or detained on a criminal charge shall be brought promptly before a judge or other officer authorised by law to exercise judicial power and shall be entitled to trial within a reasonable time or to release'. This would not include a prosecutor, who is not a judge but part of the executive branch. Indeed, the ICCPR's UN Human Rights Committee, the European Court of Human Rights and most countries' own procedural laws limit police/prosecutor detention to no more than three to four days before judicial review is required.

which the President, under article 79 of the constitution, decreed it into law.[45]

The criminal law reform working group: a new hope

Against this background, one positive example of an inclusive and transparent process stands out – the criminal law reform working group (CLRWG).

The attempt to start a systemic capacity-building process was based on the Afghanistan national development strategy law reform working group, chaired by the Minister of Justice. This was a reaction to the virtually unilateral way in which decrees were drafted during 2004 and 2005. In 2006, discussions began to implement the higher policy discussed in that working group though two subgroups, one for criminal law and one for civil and family law. Both subgroups were formed through a formal memorandum of understanding with the minister, but only the criminal subgroup, CLRWG, had any working meetings. Soon it was meeting for an entire day every week to revise drafts provided by the *Taqnin*. Both Dari and English versions were drafted, and changes were made by consensus. These revisions were then provided in the form of tracked changes back to the *Taqnin*. The CLRWG worked on a range of laws, including those for terrorism, human trafficking, juvenile code, extradition and mutual legal assistance, and the high office of oversight and anti-corruption.

The CLRWG is currently composed of representatives from the Supreme Court, the Attorney General's Office, the Ministry of Interior and the Afghan Independent Human Rights Commission, with occasional appearances depending upon the draft laws being reviewed by representatives from the Afghan independent bar association, audit office, Ministry of Justice/ *Taqnin*, and other ministries. International experts include representatives from UNODC and the US State/INL-funded Judicial Sector Support Program as comprising the co-secretariat, UNAMA, UNDP, the US and UK embassies, the Italian Cooperation Office (successor to the IJPO), EUPOL, Canadem, and, when relevant, the participation of the US Institute of Peace, UNIFEM, CSTC-A (US Department of Defence) and GTZ.

Over the course of a year, the CLRWG held regular weekly discussions on the revision of a new 2007–08 Afghan-drafted criminal procedure

---

45 Meeting between co-author Hartmann and UNODC law reform expert Matteo Pasquali and Ministry of Justice *Taqnin* director Syed Yousuf Halim, 20 May 2007.

code (CPC) intended by the government and parliament to replace the disparate codes. The ICPC, pursuant to article 79 of the constitution, was considered by the parliament. Rather than disapproving it, the *Wolesi Jirga* allowed it to remain in legal effect but instructed the government to draft for its review a new all-inclusive criminal procedure code.[46] The forum for discussion of the draft CPC had been opened in April 2008, when the *Taqnin* of the Ministry of Justice provided the CLRWG with the draft code. At a conference held in Syracusa in April 2008, the Afghan delegates, consisting of the CLRWG and the office of the president and members of parliament, after considering advice of international experts, had provided a written consensus and points of suggestion on legal policy to guide the CLRWG in its revision of the draft. The CLRWG revision of the draft CPC was aimed at implementing international human rights standards, and ensuring effective and fair proceedings in destabilising crimes, including terrorism, corruption, organised crime and narcotics trafficking. This included conforming the draft CPC to Afghanistan's legislative obligations in the UN conventions against corruption and transnational organised crime.

The working group's method of operation was to implement the legal policy formed in Syracusa by discussing each article – those originally drafted by the *Taqnin* and those proposed as amendments by the CLRWG itself. In the review process, the CLRWG adopted the paradigm of respecting, to the widest extent reconcilable with the legal policy and international legal standards, the structure and major institutional decisions as drafted by the *Taqnin*. In proposing revisions, the CLRWG did not rely on any single model of criminal procedure. Rather, it derived from the knowledge and experience of all its members solutions that were custom-designed for Afghanistan. No revision was made without an Afghan consensus that it was appropriate to the specific circumstances, institutional capacity and legal culture of Afghanistan. This process took over one year, with one or one-and-a-half days of revision sessions each week. The working group completed its task by May 2009. The next step was a series of presentations for the members of parliament in order to gain their understanding of and support for the draft.

---

46 Letter to Ministry of Justice dated 2 April 2006 by Sadiq Modaber, Deputy Minister of State for Parliamentary Affairs, referring to 30 March 2006 letter by justice and judicial, administrative reform and anti-corruption commission of *Wolesi Jirga*, copy in possession of authors.

In order to gain an introduction to the parliamentary process, the CLRWG held a week-long workshop in Vienna, attended by the senior representatives of both houses of the parliament and with the participation of world-renowned experts. The Vienna consensus paper supporting this revised CPC was then discussed in Kabul, and recommendations implemented in the form of corrections to the draft code.

The revised draft CPC addresses in detail all aspects of criminal proceedings, and has the potential to meet requirements of modern codifications in this field. Emphasis must be put in particular on the following three areas. First, the draft implements in detail the human rights protections foreseen under the International Covenant on Civil and Political Rights and the 2004 constitution. Among other things, it reinforces the presumption of innocence and links the authorisation to undertake criminal procedure actions to a quantum of proof that must be met. Likewise, it implements the constitutional principle of presumption of liberty by notionally disconnecting the carrying out of an investigation and detention of the suspect, and by providing for the requirements for grounds for arrest and detention, for a possibility to challenge the legality of arrest or detention before a court, and for a remedy for persons who are detained unlawfully. It further provides for non-custodial alternatives to detention.

Second, it provides for novel measures necessary effectively to address organised crime and thus implement Afghanistan's obligations under international conventions. The discussion in the CLRWG led to an agreement that witness protection is required by Islamic law, and relevant provisions were inserted in the draft. There was, moreover, a consensus to introduce covert and other technical measures of surveillance for the investigation of most serious crimes, and that it be accompanied by training, resources and institutional reforms necessary to ensure that these provisions are implemented with respect to the right of human dignity and privacy, protected under the constitution.

Third, the draft CPC foresees an array of measures aimed at limiting the population under incarceration, those that allow the discharge of a criminal case without holding a trial and those that are post-conviction alternatives to imprisonment.

This journey gave us an opportunity to make several observations.

We noticed that a humble international approach based on unrushed discussion and patient two-way explanation reveals far-going similarities in Western and Islamic procedural institutions and often removes points of contention, despite initially remote positions. This was in part possible due to collaboration providing insight into the matter from different angles, represented by all Afghan justice institutions and the participation of Afghans with academic expertise. This was also due to having available legally versed interpreters with experience in criminal justice legal translation. Without this combined expertise, it would not have been possible to discern disparities in approach from inaccuracies in drafting and translation.

On the linguistic side, of crucial importance was to use the Afghan draft in Dari as the base text and to adopt Dari, as opposed to English, as the language that controls the revisions. This approach is to be contrasted to the English-based approach used for the counter-narcotics law, which resulted in a significant number of provisions in the *Official Gazette* Dari version that were garbled and unintelligible to Afghan professionals.

We also noticed that Afghan participants, including the Ministry of Justice and the parliament, were much more open to accepting and incorporating foreign legal concepts and language as long as those imports concerned entirely novel institutions. This was the case even when very difficult and complex issues, such as covert measures of investigation and alternatives to imprisonment, were involved. They were less prone to accepting changes, no matter how well supported or even mandated by international standards, where they concerned traditional matter of their criminal procedure. Nevertheless, it is important to note that most of the proposed revisions were accepted unanimously, and where it proved impossible to reach agreement, an explanatory note was made, marking the disagreement and its merits, for reference by future commentators and decision-makers.

The Afghan justice and law reform institutions have been public and extravagant with their praise for the CLRWG. The chief of the Ministry of Justice *Taqnin* and Minister of Justice both gave high praise for the structured process and collaboration inherent in the CLRWG, stating that the result was the best drafting they have received from the international community. The Minister of Justice and *Taqnin* has already requested the CLRWG to work on upcoming anti-corruption legislation, the laws on special courts for ministers and Supreme Court justices, and a systemic revision and redrafting of the entire 1976 penal code that is expected to take at least a year.[47] The Ministry of Justice and senior parliamentarians

---

47 Stated by former Minister of Justice Sarwar Danish and *Taqnin* chief Halim to the co-secretariat and the Afghan and international CLRWG on the formal handover of the finished revision of the draft CPC and in a formal tripartite UNODC project review in 2009, and again in March 2010 during two meetings with UNODC. Both co-authors

have given public thanks to the CLRWG for bringing the parliament 'for the first time' into the process of lawmaking, and for explaining the rationale behind the revisions, before the President decreed it.[48]

While the very existence of the CLRWG represents significant progress, as with all progress in Afghanistan, it is fragile. At the time of writing (May 2010), the work of the CLRWG is hampered by the deteriorating security situation, which affects recruitment and movement, competing agendas with an emphasis on results now rather than quality and consensus, the lack of committed funding, and international personnel turnover. The current push to promulgate decrees, especially relating to corruption, puts unrealistic time limits on the CLRWG's reviewing role. For example, both the violence against women act and the law on special courts for ministers and Supreme Court justices were given to CLRWG with an unrealistic one-week review and revision deadline, which prevents it from providing comparative law analysis and use of international resources for research. While UNODC, with US State/INL-JSSP, has been carrying the burden of leading and moderating the CLRWG, their capacity is now at risk. Unfortunately, this is happening just when the *Taqnin* has asked the CLRWG to start a one-year-plus penal code reform process similar to the one-year process just completed for the new CPC. Moreover, the CLRWG is in talks to expand its process to include like assistance to the national assembly.

The CLRWG's existence remains precarious. No matter what its future holds, however, CLRWG will remain an example of how collaboration and consensus are built on the foundation of meticulous work, mutual respect and open-mindedness, and how the enthusiasm and dedication of a handful of legal professionals can give momentum to sustainable change.

References

Ahmed, Faiz (2005). 'Judicial reform in Afghanistan: A case study in the new criminal procedure code', *Hastings International and Comparative Law Review*, 29: 93 (LexisNexis version)

were present. Restated by current Minister of Justice Habibullah Ghalib to co-author Hartmann on 22 April 2010.
48 Stated by *Wolesi Jirga* security committee chair Ludin and *Meshrano Jirga* international relations committee chair Huqooqmal at open CLRWG meetings at UNODC HQ and the Ministry of Justice. Both co-authors were present.

Ahmed, Faiz (2007). 'Afghanistan's reconstruction, five years later: Narratives of progress, marginalised realities, and the politics of law in a transitional Islamic republic', *Gonzaga Journal of International Law*, 10: 269, available at www. gonzagajil.org

Huggler, Justin (2007). 'Afghan anti-corruption chief is drug dealer', *The Independent*, 10 March 2007, http://news.independent.co.uk/world/asia/article2344759.ece

Nader, Laura (2007). 'Promise or plunder? A past and future look at law and development', *Global Jurist*, 7(2) (Frontiers), article 1, available at www. bepress.com/gj/vol7/iss2/art1

UNODC (2004). International counter-narcotics conference on Afghanistan, 8–9 February 2004, Vienna, collected papers on UNODC's official website at www.unodc.org/pdf/afg/afg_intl_counter_narcotics_conf_2004.pdf

PART VI

Kandahar

15

No justice, no peace

Kandahar, 2005–09

GRAEME SMITH

I first arrived in Kandahar in 2005 by car, descending out of the rough hills around Kabul and onto the plains of southern Afghanistan via Highway 1, the country's main artery. In those days, the road was smooth and freshly tarmacked. We travelled without fear. The following year, with reports of Taliban roadblocks on the highway, it was considered too dangerous for a foreigner to drive – but I could still make the trip by bus, wearing Afghan clothes and hiding myself among the passengers. By 2007, however, the insurgents were also stopping the buses, as the gunmen felt confident enough about their control of the rural districts to conduct leisurely searches. The year after, I stopped allowing my Afghan staff to travel by road, preferring to buy them air tickets rather than expose them to the possibility that some Taliban fighter would get suspicious about their haircuts, their clothes, a name in their cell phone, or any of the other causes of suspicion that could get a person kidnapped or killed. Those who did venture onto the highway found it pockmarked with bomb craters and littered with the husks of burned vehicles.

During my years in southern Afghanistan (2005–09), we did not need the UN risk maps or NATO's incident data to understand that things were getting worse. The growing insurgency shaped the lives of everybody in the south, myself included. Despite many reasons being offered by military commanders and foreign commentators, nobody knows precisely why the insurgency grew so rapidly. Military commanders prefer to describe their enemies as mercenaries, claiming that Taliban foot soldiers receive generous payments for their services. Others view the insurgents through the prism of religious zealotry, calling them brainwashed products of madrasa indoctrination. For my part, I was impressed by the argument of many participants at the recent UNSW conference, which placed an emphasis on justice issues. The argument that poor delivery of justice in the Pashtun belt during Hamid Karzai's first presidential term was a major factor in the rapid growth of Taliban control resonates strongly with what I experienced and observed.

Different forms of justice

I saw six kinds of justice at work in Kandahar:

Taliban justice

For example, in Bandi Timor (south Maywand), we collected video footage of insurgents responding to a complaint about an alleged thief. They went to the suspect's house, arrested him, bound his hands and brought him before a Taliban court. An elderly judge, wearing a white turban, sat with a big Koran open in front of him and questioned the man. After some conversation, he declared him innocent. He was released. Others aren't so lucky, as we heard many reports of suspected thieves suffering amputation and suspected 'foreign spies' being hung from the trees.

Layered Taliban/tribal justice

Taliban courts don't always replace traditional *shuras*. In Shah Wali Kot district, where the Taliban are largely in control, we interviewed elders who said the village *shura* still arbitrated most disputes and administered justice. If one party is unhappy with the *shura*'s decision, however, they can take the case to the Taliban, which effectively functions as a court of appeal.

Tribal justice

This can operate in the city just as effectively as the villages. Mullah Naqib of the Alokozai tribe investigated claims that one of his tribesmen was responsible for the death of a Canadian diplomat in early 2006, and decided the man was innocent. This decision immediately took precedence over formal justice mechanisms and the suspect was set free – despite protests from Afghan national police criminal investigators, and despite the fact that Naqib's enquiries had taken only two days.

Hybrid tribal/government justice

Ahmed Wali Karzai's (AWK) house in Kandahar is the paragon of a hybrid tribal-government court. In his capacity as chairman of Kandahar's provincial council, he represents the government, and his decisions are backed by the implicit threat of violence by government and foreign forces. Officially, of course, he has no role within the government judicial system. But as an elder of the Popolzai tribe and the younger half-brother of the President, AWK is widely believed to wield enormous influence. Who knows how much power he really has; perhaps more important is that people in Kandahar are convinced that he is the highest authority to whom they have access, as evidenced by the endless stream of supplicants sitting and sprawling across the steps and halls of his house, waiting for an audience.

Government justice

I've witnessed more problems with the official police and judicial system than with any other form of justice operating in southern Afghanistan. For example, Afghan national police arbitrarily detained two men near the scene of a bomb blast in 2007, releasing one of them after his family paid bribes and torturing the other to death. His body was discovered in a canal. They'd been held in a private home, one of several unofficial jails in Kandahar. I also spent time inside the city's biggest prison, Sarpoza, interviewing men who showed me their scars and told horrible stories about torture as a routine feature of government justice.

Foreigners' justice

I've talked with former detainees who were snatched from their farms on the slightest pretext by foreign troops, who don't understand Afghanistan in general, much less the local environment. If they lack a translator, or if there's confusion about why a person has been found in a particular place at a particular time, international troops have sometimes defaulted to detaining people and sorting out the basis for detention later. This creates a presumption of guilt, as these people are often treated as battlefield combatants, regardless of whether or not there's any indication of being an insurgent. Another common reason for detention is a positive test for gunpowder residue on a man's hands, which doesn't prove much in a place where everybody is armed, and gun battles don't always involve insurgents. Even my friend Jojo was detained for eleven months by US forces, despite his status as a long-time translator for CTV, Canada's largest television network. He described being badly abused at Bagram, a facility that has become a symbol of resentment among southern Pashtuns.

Night raids by elite counter-terrorism units have also stoked local anger, because if you burst into anybody's house in the middle of the night in Kandahar, you're almost guaranteed to stir up trouble; if the homeowner wasn't already an insurgent, after the violation of the sanctity of his home, he's likely to become one. Still, on the whole, people in Kandahar generally prefer foreigners' justice to the government system because it's less deliberately predatory; its abuses result from ignorance and recklessness rather than malice. Despite the abuses detainees have suffered at Bagram, torture is less widespread – and less severe – in NATO or US custody than inside Afghan prisons. Indeed, in many cases, detainees in NATO facilities enjoy softer beds and better meals than they've previously experienced in their entire lives. But arbitrary detention and the abuses committed against those detained do great damage to the image of foreign forces, who are also blamed for their support of the more grotesquely abusive government system.

What is to be done?

The biggest obstacle to redressing this crippling pattern of injustice and abuse is what Vendrell has aptly described as the 'facile optimism' of the international community. Optimists have held up as grounds for hope progressive clauses of the constitution written by foreigners; claims that eradicating 4,000 hectares out of the 70,000 hectares of opium poppy in Helmand was a great success (I'd call such eradication a capricious and useless irritant); and hopes for a reorganised curriculum in Kabul's law school. All such measures fall into the realm of what I'd call 'technical solutions' to the problems in Afghanistan, which are at best terribly inadequate and at worst entirely beside the point. After nearly a decade of armed occupation, I don't think it's useful to wish we had better coordination, more money, and soldiers magically capable of avoiding civilian casualties. Instead, we need to admit our weakness, incapacity and ignorance.

Do any foreigners really understand what Afghans want? The polling done is criminally flawed, generating patently ridiculous claims such as that most people trust the Afghan national police. When a pilot gets implausible results from his instruments, he looks out the window to make sure he's not flying into a mountain; when governments' contractors, civil servants or soldiers deliver good news, they should take a reality check.

Every foreign observer and participant now acknowledges that the conflict is essentially political. How do you go about trying to win a political contest without any good sense of what the people want? You do what parties always do: steal your opponent's platform. What platform are the Taliban 'running' on? First, foreigners out; second, justice; and third, not much else. This third point is important, because it means the Taliban promise to leave people unmolested to grow illegal drugs, resist modern ideas about status of women, and so on. That's not much of a platform if you're trying to win over the educated people of Kabul, or even the elites of Kandahar city. But it might work in the rural Pashtun belt, where the insurgency is based.

Some well-informed observers have warned of terrible consequences if foreigners withdraw, even partially, saying the Taliban could gain momentum and destabilise areas beyond the Pashtun belt. This may happen, but perhaps it may not. The final years of the communist regime in southern Afghanistan, under the administration of Noorolhaq Oloomi in Kandahar, showed that deal-making and significant foreign subsidies are sometimes enough to prop up a moderate Afghan government. Oloomi bribed his opponents and – importantly – conceded vast swathes of territory to his opponents where they were essentially autonomous from the state. This has parallels with the apparently successful experience in Uruzgan, whose key ingredient was the military's self-restraint. The Dutch have deliberately tolerated Taliban control in some parts of Uruzgan, and security in the provincial capital, Tarin Kowt, has steadily improved, while security in the capital cities of neighbouring provinces has deteriorated sharply. The same might be accomplished in many other parts of the Pashtun belt, without creating the conditions that would allow the insurgents to topple the governments in Islamabad or Kabul.

This is not a great scenario, but it may be an option worth considering as we stare down the barrel of another fighting season in 2010 (at the time of writing). It's certainly more realistic than the four-point plan the US conceived in late 2009. I can just imagine how each of the points would make my Afghan friends laugh bitterly.

- Improve security for the population. (But you're surging troops with the expectation of higher casualties, meaning more violent deaths. Afghans don't associate more killings with more security.)
- Strengthen the link between the people and the government. (But the people hate the government. They don't want any link with it.)
- Bolster the licit economy. (But people want to grow whatever is most profitable.)

• Improve public relations. (But the people understand your actions better than you do – the problem isn't poor communication; the problem is your actions.)

Not that everything the US and its allies are doing in Afghanistan is misguided. In fact, three radical changes the US made in early 2010 show that American war planners now realise some of the crippling weaknesses of their approach in Afghanistan thus far. These developments have caught some analysts by surprise, as they have acknowledged and attempted to correct facets of the mission that had appeared permanent: rising civilian casualties, a disastrous war on drugs, and culturally unacceptable night raids by Special Forces. Among these three issues, by far the most important is the recent reversal of civilian casualty trends. The reduction in civilian deaths attributed to Afghan and international forces, down 28 per cent in 2009 from the previous year, represents an astonishing success, considering that during the same period, most other indicators showed an intensifying conflict: more insurgent attacks, the geographical spread of instability, and thousands of extra troops surging into the country. This has dramatically changed the maths that surrounds the question posed by ordinary Afghan villagers: 'Who should we fear?' The typical answer in Kandahar has been 'both sides'. Kandaharis talk of standing with a foot on two watermelons, and of being beaten by the Taliban at night and by the government during the day. That opinion could be supported by statistics in recent years that showed insurgents and pro-government forces killed comparable numbers of civilians.[1] Now that foreign forces are reducing civilian casualties, the imbalance is much more dramatic, with insurgents killing innocents in far greater numbers. Eventually, foreign forces might reasonably hope that villagers will view them as less threatening than their opposition.

But gaining popularity among rural Afghans isn't just a matter of killing fewer civilians. The threat to their livelihoods is almost as frightening as risks to their lives, which makes the issue of poppy destruction important. I've witnessed how Taliban gained popularity in places such as Bandi Timor, a region of southern Maywand district to the west of Kandahar city, by fighting off government forces sent to eradicate opium crops. A few battles made the insurgents into local heroes who were safeguarding the incomes of farmers who might otherwise be ruined by the government's

---

1 Human Rights Watch has estimated that about 60 per cent of civilian casualties are caused by insurgents, and the remainder by ISAF/US/Afghan government forces.

counter-narcotics efforts. The US special coordinator for Afghanistan and Pakistan, Richard Holbrooke, has acknowledged that eradication has been counterproductive. If farmers are allowed to harvest their crops this spring, it might help the government's reputation in key rural areas. Similarly, US commanders have indicated that they will tighten controls over counter-terrorism units that have conducted daring – but alienating – night raids in recent years. Again, if those public statements translate into a new course of action in this summer's fighting season, then it would undercut a source of grievance that drives young men to take up arms against the foreign troops.

Sadly, my personal feeling is that none of these changes will be enough to reverse the negative trends that have prevailed in southern Afghanistan since 2005. Whatever new initiatives the foreign troops implement are undermined by the fact that they're no longer viewed as reliable. Villagers often prefer Taliban justice because the insurgents are generally predictable: they follow a code that, while harsh, is easily understood. The same cannot be said of the confusing array of erratically applied models of justice that operate in government-controlled areas. Unfortunately, this serves as a metaphor for the confusion of the mission as a whole. Afghans do not understand what the foreigners are trying to achieve. At this point, many are just waiting for them to leave, and positioning themselves accordingly.

Editor's postscript: In one weekend in March 2010, bombs in Kandahar City killed at least thirty-five people. The Taliban described the bombs as a demonstration that they were ready for the next phase of the war, which ISAF has already said would move to securing Kandahar. The Interior Ministry approved Governor Tooryalai Wesa's request for 1,100 more police to help secure the city. But these police will suffer from the same poor and inappropriate paramilitary training as the police already in place. Moreover, the longstanding neglect of the state justice system in the south means there will be no functioning system to handle those the police and soldiers detain in a manner consistent with the rule of law or Kandaharis' notions of justice.

16

Kandahar after the fall of the Taliban

SHAFIULLAH AFGHAN

I was born in the district of Khakrez, in relatively secure times a two-hour drive north-west of Kandahar City. It was 1980, the year after the Soviets began unevenly occupying Afghanistan. When I was still young, my family and I, like millions of others, fled to Pakistan and began the difficult life of refugees. Most of the time we lived in Quetta, the capital of Baluchistan, the huge, underpopulated province across the border from Kandahar. In 2001 I returned to Kandahar with Akrem Khakrezwal, and had the privilege of working as his assistant as he became chief of police, successively, in Kandahar, Mazar-i Sharif and Kabul. On a visit home to Kandahar in 2005, he was killed by a huge bomb planted in a mosque. This crime was never seriously investigated. I then went to work as a governance adviser for the Canadian provincial reconstruction team. Two years later my boss there, a kind man approaching retirement named Glynn Berry, was killed by another bomb. It happened in district 5 of Kandahar City. A man was detained for that murder but Governor Khalid released him on the recommendation of Ahmed Wali Karzai, President Karzai's half-brother and head of Kandahar's provincial council. I, like everyone from Kandahar, have seen a lot of injustice. And yet, despite injustice being usual, it has never become a norm; we have continued to expect and yearn for better.

Kandahar is the country's second-biggest city and home to nearly half the people in the entire south. It was also the birthplace and bastion of the Taliban. After routing the Taliban in 2001, instead of making Kandahar a showcase for the benefits of the new order, the international community delivered it into the arms of a group of ruthless predators.

After the fall of the Taliban, nearly all the group's members, of whatever rank, disappeared from Kandahar or melted back into their villages in rural districts. Soon after the presidential amnesty of 2002, some of the Taliban who'd returned to their villages were arrested, tortured and even killed. Warlords and corrupt chiefs of police and district leaders abused

308

the former Taliban, often in private jails, and gave them little choice but to attempt to escape to Pakistan. We have hundreds of examples of such abuse, such as that of the Isaqzai tribe in Bandi Timor village of Maywand district. The Isaqzai enjoyed good relations with the Taliban when they were in power and earned a lot of money from trafficking opium and heroin. When the tables were turned, many members of the Isaqzai were tortured in jails operated by the militia of Governor Gul Agha Sherzai.

On the basis of information fed by the warlords or corrupt officials that the Isaqzai were still working with the Taliban or holding their money or drugs, Afghan and coalition forces continually raided their homes. Eventually, all members of the tribe moved to other parts of the country or to Pakistan. Ex-Taliban who remain in Afghanistan tell of having been detained and tortured five times or more by warlords or militias linked to the government. The goal of this abuse was to obtain weapons or money, even from very poor people. In response to this abuse, the ex-Taliban, and even people who had never been sympathetic to the Taliban regime, began searching for ways to protect themselves. The abuse was not counterbalanced by any development, as all money went to projects in Kandahar City or district centres rather than in the villages where most people live. Most of it ended up in the pockets of a few individuals with good connections to the international community.

Though these activities gradually led people to distance themselves from the government, for the first few years after the overthrow of the Taliban, the vast majority of people clung to hopes of a brighter future. They understood that the government was new, and believed its performance would improve. Unfortunately, these hopes went unfulfilled. Still, people were exhausted by decades of war, and they watched the disappointments multiply without reacting.

Three categories of people had power: warlords, many of whom built their power bases during the *jihad* and civil war; criminals who knew no way to make a living except by wielding an AK-47; and Afghans who returned from the US and Europe, from whom people hoped for idealistic public service but who instead focused on lining their own pockets.

The international community ignored the majority of Afghans, those who'd suffered continuously through the past three decades and lost virtually everything through the ongoing wars. No attention was paid to the poor farmers who make up 80 per cent of the population. The justice system either was too weak to protect people from predatory behaviour by the powerful, or was predatory itself. The result of all this: the Taliban rose again.

The return of the Taliban

While Afghans were becoming disillusioned by conditions in their own country, top Taliban leaders were seen in Quetta, the capital of Pakistan's Baluchistan province, renting houses and visiting mosques. Though their presence was common knowledge, neither the Afghan government nor even the countries contributing to the coalition reacted. The Taliban gradually became emboldened by the lack of reaction, and more and more of them showed themselves in public. Eventually they started to organise some small military actions along the border, riders on motorbikes attacking border checkpoints, and step by step establishing a presence in the mountains of Zabul, Kandahar, Uruzgan and border areas of Helmand province. Government security forces were strong enough to chase these small groups of neo-Taliban into the mountains, but the response was on a small scale. Low-ranking Taliban in Afghanistan and Pakistan were imprisoned and tortured, and medium-ranking men were handed over to the US, but the top leadership based in Pakistan were never touched. Those Taliban who were in Pakistani prisons were eventually released on condition that they cooperate with the ISI, and they are now working with the Quetta *shura*. It is the Quetta *shura* that makes the decisions and plans operations, which then pass through the local Taliban *shuras* and down to a command encompassing two or three districts.

The Quetta *shura*'s operations gradually increased in the south and south-east of Afghanistan. Minor Afghan government officials began accusing Taliban of attacking border checkpoints and then perpetrating violent acts on Afghan territory before returning to safety in Pakistan. Pakistan government officials vehemently denied these claims. The evidence is overwhelming, however, that the Taliban, operating in collusion with al-Qaeda in Afghanistan's Khost, Paktiya and Nuristan provinces, operate from Pakistan's Federally Administered Tribal Areas, while those operating in Afghanistan's Kandahar, Uruzgan, Zabul and Helmand provinces are directed from the capital of Pakistan's Baluchistan province.

The focus of all their operations is influencing ordinary Afghans. They are using an updated version of the strategy employed against the Soviet occupation from 1979 to 1989. In that decade, resistance began in rural villages and gradually reached the gates of the main cities. This time, under the gaze of the Afghan government's international backers, the Taliban are benefiting from the appalling corruption and incompetence of government officials at the district and provincial levels, and in particular the complete lack of any credible system of justice.

Even in provincial capitals, defendants in criminal cases languished in prison while waiting for their cases to be heard. In the Uruzgan capital of Tarin Kowt, for example, between 2002 and 2009 virtually none of the fifty-six prisoners in the decrepit provincial facility had been convicted of a crime. In many cases, the prisoners had waited years for their cases to be tried because Kabul had not supplied a judge to hear them. Someone had been provisionally offered the post in Kabul, but he had refused to pay the bribe demanded to take it up. Their continued detention was in violation of article 20 of the law on prisons, which says that if the primary court hadn't heard a case within two months of arrest, they should be released. The same law requires prison officials to notify the prosecutor if they have held a prisoner for forty-five days without having received a date for his arraignment. These requirements are restated in appendix 3 to article 6 of the interim code of criminal procedure.

No provincial officials concerned themselves with this gross injustice, and every aspect of the judicial system was complicit in this systematic violation of the laws they were charged with enforcing. The illegal imprisonment was only resolved after the UN brought senior Afghan officials from Kabul, and then continued lobbying to ensure action was taken. Significantly, the warden in the Tarin Kowt prison admitted the problem but felt the prerogatives of those who had detained and arrested the imprisoned men outweighed the force of the law. This is not surprising: the powerbrokers and police who did their bidding were familiar and close; the law was new and distant, and did not seem to be taken seriously by anyone.

From the point of view of the insurgency and Afghanistan's arrested development, such injustices and the Taliban's activities were complementary.

Despite all this, when the 2004 elections were held, many people retained some hope. Voters turned out in large numbers. But neither elections nor official censure seemed to have any impact on who was appointed to official positions. Governorships and senior roles in the police and judiciary all rotated among the same small, closed circle of people. In one egregious but in no way anomalous example, a man working as a judge in Kandahar released a prisoner sentenced to seventeen years in prison without explanation. The prosecutor launched an investigation and wanted to arrest him, but he escaped and was later appointed chief judge in Helmand province. In another instance, a prosecutor whom the governor had removed for corruption and official negligence received a letter of appreciation from the Attorney-General's office in Kabul, and on this basis was appointed Helmand's chief prosecutor.

Corruption also translated into incompetence. District leaders and chiefs of police, the state officials who had the most face-to-face dealing with people living in the countryside and the biggest impact on their lives, were appointed on the basis of their relationships with warlords and other powerbrokers rather than their abilities. After district-level officials were appointed, more senior officials had little influence over them, neither punishing bad performance nor rewarding good work. Most people in state jobs since 2001 have had no idea what their job is supposed to entail, much less how to do it. A teacher with the right connections, for instance, will be made deputy to the head detective of the counter-terrorism police or counter-narcotics police.

In addition to corruption, and the lack of any connection between a person's performance and punishment or reward, efforts to improve security were crippled by the lack of coordination among Afghan national security forces and the very halting implementation of a disarmament, demobilisation and reintegration process for hundreds of militias around the country. The process got under way before there were enough Afghan soldiers or police (ANA or ANP) to oversee it effectively.

What police there were received neither the training nor the equipment they needed. Police commanders had only a hazy idea of how many men they had. A checkpoint would report twenty officers present when there were only six. Commanders benefited from this numbers game, for the salaries, food and other allowances for all twenty men claimed as present went first to him, and he would then only distribute what was owed (or less) to the six actually there. Police leave their duty stations without permission or even notifying anyone, and join new units just as casually. About 10,000 police have been trained in the south over the past five years, but if you look for them in police posts, you won't find more than 2,000 still on the job. As soon as a policeman has a falling out with his superior or decides he doesn't like his duty station, he will wander off and present himself without explanation at another post. Such sloppiness and its corrosive effects on public confidence in the government are at the very heart of Afghanistan's ongoing travails.

The police have about triple the fatality rate of the army. Lack of proper training and equipment and the low quality and motivation of personnel[1] all contribute to this, as does their grotesquely inappropriate

---

1 Until recently, entry-level pay for a police officer was $70 a month. In late 2009 it was doubled to equal that of Afghan national army soldiers. This is still not quite enough to afford sufficient food for an average-size family. A further raise is being considered.

use in fully military operations. Police are put through a seven-week training programme run by US military contractors, mostly retired police and soldiers, that focuses on paramilitary skills rather than policing. About half of the police in the south are drug addicts who systematically ignore their duties. There is no petrol available for vehicle patrols, and many of the static checkpoints post no watch, providing an easy target for the insurgents. Because there is no system for tracking which individuals belong in which units, the Taliban will often send their own people to infiltrate police units, and after lulling the real police into a false sense of security, massacre them. Detectives who are supposed to vet police recruits have no means of obtaining information about them, and so sign a paper saying the recruit has no criminal record without any idea of whether this is true. Thus, even after a Taliban plant has gunned down a group of policemen, the authorities have no information on the culprit that might allow them to track him down.

The criminal investigations division (detectives) is the key to effective policing, but has been especially neglected. The Kandahar CID struggle to find someone to do crime scene investigations, and lack the requisite equipment, such as cameras, minidisk recorders or fingerprinting kits. Worse yet, the regular police systematically fail to close off crime scenes and instead assiduously clean them, leaving no evidence by the time the detectives arrive. This means that the police regularly lack the material evidence used in investigating and prosecuting crimes elsewhere, creating the temptation to resort to other means to win a conviction.

These shortcomings harm security and undermine the legitimacy of the government in several complementary ways. On the day of the last presidential election in August 2009, in Kandahar City alone there were twenty-eight rocket attacks and IED explosions. After the election there was at least one rocket or IED attack inside the city virtually every day. Insurgents have capitalised on the international and Afghan military forces' focus on the rural districts to concentrate on the provincial capital. On election day, the Taliban cut off half the highways leading from the districts into Kandahar City.

In the south and south-east, 50 per cent of eligible voters didn't cast a ballot because of insecurity. A quarter of those who were not deterred by security problems nevertheless chose not to vote because they had no faith in the integrity of the electoral system. Their cynicism is amply justified by the government's calamitous performance after the first, hope-filled elections of 2004.

However, President Karzai and the parliament are irrelevant to the lives of most people in the south for the simple reason that the government only controls about 20 per cent of the territory. The majority of people who live under the predominant influence of the Taliban obviously cannot look to Kabul to improve their lives, and the city-dwellers who see the same corrupt powerbrokers running state offices have not much more reason to hope.

Taliban justice

If you ask anyone in the south whether they prefer the government or the Taliban, they will tell you they don't care who's in charge – they just want peace. But if you ask about life under the Taliban, you will be disconcerted to hear far more positive comments about the insurgents than about internationally backed government. People will tell you that the Taliban provide better security and a more effective system of justice than the government. Even those who live under Taliban control prefer its system of justice to the government's. It is cheaper, faster and stronger. A case in the government system, even if not derailed by corruption, will take a year to wend its way through the system; a Taliban court will pronounce a verdict and implement the sentence immediately. If you want to expedite a court process in the government system, you have to pay a bribe; in the Taliban system, no bribes are accepted or needed. In the government system, hundreds of sentences are pronounced without ever being executed; in the Taliban system, decisions are always enforced without delay. To access the government system, you have to come to the city because it has no presence in the rural districts; the Taliban system is everywhere and easy to reach. Moreover, it is dangerous to travel in government-controlled areas, whereas Taliban areas are safe (unless attacked by Afghan or international forces). The Taliban's justice system is the main public good they provide, and the most powerful incentive they offer people to support them.

The Taliban's system of justice also includes the consistency and effectiveness with which they are perceived to apply decisions. Mullah Omar, for instance, was able to end the cultivation of poppy with a single decree, whereas the government has seen cultivation rise and rise despite spending hundreds of millions of dollars in foreign aid to end it. Corruption undoes all their efforts. With a bribe, a poppy farmer can get a district official to leave his poppy field alone and destroy that of a rival who hasn't paid. The percentage of fields destroyed is far lower than reported, because generally security considerations make it impossible for anyone to verify the claims of district leaders, who are far from disinterested.

The legitimacy of the government, already tenuous because of its miserable performance in all the areas that count the most, has been weakened still further by the overt corruption surrounding the last presidential elections. In Kandahar, the insurgents can reach any part of the city at will, and assassinate government officials and NGO workers practically on a daily basis. The Taliban cannot be beaten unless and until the government acquires the will and the capacity to deliver at least a modicum of security and justice.

PART VII

Conclusion

17

Axioms and unknowns

WHIT MASON

This book is going to press amid a long overdue sense of crisis over Western policies and practices in Afghanistan. In the memorable words of Donald Rumsfeld: 'There are known knowns. These are things we know that we know. There are known unknowns. That is to say, there are things that we now know we don't know. But there are also unknown unknowns. These are things we do not know we don't know.' Undoubtedly the same could be said for Afghanistan, and both the known unknowns and the unknown ones must keep our hopes modest even as we reflect on things we have not always known but now feel with some confidence that we do.

As the foregoing chapters make clear, much of the intervention's spectacular underperformance derives from two categories of ignorance: not understanding the link between the rule of law and security; and, even after beginning to recognise the importance of the rule of law, not knowing how to foster it. Both areas of ignorance derive, in turn, from a superficial understanding of what the rule of law means and requires in the life of a society.

Just as 'everything is connected to everything else' in the relationship between law and society, so too with lawlessness and its corrosive effects on that state of affairs that we call the rule of law.

> Public disorder, crime and violence are endemic in immediate post-conflict environments. Organised criminal activity often fills the vacuum of authority left by a failed or toppled regime, hindering institutional development and preventing the establishment of public order and the rule of law. Criminal activity undermines governmental institutions, creating weak states dominated by criminal interests and causing regional instability. This environment provides fertile ground for the growth of international terrorism, since the absence of capable law enforcement provides immunity from detection and criminal groups supply ready networks for mobilising human and financial resources.
>
> (Graduate Students Working Group 2003)

In addition to this already noxious cocktail, the repeated triumph of brute power over law cripples Afghans' ability to mount a coordinated resistance to their many predators.

Western government officials straining to find shafts of light in the Afghan gloom often cite the growth of the widely respected Afghan national army, dramatic increases in the number of children in school, improved access to healthcare and minor reductions in the growth of opium poppy. (As Hafvenstein points out, reductions in poppy cultivation benefit narcotics officials and those whose stockpiles of poppy resin have been declining in value; the number that would be meaningful to Afghans is how many people's livelihoods are illegal.) Even officials like former British Foreign Secretary David Miliband who do their best to be rigorously realistic can hardly do justice to the degree to which admitted failings in the areas of security, justice and corruption vitiate improvements in every other area. In making a general point, in 2000, about the rule of law and development, Amartya Sen (2000) might have been commenting on Afghanistan ten years later: 'We cannot very well say that the development process has gone beautifully even though people are being arbitrarily hanged, criminals go free while law-abiding citizens end up in jail, and so on . . . Development has a strong association of meanings that makes a basic level of legality and judicial attainment a constitutive part of it.'

An appreciation of the centrality of justice to the project of reconstituting the Afghan state has grown steadily over the nine years since ending the Taliban regime, to the point that the theme of the London conference of international donors in January 2010 was 'peace with justice'. Leaders of the international intervention have come to realise the role of crime and corruption in undermining popular support for the state and providing the powerful with perverse incentives to keep it weak. Internationally supported initiatives to combat crime and corruption under way by the time of the London conference include the major crimes task force, mentored by the UK's SOCA and the US's FBI; EUPol's (EU) mentoring of the Afghan national police's criminal investigation division (CID, or detectives); the high oversight office attached to the presidency; the Attorney-General's office's anti-corruption unit; and the Supreme Court's anti-corruption tribunal.

These initiatives, salutary though they may be, still constitute technocratic efforts to tinker with discrete problems; President Obama's pledge on 1 December 2009 to begin drawing down US forces within eighteen months leaves no time for more radical measures, such as challenging the widely discredited re-election of President Karzai. Despite the evolution in understanding, the piecemeal technocratic approach of 2010 perpetuates the international interveners' avoidance of confronting constitutive political pathologies.

Virtually all the problems identified throughout this book are the result of trying to mechanistically impose alien institutional models rather than seeing issues of legitimacy, compliance, security and justice through Afghans' eyes. What does 'credibility' mean in the Afghanistan context? What factors contribute to the development of legitimate authority? How many Afghans can believe in a government that includes notorious warlords, has done nothing to address years of human rights atrocities, and retained power through a discredited election? How can an international intervention help address these? As Kilcullen writes, in the insecure conditions of insurgency, popular support and compliance follow power rather than power emanating from popular support. Yet a fair share of justice programming in Afghanistan has comprised preaching about human rights and the constitution to people living under the influence of the Taliban and other insurgent groups. Such programmes ignore the famous Kantian axiom that '"ought" implies "can"' (Kant 1962) – that is, it is absurd to say someone should do something that they cannot do. This minimalist requirement that interventions take account of the realities prevailing in the societies that they attempt to change is among the most important principles of political development.

Against this backdrop, it is to be hoped that both those who make policy and those who struggle to understand it will benefit by the convergence of the contributors to this volume on the following points, which can be regarded as axioms.

The rule of law and security are indivisible from one another and central to popular support for the state, which is the key to successful counter-insurgency

Scholars of rule of law promotion have called security the *sine qua non* of post-conflict reconstruction (Stromseth, Wippman and Brooks 2006: 134). Security is not only a prerequisite for the rule of law; security, understood as broadly as it is by Afghans, can only be achieved with the rule of law. For Afghans, the Taliban are only one source of insecurity; for many, common criminals and abusive state officials represent a bigger threat. For these people, the manifold forms of injustice that litter their lives discredit every aspect of the process of state reconstruction that Western governments are working to support. By prioritising 'security', understood in narrow military terms, over justice, the intervention severely crippled its ability to tackle the insurgency as a political problem.

The rule of law is the alternative to and security from the arbitrary assertion of other forms of power. To speak of security without the rule of law is an absurdity, since at most it could only refer to being safe from one source of threat at the price of being defenceless before others.

For a state to earn the support of people, it must give them security from predatory behaviour from any quarter, especially the state itself. As Jean-Jacques Rousseau wrote in *The Social Contract*: 'The strongest is never strong enough to be always the master, unless he transforms strength into right, and obedience into duty' (Rousseau 1762). Kilcullen's story of Deioces reminds us that this is an old theme, and that creating security has been a prerequisite and means of building up support for a regime since time out of mind.

Impunity is the nemesis of the rule of law

To mean anything, the rule of law must apply to everyone, especially those who are otherwise powerful enough to violate the rights of those who are weaker. It follows that all impunity corrupts the rule of law, and absolute impunity corrupts it absolutely. As Maley, Vendrell, Stapleton and Hartmann have shown, despite recent initiatives to combat corruption, the international community has deprived itself of the political leverage to compel compliance with the law at the highest levels.

Only a balanced distribution of power will forestall impunity

Maley and Vendrell also point out that the concentration of power in the presidency deprived the nascent new state of checks and balances that would compel all powerful figures to submit to the law. Hartmann describes how international interveners aided and abetted – through acts of omission but also commission – the mutually reinforcing relationship between presidential power, impunity, corruption and the narcotics trade.

Faustian bargains do not pay

As several of the authors in this volume note, President Karzai used his extensive powers to appoint potential spoilers to positions of authority, such as Gul Agha Sherzai as governor of Kandahar and Mohammed Fahim first as Defence Minister then as Vice-President. The US-led international military forces, initially limited to pursuing al-Qaeda and garrisoning Kabul, supported such figures and contributed to their impunity. As Afghan and Smith have written, the abusive behaviour of state officials – Sherzai and President Karzai's other allies – did more than anything else to rekindle the insurgency in Kandahar.

> *People – particularly the powerful – will only act within the law when they perceive that the incentives for doing so outweigh the advantages of flouting it.*

To explain why power-holders will comply with the law, including the constitutive laws of a putatively democratic political system, Weingast (1997) emphasises the importance of both enforcement and coordination. These effectively refer to the state and civil society sides of the same coin. When individuals or groups outside the state do not expect the state to enforce the law, they will not follow it; when civil society cannot coordinate effectively to resist abuse of power by the state, the state will abuse it. Deschamps and Roe's point that the most intractable land disputes are those in which a disputant acts in bad faith, knowing they are wrong but hoping they can prevail anyway, underscores the importance of enforcement. For property rights to be effectively protected in Afghanistan, the relative power of warlords and the other supporters of the state must be changed so that warlords come to view the costs of predatory behaviour as outweighing the benefits. In other words, as long as they can get away with simply appropriating property, they will.

International interventions have reflected preconceived expectations and paradigms, and systematically failed to consider how or whether they affect Afghans' incentives to act within the law. As Peters explains, the counter-narcotics strategy has failed to grasp what drives it and whom it drives, obscuring which changes in conditions might – and which clearly will not – make growing and trafficking poppy less attractive than legal alternatives. The counter-narcotics strategy in Helmand, the leading poppy-producing province, for example, combines very weak support for alternative crops with very mild disincentives for continuing to grow poppy. Added together, they do virtually nothing to change farmers' incentives.

Another example of the importance of recognising the impact of change on actual power relations concerns control of the police. In discussing the new police law in 2005, international officials pressed for police forces in the provinces to be controlled directly by the Ministry of Interior in Kabul, rather than by their respective governors. The foreign advisers correctly noted that governors were using the police as their own militia, which is contrary to a balanced division of powers. But Afghan officials explained that without controlling the police, governors would have no authority whatsoever; the office itself, stripped of coercive power, counted for nothing.

Laws and institutions must cohere with one another and with their broader context

As Krygier anticipates and Hartmann and Klonowiecka-Milart illustrate, new laws and other changes imported without being stitched into the existing fabric of law and legal practice will be more like tumours than organs. They will not contribute positively to the existing body, but will be irrelevant to it if they are not actually toxic.

Consistency is especially important for overcoming the prisoner's dilemma every potentially law-abiding person faces in a lawless environment

The overarching importance of consistency emerges in this book, as the right to privacy in the US emerges from the space among amendments to its constitution, from the penumbra of its arguments. In societies where the rule of law prevails, one of the main reasons people comply with the law is their well-founded expectation that others will too. In a post-conflict or peri-conflict environment, the converse is true: people know others are not obeying the law and this is a compelling, rational reason not to obey it themselves, since doing so will entail costs to themselves without any benefit.

Any effort to change such perceptions and expectations of others' behaviour calls for even greater consistency in respecting and enforcing the law, especially by the most visible authorities, than would be required in a society where the rule of law is already assumed. Instead, as Stapleton, Maley, Vendrell, Hartmann and Klonowiecka-Milart have shown, the international interveners in Afghanistan have regularly displayed contempt for the country's legal framework. International support for President Karzai to remain in power for months after the constitution clearly stipulated his term was over dramatically exemplified this attitude.

We have overwhelming reasons to believe in these insights, but the challenge for policymakers and those who advise them is to believe them deeply enough. Depth of belief is alien to most discussion about the rule of law, as it is to academic thought more generally, but it is vitally important in the storm of interests that rage in conflict environments. 'For these principles to prevail in practice, in the face of the innumerable pressures to subordinate them to considerations of expediency, practitioners must understand them deeply and believe in them passionately' (Krygier and Mason 2008: 35).

All the contributors to this volume, from their diverse disciplinary and experiential backgrounds, agree about the interconnectedness of the many elements that comprise the rule of law and of the principles enumerated above. However, we must acknowledge an area of remaining uncertainty that is just as fundamental as the agreed-on axioms: we do not know how much outside intervention can achieve under contemporary conditions. Hafvenstein and Suhrke both argue persuasively that, in Afghanistan today, we can accomplish more by doing less.

Reflecting on the disappointments of most state-building interventions since the end of the cold war, many authors (including Chesterman 2005 and Von Hippel 2000) have questioned whether states can ever be built as a result of outside force. Others, though, note the role outside pressure has played in catalysing state-building processes. Suhrke in this volume points to the Meiji Restoration in Japan and the creation of the Turkish Republic as examples of modern states built in response to threats from Western imperialism. These days, strategic threats rarely loom for long enough to allow the threatened state to respond with broad state-building efforts, as did the fledgling Turkish Republic and Meiji Japan. The practice of imposing economic sanctions also cripples the threatened state's ability to modernise. China's energetic state-building process, which still derives its energy partly from historic memories of Western imperialism, may be a partial exception. A more typical response to external threats is Iran's barely clandestine efforts to develop nuclear weapons. Other than by developing weapons of mass destruction, threatened countries understand that they have no chance of competing with the West's military dominance. China and Russia also demonstrate that military strength can be achieved without politically emulating Western states.

The threat of imperialism is only one way exogenous pressure has helped catalyse state-building processes. The actual practice of colonialism has undeniably contributed to building states that today are stable. Generations of colonial administrators in British India, for instance,

helped create – albeit in the interests of Britain – many of the state institutions that today are pillars of the world's largest democracy. This sort
of sustained colonial presence is inconceivable today. Yet 'without a truly
massive effort of a type that is unlikely to be sustainable, our piecemeal
interventions around the edges not only are likely to be ineffective, but will
in many cases be counterproductive. We are insufficiently imperialistic to
carry out social transformation from abroad. And our intervention often
undermines social transformation from within' (Ginsburg 2010: 1–2).

Afghanistan today reflects a long history of imperialism without colonialism. The country has had the worst of both worlds. Its geographical
position has made it important enough to interfere with on a catastrophic
scale, but its dearth of natural and cultivable resources, combined with
its exceptionally refractory population, has discouraged the great powers
from investing in developing the state and its infrastructure through a
long-term colonial regime.

Today's huge international presence follows the historical pattern by
being overwhelmingly oriented towards the military. With the very limited
leverage the international community has over the Afghan government,
it can do little more than provide training and mentoring. What it cannot
do, in anything like its current configuration, is reshape Afghans' incentive structure so that acting within the law comes to make sense. Under
such conditions, Hafvenstein argues that any effort to combat narcotics
would be suborned by Afghan powerbrokers, and so would be worse than
doing nothing. Suhrke argues that the negative effects of the international
presence, in disrupting indigenous processes of political change, outweigh
its marginal benefits. Our ignorance of what might possibly be accomplished through exogenous pressure and support under the conditions
prevailing in the early twenty-first century compels us to acknowledge
that Hafvenstein and Suhrke may be right. If we consider the current
intervention – with its reluctant but nevertheless continuing support for
a widely discredited government, huge budgets controlled by people with
little time and less knowledge of Afghanistan or opportunity to learn
from Afghans – as the only model possible, they are almost certainly
right.

At the same time, we must also acknowledge that we do not know
what a different approach to Afghanistan, one oriented towards changing Afghans' incentive structures, might accomplish. One thoughtful and
prominent tribal elder in Kunduz, an insecure province bordering Tajikistan, opined to me in May 2010 that the arrest of any single prominent
warlord would lead to all the other warlords fleeing the country, and this

in turn would create such a surge of popular support for the state that the population would expel or smother all insurgents without any need for outside help. Such a move, which would reflect more political courage than has been seen by either Afghan or foreign players since 2001 and would signal a new political and legal order, may well have as profound an effect as the elder predicts.

For any intervention to contribute to transforming Afghanistan into a stable and reliable member of international society, it would have to put Afghans' perceptions of their own government, particularly as regards the existential issues of security and justice, at the centre of all it does. Achieving security requires the rule of law, and the rule of law requires the society to be so balanced that no one can act with impunity. In Afghanistan and other conflict-ridden environments, interveners must be mindful of the full range of issues that influence the extent to which law, rather than raw might, rules.

Law will rule when the state, the powerful and the weak all believe that the benefits of acting within the law, including the acceptance of unfavourable judgments, whether in a court, a council of elders or an election, outweigh the benefits of spurning law in favour of brute might. Achieving this state of affairs is enormously difficult, perhaps impossibly so, but in its essence, it is not infinitely complex.

How should this account of the rule of law in a post-conflict environment such as Afghanistan change interventionists' approach to fostering it? Because the rule of law is a state of affairs rather than a set of things, people charged with fostering it should listen, analyse and coordinate rather than manage programmes. Because almost everything influences the extent to which law rules in a given society, officials with 'rule of law' in their titles should sit very close to the apex of their respective institutions. Their role there would be to monitor the interplay of organic and exogenous forces to ensure the intervention was contributing as effectively as possible to reshaping the environment, so people would come to see it as first possible and then desirable to act within the law. This exercise in empathy should be applied to four types of people: the person or people at the top of the government; state officials; powerful individuals such as warlords; and a weak, poor person.

In Kosovo, for instance, a person widely considered to be a leading smuggler gave a UN official a list of changes to border security that would have to be made in order for him to be able to cease smuggling without being undercut by competitors who continued to evade the customs department (King and Mason 2006). To deliver an accurate picture, this exercise would have to be conducted in as many different environments as were relevant to the transformation of the society as a whole. In a fractured, heterogeneous environment like Afghanistan, such assessments would ideally be made in every district.

These incentive assessments of four idealised types, updated as often as changes in conditions warranted, would then become the yardstick for measuring every intervention meant to contribute to transforming the society into one where the law ruled. In Afghanistan, where the strategic aim is to create a state of affairs in which people obey the laws of the state and the state abides by the norms of international society, these yardsticks for measuring the appeal of acting within the law would be the most meaningful yardsticks for the intervention as a whole. Pundits often muse about how to measure success in a place like Afghanistan. Success is when a state of affairs exists such that the president, state officials, powerful private individuals, and poor and weak people all feel it makes sense for them to act within the law.

The intervention has not even attempted to create this state of affairs. In this sense, it has not failed so much as it has not attempted to succeed, because its architects did not understand what success consisted of. As Ahmed Wali Karzai, the president's disreputable but intelligent half-brother, once said to me: 'People in the West are always asking when the effort to bring peace to Afghanistan will end; I want to know when it will start.'

References

Chesterman, Simon (2005). *You the People: the UN, Transitional Administration and State-building.* Oxford University Press

Ginsburg, Tom (2010). 'In defence of imperialism', draft presentation at NOMOS conference, New Orleans, 6 January 2010

Graduate Students Working Group (2003). 'The missing priority: Post-conflict security and the rule of law', Woodrow Wilson School, Princeton University, report prepared for the Office of Counter-Terrorism, National Security Council, The White House, Washington DC, December 2003

Kant, Immanuel (1962). *Critique of Pure Reason,* Gregor, M. (ed. and trans.). Cambridge University Press, 1996

King, Iain and Mason, Whit (2006). *Peace at Any Price: How the World Failed Kosovo.* London: Hurst & Company

Krygier, Martin and Mason, Whit (2008). 'Violence, development and the rule of law', plenary address, delivered at the Global Development Network's

9th Annual Global Development Conference, 'Security for Development: Confronting threats to survival and safety', Brisbane, 31 January 2008

Miliband, David (2010). 'How to end the war in Afghanistan', *New York Review of Books*, 29 April 2010

Rousseau, Jean-Jacques (1762). *The Social Contract*, translated by G.D.H. Cole (undated), book 1, chapter 3, www.constitution.org/jjr/socon.htm

Sen, Amartya (2000). 'Role of legal and judicial reform in development', World Bank Legal Conference, Washington DC, 5 June 2000

Stromseth, Jane, Wippman, David; and Brooks, Rosa (2006). *Can Might Make Rights? Building the Rule of Law after Military Interventions.* Cambridge University Press

Von Hippel, Karin (2000). *Democracy by Force: US Military Intervention in the Post-Cold War World.* Cambridge University Press

Weingast, Barry (1997). 'Political foundations of democracy and the rule of law', *American Political Science Review*, 91